TOM HARTLEY was born in Belfast in 1945 and has been active in politics for over forty years. He was both the General Secretary and National Chairperson of Sinn Féin, and in May 1993 he was elected to Belfast City Council, where he chaired several Council committees, including the Arts and Tourism sub-committees and the Policy and Resources committee. From 2008 to 2009 he was Lord Mayor of Belfast. He retired from the council in September 2013 after twenty years service to the citizens of Belfast.

In his spare time, Tom pursues his love of history and interest in the environment by organising historical walks through Belfast City Cemetery for Féile an Phobail. He works to highlight the importance of our burial sites as a repository of the political, social and economic history of Belfast. His book, *Milltown Cemetery*, was published by Blackstaff Press in 2014.

BELFAST CITY
CEMETERY

THE HISTORY OF BELFAST,
WRITTEN IN STONE

Tom Hartley

BLACKSTAFF PRESS

First published as *Written in Stone* in 2006
by The Brehon Press Limited

This new and updated edition published in 2014
by Blackstaff Press
4D Weavers Court
Linfield Road
Belfast BT12 5GH

With the assistance of
The Arts Council of Northern Ireland

Typeset by KT Designs, St Helens, England
Printed in Berwick-upon-Tweed by Martins the Printers

A CIP catalogue record for this book is available from the British Library

ISBN 978 0 85640 924 0

www.blackstaffpress.com

For my parents Tommy and Hilda Hartley,
for the gifts of storytelling and history,
and my grandfather David Nelson,
a gravedigger in Belfast City Cemetery.

CONTENTS

ABBREVIATIONS

AEF	American Expeditionary Force
BA	British army
BPA	Belfast Protestant Association
CWGC	Commonwealth War Graves Commission
INTO	Irish National Teachers' Organisation
IOO	Independent Orange Order
IRA	Irish Republican Army
IRB	Irish Republican Brotherhood
ITGWU	Irish Transport and General Workers Union
ITWU	Irish Textile Workers Union
IWGC	Imperial War Graves Commission
LOL	Loyal Orange Lodge
MC	Military Cross
POW	Prisoner Of War
RAF	Royal Air Force
RAMC	Royal Army Medical Corps
RIC	Royal Irish Constabulary
RIR	Royal Irish Rifles
RN	Royal Navy
RUC	Royal Ulster Constabulary
RVH	Royal Victoria Hospital

UUC   Ulster Unionist Council
UVF   Ulster Volunteer Force
VAD   Voluntary Aid Detachment
YCV   Young Citizen Volunteers

ACKNOWLEDGEMENTS

While the writing of this book has been a journey into the history of my native city, the journey was only able to reveal itself through the support and help I received from a wide variety of individuals. Without their help I would not have been able to expose the layers of information that knit together the lives of those men, women and children of Belfast who lie in peace in Belfast City Cemetery. In my long ramble in and around the history of Belfast and its primary burial site, there are many who engaged with me on the wonderful complexity of our past. To all of them, too numerous to mention I would like to offer my deepest thanks.

In particular I wish to thank Paul McCann, my 'obituarist', whose knowledge of Victorian newspapers was invaluable. If Paul can't find you, you don't exist. Maggie Tomlinson, manager of the cemetery office in the City Hall and Patrick Sansome from the cemetery office in the City Cemetery were generous with their time and knowledge. I am also indebted to Stephen Stewart who combined his knowledge of maps and mapping with his computer wizardry to provide me with highly defined images. Jacinta Walsh persevered as I worked through numerous changes in our efforts to construct a sectional layout of the cemetery, and for her patience I will always be grateful. Robert Corbett, the archivist of Belfast City Council, was unsparing in his support. Professor George Bain, Seamus Kelters and Hilary Sloan took the time to read the first complete draft, and responded with kindness and generosity. Yvonne Murphy of the Linenhall Library was always there with her encouragement and support. *Ba mhaith liom buíochas ó chroí a ghabháil le Bríghid agus Séamus Mac Seáin. Go raibh maith agat a Shéamuis as mé a thabhairt go hOileán*

Í chun teacht ar chros chloiche, agus a Bhríghid, mo bhuíochas duit as an síorspreagadh is gríosú a thugann an tsuim atá agat féin i gcúrsaí staire dúinne a bhíonn ag streachailt le cúrsaí casta ár staire.

Gabhaim buíochas fosta le Nóilín Nic Bhloscaidh a d'aistrigh na scríbhinní Gaeilge agus Breatnaise go Béarla, to Paula Tabakin who translated a Hebrew inscription into English and Fr Francis OSB, Glenstal Abbey, who translated Greek inscriptions into English. To Hugh Russell I am indebted for his photographs and Aude Catala who encouraged my photographic skills. The mystery of headstone botany was unlocked by Professor Valerie Hall and Áine McDougal, for which I will always be grateful. A very special thanks to Steven Jaffé who took the time to provide me with the correct spelling of the names of those buried in the Jewish burial ground. A ringing endorsement is due to Harry and the late Pat Kane for their support and local knowledge. There are many more I wish to thank; these include the staff of the Linenhall library, John Walsh, Fiona Ure and Gerry Lennon of the Belfast Visitor and Convention Bureau, Brice Robertson of the Belfast Benevolent Society of St Andrew, Nicola Mawhiney of Victoria College, the Commonwealth War Graves Commission, Drew Ferris of the Ordnance Survey and David Porter for his background information on the history of Irish Presbyterianism.

My thanks to Roger Blaney, Jill McKenna, Victor Hamilton, Brian Hartley, Terence Hartley, Stiofán Ó Direáin, Carmel Mc Kinney, Tom Collins, David Byers, and Joseph McBrinn, who gave their time and knowledge. Thanks to my old friends Jim Gibney, Ted Howell and Gerry Adams, whose wisdom combined with their historical sharpness, steadied me on my journey into the complexity of our Belfast past, and to Danny Morrison for his support and interest in my research into the history to be found in the City Cemetery. For their assistance in tracking down information for this new edition, I am extremely grateful to Derek Martin for sharing his knowledge on Berkeley Deane Wise and Freeman Willis Crofts, Christopher Wilson for providing background on William McConnell Wilton, Maud Hamill for her help with William Henry McLaughlin, and John Moore for shedding light on the Morrow brothers. Michael Largey, the manager of Belfast City Cemetery, is also due huge thanks for all his help and support with the book.

The staff of Belfast City Council deserves a very special thanks. They include Peter McNaney, Mervyn Elder, Ciaran Quigley, Maurice McCann, Gerry Copeland, Maurice Parkinson, Reg Maxwell, Alan Jones, Helen McCauley, Juliet Campbell, Louise Reilly, Martin Fox, Sean McCarthy, Colin Campbell, as well as Stuart Austin and the gravediggers and gardeners of Belfast City Cemetery. For their patience and diligence when this book was first published, a big thank you to Nicola Keenan and Damian Keenan of Brehon Press. My family, especially my brother Peter, were always there with their encouragement. A special word of thanks for my partner Birgit, whose love and support sustained me through long hours of research with creative suggestions and crucial feedback on how the book should be structured. For all of this I will be forever grateful.

Above all else my journey into the history of Belfast City Cemetery represents an encounter with a wide variety of individuals and a challenge posed by the complexity of historical thought. By its very nature this fed my curiosity that led to the production of *Written in Stone*. However I alone take responsibility for what is contained in the book and I hope that my journey of historical discovery, which started all those years ago, will reveal the wonderful individuals who continue to carry in their mental rucksacks the precious knowledge of our Belfast history.

BELFAST CITY CEMETERY

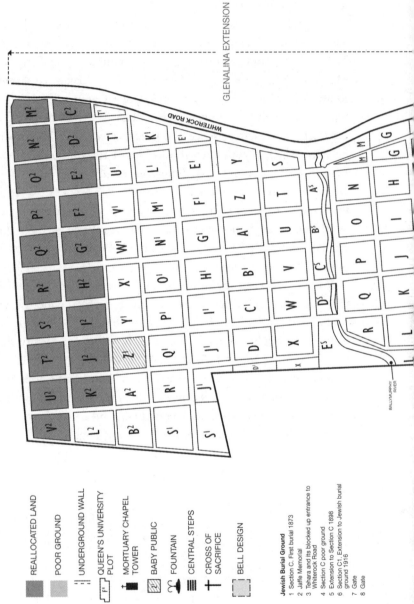

GLENALINA EXTENSION

WHITEROCK ROAD

BALLYMURPHY RIVER

Legend:

- REALLOCATED LAND
- POOR GROUND
- UNDERGROUND WALL
- F¹ QUEEN'S UNIVERSITY PLOT
- ✝ MORTUARY CHAPEL TOWER
- BABY PUBLIC
- ⚱ FOUNTAIN
- ‖‖ CENTRAL STEPS
- ✝ CROSS OF SACRIFICE
- BELL DESIGN

Jewish Burial Ground

1 Section C. First burial 1873
2 Jaffe Memorial
3 Tehara and its blocked up entrance to Whiterock Road
4 Section C poor ground
5 Extension to Section C 1898
6 Section C1. Extension to Jewish burial ground 1916
7 Gate
8 Gate

History of land acquisition
Belfast City Cemetery

- 101 acres purchased 10 December 1866 from Sinclair Family

- Belfast Cemetery opens 1 August 1869

- 57 acres of original purchase reallocated for new Falls Park 1 November 1869. The Cemetery is now 44 acres.

- 2½ designated Falls Park acres are sold to St. Patrick's Industrial School, Falls Road, 5 March 1879.

- 11 designated Falls Park acres are returned to the Cemetery by resolution 18 October 1880. The Cemetery is now 55 acres.

- 54 acres of Glenalina Estate purchased from Henry Patterson 6 June 1912. The Cemetery is now 109 acres and is renamed Belfast City Cemetery.

- 10 acres constituting 19 sections of Glenalina (C2 - K2, M2 - V2) are returned to the Parks Department 12 February 1958. The Cemetery is now 99 acres.

- 10 acres returned to Parks Department 12 February 1958 are transferred 8 March 1983 to Leisure Services Committee for the building of Whiterock Leisure Centre.

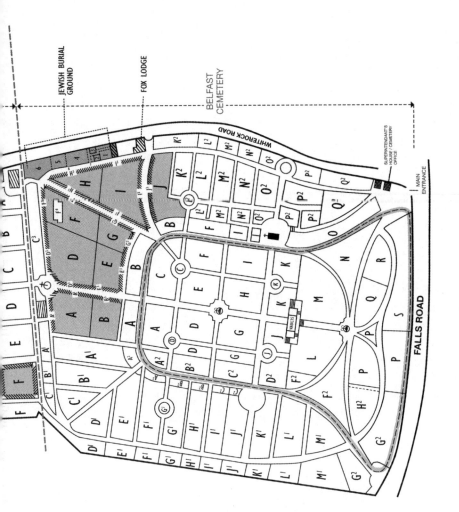

PREFACE

When I was a child I lived in a street of fifty houses inside a community of thirty streets. When someone in the area died the children would gather together and go to the wake house. There would always be a kid at the front being pushed by the kids behind, who would rap the door and ask, 'Missus, can we see the dead?' Pushed on by our curiosity we were brought into the house, but were still very reluctant to see the deceased. In those days the remains were laid out on the bed in an upstairs room, and each stair climbed increased the sense of fear. On reaching the small landing, the open door of the bedroom beckoned, and we could see the room bathed in the soft yellow light of drawn blinds and smell the aroma of burning candles. As we entered we saw the feet first and then the remains laid out on the bed; of course there was always that heavy stillness hanging in the air. We would gather round the bed, all of us looking at our feet before somehow finding the courage to peep at the corpse. We would quickly say a prayer, bless ourselves and charge down the stairs, emptying out into the street and safety.

When I look back on this experience, which was very common in our community, I see that something very important was happening to all of us kids. An experience which, though frightening, was nevertheless crucial to our understanding of the world we lived in. We were introduced to the reality of death inside the safe environment of our family and neighbours. From a very early age we knew that death represented loss, but it was also a consequence of life. As we grew older death became less frightening; in other words, we were better able to survive the sequence of loss, grief and the absence of a loved one. Death was also associated with stories of the 'olden days'. In wake houses, parents, aunts and uncles, and friends of the family would relate episodes from their lives: their experiences of childhood, growing up without electricity, the war years and rationing, the Troubles and a multitude of other tales – many of them funny – about the deceased.

These stories laid the foundations for my interest in history. Little did I realise that this interest, aided by my mother's capacity for detail and my father's talent in story-telling, would combine to reinforce my hunger for the past. But the past in Ireland often seems to find its way back to the present. As an adult my awareness of the past metamorphosed as political consciousness, so that by 1969 and the outbreak of the conflict in northern Irish society, I had become politically active.

I never made a conscious decision to do a historical walk of the Belfast City Cemetery; it was my political involvement that led me into the role. By 1973, I was working with the Sinn Féin press office in Belfast, and visiting journalists frequently asked for a tour of the British military barracks scattered around west Belfast. As someone who was born in the area, and lived on the Falls Road, I was in a position to give these tours. Initially, they were mostly walking tours of the lower and mid-Falls. As time went by, I included facets of republican history, such as Milltown Cemetery with its republican graves. Alongside the barracks and the cemetery, other aspects of the social and political history of the Falls Road emerged, and a three-hour bus tour slowly developed which had its starting point in Castle Street, at the bottom of the road, and which wound its way through the back streets and beyond Milltown to the neighbouring districts of Lenadoon, Twinbrook, Andersonstown, Turf Lodge, Ballymurphy and Beechmount, before finishing in Bombay Street in the Lower Falls.

The bus tour was eventually made part of the West Belfast Festival, which began in 1988. In its first year the tour took place a total of three times during the festival week. As the festival developed, so did the demand for the tour and, by the mid-nineties, I was bussing around west Belfast daily during the festival, Monday to Friday.

Superintendent's house at the main entrance to the cemetery

During this period other factors shaped my political and historical outlook, and these added new perspectives to the tour. Engagement with Protestants and unionists opened the door to the history of that community, and I recognised a major gap in my understanding of unionism. One way this manifested itself was in my lack of curiosity about the monuments and headstones which marked the graves of the unionist dead, in the lower end of the Belfast City Cemetery. Growing up as a nationalist/Catholic, I felt no sense of ownership or attachment to the City Cemetery, which by its location on the Falls Road was literally on my doorstep. All this changed as I began to explore these headstones and monuments, and discovered a wide variety of family and historical inscriptions, some of which I incorporated into my tour. By 1998, the extent of information I had accumulated on both the City and Milltown cemeteries was such that I decided to establish a historical walk of the two.

The walk is structured to capture the breadth and complexity of the history of Belfast. It invites us to make links and connections with a diversity that reveals itself through funerary architecture and headstone inscriptions. Visitors may either like or dislike the history they encounter, and can agree or disagree with the politics of those who lie buried in the graves they visit. But these graves, be they Catholic or Protestant, unionist or republican, represent Belfast's complex past. This book on the City Cemetery is my interpretation of that history.

There is a choice of five walks which represent a variety of themes and topics. Where possible, in each of the graves visited, I have sought to enhance the story of the individual with related information which connects with other aspects of Belfast or world history. Each grave on the walks is referenced by its section and numerical reference. Each walk is generally constructed as a journey that moves from a section to its neighbouring section. However, if an individual grave is being sought, it is easy to locate it by using the layout map to go straight to the required section. In some cases I indicate a section and grave number in bold, which will indicate to the reader connections and links.

Please remember that Belfast City Cemetery is still a burial site used on a daily basis. In your exploration of the graveyard be mindful of this and treat it with the respect and dignity that all burial sites are due. Be cautious as you move among the older headstones and monuments in the lower end of the cemetery as many of their foundations are in a vulnerable condition. Above all, try not to walk over the graves; you will notice that many of them have sunk and are exposed to the elements. Do not remove any piece of funerary architecture as a memento of your visit. Always leave a gravesite as you found it. The Belfast City Cemetery has a wealth of history to offer all its visitors through its insights into the life of the city and its citizens, so enjoy what it has to offer and leave it for others to enjoy.

BACKGROUND

During the greater part of the nineteenth century, most burial grounds in Belfast were owned by religious denominations. Friar's Bush on the Stranmillis Road was owned by the Catholic Church. The Episcopalians owned the Shankill Road graveyard. There was a Presbyterian burial ground at Balmoral and a Methodist graveyard on the Newtownards Road. The Board of Guardians owned a graveyard on the Donegall Road, which was connected to the workhouse, and the Belfast Charitable Society owned Clifton Street burial ground.

The increase in burials as a result of the Famine in the 1840s and the growth in the population of Belfast, which had risen from 70,447 in 1841 to 121,602 in 1871, combined to exhaust the capacity of the existing Belfast graveyards. In Friar's Bush human remains were buried almost on the surface, and by the 1860s mounds of remains appeared above the natural level of the ground. The resulting pressure for new burial space forced the Belfast Corporation, the predecessor of Belfast City Council, to look for a new Belfast burial site. At a special meeting of the Belfast Corporation Improvements Committee on 2 October 1865 it was decided to accept the offer from Mr Thomas Sinclair for the sale of 101 acres of his land on the Falls Road for the purpose of a public cemetery.

On 20 November 1865 the Improvements Committee asked the Town Surveyor to 'lay out a plan on forty-five acres of Thomas Sinclair's land bounded by the Falls Road and the Whiterock Road terminating in a straight line from the Falls Road to the corner of Henry's Bleach Green at the pond as the portion for which parliamentary powers would be sought'. Discussions between the Belfast Corporation and Westminster Parliament

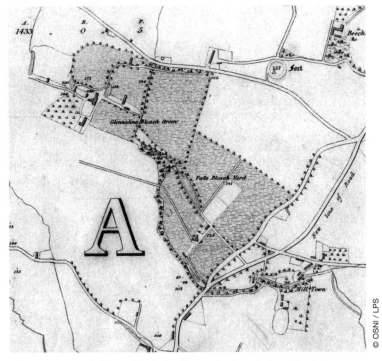

© OSNI / LPS

An 1832–3 map of the townland of Ballymurphy, later Belfast City Cemetery

led, on 28 June 1866, to a local parliamentary bill known as the Belfast Burial Ground Act.

On 29 September 1866 the Improvements Committee decided that plans and estimates for laying out the new cemetery should be advertised, to be delivered to the Town Hall by 15 November. On 10 December, the Belfast Corporation purchased five parcels of land, totalling 101 acres, on the Falls Road from the Sinclair family. This land, set in the townland of Ballymurphy, cost £12,000, with an annual ground rent of £73.5s.4d. The new site contained the Falls Bleach Works situated on the land later developed as the Falls Park tennis courts. The site also contained a number of dams, the most famous, a dry dam situated on the edge of Glenalina, later developed by the Belfast Corporation as an open air swimming pool, which to thousands of Falls Road children became known as 'the cooler'.

The 101 acres purchased in 1866 is now the Falls Park,

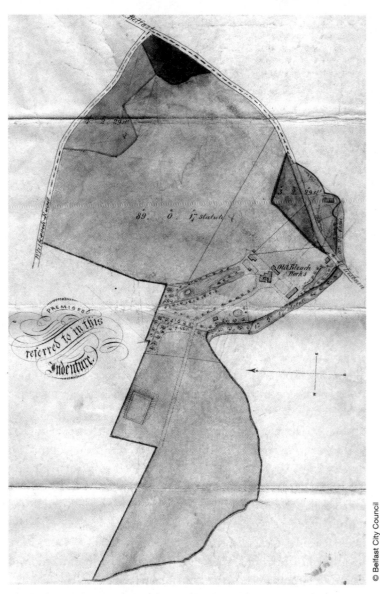

The deed map of the original acquisition bought by the Belfast Corporation

the lower end of the City Cemetery, the site today of
Maguire's Garage on the Falls Road and the old buildings of
Saint Patrick's Industrial School. Using present-day landmarks,
the western boundary of the new cemetery ran on a north-

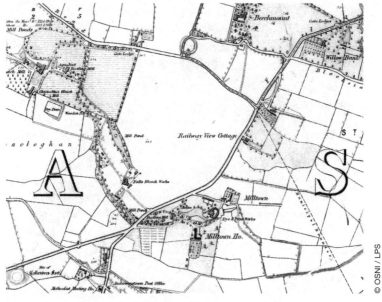

© OSNI / LPS

Map of the townland of Ballymurphy, 1857

south axis in a straight line beginning at O'Hare's farm on the Whiterock Road, through the Cross of Sacrifice and continued to the perimeter of the Falls Park; its eastern boundary was the Falls Road.

On 25 January 1867 the Cemetery Committee of the Belfast Corporation awarded William Gay of Bradford the contract to design the new Belfast Cemetery. Described as a surveyor and landscape gardener, Gay had a long association with the upkeep and design of Victorian graveyards. He had been employed by the Leicester General Cemetery Company as their first superintendent in the Leicester General Cemetery, which opened in 1849. In 1852 he arrived in Bradford where he was employed by the Bradford Cemetery Company to create their new cemetery 'Undercliffe', which opened in 1854. Having designed the cemetery, he then became its registrar and was subsequently appointed secretary to the Cemetery Company. He went on to develop the layout of two cemeteries in Liverpool, as well as cemeteries at Bacup, Wigan and Lancaster. He was also involved in the design and layout of parks. He prepared the design for the Grand Terrace in Peel Park,

Salford, named after Sir Robert Peel – the founder of modern policing in Britain and Ireland. He also designed and supervised the work on Saltair Park, near Shipley Bradford, which opened in 1871. The park was part of a purpose-built model industrial village constructed by Sir Titus Salt who wished to provide self-contained housing for the workers at his woollen mills. In the era of the Victorian garden cemetery, William Gay stands out as one of the leading figures in the development of cemetery design and layout. He died at the age of 80 at Charnwood, Eccleshill, England on 8 March 1893.

Following the successful bid by William Gay the Belfast Corporation awarded Monk & Co. the contract to provide boundary walls, roadways and drainage. Cliff & Co. of Bradford provided the wrought iron gates.

In preparing his bid to design the new Belfast cemetery, William Gay required a detailed knowledge of the ground conditions of the proposed site, its topographical features, the level of the water table, and the potential points to access the new graveyard. All this information would have been contained in the Belfast Corporation specifications and documentation, or secured by William on site visits to Belfast.

Hidden from these technical preparations is the class view that permeated the design and construction of the new cemetery. For rich Victorians death provided another way to display their wealth and personal power – they gave enormous consideration to the location of a grave and the size and design of a monument or headstone. The members of the Belfast Corporation, like Gay himself, would have been all too aware of these considerations.

The cemetery was to have two types of grave. Proprietary graves could be purchased by an individual or institution. Priced according to a defined class, they were to be located in the most desirable parts of the graveyard where the layout, combined with the lie of the land enhanced their look and status. Paupers' graves located in the Poor Ground, sometimes referred to as public ground, were the property of the Belfast Corporation. These graves were to be placed in sections out of sight, without any grave markers.

Stage one in Gay's design was to determine what land would be allocated for the two categories of graves. He then laid out the road network by using as his template the outline of a bell, in effect dividing the site into a number of sections; every section was then given an alphabetical reference. It is possible that Gay's bell design reflects the 'Bel' in Belfast. The bell as a symbol was used extensively in early seventeenth-century Belfast trade tokens and probably originates in the heraldic custom of canting or allusive arms, where heraldic forms originate in the play upon words of similar sound.

The final design stage was the mapping of the graves in each section. The standard portion of surface land required for a grave was set at 9 feet by 4 feet. The depth of a grave was set at either 9 feet or 10 feet 6 inches. In those sections designated for proprietary graves, a line of road-facing graves was planned to run along the rim of each section – today these are referred to as roadside graves. Inside the rim, lines of graves were generally aligned on an east-west axis. However, while this east-west alignment is common to the majority of graves, many sections which have a northern and southern rim have roadside graves laid out on a north-south axis. Each grave was then given a section and numerical reference. As a means of creating linear pathways through each section, lines of these numbered graves were reserved for that purpose. Today these paths are called reserves. In the Poor Ground, graves were laid out toe to head on an east-west axis; there are no linear pathways in these sections.

The orientation east-west is found in many agrarian and pagan societies whose crops depended on the sun. Thus in Ireland the orientation of the Newgrange passage grave is east-west. Many Egyptian temples have a similar orientation. The use by early Christians of the east-west orientation has its antecedent in the Roman worship of the Sun God, *Sol Invictus*. His feast day became the Christian Sunday, his birthday, and the winter solstice became Christmas. Facing eastward for worship was thus a continuation of earlier pagan practice. The feet to the east burial allows the dead to face the rising sun.

On 29 September 1868 the cemetery committee decided that

the new cemetery was to be called The Belfast Cemetery. At its meeting on 21 December 1868 the committee set the scale of charges for graves – the cost of a grave being determined by its location. The cemetery was to have six classes of proprietary grave. The most expensive cost, £9, was for a grave along the margins of walks on one of the main avenues, commonly referred to as a roadside grave. These graves were rarely bought as single graves but as plots of two, three or four graves. The grave in the second row cost £6, and for the third and fourth rows the price was £4.10 shillings. The charge for a grave in the fifth and sixth rows was £3 while graves within the sixth row in the eighth division beyond the centre walk were £2. The cheapest grave cost £1 and was located next to the margin of the public ground. These £1 graves were later to be sold as 'a special class for persons in straitened circumstances'. The small numbers of vaults in the cemetery were put up for public auction on 5 October 1869. James Carlisle (J-465) bought vaults four and five for the sum of £110. Edward Harland (M-987) purchased the vault where he is buried for £80 from the Belfast Corporation in August 1876.

The cost and location of a grave was a mark of an individual's rank in a class-ridden society. The very rich and powerful were to be buried in roadside graves, often referred to as 'select positions', which occupied the prime locations along the main avenues of the cemetery. Here their wealth could be reflected in lavish headstones and monuments. The middle classes would occupy the second, third and fourth rows, their headstones less prominent but still expensive. The working class were to be buried in rows five and six, with small headstones or cast-iron shields as grave markers. The mass of the poor were to be buried, out of sight and out of mind, in the Poor Ground.

When the cemetery opened, reference to the class of a grave was only recorded in the lease document given to the owner. From 28 June 1886, however, burial orders from the cemetery office in the City Hall to the cemetery office in the Belfast Cemetery contained a reference to the class of grave. This practice of classifying graves continued until 31 March 2001.

Religion

Initially, the Belfast Corporation intended to open the new cemetery to all religious denominations in Belfast. It planned to erect three mortuary chapels – one for Catholics, one for the Established Church and one for the Dissenters. Agreement was reached between the Belfast Corporation and the Catholic Bishop of Down and Connor, Dr Patrick Dorrian, for the provision of fifteen acres of land, a mortuary chapel and a separate entrance for the Catholics of Belfast. The Corporation also decided that thirty acres and one mortuary chapel would be provided each for the Established Church and the Dissenters. The fifteen acres allocated for Catholics were to be separated from the other sections of the cemetery by a sunken wall. As a result of a dispute between Bishop Dorrian and the Corporation the fifteen acres allocated for Catholic burials were never used for that purpose. Following the resolution of the dispute the new Belfast cemetery became a burial site just for the Protestant community. Nevertheless, a few Catholics were to be buried within its grounds.

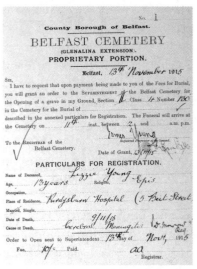

In the proposed separation between Catholics and Protestants another form of segregation was exposed. Protestants were to use the main gate at the junction of the Whiterock and Falls Road. They also had their own mortuary chapel. Catholics would have their own gate, located at the southern corner of the perimeter wall on the Falls Road. They were to be given their own mortuary chapel, located at the southern end of the main avenue. The poor, now located at the back of the cemetery, were to have their own separate entrance located 500 yards up the Whiterock Road.

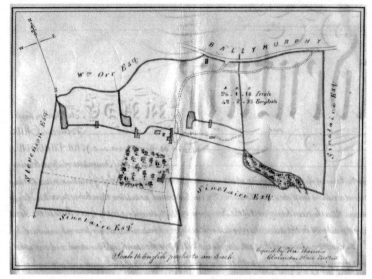

Deed map of the Glenalina land owned by the Sinclair family, 1862

A registrar for the new cemetery, Mr Calcutt, was appointed on 6 July 1869. An order of the Irish Privy Council closing other graveyards within the borough of Belfast came into force on 1 August 1869. Friar's Bush was exempt from this order, the right to inter there having being extended to 25 November 1869.

The new cemetery was opened on Sunday, 1 August 1869 to allow the public to inspect the new site. The first burials took place three days later, on Wednesday, 4 August 1869, when Annie Collins, aged 3 years and 3 months, from Browns Row, Academy Street, was buried in **H-71**. Annie's remains arrived at the cemetery at 11 a.m. but the cemetery records show that her burial did not take place until 6 p.m. On the same day Isabella McDowell, aged 10, from Mary's Place, Stanley Street was buried in **H-72** at 4 p.m. Both graves are located in the Poor Ground. The mayor of Belfast, F. H. Lewis, paid for the burial costs. Robert Tate, of 88 Hercules Street, bought the first proprietary grave for the burial of Samuel Tate, aged 14 months, who was buried on 12 August 1869 in grave **K-297**. The cost of opening a grave in 1869 was ten shillings.

On 1 September 1869 Mr J. Moran was appointed as

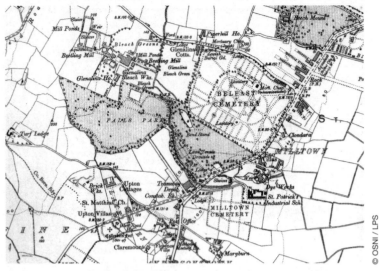

© OSNI / LPS

Belfast Cemetery and the Falls Park, 1901

superintendent of the cemetery but he resigned soon after and Thomas Leeburn was appointed as acting superintendent. By January 1871 James McLachlan had been appointed superintendent. He died on 3 July 1876 and was replaced by George McCann, who became superintendent on 1 September 1876 until his retirement in 1917.

The first reference to military ground regards two-year-old child Ellen Hurrell who was buried in **H-740** on 5 October 1869, though we don't know why she was buried here. On 5 November 1869 James Evans was the first soldier to be buried in the cemetery (**H-504**).

In January 1871, a strip of land at the very back of the new cemetery was allocated to the Jewish community. Once again subtle religious prejudice prevailed – the Jewish burial ground, located beside the Poor Ground, was effectively out of sight from the Christians of Belfast.

The Glenalina extension and Belfast City Cemetery

By the beginning of the twentieth century the Belfast Cemetery had reached its capacity to provide new graves for the population

BELFAST CEMETERY (GLENALINA EXTENSION).			
Date of Order	N A M E	Age	Day and Hour of Burial
ovember 11	Lizzie Young	13 years	Thursday
14	Jane Laws	75 year	Sunday
	Margaret McDonald	33 years	
15	Thomas Joseph Dickinson	30 yrs	Monday
19	Robert Henry McConnell	44 years	Friday
	David Gamble	12 years	
23	Sarah Reid	36 years	Tuesday
26	Emily Bingham	38 years	Friday
	John Charles Swain	4 months	
27	James Alfred Lyons	20 years	Saturday

1905

© Belfast City Council

Lizzie Young was the first burial in the new Glenalina extension

of Belfast, which by 1909 had reached an estimated figure of
484,000. The Belfast Corporation was again forced to look for
new burial space.

On 19 October 1910 the Cemeteries and Parks Committee
of the Corporation recommended that an application be made
to parliament for the right to compulsorily acquire just under
54 acres of land adjacent to the Whiterock Road from Mr Henry
Patterson, the owner of a linen beetling and bleach mill on the
site. On 6 June 1912 the Corporation bought two parcels of
land totalling 54 acres of the Glenalina estate from Mr Patterson
for £5,250. Glenalina is the English pronunciation of the Irish
Gleann an Léana, the glen of a low-lying grassy place or water-
meadow. The older residents in the Ballymurphy area call it
Glendalina, from the Irish *Gleann dá Léana*, the glen of *two* low-
lying grassy places or water-meadows. This is a more accurate
description as it describes the two meadows separated by the
Ballymurphy River.

This new acquisition of land extended the existing cemetery
westward to the slopes of the Black Mountain. With the extension
of Glenalina the Belfast Cemetery now consisted of 109 acres. In
June 1913 its name changed from Belfast Cemetery to Belfast
City Cemetery.

A grid design was the template used for the layout of sections in Glenalina. Eighty per cent of these are a standard size of 170ft by 130ft; the remainder have either a strip or triangular layout and are situated on the perimeters of the Ballymurphy River, the Whiterock Road, and the Falls Park. All sections were referenced alphabetically. Proprietary graves were alphabetically listed in sections A to Z, located between the Cross of Sacrifice and the west side of the Ballymurphy River. Sections A1 to Y1, located on the upper slopes; sections A2, to V2, located along the western boundary; and sections As to Es, located on the east and west banks of the Ballymurphy River, are all proprietary graves. Section F was earmarked as Poor Ground.

The first burial in the new Glenalina section took place on Thursday, 11 November 1915. Lizzie Young, aged 13, from 5 Beit Street, Belfast, was buried in grave **I-130 Glen**. She had died two days earlier from cerebral meningitis.

The history of land acquisition relating to the Belfast City Cemetery can be summarised as follows:

- 101 acres purchased on 10 December 1866 from Sinclair family;
- 57 acres of the original purchase reallocated for the new Falls Park on 1 November 1869. The cemetery is now 44 acres;
- 2.5 acres of designated Falls Park acres are sold to St Patrick's Industrial School, Falls Road, on 5 March 1879;
- 11 of the designated Falls Park acres returned to the cemetery by resolution on 18 October 1880. The cemetery is now 55 acres;
- 54 acres are purchased from Henry Patterson on 6 June 1912. The cemetery is now 109 acres.

The original layout of the Glenalina extension contained 74 sections. At the Belfast Corporation Parks' Committee on 30 May 1957, the Director of Parks reported that 10 acres of Glenalina were unsuitable for burial purposes. On 9 January 1958 the town solicitor reported that the issue had been raised with the Ministry of Health and Local Government, and on 12 February 1958 the Ministry agreed to the transfer of the 10 acres to the Falls Park. A new perimeter fence was raised. Beginning on the western rim of section T1, it ran to the western rim at A2, and then took in the eastern and western rims of L2, ending at the perimeter fence of the Falls Park. As there had been burials in L2 from 24 February 1951 it remained part of the cemetery. On 10 January 1980 the director of the Parks' Committee informed the committee that it would be necessary to transfer the land, now in the Falls Park, to the Leisure Services Committee for the building of the Whiterock Leisure Centre. On 8 March 1983 the Leisure Services Committee adopted a resolution to appropriate the land in question.

Catholic burials in Belfast City Cemetery

From November 1869 the Catholic population of Belfast had used Milltown Cemetery as their main burial ground. By the latter end of the twentieth century, as new graves became scarce in Milltown, pressure mounted on the city council to provide new Catholic burial space in the City Cemetery. The council met this demand by creating new lawn sections on the upper slopes of Glenalina. Lawn sections are characterised by headstones regulated to specific dimensions and the absence of grave surrounds on individual graves, thus creating the appearance of headstones set in a lawn.

By the late 1970s the cemetery, now surrounded by the Catholic housing estates of Ballymurphy, Turf Lodge and Andersonstown, was being used by Catholics. On 13 January 1979, Patrick Corrigan of 30 Beechmount Crescent, Belfast, was the first Catholic buried in section O1, Glenalina. This was followed by Catholic burials in Section W1 on 6 and 9 October 1980. This trend was accelerated by two factors – Milltown, the Catholic cemetery, was near to reaching its capacity while many Protestant families, fearful of visiting Catholic/nationalist west Belfast, which they perceived to be in the middle of a war zone, had from the 1960s used Roselawn Cemetery in east Belfast to bury their dead.

With a growing number of Catholics now using the City Cemetery, the city council began using the old reserve paths in Section Q in the lower end of the cemetery. The first burials in this section began in December 1991. The pathways in sections D, G, H, H2, L, M, P and R in the lower end of the cemetery are currently being used for burials. Fr Pádraig Murphy, Parish Priest of St John's, was one of the first Catholics to be buried here. He was interred in **R-2** on 3 June 1988.

For the purpose of recording deaths the cemetery has four administrative blocks: 'The City' refers to the original Belfast Cemetery opened on 1 August 1869; the Poor Ground in the original Belfast Cemetery, which incorporates the Poor Ground in Glenalina; the Jewish burial ground opened in 1871 and became a separate administrative block on 2 October 1889; and Glenalina, opened on Thursday, 11 November 1915, is the last and fourth block, all grave references in this section contain the word 'Glen'.

Each burial is given its own order number and is referenced in numerical sequence in one of the four administrative blocks. All burials are listed in numerical sequence in the *Register of Burials* without reference to an administrative block.

As of 30 June 2014, 91,762 burial orders have been issued for The City; 57,202 for Glenalina; 80,208 for the Poor Ground; and 273 for the Jewish burial ground. To date, approximately 229,445 burial orders have been issued, but the Register of Burials has a figure of 226,850. The difference of 2,595 is a result of burial orders being issued and then cancelled. Each purchase of a proprietary grave or plot of graves is provided with a lease document. The number of lease documents issued for The City, is 21,124 and for Glenalina 23,602 – a total of 44,726. There are 53,856 graves in use in Belfast City Cemetery – 24,130 in The City; 22,379 in Glenalina; 7,070 in the Poor ground; and 277 in the Jewish burial ground.

The last new grave, **Q2-283**, was bought for the burial of

Sarah Christie of Jude Street, Belfast, who died 30 November
2004, aged 79. The last grave used for a burial in the Public
Ground was **Z1-414 Glen** on Friday, 16 January 2004.

Funerary architecture

Three historical periods are reflected in the architecture of the
cemetery's headstones and monuments – Victorian, Edwardian
and late twentieth century.

Victorian funerary architecture usually reflected an individual's
wealth and status in society, as can be seen from a number of
ornate and lavish monuments in the lower end of the cemetery.
The main forms of Victorian funerary architecture are headstones,
monuments, urns, obelisks, broken columns and angels. This
type of architecture, referred to as neo-classical, was popular up
to the end of the nineteenth century. Influenced by ancient Greek
and Roman art, it is properly proportioned and symmetrical,
with well-defined forms. It was appreciated for its perceived
rationality, which aimed
to intellectually satisfy the
eye. There are also strong
Masonic influences to
be found in this type of
architecture.

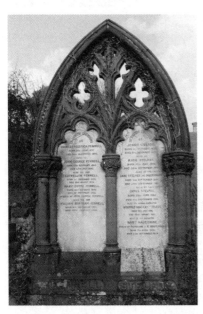

Many of the smaller
headstones are topped
by motifs which carry
a symbolic reference:
wreaths, grieving women,
clasped hands, doves and
IHS – the Latin form of the
first three letters derived
from the Greek spelling
of Jesus, 'IHCOYC' – are
but a few examples. The

M-454, James Stelfox, a good example of
Gothic funerary architecture

cemetery also contains a
number of monuments

whose architecture is referred to as Gothic Revival, which is well represented in the civic and religious buildings of the Victorians. Gothic architecture, developed in Europe between the twelfth and sixteenth centuries, is characterised by elaborate carved decoration, pointed arches, vaulting, traceried windows, rib vaults and the replacement of wall space by stained glass.

A distinctive marker for the burial site of J. Graham

Other forms of Victorian funerary architecture, found in the lower end of the cemetery, are the decorative wrought iron surrounds and cast-iron grave markers/shields, all made by local Belfast foundries. The lower end of the cemetery also contains a number of Irish stone crosses which represent the architecture from the end of the nineteenth century referred to as the Celtic Revival.

After the death of Queen Victoria in 1901, a new public attitude surfaced which resented the large amounts of money required for lavish headstones and monuments. Victorian funerary architecture gave way to the smaller headstones that emerged in the reign of Edward VII. This Edwardian style of stone can be seen in the middle sections of the cemetery. In the late twentieth century, headstones were regulated to specific dimensions and stone surrounds disappeared to facilitate the development and maintenance of new lawn sections. This form of architecture dominates a number of sections on the upper slopes of Glenalina. It can also be found in some of the reserve paths among the Victorian graves in the older sections of the cemetery.

Gravediggers

The number of gravediggers in the cemetery has fluctuated over the years. In 1898 27 men were employed in the cemetery, 19 of them as gravediggers. The remaining men carried out ground maintenance and flowering. Then, the top earnings of a gravedigger were £1,10 shillings per week. The total weekly wage bill for the twenty-seven men was £30. In 1914 27 men were employed in Belfast Cemetery and 13 in Glenalina. The total weekly wage bill for the 40 men was £42. In 1918 there were 23 men, 12 of whom were gravediggers. A record was kept for each gravedigger, documenting the number of graves dug and the number of working days. The record for 14 January 1919 shows a David Morton having worked 32½ days and dug 65 graves. Another record shows Morton having worked 89½ days and being paid £2 4s 8d. By January 1938, there were a total of 51 men employed in the cemetery, 21 of whom were gravediggers. In 2004 there were 6 gravediggers, 5 gardeners and 1 maintenance man.

Some of the employees of Belfast Cemetery gather for a group shot, *c.* 1910

© Belfast City Council

Cemetery staff, *c.* 1920

Looking for a grave

Given that similar alphabetical references for sections are used in the Belfast Cemetery, in Glenalina and in the Poor Ground, it is necessary to know in which of the three main parts of the graveyard a grave is located. As a rule of thumb many of the new graves after November 1915 are located in Glenalina. For those wishing to find a grave, a search of cemetery records is made easy by presenting to the cemetery officials a copy of a lease document, a copy burial order or a date of death or burial.

CHAPTER 1

SOLDIERS, GUNRUNNERS AND THE POOR

The first walk begins at the Falls Road entrance to the cemetery and winds its way through the lower sections finishing at the Cross of Sacrifice. Here lie soldiers of the Crimea War alongside submariners of the First World War, and highlanders whose service to the Empire brought them through the gates of Lucknow during the Indian Mutiny. We get a glimpse of the role of women but only a glimpse, as their contribution to Belfast society is rarely acknowledged on headstone inscriptions. The Ulster Volunteer Force (UVF) is well-represented, with its financers, soldiers, political supporters and gunrunners. Orangemen with their opposition to Gladstone's Home Rule Bill are found alongside newspaper proprietors and botanists. Here we begin to see the influence of the Belfast Natural History and Philosophical Society and its intellectual legacy to the city of Belfast. Banners for the twelfth of July, miniature portraits and 20,000-ton ships were made by those who lie here. Children are here, though only a few are acknowledged, as many thousands lie out of our view and consciousness. Masonic funerary architecture and symbolism is all around us – a study on its own. Headstones of every variety, grand monuments covered in symbolism, Irish stone crosses, with their intricate interlacing and ancient meanings, seek our attention. The very first monument placed in the cemetery can be found on this tour. Vaudeville stars and footballers, doctors in the East India Company, two recipients of the Victoria Cross and even the odd salesman reveal themselves. The poor are here in their thousands. The walk ends at the Cross of Sacrifice – a reminder of those soldiers, sailors and airmen from Belfast who perished during the First World War.

SUPERINTENDENT'S GATEHOUSE, MAIN ENTRANCE

Built for the cemetery's superintendent, this house was designed by John Lanyon and opened in 1873. The coat of arms of the Belfast Corporation is to the right of the side door. At the foot of the door is a black ordnance survey marker. There are two gargoyles above the spouting on the east and west face of the building. Gargoyle is from the French word for throat; *gargouille* is a waterspout often carved in the form of a grotesque winged monster.

R-474: Samuel Joseph Scott; *d.* 20 April 1910

Samuel was a 15-year-old from 70 Templemore Street in east Belfast. Employed as a 'catchboy' – junior member of a riveting squad – in the Harland and Wolff shipyard he is reputed to be the first person killed in an accident during the building of the *Titanic*. Burial records give the cause of death as a fracture of the skull. There was no stone on this grave until 2011, when one was provided by Féile an Phobail.

R-446: Maude Beattie; *d.* 16 November 1899

Maude, a 20-year-old clerk from 26 Spruce Street in the Cromac area of Belfast, died of consumption. Her headstone has an inscription to her brother John Beattie who was killed in action during the Boer War, on Sunday, 18 February 1900, at the Battle of Paardeberg Drift, South Africa. Paardeberg Drift is located on the Modder River, forty miles from the town of Kimberly.

At 7 a.m. on the morning of 18 February, a British force totalling 15,000 attacked an entrenched force of 4,000 Boers who were led by the Boer commander, General Piet Cronje. The battle lasted for ten hours, finishing at 5 p.m. the same day. The British, led by two Irish-born generals, Lord Kitchener and Thomas Kelly-Kenny, suffered heavy casualties: 303 soldiers were killed, 906 were wounded, and 61 went missing. Casualties amongst the

Boers included 100 dead and 250 wounded. Kitchener, who was junior in rank to Kelly-Kenny, had been appointed to command the attacking force. His insistence on a series of uncoordinated frontal attacks on Boer positions led to tactical blunders on the battlefield that resulted in heavy British losses and an eventual retreat behind their own lines; he was later held responsible for the high British casualty rate. No British soldier got within 200 yards of the Boer lines. It was not until 27 February that Cronje surrendered with 4,019 men, 150 of whom were wounded. The battle was one of the bloodiest of the Boer War.

There are five family headstones with memorial inscriptions to soldiers who died in South Africa during the Boer War. These are:

R.J.Wylie, Royal Inniskilling Fusiliers, *d*. 15 December 1899, Colenso	**N-674**
John A. Beattie, *d*. 18 February 1900, Paardeberg Drift	**R-446**
George McLaughlin, Imperial Yeomanry, *d*. 30 May 1900, Lindley	**F-439**
Hugh Hamilton, Queensland Artillery, RFF, *d*. 12 July 1900, Marandellas	**D-627**
Hugh Darragh, Irish Imperial Yeomanry, *d*. 26 December 1901, Winburg	**L2-5**

R-684: Cecil Kenneth Brown; *d*. 16 April 1905

Cecil Kenneth Brown, aged 18 months, from 22 Seaview Street, York Road, Belfast, died from measles on 16 April 1905, and was first buried in D-104 Poor Ground. On 21 June 1905 the Cemetery and Parks Committee of the Belfast Corporation considered a request from Mr Wm Brown of Seaview Street, York Road for permission to reinter Cecil. Permission was granted on the basis that the cause of death was non-infectious. On 22 July 1905 the remains were re-interred to **R-684**. One can only speculate that the transfer of the remains of Cecil indicate that the Brown family, faced with the sudden death of their child, were unable to meet the cost of buying a grave. The grave is marked by a brown-stoned open book. Books used as grave markers represent the embodiment of faith; they also depict learning and scholarship, and may represent the *Book of Life*, which is the symbolic book in which God records the names of the righteous.

Q2-283: Sarah Christie; *d.* 30 November 2004

Sarah McKinney was born on 14 July 1925 in Samuel Street, which runs between Winetavern Street and Millfield, in the centre of Belfast. She attended Millfield Primary School. On Christmas Day 1941, aged 16, she married Thomas Christie. The couple lived for a while in 41a Albert Street, before several moves to 49 Baker Street, 21 Farset Row and then to 3 Jude Street. Sarah had eight children and lived all her life in the Lower Falls. Her grave was the last new grave sold in the City Cemetery – since 30 November 2004 a burial can only take place in a grave that has already been used or was purchased before this date. Therefore the burial of Sarah Christie marked an historical point 135 years after its opening, when the Belfast City Cemetery ceased to provide new graves for the citizens of Belfast.

Q-48: Luis Diaz de Lasaga; *d.* 27 April 1943

Luis Diaz de Lasaga, from the Basque Country, was the captain of a ship that docked in Belfast Harbour some time late in 1937. His ship was subsequently nationalised by the fledging Basque government. This led to a dispute with the Spanish ship owners who brought the issue to the British courts. At the heart of this dispute was the legal status of the Basque government and its right to nationalise the Basque shipping fleet. On 2 May 1938, a judgement in the High Court (Admiralty Division) concerning another ship, the *Herraiz*, set a precedent in favour of the nationalist government of General Franco. The ruling of the court recognised that Franco's was the de facto government of the Basque province and that it exercised effective administrative control over a considerable portion of Spain, over most of the

Basque provinces of Alva (since the beginning of the Civil War in July 1936), Gipuzkoa (since the beginning of October 1936), and Bizkaia, including Bilbao (since the capture of Bilbao, on 19 June 1937). As a result of the dispute, Captain Luis Diaz de Lasaga and his crew were berthed in Belfast docks for over a year. During his time in Belfast the captain spoke out against the government of General Franco. At the 1938 May Day rally in Belfast he called for support for the republican government of Spain.

Later he became a captain in the British Merchant fleet. In April 1943 he was seriously injured when his ship was sunk. He was brought to St George's Hospital in London, where he died from his wounds. His remains were brought to Belfast to be buried in the City Cemetery.

Q-215: James Green; *d.* 1914

This is one of the earliest First World War graves to be found in the City Cemetery. It is the stone of Rachel Green and refers to her son James who, according to the stone, was 'submarined' in 1914 – reminding us that the expression 'torpedoed' had not yet entered into everyday use, and that submarine warfare was still in its infancy.

Q-723: Alan Campbell Carson; *d.* 17 July 1905

Q-723, Alan Carson

Alan from 'Cragalan', 75 Myrtlefield Park, Belfast, was 11 when he fell into a coma and died. His headstone, in the Art Nouveau style, is one of seven stones in the cemetery listed due to their special architectural and historic interest. Art Nouveau originated in America towards the end of the nineteenth century and then spread to Europe. It is characterised in form by sinewy and free-flowing curves, and often uses slightly tapering stems and roots, as can be seen on the Carson stone.

N-312: William Sherrard; *d*. 9 October 1895

The memorial stone was erected by members of the Cliftonville Football Club in memory of 23-year-old William Sherrard, who played for that club at the time of his untimely death from pneumonia on 9 October 1895. Along with his brothers Jack, Joseph and Connolly, he played for one of the very first Irish soccer clubs – Limavady Alexander, established in the 1870s by members of the local cricket club. Joseph Sherrard went on to play for Linfield FC, and between 1885 and 1888, played three times for Ireland. In Glasgow, on 31 March 1895, William Sherrard, playing right half, scored a goal in the 3–1 defeat of Scotland. William is buried in Limavady.

The story of Association Football in Ireland begins in 1878 with the marriage of a young Belfast businessman, John McAlery. He and his young bride went on their honeymoon to Scotland where he watched a number of football games played under Scottish Association Rules. On his return to Belfast, John immediately arranged for two Scottish clubs, Queen's Park and Caledonians, to come to the city for an exhibition match. On 24 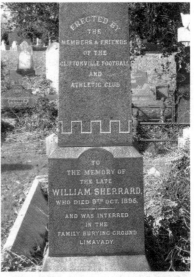 October 1878 the two clubs met in the Ulster cricket ground for their match; Queen's Park won 3–2. On 20 September 1879 an advertisement in the *Belfast News Letter* read: 'Cliftonville Association Football Club (Scottish Association Rules), Gentlemen desirous of becoming members of the above club will communicate with: J.M. McAlery, 6 Donegall Street, or R.M. Kennedy, 6 Brookfield Terrace. Open practice today at 2.30 p.m.' The first recorded game for the new club took place on 29 September 1879 against Quidnunces, a team of rugby players; Cliftonville were defeated 2–1. The first home for the new club was in the third ground of Cliftonville Cricket Club, near Oldpark Avenue. On 18 November 1880, officials of Cliftonville formed the Irish Football Association. At its first meeting, John McAlery became its honorary secretary.

N-536: Henderson Mervyn Wallace; *d*. 29 March 1904

Henderson Mervyn Wallace, from 1 University Road, was only 5 years and 5 months old when he died. The inscription on the base of his headstone refers to him as 'wee Hendie'. The headstone is a remarkable piece of funerary architecture, carved as a bushel of wheat – which represents the Body of Christ.

N-674: Emma Wylie; *d*. 8 February 1904

Emma, from 49 McClure Street, Ormeau Road, was aged 26 when she died from phthisis, a wasting disease arising from tubercular infections. The main inscription on her headstone refers to her brother, R.J. Wylie, a 35-year-old sergeant serving with the 1st Battalion Royal Inniskilling Fusiliers, a regiment of the Irish (5th) Brigade, who was killed in action during the Boer War at the battle of Colenso, on Friday, 15 December 1899.

The battle began at 4.20 a.m. on the morning of 15 December when sixteen battalions of British infantry – about 22,000 men supported by cavalry and heavy guns – attempted to break a Boer defence line of fortified trenches which had been dug along the Tugela River. Facing the British were 4,500 Boers under the command of Louis Botha.

The 4,000 men of the Irish Brigade were under the command of Major-General Fitzroy Hart. He was ordered to cross the Tugela River at a designated point on Bridle Drift, but instead led his men into the open end of a loop in the river where they suffered serious casualties as a result of heavy enfiladed rifle and artillery fire from Boer positions.

The battle lasted eleven hours, finishing at 3.30 p.m., by which time the British had failed to breach the Boer line and were forced to retreat to their base camp. British casualties at Colenso included 143 killed and 755 wounded, as well as 240 missing, presumably captured by the Boers. The failure to break the Boer line at Colenso on 15 December followed British military setbacks at Stormberg on 10 December, and at Magersfontein on 11 December. These three episodes had a very negative impact on British public opinion. Accustomed to little victories in their many colonial wars, the British public were shocked at the failure of their army to defeat what they perceived as a bunch of unruly redneck farmers on horses. One could speculate that a similar conclusion was also reached by the Kaiser in Germany.

The 2nd Battalion Dublin Fusiliers and the 1st Battalion Connaught Rangers also saw action with the Irish Brigade at Colenso.

Moreover, among the 2,000 volunteer stretcher-bearers on the battlefield at Colenso were 800 members of the Indian community of Natal, led by a 28-year-old barrister, Mohandas Gandhi, who would later become known to the world as Mahatma Gandhi.

N-696: Hugh McDowell Pollock; *d.* 15 April 1937

Hugh McDowell Pollock was born in Bangor, County Down, on 16 November 1852. He was the third and youngest son of James and Eliza Pollock. His father was Captain Pollock, a master mariner. After his early education at Bangor Endowed School, Hugh moved to Belfast to serve an apprenticeship with the firm of Andrews & Co., Shipbrokers, of Corporation Street. He then moved to McIlroy and Pollock, flour importers, which, under his management, grew into one of the largest flour importers on the island of Ireland. In 1885 he married Mrs Annie Robinson, whose father, Andrew Marshall, was from Brooklyn in New York. As a well-known member of the business community Hugh Pollock sat on the boards of a number of prominent companies associated with manufacturing, shipping and the linen industry. For many years, he was also the chairman of the Board of Governors of Victoria College. In 1899 he joined the Belfast Harbour Board, serving as its chairman between 1918 and 1921, and continuing to act as a board member until 1937. Between 1930 and 1933, when the old timber ponds on the north foreshore of the River Lagan were developed, they were named the Pollock Dock in honour of Pollock's long service to the Belfast Harbour Board. In 1917, Hugh was invited by David Lloyd George, then British prime minister, to represent the Belfast Chamber of Commerce at the Irish Convention. During this period he also acted as a financial advisor to Edward Carson. In the first Stormont elections, held in 1921, he was elected as the unionist candidate for South Belfast. In 1929 he successfully defended the seat, which had now been renamed Windsor. He retained his hold on Windsor until his death. From 7 June 1921 until the day he died, Hugh Pollock was finance minister in the Stormont government. His was the first death in the unionist cabinet since the inception of Stormont. He died from coronary thrombosis at his home in 26 Windsor Avenue, Belfast, on Thursday, 15 April 1937.

THE IRISH CONVENTION

The Irish Convention was an attempt by Prime Minister Asquith to resolve the political crisis in Ireland following the 1916 Easter Rising. On 11 May 1916, he announced that Ireland was to get self-government (Home Rule). This announcement was followed by a further statement from Asquith on 25 May that David Lloyd George, the British minister for war, had been appointed to put the cabinet's decision into operation. After a series of separate meetings with the Irish Nationalist and Unionist leaders, Lloyd George proposed that Home Rule could be implemented immediately but with an Amending bill to exclude six of the nine Ulster counties. By the end of July 1916, Britain's plan to introduce Home Rule in Ireland collapsed in acrimony, following the double-dealing tactics of Lloyd George, who offered nationalists and unionists different variations of the British proposal.

On 16 May 1917, John Redmond, leader of the Irish Parliamentary Party, and Sir John Lonsdale, who represented the unionists, received a letter from Lloyd George, who had been prime minister since December 1916. The letter contained a new proposal suggesting the immediate establishment of Home Rule for the twenty-six counties, while the six northern counties were to remain within the United Kingdom and be governed directly from London for five years. After this period the British Parliament would reconsider the question of Ireland. Alternatively, if Home Rule for the twenty-six counties was not agreeable, a convention of all Irish parties would be assembled, 'To submit to the British government a constitution for the future government of Ireland within the Empire.' Redmond rejected the proposal to implement Home Rule for the twenty-six counties but accepted the offer for an Irish convention.

A further proposal for a convention was submitted by Lloyd George on 11 June 1917. It entailed suggestions for an unelected assembly made up of 100 members, including 5 members each from the Irish Party, the Southern unionists, the Ulster Unionist Council and Sinn Féin. The churches and the Labour movement were to have 7 members each; 15 members were to be nominated by the British government and the remaining members were to be made up from mayors and chairmen of public bodies and chambers of commerce. Sinn Féin refused membership because of its stipulation that the convention should have the right to propose a wholly independent Ireland, which was rejected by the British.

The convention met for the first time on 25 July 1917 in Regent's House, Trinity College, Dublin. It had six committees and six sub-committees. In the nine months of its existence, between 25 July 1917 and its last meeting on 5 April 1918 the convention and its various committees met fifty-one times. In that period, it looked at the character of Irish self-government, including its national, financial, political, and judicial features. The convention, somewhat undermined by the perfidious approach of David Lloyd George, and the political tensions between nationalists and unionists, failed to reach an agreement. Its final report was signed by only 44 of its 100 members. There is a suspicion, held by some historians, that the 1916 proposals were an attempt at conciliating American public opinion in that crucial period when the USA was preparing to enter war against Germany. Likewise, the convention was seen as a ploy by the British to please and pacify Irish America in the immediate aftermath of the declaration of war by the United States against Germany on 6 April 1917.

N-279: William Scott; *d.* 4 April 1903

William Scott was born on 14 November 1825 in Scotstown, near Glenavy, where he served his apprenticeship before working in Murry, Son & Co., Tobacco Manufacturers, and rising to the position of managing director. An inventive man, William designed and patented the spinning machinery used in the production of tobacco, which was later embraced by the industry's leading manufacturers. Crossing the Atlantic several times to visit the American plantations convinced William to import tobacco direct from the grower, making him the first in the industry to do this. Despite many of the plantations being located in the Southern Confederacy, William publicly took the side of the North in the American Civil War. His stance was shaped by his very strong views on the abolition of slavery. His writings on this topic led to an invitation from an English deputation to give a series of public lectures throughout Britain. Like many Victorians, William had a strong sense of public duty: he was a founder member of the Belfast Total Abstinence Association, along with John McKenzie (father of William McKenzie, the portrait painter); he founded the Irish Temperance League; and he was associated with the Belfast Royal Hospital, the Skin Disease Hospital, and the Working Men's Institute. His eldest son, Dr J.M.J. Scott, served under William MacCormac (see **H-482**: Henry MacCormac) as a member of the Anglo-American Ambulances Surgeons during the Franco-Prussian War. Another son, Dr W.R. Scott, was the medical officer of Health in Bloemfontein, South Africa. William died of cardiac failure at 8 p.m. on Saturday, 4 August at his residence in Madison House, Cavehill Road in Belfast.

Q-309: Brendan Gamble; *d*. 16 July 1995

The inscription at the base of the stone states 'Beam me up Lord'; obviously a Star Trek fan.

Q-660/1: J. J. Phillips; *d*. January 1936

James Phillips, from Marlborough Park Central in Belfast, was a leading architect who specialised in the building of Methodist churches. He was also responsible for designing the Irish National Foresters' Hall at 37 Divis Street in 1906. The Foresters vacated this building in October 1972 and moved to their new premises in March 1973. Phillips designed his own memorial stone, a cross in late Gothic style. This is now listed as a having special architectural and historic interest.

Q-660/1, J. J. Phillips

Q-3: Thomas Love; *d.* 14 October 1911

Thomas lived at 39 Conlon Street and was 60 when he died. The motif above the inscription at the top of his stone is of two hands clasped together. The right hand with the plain cuff is male (possibly representing Thomas) and the left hand with the lace cuff is female (possibly representing his wife Elizabeth). The index finger of the male points to the ground. The holding of hands represents a close bond between individuals, such as in marriage. Clasped hands are also symbolic of a farewell or last goodbye.

S-215: Willie John Ashcroft; *d.* 2 January 1918

Willie John, who lived at 3 Claremont Street, Belfast, owned the Alhambra Theatre in Belfast's Lower North Street. He was born in Pawtucket, Providence, Rhode Island, USA, on 25 June 1845 – his parents emigrated from Belfast in 1840. In 1861 he joined a troupe of minstrels organised by Samuel Corey, a music-seller and publisher from Providence. For six months he travelled extensively through Newfoundland, New Brunswick, Nova Scotia and Prince Edward Island. For the next four years he travelled the same circuit with different variety, drama and minstrel groups. By 1865 he had joined the Seaver's Opera House in Williamsburg, Long Island. This was followed in 1866 by a tour organised by the Lloyds Company, reputed to be the largest minstrel group then in existence. From 1867 until 1872 he toured Canada again, and then sailed to San Francisco to play in Virginia City and Nevada. When he returned to New York he opened the Theatre Comique with himself as Principal Comic. He went to Boston and Philadelphia, and opened at the Globe Theatre on Broadway, before setting sail for England, in July 1872, where he opened at the Oxford Music Hall, London, that September. After London he played Liverpool, Manchester, Hull, Sheffield and Birmingham. He returned to New York but was back in England by June 1875, playing at the Cambridge and Metropolitan Music Halls in London.

In 1876 he achieved huge success with the song 'Muldoon the Solid Man', a rewritten version of an American hit originally penned by John Poole of New York in 1870 and sung by a Tony Pastor. The inscription, 'The Solid Man', which can be found on the base of the cross marking his grave, was first used in 1876 in a Liverpool advertisement.

In 1879 Ashcroft bought the Alhambra Theatre of Varieties in Lower North Street, Belfast, from Dan Lowrey for the sum of £2,000. John Stamford, the manager of the Alhambra, wrote the song 'Macnamara's Band' for Ashcroft.

Ashcroft led a turbulent existence. His wife, the English actress Kitty Brooke, accused him of having an affair with a female cross-dresser and brought him to court. The ensuing, very public, battles of the couple included rows on the stage of the Alhambra. In October 1895 he tried to commit suicide by cutting his throat – he failed but was immediately taken to the Belfast Asylum. In September 1900 he was bankrupted to the tune of £2,450 and subsequently sold the Alhambra. After this, he was committed to the asylum a number of times and died in Purdysburn Asylum on 2 January 1918.

The face of the cross is inscribed 'Laura'. Laura Jane Brooke lived at 13 Eglinton Place until her death at 22 years from pleurisy on 6 December 1887. In the burial records the owner of the grave is registered as Mrs Kate Brooke Ashcroft, the wife of William John Ashcroft.

The Alhambra was one of the first theatres to show films in Belfast, opening its doors to filmgoers in 1896. John Yeats Moore, a cousin of W.B. Yeats, bought the theatre in 1918 and immediately converted it into a cinema. In 1955 the Rank Organisation bought the Alhambra. In September 1959, it closed after a fire caused serious damage. It was later used as a bingo hall.

P-160: Annie Bridgett; d. 25 August 1915
William Bridgett; d. 7 June 1917
William Bridgett; d. 14 June 1932

Annie Bridgett lived at 98 Great Victoria Street, Belfast. She was a member of a well-known Orange Order family and is described on her headstone as 'First Worshipful Mistress Ireland's First Ladies LOL No1'. Annie was married to William Bridgett who, for sixty years, was a designer and painter of banners commissioned by Orange lodges throughout Ireland, Britain, Canada and the United States. William was also a senior Orangeman who held a number of positions in the Orange Institution, including Deputy Grand Master of the Grand Orange Lodge of Ireland and trustee of Sandy Row Orange Hall. He was a senior member of the Freemasonry and had been a member of the Masonic Province of Down. One of his death notices reads 'from Grand Black Chapter represented by Sir Kt John Hume'. He died, aged 79, on 14 June 1932. His address in the burial records is given as 65 Botanic Avenue and 106 Great Victoria Street. Above the inscriptions is the symbol in the degree of a

Master mason; the Masonic symbol of the 'All Seeing Eye' set inside a square and compass.

On the right side face of the stone is an inscription remembering their son, William H. Bridgett. He was a member of the 17th Battalion Royal Irish Rifles, and died in battle on the Ypres salient, Flanders, on 7 June 1917. He is buried there, in Belgium, in the small military cemetery at Spanbroekmolen. The Orange Order named the Bridgett Memorial Sandy Row Guiding Star Loyal Orange Lodge in memory of him. The Commonwealth War Graves Commission (CWGC) lists his regiment as the 9th Battalion Royal Irish Rifles.

On 7 June 1917 the British army launched an offensive against German positions on the Messines-Wytschaete ridge (often pronounced Whitesheet by British soldiers). In this operation, the 16th Irish Division and the 36th Ulster Division were deployed alongside one another, on both sides of the road to Wytschaete, the 16th being on the left of the 36th. They placed 22 mines under German trenches. At 3.10 a.m., 19 of these mines exploded with devastating effect in the German positions facing British army trenches – 10,000 German soldiers were killed or buried alive, and over 7,000 were taken prisoner. One of those who died that day was Willie Redmond, Nationalist MP for Waterford and younger brother of John Redmond. The number of soldiers from the two Irish divisions who were killed and wounded in this operation amounted to 1,448.

British formations were ordered to begin their advance at precisely 3.10 a.m. so that they would reach the German lines moments after the explosions, when the German military units would be in a state of utter confusion. In the case of William Bridgett's unit, the mine they were advancing towards was inexplicably delayed for seventeen seconds and elements of his unit were caught in its blast.

The Germans discovered one of the unexploded mines before 7 May 1917, another was found and detonated in 1955 and one remains lost in the region of Ploegesteert Wood.

John Redmond MP was born on 1 September 1856 in Ballytrent, County Wexford. He was the eldest son of William Redmond, MP for Wexford. John was first elected to Westminster parliament in 1881, to represent the constituency of New Ross. In 1900 he was chosen to lead the Irish Nationalists in Westminster. A strong advocate of Home Rule in September 1914, he called on the members of the Irish Volunteers to join the British army and help Britain in its war effort; 170,000 Irish men responded to his call.

H2-190: Alexander Robert Hogg; *d.* 25 August 1939

Alexander Robert Hogg, the first son of David and Mary Hogg, was born on 1 March 1870 in Tullywest, County Down. His younger sister Lizzie was born around 1872 and a younger brother, David James, was born in 1873. By 1891 the family had moved to 3 Trinity Street, off Clifton Street, in north Belfast. Little is known of Alexander's early life and education, but we do know that he served his time with his uncle, James Hogg, in James Hogg Sons & Co. Ltd., grocers and druggists, at 173 York Street in Belfast, before moving to Dobbin & Co, grocers, druggists and general merchants, at 45–47 North Street, next door to the Alhambra Theatre. By the age of 30 he had left the security of his full-time job to pursue a professional career in photography, a subject in which he had been interested since his teens. By 1901 he had established his own studio at 13 Trinity Street, where he remained for twenty years. As a result of the political conflict raging in Belfast in the early 1920s Alexander decided, in 1921, to move his studio to a vacant studio on the top floor of 81 High Street in the city centre. In 1934 both home and business relocated to 67 Great Victoria Street, which

© Belfast City Council / PRONI

Christian Place by Alexander Hogg

he made his address until his death from pulmonary tuberculosis on 25 August 1939.

On 22 September 1903, at Strand Presbyterian Church (2nd Derry), he married Sara Marion Houston, who had been born in San Francisco. The newly-married couple moved to a new house at 3 Chichester Road in north Belfast before moving in 1912 to 10 Thorndale Avenue. Sara died on 15 April 1932. Two years later, in 1934, at the age of 64, Hogg married again, at Rosemary Street (3rd Congregation) Presbyterian Church in Belfast on 28 April 1934. This time his bride was Margaret Mann who for many years had been employed as a retoucher in his photographic business. Retouching was used by photographers to give a sharper definition to their photographs.

In his career as a professional photographer Alexander emerged as one of the two great photographers of late Victorian Belfast, the other being his friend and colleague Robert John Welch (see **A-512**). Alexander specialised in technical photography, becoming, between 1928 and 1935, the official photographer for the shipbuilding yard of Workman Clark & Co. His early photographs reflect the industrial development of Belfast City, with its new electric trams, motor cars supplied by Harry Ferguson, and the launch at the Harland and Wolff shipyard on 15 June 1912 of the passenger and cargo ship, the *Oxfordshire*. His numerous images of linen workers remind us why Belfast was often referred to as 'Linenapolis'. However, like any working photographer, Alexander's practice brought him into contact with all aspects of the life of the city. In 1907 his coverage of the dockers' strike included a stark picture of a riot on the Grosvenor Road, where a crowd attacked soldiers of the Cameronian regiment. In 1912 he captured the historic signing of the Solemn League and Covenant in the City Hall on 28 September. His haunting images of the slums, commissioned by the Belfast Corporation between 1912 and 1915, are a startling reminder of the atrocious housing conditions which prevailed among the ranks of Belfast's inner-city poor. One of his more haunting images is that of two men sleeping in the kilns of Springfield brickworks. His diverse portfolio ranged from scenes of the River Lagan, aeroplanes at the short-lived Balmoral aerodrome (see **K1-300/1**: Berkeley Deane Wise) to Gallaher's tobacco factory in York Street, and First World War soldiers to a horse-drawn ambulance of the Belfast Fire Brigade. Outside of Belfast he photographed the burial mound at Newgrange and brickworks at Killough.

Alongside his regular business Alexander had, from an early age, shown a keen interest in the use of photography as a tool for education and entertainment. To this end he taught himself how to make lantern slides, and in his promotional literature, he referred to himself as a 'lanternist'. One of his slide shows, *The River Lagan from Source to Sea*, contained more than two hundred illustrations. Coincidentally, the earliest of his photographs to survive is a scene of the Lagan taken in 1888.

Hogg was associated with many cultural and philosophical societies, including the Belfast Arts Society (later to become the Ulster Academy of Art), the Ulster Arts Club, the Belfast Natural History and Philosophical Society, the Belfast Naturalist Field Club, and the Belfast branch of the Professional Photographers Association. A collection of his photographic plates are lodged with the Ulster Museum alongside those of Welch.

—— ENTRANCE TO GRAVEYARD BESIDE ——
FALLS PARK WALL

In the initial planning of the Belfast Cemetery, this entrance was intended for Catholic burials only.

M1-18: William James McCausland; *d.* 31 May 1916

William James McCausland, a member of the Royal Marine Light Infantry, was lost on the battle cruiser HMS *Indefatigable*, 31 May 1916, during the battle of Jutland – the first encounter between the German and British fleets. *Indefatigable* was hit five times by the German battle cruiser *Von Der Tann*. One of the hits on the fore turret of *Indefatigable* penetrated the magazine space causing a major explosion that sliced the ship in half. The battle began at 3.45 p.m. and by 4.05 p.m. the *Indefatigable* had sunk with a loss of 1,017 crew – four survived.

THE BATTLE OF JUTLAND

The Battle of Jutland was the largest naval battle of the First World War, involving 258 warships and 70,000 seamen. The first engagement of the battle began on 31 May 1916 when scouting squadrons of battle cruisers belonging to the British Grand Fleet and the German High Seas Fleet opened fire on each other at a range of 15km. By the time the fighting ceased, at 3 a.m. on the morning of 1 June, the British had lost 3 battle cruisers, 3 armoured cruisers, and 8 destroyers – 6,094 men. The Germans lost 1 battle cruiser, 1 battleship, 4 light cruisers, and 5 destroyers – 2,551 men. Although the British suffered the greatest losses, they won a strategic victory. As a result of Jutland, the German High Fleet remained bottled up in the security of its homeports for the rest of the war.

One of the ships that took part in the battle of Jutland was the light cruiser HMS *Caroline*, which is presently berthed in the Alexandra Dock, Belfast Harbour, where she was used as a training facility for the Royal Naval Reserve until she was decommissioned in 2009. Launched on 21 September 1914, *Caroline* was commissioned on 14 December with a crew of 17 officers and 272 ratings. She was based with the British Grand Fleet at Scapa Flow where she was part of the 4th Light Cruiser Squadron. At Jutland she saw action against a Deutschland Class German battleship and was involved in a torpedo attack.

On 27 March 1918 a platform built over the forward six-inch gun on HMS *Caroline* was used in an experiment to launch a Sopworth Camel biplane. This experiment, using a high performance land plane in a ship-borne operation, was part of a research programme that would eventually see the development of the modern aircraft carrier.

G2-71: Thomas Gibson Henderson; *d.* 14 August 1970

Thomas Gibson Henderson was born on 13 October 1887 at 12 Dundee Street, Shankill Road in Belfast. He attended Jersey Street and Hampden Street National schools. His father John was a painter by trade as well as a drum-maker and banner painter. After leaving school Thomas joined Harland and Wolff, first as a liner boy and then as a catch boy. In 1903, at the age of 16, he joined the Orange Order; he was a founder member of the first Juvenile Orange Lodges. In June 1918, the leader of Ulster Unionism, Edward Carson, created the Ulster Unionist Labour Association as a working-class platform for labour unionists; Thomas became one of its first members. On Christmas morning 1919 he was sacked, for reasons that are unclear, from Harland and Wolff. After a variety of jobs, including shirt and collar cutter, salt packer and machinist, he eventually opened his own small business as a painter. As a painter and an Orangeman, he has the distinction of having painted the very first King Billy on to the gable wall of a grocery and confectionery shop in Weir Street in the Shankill area of Belfast.

Prior to the local government elections held in January 1920, he attempted to get the Ulster Unionist nomination to contest the Shankill Ward, but was rejected. As a consequence, he resigned from the Unionist Party and immediately sought the support of his local Orange lodge, Old Boyne LOL 633; on 15 January 1920 he was elected as an independent unionist to the Belfast Corporation. His election was the beginning of his lifelong involvement in local and regional politics. On 3 April 1925 Thomas won a seat as an independent unionist in the Stormont parliament for Belfast North, coming in with 3,696 votes ahead of the nearest official Unionist candidate, W. Grant. This was the last Stormont election that used proportional representation. In the 1929 Stormont parliamentary elections, held on 22 May, he won the single seat constituency of Shankill, winning by 281 votes over the Unionist Party candidate, S. McGuffin. He held this seat until 22 October 1953 when, in a three-cornered contest, he lost by 2,270 votes to the official Unionist candidate, Henry Holmes.

One of his great public speaking feats in the Stormont parliament occurred on 26 May 1936. Rising to talk at 6.32 p.m. on a finance bill he continued until 3.55 a.m. on 27 May. Tommy was renowned as a colourful political figure with a great turn of phrase, always remembered for mixing metaphors. He was suspended by the Speaker at Stormont on two occasions: once on the issue of 'means testing' and, on 26 October 1938, for making 'a scene' during a debate on the Marketing of Potatoes Bill.

As a city councillor he campaigned for the provision of books and free meals for disadvantaged children throughout Belfast. He proposed the reclamation of 1,000 acres of the northern foreshore of Belfast Lough for the development of a promenade, a bathing pool and all the amenities of a 'Lido'. Moreover, he suggested a new swimming pool at the Grove and persistently called for the reclamation of the Bog Meadows. Over his fifty years as a councillor, Tommy sat on a variety of council committees, including the Health, Education, Libraries and Museums, and the General Purposes Committees. In 1936 he was elected as an alderman and, in 1942, became High Sheriff, followed a year later by his ascension to the role of deputy lord mayor. In October 1963 he was made a 'Freeman of the City', a title conferred on him at a ceremony in the Belfast City Hall on 21 February 1964. He held the Shankill seat for fifty years until his death in 1970.

INDEPENDENT UNIONISTS

From its formation in early 1905, the Ulster Unionist Council sought to create a political monolith that would consolidate the efforts of unionism and defend the political, social and economic interests of unionists within the Union. Despite the early success of the council in achieving this goal, there always existed a group of independent unionists, outside the formal structures of the council. These independents held a variety of political positions, frequently reflecting the fusion of strongly held evangelical Protestant beliefs inside a traditional unionist mindset. There was also an underlying working-class opposition to big house unionism.

On 14 December 1933, a short article in the *Northern Whig*

reported on the formation of a new political party to be known as the Northern Ireland Independent Unionist Association. In effect, this was an attempt to create an umbrella group for independent unionists and Thomas Henderson became its first president. On 15 January 1934 they contested a small number of seats in the local government elections. In January 1938 they announced their intention to contest 15 seats in the forthcoming Stormont elections, to be held on 9 February 1938. By election day there were just 7 independent unionists contesting 6 seats. Winning just 2 seats, their lack of success ended their attempt to create a more cohesive political force from among those unionists operating outside the formal structures of the Unionist Party. In the same election, the Progressive Unionists, another element of disgruntled unionism, failed to win any of the 12 seats they had contested.

Independent unionists, who drew their support from their local community, have always had limited electoral success at the polls in Belfast City, beginning with Thomas Sloan (**R1-141 Glen**) who held the Belfast South seat from 1902 until 1910. On 2 May 1923 Philip Woods won a by-election for the Belfast West seat in the Stormont parliament. In 1925 James Gyle won the Belfast East seat. In the Stormont election of 1929 Robert McNeill represented Queen's University, and John William Nixon won the Woodvale seat. Nixon, who had been dismissed from the Royal Ulster Constabulary in 1924, had been elected a Belfast Corporation Councillor for the Court Ward on 26 August 1924, a post he held until 14 May 1936. He retained his Stormont seat until his death in May 1949.

In one sense the independent unionists acted as a safety valve for unionism. They channelled religious, class, and political tensions through a number of local politicians whose political activity was firmly entrenched in the broad family of unionism.

G2-180/1: Reverend Charles Davey; *d.* 26 March 1919
Reverend Ernest Davey; *d.* 17 December 1960

The Reverend Charles Davey was born on 9 April 1857 in the locality of Carrickfergus, County Antrim. In early life he had been associated with the Irish Evangelisation Society. He attended Queen's College, Belfast and graduated in 1881. He continued his theological studies in the Assembly College, Belfast and then in London's Presbyterian College. In 1886 he was licensed to preach by the London Presbytery and in August 1887 he returned to Ireland and was ordained in First Ballymena Presbyterian Church. He then moved to St Enoch's in Belfast where he was installed on 7 January 1892. In 1900 he moved to Fisherwick Church, where he ministered for eighteen years. He lived at 17 Wellington Park, Belfast.

Reverend Ernest Davey, the son of Charles Davey, was born in Ballymena on 24 June 1890. He was educated at Methodist College and Campbell College, Belfast. In 1908 he was awarded a scholarship to Queen's College, Belfast, where he studied for a year before moving to King's College, Cambridge, graduating there in 1913. He completed his education in Edinburgh, Heidelberg and the Presbyterian College, Belfast. Licensed by the Belfast Presbytery in 1916, he was appointed an assistant in Agnes Street Church and then in Fisherwick. In 1917 he was appointed by the General Assembly as Professor of Church History in the Presbyterian College.

In 1927 he was charged with heresy and brought before a commission appointed by the Belfast Presbytery. The Reverend Hunter of Knock Presbyterian Church in east Belfast, using material from Ernest's student notes and his books, *The Changing Vesture of Our Faith* and *Our Faith in God*, put together five charges of heresy. Davey pleaded not guilty to one charge and claimed 'justification' on the remaining four. He was acquitted after a very successful defence in front of the Presbytery and Assembly.

The Reverend Hunter resigned his membership of the Irish PresbyterianChurch and went on to help found the Irish Evangelical Church. In 1942 Ernest Davey became Principal of the Presbyterian College in Belfast and in 1953 he was elected moderator of the Irish Presbyterian Church. He lived at 3 College Park, Belfast.

There is an inscription on the Davey headstone remembering

William, the son of the Reverend Charles Davey, who was a soldier of the First World War.

The Presbyterian College, designed by Charles Lanyon, was opened on 5 December 1853 as a training college for the Presbyterian ministry. Previously students wishing to become clerics in the Presbyterian Church had to attend the Royal Belfast Academical Institution. In 1881 the college was granted the right to confer degrees through Royal Charter. Between 1921 and 1932 the library of the college was used as the home of the Northern Ireland parliament. Today the college is known as the Union Theological College.

M1-1002: Herbert Barnes; *d.* 22 Feb 1919

At age 28 Herbert Barnes died of pneumonia at the Military Hospital, Clifton Street, Belfast. Reference is made on the family headstone to his connection with the Fourth Hussars. The family of Herbert is listed in British military records as serving continuously with the Fourth Hussars since 1715.

The Fourth Hussars were raised in 1685 and known by their colonel's name, Berkeley's Dragoons – only becoming the Fourth Hussars in 1861. During the Crimean War they took part in the Charge of the Light Brigade and with the support of the King's Royal Irish Hussars, they silenced the Russian guns. Winston Churchill served as an officer in this regiment.

MI-869: Peter McKay; *d.* 4 September 1898

Peter, who lived at 47 Dock Street, Belfast, died at the age of 71. The inscription on his headstone describes him as 'One of the Thin Red Line'. At the battle of Balaclava in the Crimea, 25 October 1854, four hundred Russian cavalry made up of Cossacks and Ingermanlandsky Hussars charged a section of the British line defended by the 93rd Regiment Sutherland Highlanders. Immediately the 93rd were deployed as a straight line. The Russian cavalry, 600 yards out from the British line, were met with an ineffective volley fired from the *Minié* rifles of the Highlanders. At 150 yards a more devastating volley was fired into the ranks of the cavalry and broke its charge.

This action was witnessed by a journalist, William Howard Russell. From Tallaght in County Dublin and acknowledged as the first modern war correspondent, Russell was reporting for *The Times* of London. In his report he wrote, 'As they [the Russians] dash on towards the thin red streak topped with a line of steel'. In time the 'thin red streak' became the 'thin red line'.

Shortly after the defence of the British line by the 93rd, the Heavy Brigade broke through the Russian line. Among the regiments of the Heavy Brigade were the 6th Enniskillen Dragoons and the 4th Royal Irish Dragoon Guards. Later, on the same battlefield, the disastrous Charge of the Light Brigade took place. The Russians were attempting to recapture Russian guns taken by the British earlier in the battle. The Light Brigade was ordered to recover these guns, which lay to their right – instead they attacked another heavily fortified Russian position. Within twenty-five minutes 107 men and 397 horses were killed, among them soldiers of the 8th King's Royal Irish Hussars. This military disaster is remembered in Tennyson's poem when he writes, 'into the valley of death rode the six hundred'.

William Howard Russell went on to report the Indian Mutiny in 1857; the American Civil War in 1861, where he would report on the first battle of Bull Run on 21 July of that year; the Franco-Prussian war of 1870; and the Zulu wars in South Africa in 1879. In 1860 he founded the *Army & Navy Gazette*.

Throughout the cemetery there are numerous family headstones carrying a wide range of memorial inscriptions for dead soldiers, naming battlefield sites and theatres of war. A study of the inscriptions in the lower end of the cemetery reveals the extent of loss during the First World War of soldiers, sailors and airmen, sons of the Protestant and Unionist establishment.

While inscriptions of the First World War dominate, there are also soldier references to the Crimean War (1854–5), the Indian Mutiny (1857), China (1860), the New Zealand Wars (1863), the anti-Home Rule riots in Belfast (1886), the Boer War (1899–1902), the conflict on the North Western Frontier of India

(1921), and the Second World War (1939–45). There are also a small number of inscriptions that refer to soldiers garrisoned in Belfast.

F2-44: James Stewart; *d.* 6 January 1942

James Stewart was the son of Robert Stewart, a weaver from Lissue in the parish of Blairis outside Lisburn. Robert came to Belfast in 1861 and lived in Marine Street in the docks area of Belfast, where James was born on 11 July 1866. Some time after his birth the family moved to Lincoln Street, off the Falls Road. Here the young James came into contact with republicanism. In 1880 the family moved to Leopold Street in the staunchly unionist area of the Shankill Road. James, a member of the Church of Ireland met and married Catherine Alexander Hamilton, a Presbyterian from Wilton Street, Shankill Road. The young couple moved to Canmore Street, Shankill Road, where James lived until his death in 1942. They had five children, Jimmy, Fred, Bobby, Charles and Kate. All his life James was passionate about Irish, left-wing politics and cricket – he played for Woodvale Cricket Club. On the top left of his headstone is the figure of a batsman and wicket-keeper. His politics are reflected in the inscribed 'Organise our strength at the point of production', a quote used by the socialist

movement commonly referred to as the 'Second International'.

During the Irish War of Independence, 1919–21, his son, Charles Stewart, was an active IRA volunteer in the 2nd Battalion Belfast Brigade then active in the Marrowbone area of north Belfast. Charles fought with the East Mayo Roscommon Brigade and was wounded by the Free State army outside Kilkelly, County Mayo, during the Irish Civil War. Smuggled back to Dublin by a friendly nurse, he eventually made his way back to the North where he was imprisoned in Crumlin Road jail, Belfast. He was then transferred to the prison ship *Argenta* before ending up in Derry jail, where he was released in 1924. Charles is buried in grave **WA-321.B**, Milltown Cemetery.

H2-677: Margaret Byers; *d.* 21 February 1912
H2-678: John William Byers; *d.* 20 September 1920

Pioneer of women's education and founder and principal of Victoria College, Margaret was born on 15 April 1832 into a family of Presbyterian farmers in Rathfriland, County Down. She went to England after her father's death in 1840, returning in 1852 to marry the Reverend John Byers on 24 February. Soon after their wedding, the young couple sailed to China, where in Shanghai she gave birth to a son, John. The day before her son was born doctors informed Margaret that her husband was seriously ill with little hope of survival. She immediately organised for the family to return to Ireland by ship. Unfortunately, her husband died on the journey home, eight days from New York. His remains were brought to New York and buried there, in Greenwood Cemetery.

Back in Ireland, Margaret took up her first teaching post at the Ladies Collegiate School, Cookstown, County Tyrone. During this period she was encouraged by the Reverend John Edgar, Professor of Theology at the Assembly College, and the Reverend William Johnston, minister of Townsend Street Presbyterian Church, to open her own school.

In 1859 Margaret opened the Establishment for the Boarding and Education of Young Ladies, 13 Wellington Place, Belfast.

The school subsequently moved to 10 Howard Street, then to 74–76 Pakenham Place, off the Dublin Road, and then to Lower Crescent in 1874. It was named Victoria College in 1887. In 1876, Margaret was appointed as the first secretary of the Belfast Women's Temperance Association, a prison-gate mission for women. Discharged female prisoners were encouraged to stay at its premises at Tudor Lodge, on the Crumlin Road, which had room for twenty-five to thirty women, who worked at laundering and sewing.

Margaret campaigned for the rights of women to a university education, and largely as a result of her efforts the Royal University of Ireland, in 1881, offered to include women in its degree courses and examinations. On the foundation of Queen's University, she was the first woman appointed to its Senate.

Teacher, temperance reformer, businesswoman, philanthropist, suffragette and devout Presbyterian, Margaret supported the Ulster Women's Liberal Unionist Association, and was secretary of the Ulster branch of the National Society for Women's Suffrage. She was also a member of a committee headed by Margaret Pirrie (**K-468/9**) which helped raise funds to build the Royal Victoria Hospital.

John Byers, Margaret's son, was born in Shanghai on 9 November 1853. He was educated at Royal Belfast Academical Institution and Queen's College, Belfast, from where, in 1878, he graduated with his medical degree.* He continued his studies in London and Dublin, returning to Belfast in 1879 to set up his own practice; in that year he was appointed to the Hospital for Sick Children in Queen Street. In 1882 he organised the Department for Diseases of Women in the Royal Hospital, Frederick Street – later to become the Royal Victoria Hospital. John was physician to the Belfast Maternity Hospital and consulting physician to the Victoria Hospital for Diseases of the Nervous System, and held the Chair of Midwifery at Queen's University. He was a member of the Belfast Natural History and Philosophical Society and was elected as its president in 1908. He was twice President of the Belfast Literary Society and was also an Irish speaker. He took a keen interest in Irish folklore and the early history of Ireland – culminating in his book, *The Dialect and Folklore of Ulster*. He lived at Dreenagh House, Lower Crescent, Belfast.

H2-683: Andrew L. Horner; *d.* 26 January 1916

Andrew Horner was born in Limavady, County Derry, on 7 April 1863. His family had settled in County Derry during the plantation, where one of his forefathers took part in the Siege of Derry. He was educated at Londonderry Academical Institution which later amalgamated with Foyle College. On leaving school he entered Queen's College, Belfast, where he graduated in 1881. For a short period he attended the Assembly College with the aim of becoming a Presbyterian minister, but then decided to train as a barrister.

---

* See John Carlisle **K-464** for explanation of name change of Belfast Academical Institution to Royal Belfast Academical Institution.

A convinced and ardent unionist, he was sent by the Irish Unionist Party to Hartlepool, England, during the period of the second Home Rule Bill, 1893, to highlight unionist opposition to Home Rule. In the general election of 1895 he was sent by the Irish Loyalist and Patriotic Union to organise 150 Irish Unionists to speak and canvass in the east of England. In November 1906 he stood against an established unionist, as an anti-Home Rule candidate, for the constituency of South Tyrone but was defeated by 283 votes. After this he helped reorganise the South Tyrone Unionist Association. Following an intensive registration and canvassing operation, where every unionist voter was visited, he won the seat in January 1910 with a majority of 284 votes. He held the seat until his sudden death at Crewe, England, while returning to Ireland.

F2-60: Benjamin Peebles Davidson; *d*. 23 November 1949

Benjamin was 77 years old when he died. He lived at 67 Bawnmore Road, Belfast. His headstone is an example of the 'Egyptian Revivalist' architecture. The stone is topped by a symbol of the Winged Sun disc. On each side of the stone are vertical representations of the lotus flower. Egyptian Revivalist architecture takes its name from the use of ancient Egyptian architectural forms and symbolism. This trend in architectural design emerged in the middle of the eighteenth century; its development was accelerated by the interest spawned after the decoding of Egyptian hieroglyphics in the early part of the nineteenth century. There are strong Masonic influences in the use of this form of architecture.

F2-79/80: John Kirkwood; *d*. 7 January 1906

John Kirkwood, from 23 Agnes Street off the Shankill Road, was born in Ligoniel where he served an apprenticeship with the Wolfhill Spinning Company. Later he became a cashier at the John Savage & Co. Prospect Mill. In 1878 he became general manager at Kirker, Greer & Co. Distillers. John was a unionist and belonged to the Ulster Reform Club. He was also a Prince Mason and a governor of the Masonic Orphan School in Dublin. His headstone is a polished red granite obelisk. The symbol above the inscription is the Masonic symbol of a compass set on a square, with a G in its centre.

There are a number of stones scattered throughout the bottom end of the cemetery that carry a reference to the Masonic order, the most prevalent being the obelisk. The square and compass – the most common of all Masonic symbols – are emblems of Ancient Craft Masonry, which represents the union of opposites: the square is the earth and the compass is heaven. The square makes angles and the compass creates arcs – G is the geometry that binds them together. In the old Masonic manuscripts, known as *The Old Charges*, Freemasonry is equated with geometry. The square equates to the earth and matter, the compass to the circle, heaven and matter.

The obelisk was the Egyptian symbol of eternal life, resurrection and regeneration. The word obelisk comes from the Greek word '*obeliskos*', meaning a prong for roasting. Associated with the Egyptian sun god Ra, they were often cut from the red sandstone of Syene. Many obelisks carry incised hieroglyphics.

UNDERGROUND WALL

Dividing sections P and H2, the wall runs on a west-east line from the main path to the Falls Road. It is 9 feet deep, which is also the depth of a grave in this section. Prior to the opening of the Belfast Cemetery in 1869, this sunken wall was meant to be the dividing line between blessed and unblessed burial ground, in effect separating the Catholic and Protestant sections of the new graveyard.

As a result of a dispute between Bishop Dorrian and the Belfast Corporation over having the final say regarding who could be buried in the section allocated for Catholic burials, the ground was never actually used for its intended purpose. The dispute was brought before the Judicial Committee of the Irish Privy Council, which met in Dublin Castle on 23 June 1869. Isaac Butt represented Bishop Dorrian.

Butt was born in Glenfin in County Donegal on 6 September 1813. Educated at Trinity College Dublin, he became Professor of Political Economy there in 1836 and was called to the bar in 1838. Initially he supported the unionist opposition to Daniel O'Connell's Repeal movement. However, the famine in the 1840s brought a new direction to his politics, and in 1847 he defended members of the republican Young Ireland organisation. He first entered the Westminster parliament in 1852 as the MP for Harwich. In 1865 he defended members of the Irish Republican Brotherhood (IRB) and in 1870 he founded the Home Rule movement. By 1871 he had been elected MP for Limerick.

Also there on 23 June to support the bishop was Bernard Hughes, bakery owner and pre-eminent Belfast Catholic businessman. The dispute concerned the burial, in blessed ground, of Catholics who had been excommunicated or had committed suicide, or of stillborn babies who were never baptised. In the eyes of the Catholic Church such burials in blessed ground were a desecration. The bishop also wanted those in charge of the Catholic section to be under his control – to be appointed or dismissed by him; a portion of the council fees to be paid to him for the support of a Catholic chaplain who would officiate at burials; and finally a commitment that earth from the consecrated ground would not be carted away.

The dispute was eventually resolved when the Corporation bought from Bishop Dorrian, for £4,000, the right to bury Protestants in the ground previously allocated for the burial of Catholics. The bishop then purchased, from James Ross at a cost of £4,200, fifteen acres of land on the eastern side of the Falls Road. Eight acres of this land were used as a burial site, Milltown Cemetery, while the remaining seven acres went to St Patrick's Industrial School. The first person buried in Milltown was Fr Patrick Clark, who died on 15 November 1869.

F2-433: Alexander Kerr; *d.* 12 March 1917

Alexander Kerr was lost on HM submarine *E-49*. Launched in 1916, it was mined off the Shetland Islands on 12 March 1917.

There is also a stone to Kerr's memory in Portsmouth Naval Memorial Cemetery B.

The first Royal Navy submarine was launched in 1902, and was developed by John P. Holland, originally from Liscannor, County Clare, who had immigrated to the United States. Holland was a Christian Brother and schoolteacher. He first suggested to the Irish revolutionary organisation, Clan na Gael, through John Breslin, a member of the 'Clan' in New York, that he had a submersible boat that could attack British warships. Holland secured $16,000 from Clan na Gael to develop three submarines between 1876 and 1881. However, with the decline of political conflict in Ireland and the demise of the Fenian movement, interest from the Irish Americans waned. Then, by 1897, the United States government became intrigued, and purchased the third Holland submarine. This was named USS *Holland*.

F2-122: Marjorie A. Robinson; *d.* 22 October 1924

From a very early age Marjorie was interested in art, which led to an introduction to Vere Foster (**F-527**), who in turn introduced her to the designer and illuminator John Vinycomb, head of the art department in the Belfast firm Marcus Ward & Co. Under his guidance she became skilled in the art of illuminating and took up miniature painting. In 1907 she left for London, where she spent the next seven years. She returned in 1914 and lived at 139 Antrim Road. In the burial records her address is also given as 1 Queen's Elms, Belfast.

P-843: George Sayers; *d.* 20 February 1880

George was born on 12 March 1865 and came from the Malone area of Belfast. He died aged 14 from pneumonia brought on by an accident during a rugby match. In the motif at the top of his headstone are two rose flowers, two rosebuds and a sickle. One of the rose buds is broken at its stem. The two flowers represent his parents; the bud may represent a sibling; the sickle

P-843, George Sayers

is death, and the rose bud broken at its stem represents the life of George tragically cut short.

P-840: Julius Loewenthal; *d.* 5 February 1916

Julius Loewenthal was born and educated at Ludwigslust, near Schwerin in Mecklenburg, not far from the German Baltic coast. When he was 18 he entered the firm of Moore & Weinberg, Linenhall Street, Belfast – one of three new Jewish linen houses (the other two were Jaffé Bros., and George Betzold & Co.). Several years later he was made a partner. After the death of Mr Moore and the retirement of Mr Weinberg he assumed control of the business. He became chairman and treasurer of the Linen Merchants' Association, and he was also a member of the Chamber of Commerce. In the burial records his religion is given as Presbyterian, however Loewenthal is a German-Jewish name, which literally means 'the valley of the lions'. Julius died at his residence Lennoxvale, Malone Road, aged 81.

In 1892 the linen warehouse of Moore & Weinberg became the Linen Hall Library.

F2-638: John Kelly; *d*. 15 September 1904

The first member of the Kelly family associated with coal boats was Samuel Kelly who was born in Ballinderry, County Antrim, in 1818. When he was 22, Samuel set up a business as a grocer and coal merchant in Queen's Quay in the Belfast Docks. His son John was born in or around 1841. By 1861 Samuel bought the ship, the *Brigantine William*, the first of what became known as Kelly's Coal Boats. Samuel died in 1877 and John took over the business, which began to prosper. John, who lived most of his life at Bellavale, in Mountpottinger, east Belfast, was a member of the Orange Order, the Duke of York Masonic Lodge number 666, and the Belfast Conservative Association. He died in Harrogate, England.

It was John's son, Sam, who purchased the gunrunning ship the SS *Clyde Valley* for £4,500. The *Clyde Valley* brought the UVF guns into Larne on 24 April 1914. The guns were purchased in Hamburg, shipped as far as the Tusker Rock, off the southeast coast of Ireland on the SS *Fanny*, and were then transferred to the *Clyde Valley* in the late evening of 19 April 1914.

There was a Watson-class lifeboat named the *Samuel Kelly*. A gift from Lady Mary Kelly, of Crawfordsburn, it was built in 1950 by Samuel White & Co. of Cowes, Isle of Wight, and named after Sir Samuel Kelly, the coal importer and owner of Kelly's Coal Boats. Operating out of Donaghadee, it was involved in the rescue of passengers from the ill-fated *Princess Victoria*, which went down in the Irish Sea on 31 January 1953.

L-752: Josias Cunningham; *d*. 5 September 1895
L-754: James Cunningham; *d*. 1 November 1924

The Cunninghams' connection with Ireland began when Thomas Cunningham left Scotland during the troubles of 1670 and secured a property at Crookedstone, County Antrim. In 1796 his son, Samuel, was killed in an engagement with a French privateer. One of his grandsons, Samuel, was involved in trading with the West Indies. The family had a tobacco manufacturing and import business in Belfast in the early part of the nineteenth century.

Josias was born on 19 January 1819, and educated at Royal Belfast Academical Institute. In 1843, now a stockbroker, he founded Josias Cunningham & Co. which had its office at 41 Waring Street, Belfast. The family owned a large estate in Glencairn, north Belfast, where Samuel Cunningham built Fernhill House in 1899. The family had a long tradition of being active unionists. Their plot contains nine graves, reference L-752/760. The grave reference for Josias, who died on 5 September 1895, was originally L-120, but is now L-752. Graves L-119, L-120 and L-121 were incorporated into the Cunningham plot and each given a new reference.

James Cunningham, who became the head of Josias Cunningham and Co., was a member of a special committee set up within the UUC in 1911 to consider the question of armed resistance to the imposition of Home Rule. The money required for the purchase of weapons by the UVF was channelled through James, and some of the weapons and ammunition smuggled into Ireland by the UVF were stored in the stables at Fernhill House where, on 6 June 1914, a review of the UVF was held. In the 1990s the house was opened as a community museum reflecting the political and social history of the greater Shankill. It emphasises the tradition of service in the British military, especially the history of the 36th Ulster Division.

M-74: Elisha Scott; *d.* 16 May 1959

Elisha, born on 24 August 1894, was one of a family of ten, and was educated at St Simon's School, Donegall Road, Belfast. His lifelong association with football began with the 4th Belfast Company Boys' Brigade, where he played as an inside forward and centre forward, eventually becoming their goalkeeper. From the Boys' Brigade he moved to Broadway United, and then played as goalkeeper for Liverpool Football Club. He played his first Liverpool match against Newcastle United on New Year's Day, 1913. His association with Liverpool lasted twenty-two years, with a short break during World War I when he returned

M-74, Elisha Scott

to Belfast, playing two games with Linfield and helping Belfast Celtic win the Irish Cup, Gold Cup, City Cup, County Antrim Shield and the Belfast and District League. By 1921 he gained his first international cap for Ireland in a match against Scotland. His international career spanned 11 matches against Scotland, 9 against England and 10 against Wales. He played 429 games for Liverpool's First XI before returning to Belfast in 1935 to become player/manager with Belfast Celtic. In 1936, after a Celtic match with Distillery in Grosvenor Park, he quit active football to focus on a management role. He is best remembered as the manager of Belfast Celtic in the years 1935–49, the period of Celtic's Irish League triumphs of 1935–8, 1940 and 1945. He died, aged 66, at the City Hospital in Belfast.

M-61: Clara Copley; *d.* 14 March 1949

Clara Peddis, later known as Ma Copley, was born to Jonas and May Peddis in Clough, Masbrough, near Rotherham, Yorkshire, England, on 14 May 1865. Her father was a greengrocer, and she had one sister. Following Clara's marriage to Joseph Copley, a

timekeeper in the nearby Phoenix Steel Works, she gave birth to two children, Percy and Harold. Some time after the First World War, 'Ma' Copley moved from Liverpool, where she had a wax museum, to Belfast, where she founded a travelling funfair and became a boxing promoter. During the winter months the fair was permanently based in the Chapel Fields, which existed then between the Markets and the Donegall Pass areas of Belfast. During her years as a circus owner and boxing promoter, Ma Copley lived in a caravan before settling at 56 Donegall Pass. Her son Percy married Annie Stankiich on 13 April 1921, and the couple had eleven children. Four of Ma Copley's grandchildren were born in the football grounds that held the funfair during the summer months. These grandchildren included Robert Celtic Copley, who was born in Celtic Park, the home ground of Belfast Celtic; Percy Copley, who was born in the grounds of Banbridge Football Club; Cecil Copley, who was born in Dundella football grounds; and Doreen, who was born in Bangor football grounds.

In the 1930s Ma Copley opened a boxing booth on the Chapel Fields and later built a hall on the same site. Boxers like Tommy Armour, Jimmy Warnock, Ginger Welsh, Tiger Smyth, Jackie Mussen, Buckets Megahey and 'Machine Gun' Mackenzie fought in her booth. The winner received a prize of five shillings. Eventually the local constabulary closed down the hall after complaints that it was a fire hazard. She died aged 83. There is no stone or grave marker on Clara Copley's grave. In 2002, fifty-three years after her death, Jill McKenna, a local historian and writer, who maintained a deep interest in the life of this remarkable woman and her sons, placed three small markers on her grave.

M-960: Cecil Vincent Boyd; *d*. 23 November 1917

Cecil's inscription reads 'Killed in action near Cambrai, France'. The battle of Cambrai is remembered as the first battle in history where large numbers of tanks were used in formation. Tanks were first deployed in small numbers on the Somme when, on 15 September 1916, during the battle of Flers-Courcelette, 49 tanks saw action. They were again deployed at Messines in June 1917. At Cambrai, 476 tanks were deployed on 20 November 1917, when 250,000 British soldiers attacked German lines along a six-mile front. By the end of the battle, on 7 December 1917, the German army had retaken most of the ground gained by the British at the start of the engagement.

M-962: Robert Hugh Hanley Baird; *d*. 8 October 1934

Robert Baird, born on 9 February 1855, was the son of William Savage Baird (**K-258**). He was educated at the Model School and the Royal Belfast Academical Institution. On leaving school in 1869, he became an apprentice compositor in the Ulster Printing Company, Arthur Street, Belfast, owned by his father and Uncle George. On 1 September 1870 he is reputed to have set the type on the very first contents bill of the *Belfast Evening Telegraph* and sold the first copy of the new paper to the Reverend N. E. Smith of Drew Memorial Church, Grosvenor Road. On the completion of his apprenticeship, he moved to the literary department of the *Belfast Telegraph*, where he eventually became sub-editor. After the death of his father from typhoid in 1886 and his uncle in March 1890, he assumed the sole management of the printing and newspaper business. In 1894 he brought out *Ireland's Saturday Night*, a popular sporting newspaper.

A senior member of the Masonic Order, he was initiated into the Excelsior Masonic Lodge CIX in 1885. He was the founder and the First Master of Press Lodge 432, a Royal Arch Mason, a Knights Templar and a member of the Prince Grand Rose Croix Chapter 12, and a 32nd degree Mason. A prominent Orangeman, he was Deputy Grand Master of Ireland and a Deputy Grand

Master of Scotland. On a number of occasions he represented the Grand Lodge of Ireland on the Imperial Grand Orange Council of the World. After his death the Oldpark Temperance LOL 1045 changed its name to the Robert Baird Memorial Temperance Lodge. A new banner made by the Bridgetts (**P-160**), then at Pakenham Street, between Dublin Road and Donegall Pass, was unfurled and dedicated. Arrangements were made for the banner to be flown on 6 June 1935; however, due to bad weather, the banner was not flown until Tuesday, 2 July 1935, when it was paraded along Clifton Street. Robert lived at Park Lodge, Antrim Road.

W & G Baird were letterpress and lithographic printers and bookbinders. They published the *Belfast Telegraph*, the *Irish Daily Telegraph*, the *Belfast Weekly Telegraph*, the *Larne Times*, the *Ballymena Weekly Telegraph* and *Ireland's Saturday Night*.

M-962: William Robert Baird; *d*. 25 July 1953

William Robert Baird, the son of Robert Hugh Hanley Baird, was chairman and managing director of the *Belfast Telegraph*. Educated privately in England, he received his early training in newspaper management while serving on the staff of the *Brighton Herald*. Returning home to Belfast, he joined the family newspaper business as part of its management and Board of Directors. On his father's retirement in 1951, he became the chairman and managing director of the *Belfast Telegraph*. A passionate interest in cars led to his lifelong involvement in racing. At the age of 22 he drove his Riley car in the Tourist Trophy race on the Ards Circuit. He drove an Emeryson in the 1947 Coup de Lyon, and later a Ferrari in the Ulster Trophy at the Dundrod circuit. His hobby killed him aged 41 when his Ferrari skidded and turned over. He was able to extract himself from under the car but died fifteen minutes later in the ambulance. At the post-mortem the coroner reported that Baird died as a result of a lung injury caused by a broken rib. Baird was a Freemason and a member of the Press Masonic Lodge, Avonmore Royal Arch Chapter and the Downshire Preceptory.

M-955: John Glancy; *d.* 27 July 1901

John Glancy, born on 16 March 1825, in Dublin, joined the British army as a boy soldier. He served with the 14th Prince of Wales' Own Regiment and was highly decorated. On 18 June 1855 he fought with his regiment at the heavily reinforced fortification – the Great Redan – in the battle for Sevastopol in the Crimean War. He also fought in the New Zealand Wars of 1863–6. The reference to Kohevoa (correct spelling Koheroa) and Rangiriri on the stone of John Glancy refers to military engagements in the Waikato area of New Zealand's North Island.

His inscription refers to his connection with the Royal Victoria Hospital (RVH) for nearly a quarter of a century until his death in 1902. John was appointed chief medical superintendent of the Belfast Royal Hospital in 1880. The hospital, in Frederick Street, was renamed the Royal Victoria Hospital in 1899. In 1903 a new RVH was opened on four acres of land acquired from the Belfast Corporation. The new site, between Grosvenor Street (now called Grosvenor Road) and the Falls Road, originally belonged to the Belfast District Lunatic Asylum.

M-955, John Glancy

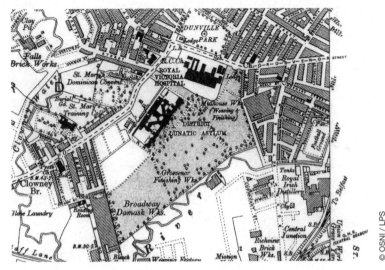

Map of the RVH and the Belfast District Lunatic Asylum

The grave slab at the base of the cross has a crossed sword and flag with three campaign medals – the Crimean War medal with the Sebastopol Clasp, the Turkish Crimea Medal, and the New Zealand medal, all in relief – accompanied by a stone pith helmet.

THE CRIMEAN WAR

The Crimean War began as a dispute between France and Russia over religious sites in the Holy Land. In 1852 France secured, from the sultan of the Ottoman Empire, privileges for the Latin churches in Palestine. Russia then made a series of counter demands in 1853, which the sultan turned down. By July 1853 Russia had invaded the Ottoman states of Moldavia and Walachia. In October the Ottoman Empire declared war on Russia. This was followed in 1854 by England and France declaring war on Russia, and in September 1854 French and British armies landed in the Crimea. There were four main battles: the Alma, Balaclava, Inkerman and Sevastopol. Peace negotiation between Russia and the Allies led to the Treaty of Paris in February 1856. In the lower Falls area of Belfast, a number of streets were named in memory of the Crimean War –

including Alma, Balaclava, Varna, Inkerman, Sevastopol, Raglan and Odessa Streets.

The Great Redan, Malakov Tower

The British and French armies surrounded Sevastopol, the main town in the Crimea, on 24 September 1854. It fell to the French the following year, 8 September 1855. During the year-long siege Sevastopol endured seven major bombardments. The English and French generals decided that the town could be taken from the east and south. Here, two heavily reinforced fortifications, the Great Redan and Malakov Tower, confronted their armies. The two fortifications were part of a defence line built by Russian engineers that linked a series of bastions, all connected by a line of entrenchments. The British were given the task of taking the Great Redan and the French the Malakov. It was decided to attack these two fortifications on 17–18 June 1855 but the Russians repulsed the two armies – who suffered heavy losses. On 8 September 1855 the French took the Malakov while the British were pushed back, at the Great Redan. The Russians evacuated the south side of Sevastopol on 9 September 1855.

THE NEW ZEALAND WARS

There were three major periods of conflict, over land, between the Maoris and the British Colonials: 1846–7, 1860–1 and 1863–6. The Maoris feared that white settlers would encroach on their land and threaten their way of life. The Waitara land wars of the 1850s were followed by a volatile period in the history of New Zealand. The reference to Koheroa (Kohevoa on the stone) and Rangiriri on the stone of John Glancy refers to military engagements in the Waikato area of New Zealand's North Island. Waikato is a province that lies just south of Auckland.

Koheroa

This is a range of hills in the Waikato area of New Zealand's North

Island, which rise above the town of Mercer. It was here, on 17 July 1863, that a British force numbering five hundred clashed with a much smaller Maori force.

Rangiriri

This was the site of a Maori *Pa* (fort) on the banks of Waikato River. On 20 November 1863 a British force of 850 stormed the *Pa*. They were repulsed eight times before the *Pa* fell, with the British losing 41 men and 72 wounded. Rangiriri was a turning point in the war of 1863–6. The Maoris never recovered from their defeat – although the conflict continued for another nine years as a guerrilla war between colonial militia and the Maoris. Many of the militia were recruited on the promise of receiving free grants of confiscated Maori land. By the end of 1863, 1,475 militia recruits had arrived from Australia; this was soon followed by another 1,200 along with 1,000 wives and children. These soldiers were to settle and defend the land against the Maori. Maori opposition had all but fizzled out by 1885.

The last regiment of the British army to withdraw from New Zealand in this period was the 18th (Royal Irish) Regiment of Foot. It arrived in New Zealand in 1863 and departed in 1870. This regiment, raised in 1683, fought against the Irish Brigade in Flanders and the Spanish Irish Regiments at Gibraltar.

M-945: Richard Rutlidge Kane; *d.* 20 November 1898

Richard Rutlidge Kane, born in Omagh on 10 June 1841, spent most of his youth in the County Cavan town of Belturbet. For many years he was a minister of the Primitive Methodist Church before entering the ministry of the Church of Ireland. He was ordained as a deacon in the diocese of Down in 1868 and as a priest in 1869. His first curacy was in Dundonald, which he left in 1868; he also married a Miss Greenslade on 1 September of that year. In 1869 he moved to Walditch, Dorset, in the south of England. By 1871 he had returned to Tullylish, County Down, to become its rector in 1872, remaining there until 1882. In his early

thirties he completed his education at Trinity College Dublin, where he took his Bachelor of Arts and Doctor of Law degrees in 1877 and a Master's degree in 1880. By 1882 he was rector of Christ Church at the corner of Durham Street and College Square North, Belfast – a position he held until his death.

As the Grand Master of the Orange Order in Belfast he played a pivotal role in the campaign against Gladstone's first Home Rule Bill. He was a member of the Grand Lodge of Ireland, Vice-President of the Ulster Loyalist Union and Belfast Conservative Association and a member of 314 Masonic Lodge. As a leading opponent of Home Rule he and the Reverend Hugh Hanna accompanied Lord Randolph Churchill on to the platform at a public meeting of Conservatives and Unionists in the Ulster Hall, Belfast, on 22 February 1886. Speaking on behalf of the Grand Orange Lodge, Reverend Kane opened the proceedings by outlining Unionist opposition to Home Rule:

> In regard to the policy of weak concession to Irish rebel clamour which we have long deplored, Irish loyalists, to the number of a million and a half, have drawn the line at repeal of the union and the establishment of a separate parliament in Dublin.

A Catholic priest, Fr Tohill, publicly accused Kane and Hanna of inciting Protestants during the anti-Home Rule riots of 1886.

After Hanna's death, on 2 February 1892, Kane chaired a meeting in Clifton Street Orange Hall to raise money for the erection of a statue in his memory. On 31 March 1894 a bronze statue of Hanna was elevated in Carlisle Circus, remaining there until it was blown up by the IRA on 1 March 1970.

A leading Orangeman, also reputedly an Irish speaker and a patron of the Gaelic League, Kane is named in the *Gaelic Journal* issued on 1 December 1895 as being one of its patrons. In the Unionist Convention, held on 17 June 1892, Kane was thought to be responsible for the prominent display of the Irish slogan '*Erin go Bragh*'. At this convention he seconded a resolution proposed by Reverend Lynd, the father of Robert Lynd (**M-495**). This resolution pledged the support of the Ulster unionists to Southern unionists.

On 22 April 1898 Rutlidge Kane laid the foundation stone for the West Belfast Orange Hall on the Shankill Road. An Orange lodge, the Kane Memorial Temperance Independent Lodge, was named after him. He lived at 2 Royal Terrace, Belfast.

An important Irish unionist, he is described on his headstone as 'A faithful Pastor, gifted orator and loyal Irish Patriot'. The inscription on the right side face of the stone reads:

> His great talents as orator and divine were devoted to the service of his country by the faithful preaching of the gospel, the defence of constitutional principles and especially with courage and success contending against the 'Home Rule Bill' as a proposal calculated to lead to the dismemberment of the British Empire and the disruption of the United Kingdom.

M-941/2: Reverend James Ferris; *d.* 28 August 1898

There are three inscriptions on the surrounds for the three sons of Reverend James Ferris of Windsor Presbyterian Church. His eldest son, Lt John Ferris, died first, on 15 June 1903, in Poona, India. His second son, Hugh Ferris, died last, on 17 July 1925, while serving with the South African Heavy Artillery in Vence, France. His youngest son, William Ferris, died on 7 June 1917 (fourteen years after his oldest brother), at Messines Ridge serving with the 36th Ulster Division.

M-933: Samuel Alexander Stewart; *d.* 15 June 1910

Samuel Alexander Stewart was born in 1826 and lived with his sister, Mrs Allen, at 342 Springfield Road, Belfast.

Samuel's family, originally from Scotland, had settled in the Ballymena area in the seventeenth century. His grandfather had emigrated to Philadelphia. Samuel himself was born in North America but returned to Belfast in 1837, when he was eleven years old, with his father. He began his working life that year, as an errand boy, and later worked as a trunk-maker in his father's business in North Street, where they also sold leather goods. A self-educated man, he obtained a sound knowledge of science through his love of books, and through night classes. As a result of attending lectures organised by the Department of Science and Art between 1860 and 1864, given by J. Beete Jukes and Professor R. Tate, he developed a strong interest in botany, zoology and geology.

A renowned botanist, Samuel made many trips into the countryside of Down, Antrim and Derry in search of the wide variety of flora to be found in these counties. In the course of this work, he made extensive notes and collected a large number of specimens. A founder member in 1863 of the Belfast Naturalists' Field Club, he presented the paper 'On the Occurrence of Some Rare and Little Known Plants in the Belfast District'. He was also interested in the variety of rocks to be found in the Belfast region, and as a result of excavations in the Belfast dock area, was able to research glacial deposits in the Lagan estuary. In 1874 he published a list of the mosses that can be found throughout the North.

Soon after, he joined a small team whose botanical exploration of the lesser well-known parts of Ireland was compiled for a new edition of *Cybele Hibernica*, research for which was funded by

M-933, Samuel Alexander Stewart

the Royal Irish Academy. In 1882, on the completion of a report on Fermanagh, he conducted further research for a report on Rathlin Island, which was completed in 1884. It was during this period that he met a brilliant young botanist, Thomas Hughes Corry, who was later drowned in Lough Gill, County Sligo, on

9 August 1883 (**H-31/2**). Reports on Lough Allen and Slieveanieran were finished in 1885, and by 1889 he had carried out extensive research on South Clare and the Shannon. In 1888 his book *Flora of the North East of Ireland* was published.

By 1880 he had been appointed assistant curator in the museum of the Belfast Natural History and Philosophical Society in College Square North; in 1891 he became curator, a post he held until 1907. In 1892, with the help of Robert Loyd Praeger, he reported to the Royal Irish Academy on the botany of the Mourne mountains.

While crossing Ann Street in the centre of Belfast at 2.45 p.m., 15 June 1910, Samuel fell down on his left side and hit his head. It was originally thought that he had been knocked down by a horse-drawn van, which passed him as he fell. He died four hours later of shock and heart failure in the Royal Victoria Hospital. He was 84.

At a meeting of the Belfast Naturalists' Field Club on 22 June 1910, it was decided to raise funds to erect a stone over the grave of Alexander Stewart. £56.13s.6d was raised by subscription with a further £11.14s.6d added from the funds of the Field Club. His headstone is in the style of a megalith or possibly a portal stone of a dolmen. It originally carried an oval bronze portrait medallion, which was designed by Rosamond Praeger. The medallion has since been stolen.

— THE BELFAST NATURAL HISTORY SOCIETY —

On 5 June 1821 eight men met in the house of Dr James Drummond, 5 Chichester Street, Belfast — Francis Archer, Robert Simms, James Grimshaw, James Drummond, Robert Patterson, George Hyndman, William McClure and James MacAdam — to form 'The Belfast Natural History Society', and for the first sixteen months of its existence the society continued to meet in this house. Between October 1822 and September 1823, apart from one meeting in James MacAdam's house, meetings were held in the natural philosophy classroom of the Academical Institution. By 17 September 1823 the society was viewing the premises of the New Commercial Buildings (later to be occupied by the *Northern Whig*) situated in the locality known as the Four Corners. Soon after, an agreement was reached between the society and the committee of the Commercial Building for the letting of two rooms at a rent of £10 per year, with £1 extra being charged for the supply of coal. By May 1826 there were sixty members, and by September 1827 the society agreed to draw up plans for its own premises. In the same year it secured a small plot of ground near the Malone turnpike for the purpose of creating a botanical garden. On 13 May 1829 the society bought ground in College Square North from Thomas McCammon. The deeds of the new property, dated 17 April 1830, listed James Drummond, Edmund Getty and William Tennent as the trustees.

On 18 January 1830 an advertisement was placed in the local newspapers seeking tenders for a new building; Duff & Jackson of 18 Commercial Buildings were the architects. Finally, on 1 May 1830, the society left its rooms in the Commercial Buildings.

Three days later, the Belfast Natural History Society marched from Commercial Buildings to the Castle Office where the Marquis of Donegall joined them; they proceeded to College Square where the foundation stone for the new museum was laid. A container was set into the foundations, secured within which were a document in Latin stating who the building was erected for and the date of its foundation, papers of the society, a membership and subscribers list, an 1830 *Belfast Almanac*, coins carrying the Belfast Corporation seal, and four verses from the twelfth chapter of Job in Irish, Welsh, English, Latin, Greek, Hebrew, Arabic, German Hebrew, German, Italian, French, Spanish, Portuguese, Danish and Romaic. On 27 July 1831 John Montgomery was appointed as porter. That November the new building was formally opened. It was the first museum in Ireland built as a result of voluntary subscriptions. John Cassidy became the museum's first curator on 1 May 1834, with a salary of £21 for his first year. On 23 August the society became known as the Belfast Natural History and Philosophical Society. In 1844 William Darragh (J-387) was appointed curator, a post he held until 20 June 1891.

On 7 July 1907 monies held by the Belfast Natural History and Philosophical Society were offered to the Belfast Corporation who, two years later, decided to build a new museum. On 27 July 1910 the cash was legally transferred to the Belfast Corporation, which then rented from the Philosophical Society the old museum in College Square North. By 1914 the Belfast Corporation had agreed to the design by architect J.C. Wynnes for a new municipal museum. However, with the outbreak of the First World War, building was delayed. Eventually, in May 1923, the first section of the new museum on the Stranmillis Road was begun, with the foundation stone being laid by the Duke of York on 22 July 1924. The new museum was officially opened 22 October 1929.

M-915/6: Cairns Children Headstone

The inscription on this stone commemorates the four Cairns children from Ligoniel who died in November 1882. Lizzie was aged 9, John, aged 8 (described as 7 in the burial records), William, aged 6 (described as 5 in the records), and Hugh was just 1 year old. All died from scarlatina – scarlet fever – and were buried on 13 January 1883. There were 195 deaths from scarlatina in Belfast during 1882, with 135 occurring within three months, between the beginning of October and the end of December.

   This headstone is a reminder of the vulnerability of children in an age when countless youngsters died at birth and thousands died in their very early years from infectious diseases such as smallpox, chickenpox, mumps, whooping cough, measles, diphtheria, German measles, diarrhoea and tuberculosis. Some of these diseases came with regularity in certain seasons of the year. Diphtheria and scarlatina were associated with autumn, their symptoms emerging in the months of September, October and November. Whooping cough was associated with springtime, while measles tended to emerge mid-summer and in December. By the 1950s better housing and sanitation, a healthier diet and improved economic conditions, and the introduction of penicillin combined with an increase in public health measures, contributed to the eventual control of these infectious diseases.

M-818: William Gray; *d*. 6 February 1917

William Gray was born in County Cork in 1830. At 16 he began his apprenticeship in the building trade, and also enrolled as a student in the Cork School of Design. He later worked with the Royal Engineers on military fortifications in Portland, England. It was here that he developed an interest in geological study and started to collect fossils. In 1862 he returned to Ireland to work in the Belfast office of the Board of Works. Maintaining his interest in geology, he began to research stone-age flint implements. This led to the publication of a pamphlet, *Irish Worked Flints, Ancient & Modern*. As a member of the Belfast Naturalists' Field Club he helped research a number of important stone age sites, the most notable being Mount Sandel in County Derry. In 1874 he became a member of the Royal Irish Academy. On his death his collection of Irish antiquities and flint implements were left to the Belfast Municipal Museum.

K-271: Robert McMordie; *d*. 25 March 1914

Born on 31 January 1849 and educated at Royal Belfast Academical Institution and Queen's College, McMordie became a solicitor in 1874. He was a member of the Belfast Corporation from 1907 until his death in 1914. From 1910 to 1914 he served as lord mayor, elected no less than five times to this position. By 1911 he was also elected as MP for East Belfast. At the inaugural meeting of the Young Citizen Volunteers (YCV) in Belfast City Hall on 10 September 1912, McMordie became its first President. The YCV eventually merged with the UVF and became a battalion of its Belfast Regiment. During the First World War it became the 14th Battalion Royal Irish Rifles. A committed unionist, the mourners at his funeral included members of the standing committee of the Ulster Unionist Council, Captain Craig MP, and a detachment of the UVF.

K-258: William Savage Baird; *d*. 21 July 1886

William Savage Baird, newspaper proprietor and co-founder

of the *Belfast Telegraph*, and father of Robert Baird (**M-962**), lived at Avonmore, Fortwilliam Park, Belfast. He was a unionist and a member of the Enniskillen 645 Orange Lodge.

He was born on 9 September 1824 in Randalstown, County Antrim. In 1838 at the age of 14 he arrived in Belfast to serve as an apprentice printer at the tri-weekly newspaper, the *Ulster Times*, then published in Arthur Place, and edited by a young barrister, Isaac Butt. In 1844 he moved to work for a John Henderson of Castle Place, which later became Henderson & Russell of High Street, where he specialised in printing musical publications. A later move to the book-publishing house of Simms & McIntyre was followed by a job as foreman with a Mr Abner Walsh of Arthur Square, which in turn was followed by a management position in the job-printing department of the *Belfast Mercury*, a daily newspaper. Following the closure of the *Belfast Mercury*, on 2 November 1861, he and his brother George bought the job-printing department of the defunct newspaper.

It had long been William's ambition to own a newspaper, and in January 1870 he publicly announced his plans to start one – the *Belfast Daily Mail*. However, when he noticed an advertisement in August 1870 for a new Belfast evening paper, he decided to set up his own. Four days later, on 1 September 1870, the *Belfast Evening Telegraph* was launched. It was the first evening newspaper in Ireland and cost a halfpenny. It had four pages and its first edition sold 30,000 copies. It was six days ahead of its rival. In the same year the first English evening newspapers were launched – the *Boston Evening News* and the *Bradford Evening Telegraph*. In 1886 the paper moved to purpose-built premises at Royal Avenue. That same year, William died of typhoid fever, on 21 July.

The Baird headstone carries a beautiful example of angel architecture. Angels are agents and messengers of God, representing divine communication and spirituality, and they guard the dead. Seven angels can be identified: Michael, with his sword or spear; Gabriel, who carries a lily or a horn; Raphael, who carries a pilgrim's staff; Uriel, who carries a scroll or book; Jophiel, who carries a flaming sword; Chamel, who carries a staff and cup; and Zadkiel, who carries Abraham's sacrificial knife.

Many of the angels in the City Cemetery were commissioned from the quarries of Carrara in Northern Italy, which were famous for their stonemasons. As a result, angels carved by Carrara stonemasons are to be found in many graveyards in Ireland and Britain, and are identical in their design.

K-194: Sir William Whitla; *d.* 11 December 1933

William Whitla, of 14 Lennoxvale, Malone Road, Belfast, was born in Monaghan, on 15 September 1851. He began his education at the model school in Monaghan and then came to Belfast, where he became an apprentice in a firm of dispensing pharmacists. In 1872 he entered Queen's College, graduating in 1877 with his medical degree, and then qualified in the same year as a Licentiate of the Royal College of Physicians and Surgeons, Edinburgh.

In 1882 he was appointed physician to the Belfast Royal Hospital and had his first book *Elements of Pharmacy, Materia Medica and Therapeutics* published. He also served on the staff of the Belfast Ophthalmic Hospital in Great Victoria Street and the Ulster Hospital for Women and Children in Templemore Avenue. In 1886 he was appointed as a senator of the Royal University, and became an examiner of that institution in 1889. In 1887 he was appointed examiner by the University of Glasgow. In 1890 he was appointed Professor of *Materia Medica* at Queen's College. One year later he published a *Dictionary of Medical Treatment*.

In 1913 he was selected chairman of the demonstration of the Methodist Anti-Home Rule Campaign held in the Ulster Hall. His speech delivered at that demonstration was later issued as a pamphlet, *A Message to the Non-Conformists of England*, which he used for a number of public meetings in Britain. An indication of the strength of his politics can be seen in that part of his will which bequeathed £1,000 to the gunrunner Fred Crawford (**K-73/4**) 'as a token of appreciation for what he has so heroically done for Ulster and the empire'. In 1917 he was appointed Honorary Physician in Ireland to the King, and was

elected president of the British Medical Association. He served as a member of the Irish Convention from 1917 to 1918 (see Hugh McDowell Pollock, **N-696**) and went on to represent Queen's University Belfast in the British parliament from 1918 to 1923.

The Latin inscription on the top of the stone translates as 'Rest in Heaven'; the Greek at its base translates as 'For he was given to love of men and to love of his art'. Whitla Hall at Queen's University is named after him.

K-73/4: Fred Crawford; *d*. 5 November 1952

Born on 21 August 1861, Fred was educated at Methodist College in Belfast and University College, London. At the age of seventeen he became an apprentice with Harland and Wolff and later served as an engineer with the White Star Shipping Line in Liverpool.

In 1892 he returned to Belfast and joined the Ulster Loyalist Union. Not content with this level of activity he also organised his own secret society that year, Young Ulster. Membership depended on ownership of a .455 revolver, a Martini, or a USA Cavalry Winchester Rifle, and all members were required to have a hundred rounds of ammunition each. The following year he put forward a proposal to Lord Ranfurly, a staunch unionist, to kidnap Prime Minister Gladstone. This proposal was abandoned after Ranfurly refused to give the £10,000 required for the venture.

Crawford helped the Conservative Party in the Brigg by-election in 1894 and ran the Brigade of Unionist Workers in North East England during the general election of 1895. He began to smuggle Mauser Rifles into the North of Ireland and formed his own rifle club, based in his Mill Street factory, where a miniature rifle range existed. He founded several rifle clubs and revived the North of Ireland Rifle Club firing range on waste ground beside the LMS Railway in Belfast. From 1895 to 1897 he was active as secretary of the Unionist West Belfast Registration Committee.

Crawford had been commissioned as second lieutenant in the Mid-Ulster Artillery in 1894. Four years later he moved to the Donegal Artillery and was promoted to captain. In March 1900 he served with the British army in South Africa as second-in-command of a service company until July 1901. From January 1901 until his demobilisation seven months later, he also acted as adjutant of the Irish Brigade Division, Militia Artillery.

By 1906, while secretary of the Ulster Reform Club, he advertised in French, German, Austrian and Belgian newspapers under the name of Hugh Matthew – looking to buy 10,000 second-hand rifles and two million rounds of ammunition. By November 1910 he became an agent for the Ulster Unionist Council (UUC). That same month the UUC set up a special committee with the task of considering armed resistance in the event of the Home Rule Bill being passed through the Westminster parliament. By 1911 Crawford was a member of the Ulster Unionist Council.

He led the West Belfast Volunteers into the Balmoral show grounds on Easter Tuesday, 9 April 1912. On Covenant Day, 28 September 1912, he commanded the guard which escorted Lord Carson and signed the Covenant in his own blood. Following the decision by the UUC in January 1913 to form the UVF, Crawford was appointed director of ordnance to UVF headquarters staff.

In 1913 he smuggled into Ireland six maxim machine guns that he purchased in London. He is best remembered for smuggling 25,000 rifles and 2.5 million rounds of ammunition from Germany, transported to the coast of southeast Ireland by the SS *Fanny* and brought to Larne harbour by the *Clyde Valley* on the night of 24 April 1914. The German arms dealer who secured the weapons for him was a Jew, Bruno Spiro. The Nazis confiscated Spiro's company in 1934 and he is thought to have committed suicide in a concentration camp.

In the aftermath of the First World War, Crawford, with the consent of James Craig, reorganised the UVF. In October 1920 the British government established the Ulster Special Constabulary, consisting of A-, B- and C-Specials. In effect the UVF was to be absorbed into the British state apparatus. In late 1921 the British government authorised the setting up of a new section of the Ulster Special Constabulary. Named C1, it was again designed to absorb the reorganised UVF. Crawford served as a district commandant in the B-Specials. The A- and C-Specials were demobilised in December 1925, but the B-Specials were not demobilised until 1970 when they were replaced by the Ulster Defence Regiment. Their last night of duty was 31 April 1970.

K-55/6: Victoria Davis; *d*. 23 November 1869

Victoria, from University Road, was aged 7 when she died. In the burial records she is described as the 'daughter of The Belfast Man'.

'The Belfast Man', Francis Davis, was born on 7 March 1810 in Ballincollig, County Cork. When he was 7, his family moved to Hillsborough, County Down. Following the death of his mother, 12-year-old Francis went to live with relatives. Within the next couple of years he became a weaver and moved to Belfast. At 20 he moved first to Glasgow and then Manchester to develop his skill in the craft of muslin weaving. A self-taught man he first came to the notice of the public through the publication of his ballads and poetry in support of Catholic Emancipation. In the 1840s he became active in the Young Ireland Movement and many of his poems and songs were printed in their newspaper,

The Nation. To distinguish himself from Thomas Davis, leader of Young Ireland, Francis used the name 'The Belfast Man'.

In 1845 he returned to Belfast and became editor of the *Belfast Man Journal*. Later he worked as the librarian for the People's Institute and then as assistant registrar for Queen's College. His first book, *Lispings of the Lagan*, was published in 1849. When Egyptian mummy Kabooti (now known as Takabuti) was brought to the museum in Belfast, Davis was present when it was unwrapped, an experience reflected in his poem 'Kabooti'. Curiously, for someone associated with Young Ireland, he wrote a eulogy in memory of Prince Albert, the husband of Queen Victoria, and for this he received a medal from the Queen and a public dinner. An extensive collection of his poems and songs, *Earlier and Later Leaves*, was published in 1878. He converted to Catholicism in the last eight years of his life. He died on 7 October 1885 and was buried in Milltown Cemetery on 11 October (**YC-122.A**).

K-5: William Burden; *d*. 4 April 1879

William Burden was born in 1798 in India, where his father Henry was a doctor. Both his parents died when he was 12 so he moved to Belfast to live with his aunts. He was educated at Belfast Academy. His family were descendants of Huguenots who settled in Lisburn around 1680. He began his working life as an apprentice in Vance & Stockdale, but left soon after to continue his studies. He obtained his medical degree from Glasgow University and was elected a member of the Belfast Medical Society in 1829. In 1830 he moved to Newry, spending his first three years as a doctor there. By 1838 William, now living at 16 Alfred Street, Belfast, was appointed physician to the Belfast Maternity Hospital. From 1840 to 1849 he was a member of the Faculty of Medicine at the Royal Belfast Academical Institution, where he lectured on diseases of women and children, and on midwifery. With the founding of Queen's College he became its first Professor of Midwifery. There is no headstone for his grave.

K-11: Lucy Layton Hamilton; *d.* 18 July 1878

Lucy Layton Hamilton was
from Ellens Ville in Bangor,
County Down, and died aged
16. The headstone is sculpted
as an anchor.

K-11, Lucy Hamilton

The anchor as a symbol
dates back to the early
Christian period when it was
used as a disguised cross and
as a marker to guide the way
to secret meeting places. An
early Christian symbol of
hope, confidence and safety,
an anchor entangled in a rope
symbolises death.

K-503: James Crawford; *d.* 23 October 1903

The lower end of the cemetery reveals a widespread use of urns
as symbols of mourning. Urns come from the ancient Greeks and
Romans who, after cremating their dead, placed the ashes in a
vase which they covered with a shroud. Urns are often draped
with a cloth, a garland or wreath. There is a wide variety of urn
design in the cemetery, as exemplified by this grave.

K-316: Thomas Cousins; *d.* 13 December 1875

Thomas Cousins, whose gravestone is designed as a sarcophagus,
lived in Holywood, County Down, and was 41 when he died of
diphtheria.

Sarcophagus, from the Greek word *sarkophagos*, signifies an
ornamental stone coffin, originally named after a special kind
of limestone used for caskets, which was believed to have flesh-
consuming properties.

K-346: Frank Workman; *d.* 14 November 1927

Frank Workman was born on 16 February 1856, the fourteenth child of Robert Workman, a linen merchant who lived in Windsor Avenue, Belfast. He was educated at the Royal Belfast Academical Institution, and at 17 he joined Harland and Wolff shipbuilders as a gentleman apprentice. In 1879 he set up his own small shipbuilding yard on a 4-acre site on the north bank of the River Lagan. A year later, George Clark (H-21), another former Harland and Wolff apprentice, became his business partner and so began the Workman Clark Shipbuilding Company. The first order for the new yard was from D. Macbrayne for the 265-ton coaster *Ethel*. In 1891 a new site – close to Harland and Wolff on the southern side of the river – was acquired for the construction of engine and boiler shops. In 1894 the company bought another yard beside their engine and boiler shops, formerly owned by McIllwaine & McColl. Workman Clark specialised in the building of cargo ships and was also instrumental in the development of refrigeration ships.

One of its main customers was the firm of J.P. Corry, the timber merchants, whose first order in 1886 was for a 1,708-ton sailing ship, *The Star of Austria*. In 1884 Workman Clark completed their first sailing ship, the 1,756-ton *Fort George*, for Clark & Service. The last sailing ship built by the yard was the 2,270-ton *Lord Dufferin*, completed in 1896 for John Herron & Co. In its lifetime, Workman Clark built 535 ships of varying sizes and tonnage, ranging from the 102-ton schooner yacht *Lenore*, built in 1882 for a George Smith, to the 20,000-ton liner *Bermuda*, built in 1927 for the Bermuda and West Indies Steamship Co.

Its production peaked in 1919 when, with a workforce of 10,000, it built thirteen ships with a gross tonnage of 87,600. With the reorganisation of the shipbuilding industry in the late 1920s and early 1930s, Workman Clark was dismantled and its sites on Queen's Island absorbed by Harland and Wolff. The 8,010-ton *Acarus*, built for Anglo Saxon Petroleum and completed in 1935, was the last ship it produced.

A strong unionist, Frank was President of the Victoria Unionist

Association. In 1908, he was elected to Belfast City Council and became High Sheriff in 1913. Some of the guns smuggled into Larne for the UVF in 1914 were stored at the Workman Clark yard. George Clark chaired a secret sub-committee of the Ulster Unionist Council whose purpose was the acquisition of arms for

K-346, Frank Workman

the unionist cause. From 1925 to 1935 Clark was a member of the Northern Ireland Senate.

The base of the cross carries an inscription to the memory of Frank Workman's son, Lieutenant Edward Workman, who died from a head wound received during a raid on German trenches. Before the outbreak of the war in 1914, Edward, who had been educated at Charterhouse and Cambridge University, had managed the Workman Clark yard. He also served as a company commander in the 6th Battalion East Belfast regiment of the UVF. The cross also carries an inscription in memory of Squadron Leader Frank Workman Lindsay, Frank's grandson.

The Workman Cross looks like it is made from speckled limestone but it might actually be reconstituted limestone. If so, a mould of the cross would have been prepared. Then, the original rough limestone would have been ground down into a granular form and mixed with a binding agent to create a liquid substance, and this substance would have been poured into the mould and left to harden.

H-482: Henry MacCormac; *d.* 26 May 1886

Henry MacCormac lived at Fisherwick Place, Belfast. The son of Royal Navy officer Cornelius MacCormac, Henry was born in 1800, in Fairlawn, County Antrim. He was educated in Dublin and Paris and graduated as a medical doctor from Edinburgh University in 1824, the same year he became a Licentiate of the Royal College of Surgeons, Edinburgh. Following the completion of his studies, he travelled by sailing ship to South Africa and then by land to Sierra Leone. He also travelled to North America.

In 1828 he returned to Belfast where he set up a practice in Upper Arthur Street. In 1831 he was appointed attending physician to the Belfast Infirmary and Fever Hospital in Frederick Street, which had opened that August. During the cholera epidemic that raged through Belfast in 1832, Henry secured a small building on Lancaster Street, at the back of the Infirmary, as an isolation block and quarantine house. In 1836 he became Dean of Medicine at the Royal Belfast Academical Institution and from 1840 to 1845 was Dean of the Faculty. He also acted as visiting physician to the Belfast District Lunatic Asylum situated in Grosvenor Street, now Grosvenor Road. He wrote a book about consumption, suggesting that it was an airborne disease that could be prevented by fresh air and proper ventilation.

Henry's son, William, was the attending surgeon to the Belfast General Hospital from 1864 to 1870. He entered Queen's College in 1851 and completed his education in Dublin, Paris and Berlin. He saw war service in South Africa and Serbia. In the Franco-Prussian war of 1870–1, William served with an American ambulance contingent and witnessed the French surrender at the Battle of Sedan. Well-known through his work on the subject of gunshot wounds, he was also the first Irishman to become president of the Royal College of Surgeons.

The nineteenth century witnessed a growth in the provision of medical care. Accordingly, there was an increase in the number and range of hospitals in Victorian Belfast: the Belfast Infirmary and Fever Hospital (1817), the Belfast District Lunatic Asylum (1829), the Union Fever Hospital (1846), the Belfast Hospital for Cutaneous Diseases (1865), the Belfast Ophthalmic Hospital (1868), the Ulster Eye, Ear and Throat Hospital (1871), the Ulster Hospital for Women and Children (1872), the Samaritan Hospital (1874), the Belfast Hospital for Sick Children (1879), the Victoria Hospital for Diseases of the Nervous System (1896), and the Foster Green Hospital for Consumption (1897).

H-252: Edward Bunting Hart; *d.* 7 November 1907

Edward Bunting Hart was 72 when he died at his residence Lisnacree, Strandtown in east Belfast. After an early visit to South Africa he returned to Belfast and worked for the Belfast & County Down Railway. Later, together with a Dr Ritchie, he founded Ritchie, Hart & Co., an iron and brass foundry in Mountpottinger Road, which had previously been called Reeds Foundry. In his early fifties, Edward cut his connection with the foundry and succeeded his father Joseph in his business Hart & Churchill, pianoforte and music dealers.

The Hart name had been associated with the music business since 1792, when William Howard Hart advertised as a teacher of the flute. By the 1820s he was trading as Robert Hart & Son, describing himself as a professor of pianoforte and pedal harp. By 1839 the company had moved to 18 Castle Street, where, in 1842, Joseph Hart was advertising his piano warehouse. In 1858 William Grant Churchill, a piano tuner, advertised for business, giving his contact address as the premises of Robert Hart & Son. With the marriage of William Grant Churchill to the daughter of Edward Bunting Hart, the company became Hart & Churchill. The company moved to Castle Place and eventually to 16 Wellington Place.

Edward Bunting Hart does not appear to have a family connection with Edward Bunting, the collector of Irish music – though perhaps the Hart family had a strong connection with Bunting through their music business. In naming his son Edward Bunting Hart, Joseph may have been recognising this connection.

I-199: William Child; *d.* 27 November 1878

William Child, born in 1806, lived at 35 Botanic Avenue, Belfast. William was a lieutenant colonel in the 46th (South Devonshire)

I-199, William Child

Regiment and then staff officer of pensioners from 1852 until 1875. The Masonic symbol on his headstone is a square and compass set inside a six pointed star. The arms of the compass sit below the arms of the square. The symbol is located inside a ring that has seven flowers; each flower has four petals. Flowers with four petals belong to the plant family, Cruciferae; their petals are arranged in the shape of a cross. The use of the Cruciferae suggests that William Child was connected to the Masonic Knights Templar. The crucifix is a necessary piece in the furniture of a Priory of the Knights Templar. Masonic furniture is the moveable content of the floor space associated with Masonic ritual.

I-319: Robert Lloyd Patterson; *d*. 29 January 1906

Robert Lloyd Patterson, the second son of Robert Patterson (**L-136**), was born on 28 December 1836 at 3 College Square North, Belfast. Robert Lloyd came from a family which was involved in the mill furnishing business, which his grandfather began in 1786 in High Street. His father, also called Robert, had joined the family business at a very early age.

Robert Lloyd began his education with a Miss Mahon of College Street South (now Grosvenor Road), and then with a Reverend John Porter in College Square East, and finally at the Royal Belfast Academical Institution. In 1851 he was sent to school in Stuttgart, Germany, for one year. Returning to Belfast, he became an apprentice at Richardson Brothers, flax and linen merchants. By 1858 he had enough experience to set up his own company, R. Lloyd Patterson & Co., in partnership with a George McIntyre. On 12 November 1861 he married Frances Sarah Caughey. Robert served as a director of the York Street Flax Spinning Company and as chairman of the Board of Superintendents of the Belfast Bank, and also as a member of the Belfast Chamber of Commerce from 1864. A liberal unionist, he was one of the original members of the Ulster Reform Club.

Robert Lloyd's father was 19 when he became a founder member of the Belfast Natural History Society. Young Robert shared this love of natural history and he joined the Belfast Natural History and Philosophical Society. He was its president in 1881–2 and 1894–5. A keen ornithologist, he was considered an authority on Irish birds, and in 1880 his book, *The Birds, Fishes and Cetacea of Belfast Lough*, was published. He was also a keen art collector and accumulated a large collection which he left to the Belfast Corporation.

Robert's brother, William Hugh Patterson (**L-136**), who also worked in the family business in High Street, was a founder member of the Belfast Naturalists' Field Club and a member of the Belfast Natural History and Philosophical Society.

I-318: Valentine Mumbee McMaster, VC; *d*. 22 January 1872

Valentine Mumbee McMaster was born on 16 May 1834 in India. He was a surgeon with the 78th Regiment the Seathforth Highlanders in 1855 when it was on active service in South Africa. He then moved with his regiment to Persia and India. He briefly left the 78th and joined the 6th Dragoons (Inniskilling), rejoining the 78th when it was stationed in Nova Scotia. The regiment was posted to the military barracks in North Queen Street, Belfast, where he died from an infection of the lungs, aged 37.

Mumbee McMaster was given a full military funeral. A firing party with arms reversed, one hundred-strong and four deep, led the procession. Behind the firing party came the muffled drums of the regimental bands of the 78th and the Antrim Rifles, followed by his remains carried on a gun carriage drawn by four black horses. On the lid of the coffin, which was covered with the regimental colours, were his sword, spurs and bonnet. The pallbearers who flanked the gun carriage were six senior officers from the 78th in full dress uniform. His horse, draped in black followed the remains, just ahead of the chief mourners, who were followed by the soldiers of the Antrim Rifles and the 78th.

During the Indian Mutiny he was awarded the Victoria Cross (VC). On 25 September 1857, the Seathforth Highlanders penetrated Lucknow, the capital of Oudh. Their objective was to relieve the British garrison, which had been under siege for ninety-two days, and while their entry in Lucknow strengthened the garrison, it failed to lift the blockade. Nevertheless, the regiment won the VC and decided that Mumbee McMaster would receive the decoration on their behalf. The military records name him

I-318, Valentine Mumbee McMaster

as Valentine Munbee McMaster and suggest that Munbee is his mother's name. On the headstone the name is Mumbee, which may be derived from the Indian name for Bombay, Mumbai. His death notice gives his name as Valentine Murtee McMaster.

Belfast has two further VCs from the Indian mutiny – Private Bernard McQuirk, who is also buried in the City Cemetery (J-233), and Private Patrick Carlin, who is thought to be buried in Friar's Bush. On 29 January 1856, Queen Victoria initiated the Victoria Cross, which was designed by her husband, Prince Albert – a Maltese cross embossed with a Royal Crest and a scroll inscribed with the words 'For Valour'. The medal is still made from the bronze of Russian cannon captured at Sevastopol in the Crimean War and is the highest decoration that can be gained in the British armed services. The very first VC was awarded to an Irishman, Charles Davis Lucas, from Druminargale House, near Poyntzpass, County Armagh. A midshipman on HMS *Hecla*, operating off the island of Bomarsund in the Gulf of Bothnia on 21 June 1854, he successfully hurled a live Russian shell over the side of his ship, thus saving many lives.

THE FIRST WAR OF
INDIAN INDEPENDENCE

In the late 1850s the British army in India introduced a new Enfield rifle, which used a paper cartridge, containing both ball and powder. To load the rifle, the cartridge had to be bitten off at its end and then rammed down the muzzle. The cartridge was heavily greased with animal fat and Indian soldiers in the *Seapoy* Regiments believed the grease was made from cow and pig fat. Cows are sacred to Hindus and pig meat is abhorrent to Muslims. Therefore, in biting such a cartridge, a Hindu would break their caste and a Muslim would feel defiled.

By the end of March 1857, the rumours were at their height when a young *Seapoy*, Mangel Pande, of the 34th Native Infantry, shot his sergeant-major on the parade ground of Barrachpore and then tried to shoot himself. He was court-martialled and hanged on 6 April 1857. The 34th Native Infantry were considered a disgraced regiment and were disbanded, their shame proclaimed across every barrack square in India. This regimental humiliation deepened the discontent already existing among the *Seapoy* Regiments.

A few weeks later eighty-five troopers from the 3rd Light Cavalry in Meerut refused orders to handle the new cartridge. They were court-martialed and each was sentenced to ten years' hard labour. Paraded in front of the Meerut garrison, the eighty-five, shackled in leg and arm irons, were stripped of their uniforms before being led to prison. As a consequence of this, serious rioting led by *Seapoys* of the 3rd Light Cavalry broke out in Meerut. Within a short period of time the mutiny spread to other garrisons of *Seapoys* in Delhi, Cawnpore and Lucknow. In the aftermath of the mutiny, which ended on 8 July 1858, the British East India Company was dissolved and control of India was passed directly to the British government, commonly referred to as the *Raj*.

In the Clonard area of west Belfast, Kashmir Road, Benares, Lucknow and Cawnpore streets were named after battle sites of the Indian mutiny.

I-328: John Hopkinson; *d.* 30 November 1869

John Hopkinson lived at 184 Leeson Street and worked as a cashier in the Ulster Railway goods department. The obelisk over his grave was the very first stone erected in the cemetery, on 1 January 1870. William Firth, of the same Leeson Street address, is listed as the owner of the Hopkins grave.

I-178: Elizabeth du Mesney; *d.* 14 February 1917

Elizabeth served in the Surrey 56 Voluntary Aid Detachment (VAD) at Waverley Abbey Military Hospital. She died there, on 14 February 1917, from appendicitis. Burial records give her name as Winifred Elizabeth Atkinson from Ard-stratha, Antrim Road, Belfast. There are two VADs buried in the City Cemetery, the other being Gertrude Annie Taylor (**L-391**).

Voluntary Aid Detachments were formed in 1909 with the objective of providing support in times of war. At the outset of war in 1914, VADs were essentially nursing orderlies – they scrubbed floors, cleaned and dusted. By May 1915, those over the age of 23 were sent to work in field hospitals on the Western Front where they were used as ambulance drivers, stretcher-bearers and nurses' aides.

I-59: James McCleery; *d.* 1875

This obelisk on this grave is a memorial stone in remembrance of James McCleery, a pawnbroker, but he is not buried in this plot. The word 'Cenotaph' is cut into the stone above the inscription, which can either mean an empty grave or a memorial stone to commemorate someone who is buried elsewhere.

——————————— MORTUARY TOWER ———————————

Samuel Carson, contractor, built the Mortuary Chapel in 1874 at a cost of £1,040. Today, all that remains of the chapel is its tower.

A victim of vandals for years, the chapel was set on fire on 7 July 1980. Five years later, on 22 February, the remains of the chapel were demolished.

The tower of the mortuary chapel

I-62: Margaret Seeds; *d*. 17 May 1887

Margaret Seeds lived at Crescent Terrace, University Road, Belfast. She was the daughter of Poyntz Stewart, referred to on the headstone as 'Of East India Company's Service'.

The East India Company was set up in 1600 by Elizabeth I and given a monopoly on the trade between India and England. As the company developed, it developed its own army and navy, and ruled large parts of India. In the aftermath of the Indian mutiny in 1857, the British government enacted the India Act of 1858 which abolished the East India Company and established full British government control of India.

I-519: John Kirker; *d*. 21 January 1891

The Kirker monument is cut from one block of Irish limestone and is an ornamental cross. Each side of its shaft has four panels, and each panel has its own distinct design of interlacing and geometric spirals cut into stone. Some of its panels depict figures of animals. The complexity of the design is also reflected on its east and west face.

In the nineteenth century Irish stone crosses were popularised as funerary architecture and thousands can be found in burial sites here in Ireland, and in countries where Irish people have settled. The City Cemetery contains many examples of this type of cross, the most striking of which can be seen in the lower end of the cemetery among the Protestant and Unionist establishment.

The first traces of this stone cross in Ireland date back to the eighth and ninth centuries. They are thought to have evolved from wooden or metal crosses. Some scholars think they were used to mark out the boundaries of monasteries, others that they were associated with miracles or places of prayer and penance.

There are three basic types of cross, all of which can be found in the cemetery – plain, with little or no decorative work on its surface; ornamental, with a surface covered by interlace and Celtic geometric spirals; and scriptural, where panels carry

I-519, John Kirker

multiple figures reflecting symbolic elements of the old and new testaments.

The crosses have a number of common features. The shaft of the cross is set in a large base, thought to represent the stone of Golgotha on Calvary. The majority of crosses are ringed, an innovation that scholars think was aimed at supporting the arms of the cross while symbolically representing the Cosmos. A stone, representing a shrine or chapel, often caps the top of crosses. Whatever their meaning, there is no doubt that they are an enduring cultural and religious symbol.

P2-227: Fanny Craig; *d*. 8 May 1887

Fanny Craig, from 49 Parkmount Street, York Road, Belfast, was 29 when she died of convulsions on 8 May 1887. The inscription on her headstone reads 'John Hair in memory of his beloved wife Fanny Craig'. How should this inscription be understood? Was Fanny an independent woman who kept her own surname while being married to John Hair? Or does this inscription reflect the sensitivity of John who understood the black humour of Belfast wits and foresaw the fun they would have with his wife's married name, Fanny Hair? His sensitivity also extends to the burial register where the name entered is 'Fanny Haire'.

O2-47–50: Belfast Benevolent Society of St Andrew

There are six graves in this plot. The first burial took place on 24 July 1898. The large X set in the half-moon shape of rough-hewn stone is the Cross of St Andrew. John Arnott from Auchtermuchty, Scotland, and David Taylor from Perth were instrumental in founding the Society in Belfast. Both had also founded Arnott's Store, drapers and outfitters, in Bridge Street. John became mayor of Cork while David became mayor of Belfast. On 14 September 1867 a meeting was called in the Belfast Athenaeum, at 22 Castle Place, about forming a St Andrew's Society. One week later a rulebook was produced.

On 30 November 1867 the first AGM of the Society was held. Membership was open to those of Scottish birth or those who had a parent or grandparent born in Scotland. In the course of its history the society has engaged in wide-ranging acts of benevolence. It provided coal allowance, spectacles, and boots and tools for workmen in the early days. Then, in 1974, it built ten bungalows for older people. It continues to this day with its charitable works. (See the headstone of the Belfast Benevolent Society of St Andrew **D-182/3**.)

Andrew, the apostle, was a fisherman and lived with his brother Peter in Capernaum, on the shores of the Sea of Galilee. He died in 60 AD in Greece, when the Roman Governor Aegeas sentenced him to death and had him crucified upside-down on a cross shaped like an X – a Saltair. St Andrew is the patron saint of Scotland; King Hungus of Scotland claimed to have been inspired by St Andrew to win a battle over a Saxon army. After the battle the king proclaimed the white cross on a blue field as the flag of Scotland. Andrew's feast day is 30 November.

O2-195/6: Belfast Masonic Charities

There have been eight burials in this plot. The first was Charles Stewart, who died on 27 June 1914, and the last was William Geary, who died on 20 August 1920.

N2-483: Arthur Stanley Tinsley; *d.* 8 March 1934

Arthur Tinsley was a retired bank official who lived at 6 Sans Souci Park in Belfast. He died aged 65.

The Tinsley cross is a smaller replica of St Martin's Cross, a mid- to late-eighth-century ringed cross on the island of Iona. The north face of the cross is covered with snakes and bosses. The south face has a mother and child and four panels, thought to represent Daniel in the lions' den, Abraham about to sacrifice Isaac, and David playing his harp with a piper. The lowest panel with two representations of David may be David killing Goliath, and David before Saul. (See the Cowan Cross **G-241**, which is also a replica of St Martin's Cross.)

M2-224/5: Armagh True Blues LOL 154

There have been two burials in this plot: James Waters, 86 Aberdeen Street, Belfast who died on 12 March 1892, and William John White, 50 Riga Street, Belfast, who died on 15 June 1909. Both men were from the Shankill Road area. Armagh True Blues is an Orange lodge attached to Number 1 District, Belfast. The warrant (document that authorises the setting up of a lodge) for this lodge was originally issued to the Cavan Militia in 1798, the year of the United Irish Rebellion. The Belfast lodge

may have come into existence in 1829 and was probably formed by Orangemen from County Armagh who had settled in the town. The number of the warrant issued by the Grand Lodge of Ireland, under which the lodge exists, was 154, but if a lodge becomes dormant the warrant can be reissued, as is the case with Armagh True Blues.

The Cavan Militia was raised in 1793, and had its headquarters in Cavan town. Like most other Irish militia regiments it was disbanded in 1802 in the aftermath of the United Irish Rebellion. It was reformed in 1803, and in 1881, it was affiliated to the Royal Irish Fusiliers, becoming its 4th battalion.

F-700: Robert Cherry; *d*. 10 March 1870

The design of this headstone was typical of late eighteenth and early nineteenth century English funerary architecture. The style is based on architectural forms associated with furniture; this type of headstone is referred to as a bedstead, taking its name from a popular style of headboard then in use. The cemetery has a small number of these stones in section I, but they tend to be more common in older churchyards throughout Ireland.

F-677: R. B. Andrews; *d*. 13 March 1921

Robert Beattie Andrews lived at 118 Cliftonpark Avenue, north Belfast, and worked as a traveller (salesman) in Coombe Barbours. As a senior member of Freemasonry, Andrews was a Life Governor of the Masonic Female Orphan School, the Orphans' Boys School, the Belfast Charity Fund and the Belfast Widows' Fund; he held these positions until his death. A founder member of the Crumlin Road Masonic Hall, he was the local secretary of the Lodge of Research 200, a Past Master of Lodge 259, and a founder member of Number 21 Lodge and the Shaftsbury Lodge 327 where he acted as registrar. He was a Past Master of the Masonic Province of Antrim and was a Past Knight of Royal Arch Chapters 21, 226, 327 and 513. He was also a Past Second Grand Principal of the District Grand Royal Arch Chapter of Antrim. A High Knight Templar, he was also a member of the Belvoir Preceptory.

An active unionist, he had been a member of the old Conservative Association and later acted as treasurer for the Shankill Parliamentary Association, which he represented on the UUC. For many years he was president of the Crumlin Road and District Unionist Club. He was also a member of the Empire Orange Lodge. There is a death notice in the *Belfast Telegraph* on

F-677, R.B. Andrews

Monday, 14 March 1924, from the Falls Royal Arch Chapter 226.

His grave stone has a base, a pedestal and a plain column with a Gothic crocket capital, upon which is a globe. The design of the column originates in a sixteenth-century Masonic representation of the two pillars, Jachin and Boaz, which stood either side of the entrance to Solomon's Temple. The right-hand pillar, Jachin, signifies establishment and legality, and the left-hand pillar, Boaz, signifies strength. The globe on top of the pillar denotes the earth and the heavens.

The column's pedestal is full of Masonic symbolism. On its eastern side, at the grave's head, a G is set inside the compass and square, with the legs of the compass laid on the square; this represents the degree of Master and also the union of opposites (F2-79/80, Kirkwood). On the pedestal's northern side a crowned Maltese cross with a lion is set at each of the acute angles of the cross, representing the Order of Knights of Malta. The arms of the cross are set on a ring which encircles a Tau Cross, symbolising a Royal Arch Mason. On the western side is a bishop's mitre, set inside a triangle with the lettering D-G, R-A and G-ANT. A Prelate in the Priory of Knights Templar uses the Episcopal mitre. The triangle is a symbol used in Craft Masonry and in the Royal Arch. D-G may refer to the role of District Grand Master; R-A to Royal Arch and G-ANT to Grand Master Antrim. On the southern side the symbolism is difficult to determine; it might be a bishop's mitre, and what looks like a small tag on the lower rim of the mitre carries a shamrock. Set inside the mitre is a circle containing possibly two hands and an interlaced square and compass. Text surrounds the circle. Above the mitre is a banner inscribed with text which is, unfortunately, unreadable.

L2-18: Hugh McKibbin; *d*. 8 December 1914

This headstone carries a memorial inscription for Hugh McKibbin from 3 Newington Street, Belfast. Hugh was the third engineer on the SS *Vedra* who died after an explosion and fire ravaged the ship from stem to stern. Of the 36 crew members, only 2 were rescued, 32 lost their lives in the fire, while 2 others drowned in their attempt to swim away from the burning ship. The *Vedra*, with a gross tonnage of 4,057, and chartered by the Anglo-American Petroleum Company, was en route from Sabine, Texas, to Barrow on the west coast of England. She was carrying 6,000 tons of benzene. At 8 p.m. on the evening of the seventh she ran ashore at Walney Island, a few miles from her destination. At 3.30 a.m. on the following morning, a local tug tried to pull the stranded ship of the shore. She was hauled and bumped over a stony bottom, causing her coffer dam bulkheads to break which resulted in the benzene flooding the engine room. The ship was immediately engulfed in flames; the majority of her crew were trapped in the forecastle and could be heard screaming for help. The inscription on the headstone which is difficult to read, refers to Hugh 'who perished in the burning of the SS *Vedra* 8 Dec 1914'.

L2-472: Elizabeth McDermaid; *d.* 7 July 1926

Elizabeth, a native of Glasgow who resided for a year at 2 Ava Street, off the Ormeau Road in south Belfast, died of a cerebral haemorrhage on 7 July 1926.

One of the most unusual events in the history of the Belfast City Cemetery took place at her grave three weeks after her death. On Wednesday 28 July her son John, who was president and medium of the Belfast Christian Spiritualist Association, led an evangelical service at her grave. Up to one hundred members of the Belfast Christian Spiritualists Association were in attendance, including their secretary Edwin Graham (**F2-145**). As John McDermaid conducted the service of prayer, singing, and an address, photographs were taken in an attempt to capture on film the images of the spirits of the departed friends of those around the grave. On Tuesday 17 August 1926, the photographs were released to the press. They were apparently out of focus but showed small white clouds over those assembled round the grave. John McDermaid claimed that he was able to see the spirit forms of three departed relatives in these photographs, while Edwin Graham was convinced that he could see his brother. The following day, Wednesday 18 August, a summons issued by Detective Constable W.J. Elliott against John McDermaid was adjourned for a week at the Belfast Summons Court. The summons stated 'that you on the 5 August did pretend to tell fortunes to deceive and impose on His Majesty's subjects'. In court it transpired that a policewoman had gone to McDermaid for a 'reading' and had been promised 'romantic adventures' – McDermaid accepted a fee of two shillings. One week later, on Wednesday 25 August, John McDermaid was bound over on his own bail of £10 to keep the peace.

K2-449/508: Belfast Charitable Society

There are 59 graves in this plot, containing 232 remains. Ann Ferron, who died on 18 October 1892, was the first burial, and John McAfee, who was buried on 15 November 1930, was the last interment. A new plot was then purchased by the Charitable Institution in section J3.

The foundation stone for the Belfast Charitable Society building, Clifton House, thought to be designed by Robert Joy, was laid on 2 August 1771. The building, completed in 1774, was officially described as a Poor House and Infirmary. Its first inmates were received on 11 February 1775 when twenty-five Belfast poor took up residence. A local act of parliament enacted in 1774 gave powers to the 'president and assistants of the Belfast Charitable Society to make laws, rules, orders and regulations for the government and management of the infirmary and poor house now known as Clifton House to make bylaws and regulations and to exercise the same powers with respect to all idle and sturdy beggars within Belfast'.

Sections A, B, D, E, F, G, H, I and J Poor Ground

The very first recorded burial to take place in the Poor Ground was Annie Collins, aged 3 years and 3 months, from Browns Row, Academy Street, Belfast, who was buried in **H-71** on 3 August 1869. At the meeting of the Cemetery Committee, on 21 September 1869, it was decided that in Poor Ground section H (the first section to be used for burying the poor), graves would not be filled in until five interments had taken place. The last burial in these sections of the Poor Ground took place on 8 January 1929 when 7-week-old Sarah Smyth was buried in **F-695**. From the burial of Annie Collins to the burial of Sarah Smyth, 62,792 burial orders were issued. There is absolutely nothing to mark these graves other than sections of open ground. Today, these sections contain some roadside proprietary graves. In these cases, the number 3 is added to the alphabetical reference.

J-233 Poor Ground: Private Bernard McQuirk, VC; *d.* 5 October 1888

Bernard McQuirk lived at 72 Urney Street on the Shankill Road. A member of the 95th Regiment, the Sherwood Foresters, he had joined the British army in 1853 and served in the Crimean War. It was during the Indian Mutiny that he received his VC. On 6 January 1858, McQuirk's regiment captured the town of Rowa. During hand-to-hand fighting he received five sabre cuts to his head and body and was also wounded by a musket ball. He lies in an unmarked grave in the public ground. Burial records describe his occupation as 'labourer' and show his name as Bernard McCourt. He was 50 when he died.

FOX LODGE

Built beside the entrance on the Whiterock Road soon after the opening of the cemetery in 1869, the Lodge housed the cemetery foremen. Its last resident, Larry Ferguson, employed in the cemetery as a scythes man, died on 17 February 1993. After Larry's death the house fell into a state of disrepair.

I-434 Poor Ground: Unknown Man; *d.* 11 June 1921

Burial records tell us that this unknown man was 45 years old and died on 11 June 1921. His burial in the Poor Ground took place on Friday, 16 June 1921. Among the nationalist residents in the Lower Falls at that time there was a widespread belief that the unknown man was Edward Fitzgerald, who had lived at 122 Dover Street; they also believed that he had died in suspicious circumstances, and that the police had suppressed evidence of his identity. Edward, a Catholic, had been a soldier in the British army for 13 years, including 4 years of service in the Great War. He served in India, China and Egypt, was demobbed and then re-enlisted in 1914 at the outbreak of the First World War. As a result of injuries he sustained during the First World War, his leg was permanently stiff. Returning to Belfast he found employment with the Great Northern Railway Company. He also worked part-time in a betting shop.

On Tuesday, 13 June 1921, the *Irish News* carried a report that an unknown man, arrested under curfew regulations by a patrol of the Ulster Special Constabulary, on the night of Friday, 9 June, jumped from a Crossley tender armoured car while it was turning into Wellington Place in the centre of Belfast. The man had suffered serious injuries to the back of his head and had been taken to the Royal Victoria Hospital in a state of unconsciousness. He was described as 5 foot 8 inches in height, aged about 40, and wearing a dark tweed suit and a cap. On Sunday 11 June, the unknown man died without regaining consciousness. The same edition of the newspaper also reported on the inquest of the unknown man. A police witness gave evidence that he saw a man acting suspiciously near College Square North in the centre of Belfast. He was arrested but refused to give details of his name and address. On his way to the police barracks he had jumped out of the Crossley tender on to the footpath, the tender was stopped, and the man conveyed to the Royal Victoria Hospital. Medical evidence to the inquest indicated that the unknown man had died as a result of a fracture to the base of his skull. The inquest was then adjourned until 20 June to give the police time to identify the unknown man. At the adjourned inquest a police witness stated that the police were unable to identify him. The verdict returned was death from a fracture to the skull.

On 2 July 1921, the *Irish News* revisited the story of the unknown man with the headline 'The Unknown Victim – How Brave Ex-Serviceman met his fate in Belfast'. The West Belfast MP, Joe Devlin, raised the issue in the Westminster parliament. In response, the solicitor-general outlined the facts relating to the arrest and detention of the unknown man and admitted that betting tickets bearing the name of Edward Fitzgerald, commission agent, had been found in the unconscious man's clothes. It later transpired that the trousers of this man had been the type used as the uniform of employees of the Great Northern Railway. The burial register containing details of the unknown man states 'enquires made about this man 5.7.21'.

H-119 Poor Ground: Rose Dilworth; *d.* 9 October 1869

Rose was a mill worker who lived at 62 Tea Lane in the Sandy Row area of Belfast. Her death certificate (which gives her name as Dalworth) records that she died in the General Hospital from a head injury. Burial records state that she was killed in 'T lane mill' and that three to four thousand people – presumably her work mates – attended her funeral. She is buried in an unmarked grave.

Tea Lane, built in the 1820s, ran from Sandy Row to Linfield Road. The houses were for the mill workers who worked in the surrounding textile mills and brickworks. Tea Lane changed its name to Rowland Street. Six of the original houses can be found in the Ulster Folk and Transport Museum at Cultra.

— POOR GROUND, SPANISH LADY FLU, 1918 —

The word 'influenza' originates in Italy, where in the seventeenth century Italians believed that the disease was caused by the influence of the stars. There are three different strains of influenza: A, B and C. A is the most severe and often jumps from animals to humans. In the process, it emerges as a new variety of the virus. 'Spanish Lady Flu' was such an A-strain. The first outbreak occurred in the Allied Military camp at Etaples, northern France, where in December 1916, a number of soldiers died of a deadly flu-like disease, incorrectly described as purulent bronchitis. On 8 March 1918, a soldier of the United States army serving in Camp Funston, Kansas, became the first officially recorded victim of Spanish Lady.

Facilitated by the enormous mobility of people and armies in the wake of the First World War, the virus spread quickly with devastating results. It particularly affected those between the age of 20 and 40. By the time the flu had run its course it had infected up to a billion people worldwide and killed fifty million. While the majority of its victims suffered from the normal symptoms of flu, such as headaches, muscle pain and fever, a substantial number died quickly as their lungs filled with fluids. As the lips, ears, fingertips and toes of victims turned blue, they literally drowned as a result of internal haemorrhaging and excess lung fluid.

The life of the flu can be broken down into three periods: its beginning and mild period, stretching from March 1918 to July 1918; its middle and its devastating period, which lasted from September through to December 1918; its final and less virulent period from February to April 1919.

When the flu first appeared, the press generally failed to report on it as a result of wartime censorship, but as Spain was a neutral, non-combatant nation, the press there carried some of the earliest reports of the pandemic. When *Pravda*, the Russian newspaper, covered the story of the flu it reported that 'Ispanka' (the Spanish Lady) had come to town. The Spanish Lady flu reached Belfast in May 1918.

It is impossible to say how many died in Belfast at this time; however, comparing the number of deaths in the cemetery during the lifetime of the flu to the same period in 1917 shows an increase of over 1,038 burials during 1918. Initial research appears to indicate a correlation between the three periods that span the lifetime of the flu and the increase in burials during these periods.

Today we tend to associate the period of the Spanish Lady Flu with burials in the Poor Ground, and this is reflected in the Poor Ground burial records for 1918, which list many deaths from influenza and pneumonia. However, the burial records for proprietary graves reveal that substantial numbers of flu victims were buried in family graves in Sections C, H, I, J and P Glen.

During the first period of the flu, burials increased from 4 June 1918, reaching a peak by 2 July. They decreased thereafter until settling to a 'normal' figure by late August. There were 755 burials: 260 buried in Poor Ground and 495 in proprietary graves. In the same period of 1917, 423 deaths had been registered; 178 in Poor

Ground and 245 in proprietary graves. In the two weeks prior to 30 July, 30 remains were received from Queen's University.

By 24 September 1918, during the second period, burials were again on the increase. They reached a peak by 30 November and thereafter decreased. This period saw 1,124 burials: 364 buried in Poor Ground and 760 in proprietary graves (21 of these were American soldiers who drowned when the troop ship *Otranto* sank; see D-58–75 Glen). In the same period of 1917, 580 deaths had been registered of which 275 were in Poor Ground and 305 in proprietary graves.

By the end of January 1919, during the flu's third and final period, burials were once again on the increase, reaching a peak by 11 March. During this period there had been 748 burials: 256 buried in Poor Ground and 492 in proprietary graves. In the same period of 1917, 586 deaths had been registered, of which 234 were in Poor Ground and 352 in proprietary graves.

In total, over 2,627 burials had taken place in the cemetery during the lifetime of the flu compared to the 1,589 burials for the same period in 1917–18, an increase of 1,038 burials.

	1917 burials	1918 burials	Differential
Period 1	423	755	+332
Period 2	580	1124	+544
Period 3	586	748	+162
Total	1,589	2,627	+1,038

Epidemics and pandemics in Belfast

An epidemic is a disease characterised by sudden invasion of the population, rapid and extensive spread, and sudden decline. A pandemic is a disease that affects a whole country, though today the term is generally applied to a disease that affects the whole world.

There were three major pandemics in the twentieth century: the Spanish Lady Flu in 1918–19, the Asian Flu in 1957 and the Hong Kong Flu in 1968. In 1976 a soldier died in Fort Dix, New Jersey, from a flu thought to be descended from Spanish Lady. In 1997 flu was detected in Hong Kong, which had jumped from chickens to humans and was only contained after the Hong Kong government slaughtered over a million chickens.

Spanish Lady was the first pandemic to affect Belfast, but Belfast had been previously hit by several epidemics. On 18 March 1832 the first Irish cases of Asiatic cholera were recorded. Of the 2,827 cases treated in the Fever Hospital, Frederick Street, 418 died. A further outbreak occurred in 1834, and again in the famine years 1847–49. In the early months of 1847 there was also a serious outbreak of smallpox and dysentery among the poor of Belfast. Later that year the *Swatara*, en route from Liverpool to New York, was forced to return to Belfast after the outbreak of fever among her passengers; the sick were transferred to the Fever Hospital. On 9 December 1847, Mary Sherry was taken ill at 6 a.m.; by 3 p.m. she was dead in the Fever Hospital, the first victim of the cholera epidemic. By the time the epidemic had run its course, towards the end of 1849, the Fever Hospital had treated 15,000 cases, with 3,000 dead.

Then, in 1853, the *Guiding Star*, on its voyage from Liverpool to New York (carrying 600 passengers, some suffering from cholera), was forced by bad weather to dock in Belfast. The disease soon spread to the inhabitants, who suffered another epidemic that lasted until December 1854, with 8,000 cases being treated in the Fever Hospital. Of these, approximately 2,000 died. Cholera returned to Belfast again in 1866.

Typhus, associated with lice from rats, was recorded in 1816 and existed in Ireland until the 1920s, and typhoid was widespread in Ireland until the 1950s. A Dr Gerhard in Philadelphia made the distinction between the two diseases in 1836: typhus is a disease associated with overcrowding and poverty, whereas typhoid is linked to the contamination of food or water by the bacillus of the disease.

The year 1919 saw an epidemic of scarlet fever in Belfast, which began in the early part of the year and reached its peak in the winter months of 1919 and the early part of 1920.

The following is an excerpt from a notice printed in the *Belfast News Letter* on 15 March 1875:

Regulations to be observed by persons in whose houses contagious diseases have arisen

Sanitary Department, Town Hall, Belfast,
16 February 1875.

- To prevent the spread of infectious diseases it is imperative that the following rules shall be strictly observed:

- When a case of typhus fever, smallpox, scarlet fever, or any other infectious disease shall occur in any house occupied by poor persons, the patient under the advice of the medical attendant should be promptly removed to hospital.

- When the patient has been so removed, or has, unfortunately, died in the house, the entire clothing used about the person should be put into a tub of cold water, or, still better, a mixture of 'Condy's Fluid' one part to a hundred of water and kept outside the house for twenty-four hours. The house floors and woodwork should immediately be thoroughly washed and cleansed with hot water and soap. The walls, when practicable, lime washed, and every apartment fumigated with chloride of lime and vitriol in proper proportions. The operations should be under the supervision of a sanitary sub-officer.

- The personal and bed clothes, after having remained in the cold steep for twenty-four hours, should be carefully washed with hot water and soap, and dried before a strong fire.

- The bed, if of straw, chaff, or shavings, as well as ticking, if very dirty, and saturated with any discharge from the patient, should be burned. This should be done within the yard attached to the house, and under the direction of a sanitary sub-officer.

- Woollen articles in the house should be cleansed, and exposed to a strong dry heat.

- During the carrying out of all these precautions, a free current of fresh air should pass through all the rooms of the house, by having the doors and windows kept open.

Samuel Brown, LK QCPI, &c.,
Consulting Sanitary Officer.

H-531/545/525, Poor Ground: First World War Memorial

In 1914 a plot of 19 graves in section H Poor Ground was allocated for the burial of First World War soldiers; there are 74 soldiers buried in this plot. The first burial was Rifleman Sturgeon, of the Royal Irish Rifles, who died on 1 December 1914.

During the First World War a number of cemetery staff enlisted in the British army. In the cemetery records for 1916 there is a reference to Charles Bell killed in action in Ypres, Belgium, on 25 April 1915. Reference is also made to James McNenemy, who had been discharged from the Royal Irish Fusiliers on 11 January 1916

The First World War memorial screen wall

and was no longer physically fit for war. On 9 October 1917 the Parks Committee was informed that John McFadden, foreman of Dunville Park, had returned home after two years imprisonment in Germany. On 23 April 1918, mention is made of Andrew McMullan, who re-enlisted, having been discharged after nine months service.

On 12 February 1918, Daniel McCann, superintendent of the cemetery, reported that the military authorities had delivered wooden crosses for the graves of soldiers interred in the cemetery. On 12 March he reported that a further seven crosses had been delivered.

On 24 January 1927 a letter to the Belfast Corporation from the Imperial War Graves Commission (IWGC) – later to become the Commonwealth War Graves Commission (CWGC) – submitted proposals for the erection of a 'stone curb wall' which would carry the names and military details of those buried in the memorial plot. At a meeting of the Parks Committee on 17 August 1927, it was agreed that the IWGC be permitted to erect the memorial wall. The memorial carries the names of 74 soldiers who are buried in the plot, 58 soldiers who are buried in unmarked graves in the Roll of Honour ground in sections H3 and I3, and 8 soldiers who are buried elsewhere in the cemetery.

Of the 296 First World War graves in the cemetery, 133 of these are buried in unmarked or family graves, which are often referred to as 'Roll of Honour' ground. There are soldiers' graves marked with military stones scattered throughout sections A, B, C, C3, D, F, G, H, I, J, K, L, M, O and P in The City and sections P and Q Glenalina. There are also five headstones in the memorial plot for soldiers who are buried in other graveyards.

All IWGC headstones are of a uniform shape and size – 15 inches wide, 3 inches thick, and stand 2 feet 8 inches out of the ground. Each headstone is engraved with a name and rank, the date of death if known, a regimental badge and a religious symbol. Many of the stones carry inscriptions from deceased's family. Details of all these soldiers can be obtained from the CWGC.

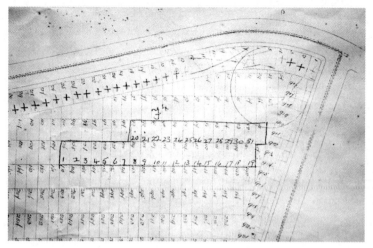

The Queen's University section of the Poor Ground

F4-1/31 Poor Ground: Queen's University Section

These graves form a sub-section within a section. They are located in Section F Poor Ground and run on a north-south axis from roadside graves **F-911–4**. The only section in the cemetery with a '4' after the alphabetical reference, these graves are owned by Queen's University and contain 139 remains used to further medical science. Burials records indicate that many of those buried here came from the Belfast Asylum or the Work House. The remains of the insane and the poor provided Queen's medical researchers with a resource for their studies, at the same time relieving the Asylum and Work House of the burial costs. The first burial in this section took place on 19 July 1918. Originally these graves were numbered **F-81/93** and **F-108–126**.

─────── RED BRICK HOUSES 2A AND 2B ───────
WHITEROCK ROAD

The red-bricked houses at 2a and 2b Whiterock Road were part of the estate of Henry Patterson and housed his mill foremen. They were acquired when the estate was sold to the Corporation on 6 June 1912 and then rented to cemetery staff. The Corporation sold the two houses: Geraldine and Robert McManus bought 2a on 31 July 1991, and William Tully bought 2b on 30 January 1997. Seven cottages also belonging to the estate of Henry Patterson were situated directly behind the two red brick houses but they were demolished shortly after the Corporation purchased the estate.

C3-799: William Gillespie; *d*. 15 October 1914

William Gillespie, whose family came from Dunmurry, was a stoker on the cruiser HMS *Hawke*, which was torpedoed by the German submarine *U-9* off the coast of Scotland on 15 October 1914. The *Hawke* had been launched at Chatham dockyard in 1891 and weighed 7,350 tons. She was hit near her magazine and sank in eight minutes – 525 crew were drowned, with only 73 surviving. William Gillespie was among the 51 Belfast men who lost their lives that day. The *Hawke* had another connection with Belfast. On 20 September 1911, she collided with the White Star liner, the *Olympic*, and in command of the *Olympic* was the future captain of the *Titanic*, E.J. Smith.

U-9 was one of the most successful German U-boats of the First World War. Built in 1910, she was a patrol-type submarine powered by two heavy oil engines. On 22 October 1914, about 40 miles off the Hook of Holland, she sank 3 British cruisers, the *Aboukir*, the *Hogue* and the *Cressey* – 1,459 sailors were lost and 837 were rescued from the North Sea. The result convinced naval strategists that the submarine had enormous fighting capabilities and that warships of the Royal Navy were vulnerable to them. *U-9* was used on operational duties until November 1915, returning to Kiel in Germany to be used as a training boat in April 1916. She survived the war and surrendered to the British Navy. She arrived in Morecambe on 30 May 1919, where she was broken up for scrap.

By 1905 the Germans had designed submarines with real fighting potential. In 1913 Germany launched its first diesel-powered *unterseeboot*, more commonly known as U-boats. At the outbreak of the First World War Germany had 10 U-boats and 17 more under construction; the French had 77 and the British, 55 submarines, most of which had four torpedo tubes in the bow and another two in the stern. The first sinking by a U-boat was on 5 September 1914 when *U-21* sank the small cruiser HMS *Pathfinder* off the Scottish coast. The last torpedo fired by a U-boat at the end of the First World War was on 21 October 1918, when the British merchant ship *Saint Barcham* was sunk in the Irish Sea with a loss of eight lives.

D3-23: The McCutcheon Children

This grave holds the remains of eight McCutcheon children – the youngest was 6 months old, the eldest, 7 years old – and one adult. It is probably safe to assume that the children were siblings, but there is no indication of that in the burial records. Louisa, aged 21 months, from 15 Barrington Street, Donegall Road, Belfast, died from diarrhoea on 17 July 1895; Margaret, aged 11½ months, from 27 Ayr Street, York Road, Belfast, died from convulsions on 11 June 1897; William, aged 4½ months, from 65 Britannic Street, Sandy Row, Belfast, died from marasmus on 5 September 1899; Daniel, aged 7 months, from 38 Tavanagh Street, Donegall Road, Belfast, died from diarrhoea on 5 October 1902; Mary Jane, aged 18 months, from 38 City Street, Sandy Row, Belfast, died from whooping cough on 4 February 1910; Mary Lenora, aged 7 years, from City Street, Sandy Row, Belfast, died from whooping cough on 6 February 1910; Hanna, aged 6 months, from 160 Matilda Street, Sandy Row, Belfast, died from pneumonia on 15 January 1911; and Samuel, aged 18 months (burial records give his age 14 months), from 1 Lawyer Street, Sandy Row, Belfast, died on 4 January 1916 from diphtheria.

The adult was 61-year-old Agnes Cairns from 12 Rowland Street, in the Sandy Row, who died from bronchitis.

This headstone reminds us of children's vulnerability to the range of diseases and infections that ravaged working-class Belfast in the nineteenth and early twentieth centuries. Children dying in large numbers was a common enough occurrence; an example of this is the year that Margaret McCutcheon died

from convulsions. On 1 September 1897, Henry Whitaker MD, medical superintendent for the City of Belfast, reported to the Belfast Corporation on the number of deaths between 22 July and 25 August of that year. In this thirty-five-day period 370 children died in Belfast – 276 of these were less than a year old and 94 were aged between 1 and 5 years. The main killer was diarrhoea, followed by the wasting disease phthisis, which in turn was followed by diseases of the respiratory organs. In his report Whitaker states that 'the health of the city is very unsatisfactory and its death-rate abnormally high'. He goes on to report 'the epidemic of measles and scarlatina seems to have died out'.

In the ten-year period between 1884 and 1894, Belfast, at the pinnacle of its wealth and industrial power, had a higher percentage death rate per thousand than London, Manchester, Birmingham, Newcastle, Oldham, Bolton, Leeds, Sheffield, Bristol, Bradford and Glasgow. In this period the death rate in Belfast had either increased or remained stationary, while in the other cities it had diminished. Between 1891 and 1895 Belfast had a higher percentage death rate per thousand for typhoid, typhus, scarlatina, diphtheria and diarrhoea than London, Liverpool,

Manchester, Birmingham, Leeds, Sheffield, Bristol, Bradford, Dublin and Glasgow. Appalling housing and sanitary conditions; the building of slum dwellings on sites previously used as dumps; large numbers of open sewers, drains and cesspools; inadequate supervision of the construction of streets; the ineffectual administration of Public Health Acts; widespread poverty and hunger; long working hours in mills and factories, especially for women and children; and inadequate health provision are some of the main factors which put Belfast top of the death rate list in the industrial cities of the British state.

SECTION C3-ISLAND CROSS OF SACRIFICE

On 24 January 1927 a letter from the IWGC to the Belfast Corporation submitted a proposal for the erection of a 'War Cross' in section C3-island site; this was approved by the Corporation at its meeting on 1 April 1927. The contract to build the cross was given to Messrs Haslett Bros., Abercorn Road, Derry City. Designed by Sir Reginald Blomfield, it was erected to remember the soldier

The Cross of Sacrifice

dead of the First World War and is at the very back of the original Belfast Cemetery. The cross, with its downward pointing sword, is made from Carlow limestone, and sits on an octagonal base resting on three steps. There are four cross sizes, depending on the number of graves in a cemetery.

CHAPTER 2

THE JEWISH BURIAL GROUND

This short walk reveals the journey of the Jewish community from its arrival in mid-nineteenth-century Belfast, its growth in the early part of the twentieth century and its decline after 1940 – today there are approximately 130 members of the Jewish community living in Belfast with another 80 or 90 throughout the north of Ireland. A great sadness pervades the Jewish burial ground – in its own way it tells the story of the Jewish Diaspora.

In the minutes of the Cemetery Committee of 5 October 1869, reference is made to a letter from Mr D. Jaffé requesting a meeting regarding an application for burial ground on behalf of the Jewish community. In the minutes of the same committee, dated 16 January 1871, permission is given for the allocation of land for the burial of members of the Jewish community.

© Belfast City Council / PRONI

The minutes of the Belfast Corporation's Cemetery Committee, 5 October 1869

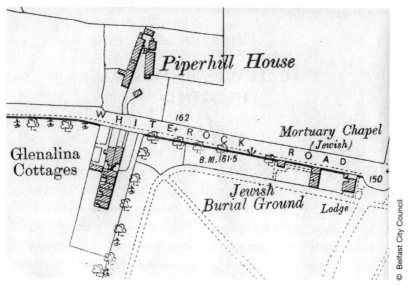

© Belfast City Council

A map of the Jewish burial ground, 1901

There are three distinct phases of development regarding the Jewish burial ground. The first phase is the acquisition of section C in 1871, which has proprietary graves and Poor Ground. The second phase is an extension of section C in 1898 and the last phase is the acquisition of section C1 in 1916.

Jewish Burial Ground

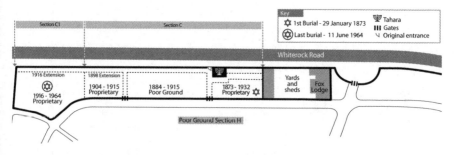

Jewish burial ground, Section C – Acquired 1871

Proprietary graves layout 1873–1932

All names are spelt as they appear in burial orders.
When only a grave reference is given, this indicates an unused grave.

C-166	C-340	C-521
C-167	C-341 Daniel Jaffé 28.01.1874	C-522
C-168	C-342	C-523
C-169	C-343	C-524
C-170 Arthur Betzold 28.04.1877 Florence Betzold 05.09.1880	C-344 Norah Veitil 29.11.1879 Lucy Veitil 30.05.1883	C-525
C-171 Behjamin Marks 01.06.1878	C-345 George Betzold 10.02.1890	C-526 David Buchinsty 21.06.1903
C-172 (S/B) Rubenstein 07.08.1883	C-346 Julia Phillips 26.06.1932 Last burial in this section	C-527 Ester Circorsky 17.03.1903
C-173 Lewis 12.01.1892	C-347 Michael Cohen 13.04.1887	C528 Bernard Brown 26.02.1903 Jacob Hyman 08.03.1903
C-174 Elias Silver 17.01.1892	C-348 Louis Solomon 17.08.1893	C529 Edith Slack 28.10.1902
C-175 David Natalie 13.06.1897	C-349 Eda Myers 15.09.1898	C-530 Harry Freeman 19.06.1902

C-176	C-350	C-531
Berty Levey	Alfred Lewis	Marion Kruger
13.06.1897	01.10.1898	25.02.1900
C-177	**C-351**	**C-532**
Jussman Clarke	Israel Bogan	Solomon Wiener
23.05.1898	20.11.1898	16.06.1902
C-178	**C-352**	**C-533**
Gertrude Lazarus	Sarah Clarke	Annie Appleton
17.08.1898	13.07.1899	24.02.1900
C-179	**C-353**	**C-534**
	Moses Blogh	Henry Lewis
	30.12.1899	10.01.1900
C-180	**C-354**	**C-535**
Aaron Altshular	Saul Bernstein	Fisher Sergie
25.02.1904	02.05.1904	16.11.1904
C-181	**C-355**	**C-536**
(S/B) Herschman		
29.1.1873		
First Burial in Jewish Ground		
C-182	**C-356**	**C-537**
C-183	**C-357**	**C-538**
C-184	**C-358**	**C-539**

The first burial was a stillborn (S/B) child by the name of Herschman from 57 Divis Street, Belfast, who died on 29 January 1873 and was buried in **C-181** on the 31st of that month.

The 1873 burial register with Herschman reference, 31 January 1873

© Belfast City Council

The following is a summary by year of the names and addresses of those members of the Jewish community buried in the Jewish burial ground. It becomes obvious in a study of the burial records that the spelling of a name was often registered as it was heard. There are also differences in spellings between the burial order, which was kept at the City Hall, and the burial register, which was kept in the City Cemetery office. If a name is incorrect, the correct spelling is placed in brackets.

1873	**(S/B) Herschman.** 57 Divis Street. *d.* 29 January 1873.	C-181
1874	**Daniel Joseph Jaffé.** Merchant. 65 years. *d.* 28 January.	C-341
1877	**Arthur Betzold.** 2 months. 6 Wellington Park. *d.* 26 April.	C-170
1878	**Benjamin Marks.** 5 months. 4 Carrickhill. *d.* 1 June.	C-171
1879	**Norah Henrietta Veitil (Veital).** 7 weeks. 48 Ulsterville Avenue. *d.* 29 November.	C-344
1880	**Florence Betzold.** 3 weeks. 6 Wellington Park. *d.* 5 September.	C-170
1881	**Edward Benjamin Boas.** 6 years, 5 months. *d.* 6 June.	C-163
1883	**Lucy Jeannette Veitil (Veital).** 13 years. 48 Ulsterville Avenue. *d.* 30 May.	C-344
	Rubenstein. 6 weeks. 44 Regent Street. *d.* 7 August.	C-172
1884	**Lewis.** 9 hours. 56 Israel Street. *d.* 12 January.	C-173
	Israel Cohen. 5 months. 55 McClure Street. *d.* 12 February.	C-150
1885	**Walaia Cohen.** 8–17 days. 55 McClure Street. *d.* 27 December.	C-150

1887	**Michael Cohen.** Moneylender. 68 years. 23 Magdala Street. *d.* 13 April.	C-347
	Abraham Rutenberg (Ruttenberg). 4 months. 123 Hillman Street. *d.* 6 August.	C-151
	(S/B) Friedman. 53 Eglinton Street. *d.* 10 August.	C-152
1888	**Goldfus Soul (Saul).** 8 months. 25 Hillman Street. *d.* 23 March.	C-153
	Bennet Gleazer (Glazer). 18 days. 147 Cullingtree Road. *d.* 11 April.	C-154
	Abraham Francis Rubinstein. 13 months. Armagh. *d.* 26 October.	C-155
	Bennet Lewis Rabimoutteh. 1 year. Armagh. *d.* 8 November.	C-324
1889	**Simon Lewis.** 10 weeks. 36 Hillman Street. *d.* 12 March.	C-325
	Rachel Silver. 16 months. 135 New Lodge Road. *d.* 2 October. *First Jewish burial order*	C-326
1890	**(S/B) Lewis.** *d.* 12 January.	C-327
	Emma Clarke. 6 weeks. 47 Eia Street. *d.* 30 January.	C-328
	George Betzold. Linen merchant. 54 years. Derryvolgie Avenue. *d.* 10 February.	C-345
	Israel Sloan. Hawker. 38 years. 52 Israel Street. *d.* 12 August.	C-329
	(S/B) Jaffé. 9 Israel Street. *d.* 14 August.	C-505
1891	**Louis Millar.** 2 years, 4 months. 137 Divis Street. *d.* 1 January.	C-506
	Maria Robinson. 5 months. 27 Harding Street, Derry City. *d.* 30 March.	C-507

Annie Rutenberg (Ruttenberg). 6 months. C-508
73 Bristol Street. *d*. 7 December.

Abraham Lavine (Levine). 8 days. C-509
201 Upper Meadow Street. *d*. 9 December.

1892 **Elias Silver.** Dealer. 34 years. C-174
45 Twickenham Street. *d*. 17 January.

(S/B) Krayzman. 142 Divis Street. C-510
d. 3 February.

Isaac George Purcell. 18 weeks. C-156
88 Dover Street. *d*. 9 September.

(S/B) Earlstein. 27 Penrith Street. C-330
d. 26 October.

(S/B) Bermstayom (Bernstein). Armagh. C-511
d. 29 November.

1893 **(S/B) Brook.** 137 Divis Street. *d*. 9 February. C-157

Michael Elliott. 3 years, 6 months. C-331
52 North Boundary Street. *d*. 24 March.

Daniel Davis. Manager, Reform Club. C-158
d. 11 April.

Abraham Rutenberg (Ruttenberg). C-512
3 years, 6 months. 63 Bristol Street. *d*. 10 July.

Haris Jacobson. 11 months. C-332
28 Bedeque Street. *d*. 15 August.

Louis Solomon. 9 months. Ballyhackamore. C-348
d. 17 August.

Jacob Cohen. 10 days. Conlig Street. C-513
d. 23 December.

Edith Berman. 2 years. 161 Divis Street. C-159
d. 28 December.

1894	**Gershon Hirsch Seilin.** 16 months. 13 Arkwright Street. *d.* 24 July.	C-333
	Eihel (Ethel) Parke. 3 months. Edward Terrace, Armagh. *d.* 4 November.	C-514
	Sarah Berwitz. 28 years. 180 Hillman Street. *d.* 16 November.	C-160
	Judah Herson. 15 months. 19 Divis Street. *d.* 21 December.	C-334
1895	**David Fastovsky.** 7 months. 42 Gloucester Street. *d.* 22 January.	C-515
	Lazerus Cohen. 6 months. 27 Fortingale Street. *d.* 4 February.	C-335
	David Brooke. 6 months. Union Street, Cookstown. *d.* 7 April.	C-161
	Aaron Elliott. 20 months. 36 Bedeque Street. *d.* 5 June.	C-516
	Rose Rutenberg (Ruttenberg). 10 months. 17 Bandon Street. *d.* 9 July.	C-162
	Leah Purcell. 14 months. 25 Salisbury Street. *d.* 19 September.	C-336
	(S/B) Bass. 19 Perth Street. *d.* 11 November.	C-517
	Clara Leinkram. 11 weeks. 77 Hopewell Street. *d.* 15 December.	C-690
1896	**Abraham Elliott.** 4 years. 36 Bedeque Street. *d.* 9 January.	C-691
	Henry Ruttenberg. 9 months. 3 Vicinage Park. *d.* 24 March.	C-692
	Samuel Edstene. 4 months. 15 Mountjoy Street, Derry City. *d.* 2 June.	C-693

Louis Leinkram. 14 months.   C-694
77 Hopewell Street. *d*. 31 October.

Catherick (Catherne) Glick. 10 months.   C-695
Armagh. *d*. 1 December.

(S/B) Leventhall. 19 Perth Street.   C-696
d. 11 December.

1897   **David Natalie (Natalia).** Shopkeeper from   C-175
Manchester, found dead in York Street.
26 years. *d*. 26 May.

Berty Levy. 17 years. 43 Analea Street.   C-176
d. 13 June.

Blenny (Benny) Barron. 4 months.   C-697
41 Bristol Street. *d*. 27 June.

Liny Wolff. 10 months. 30 Bedeque Street.   C-698
d. 28 July.

Rebeca Leinkram. 7 months.   C-699
77 Hopewell Street. *d*. 2 August.

Nathan Rosenfield. 5 weeks.   C-700
25 Newington Avenue. *d*. 17 September.

1898   **Mendel Parks.** 36 years. 12 Conlig Street.   C-701
d. 20 April.

(S/B) Miller. 45 Analea Street. *d*. 11 May.   C-702

Jussman (Zussman) Clarke. 50 years.   C-177
31 Lonsdale Street. *d*. 23 May.

Gertrude Lazarus. 7 months. Lurgan.   C-178
d. 17 August.

Eda Myers. 49 years.   C-349
73 Great Victoria Street. *d*. 15 September.

Alfred Lewis. Traveller. 21 years.   C-350
3 Churchill Street. *d*. 1 October.

Arron Chipkin (Chiplins). Traveller.   C-149
30 years. *d.* 11 November.

Israel Bogen. Shopkeeper. 45 years.   C-351
14 Eglinton Street. *d.* 20 November.

David Wulfson. 3 years, 6 months.   C-148
19 Fortingale Street. *d.* 29 November.

1899   **Dalby (Dally or Dolly) George Blank.**   C-147
1 year. 21 Broughton Street,
Dundalk. *d.* 8 January.

Isaac Solomon. 10 months.   C-146
62 Groomsport Street. *d.* 9 September.

(S/B) Rostow. 1 Vicinage Park.   C-145
d. 17 November.

Moses Blogh. 58 years. 15 Mountjoy Street,   C-353
Derry City. *d.* 30 December.

Sarah Edith Clarke. 20 years.   C-352
Armagh Asylum. *d.* 13 July.
Burial order lists **C-350** *as grave number.*

1900   **Henry Lewis.** Jeweller. 45 years.   C-534
Thompson Home, Lisburn. *d.* 10 January.
Burial order lists **C-346** *as grave number.*

Annie Appleton. 33 years.   C-533
Mater Infirmary Hospital. *d.* 24 February.

Marion Rebecca Kruger. 50 years.   C-531
89 Fortingale Street. *d.* 25 February.

Marks Rutenberg. 1 year.   C-144
39 Fortingale Street. *d.* 27 March.

(S/B) Elliott. 6 Vicinage Park. *d.* 30 March.   C-143

(S/B) Davis. Clifton Street Hospital.   C-144
d. 5 November.

May Morris. 5 years. 59 Newport Street.   **C-143**
d. 27 November.

Dina Cohen. 18 months.   **C-142**
14 Fortingale Street. *d.* 18 December.

1901   **Fanny Robinson.** 11 months.   **C-141**
Groomsport Street. *d.* 25 February.

(S/B) Sheir. 19 Lincoln Avenue. *d.* 8 March.   **C-140**

(S/B) Philip Hodes. 38 Groomsport Street.   **C-137**
d. 3 April.

(S/B) Godea. 8 Frederick Street. *d.* 30 April.   **C-136**

Harris Levinthal. 16 months.   **C-135**
113 Bristol Street. *d.* 7 July.

Harry Benjamin. 8 months.   **C-323**
85 Fortingale Street. *d.* 19 July.

Sarah Paradise. 4 months.   **C-322**
25 Carlisle Street. *d.* 3 September.

1902   **(S/B) Sherskie.** 4 Vicinage Park.   **C-321**
d. 21 January.

Joseph Glasser. 10 months.   **C-320**
18 Southport Street. *d.* 5 February.

Louis Blank. 3 months. Dundalk. *d.* 20 May.   **C-319**

Solomon Jacob Wiener. 4 years and   **C-532**
6 months. 2 Fairview Street. *d.* 16 June.

Harry Freeman. Apprentice. 16 years.   **C-530**
25 Carlisle Street. *d.* 19 June.

(S/B) Gorfunkle. 26 Groomsport Street.   **C-318**
d. 12 July.

(S/B) Jacobson. Clifton Street Hospital.   **C-317**
d. 25 August.

(S/B) Sherlock. 20 Regent Street.   C-316
d. 30 August.

Edith Slack. 54 years.   C-529
180 Old Lodge Road. *d.* 28 October.

1903   **Joseph Leventon.** 11 years.   C-315
24 Fortingale Street. *d.* 14 January.

Bernard Brown. Drapier. 32 years.   C-528
34 Vicinage Park. *d.* 26 February.

Jacob Hyman. 10 months.   C-528
94 Great George's Street. *d.* 8 March.

Esther Leah Percorskie. 28 years.   C-527
4 Bellview Avenue. *d.* 16 March.

(S/B) Jacobs. 29 Newington Street.   C-314
d. 2 May.

Sophia Writson. 2 years.   C-313
143 Fortingale Street. *d.* 18 May.

David Buchainsky (Budzosky). Tailor.   C-526
39 years. 107 Fortingale street. *d.* 21 June.

Shulla Levine. 45 years. 29 Lincoln Avenue.   C-337
d. 26 June.

Bernard Grosse. 58 years. 73 Bristol Street.   C-518
d. 17 December.

1904   **(S/B) Rapaport.** 61 Great Patrick Street.   C-312
d. 6 January.

(S/B) Hyman. 94 Great George's Street.   C-311
d. 17 January.

Jacob Smyth. 25 days. 25 Buckpark Street.   C-310
d. 3 February.

Aaron Altshular (Atshular). 56 years.   C-180
4 Abercorn Terrace, Derry City. *d.* 25 February.

Saul Bernstein. Traveller. 28 years.   C-354
8 Perth Street. *d.* 2 May.

Blank. 6 months. Child of George   C-504
and Sarah, Dundalk. *d.* 16 August.

Morris Samuel. 9 months.   C-503
18 Great Patrick Street. *d.* 26 September.

Edie Ratthaws (Rathus). 10 months.   C-502
44 Violet Terrace, Crumlin Road.
d. 4 October.

Ellina Harris. 5 months. Dublin Street,   C-501
Dundalk. *d.* 4 October.

Fisher Sergie. Traveller. 53 years.   C-535
62 Newtownards Road. *d.* 16 November.

Paulina Gordon. 2 years, 8 months.   C-500
54 Groomsport Street. *d.* 12 December.

(S/B) Jacob Solomon. 240 Old Lodge Road.   C-499
d. 19 December.

Mollie Cohen. 63 years. 15 Vicinage Park.   C-109
d. 24 December.

1905   Harry Winegood. 14 weeks.   C-498
88 Great George's Street. *d.* 12 March.

Kate Barker (Baker). 26 years,   C-110
and her (S/B) baby. 65 Fortingale Street.
d. 13 April.

Joseph Daitch. Cigarette manufacturer.   C-497
34 years. Oldpark Road. *d.* 6 May.

Henry Lewis. 1 year, 8 months.   C-496
93 Fortingale Street. *d.* 15 June.

(S/B) Morris Hynman (Hyman).   C-495
94 St George's Street. *d.* 25 June.

Bessie Dinah Eitman. 1 year, 9 months.   C-494
65 Bristol Street. *d*. 25 June.

Joseph Freeman. Manager. 57 years.   C-118
Lever Street. *d*. 2 August.

1906   **Jane Diamond.** 8 years. *d*. 2 March 1906.   C-493

Leah Clarke. 23 years.   C-111
37 Packenham Street. *d*. 6 March 1906.

(S/B) Leah Morris Hynman (Hyman).   C-492
94 Great George's Street. *d*. 29 March.

Helina Karp. 22 years. 7 Summerhill Street.   C-112
d. 12 June.

(S/B) Eban. 26 Antrim Road. *d*. 2 July.   C-491

(S/B) Gordon. *d*. 20 August.   C-490

Louis Goldberg. Soldier. 22 years.   C-489
Ballykinlar Camp. *d*. 23 August.

Sarah Lukowsky. 70 years.   C-113
2 Twickenham Street. *d*. 25 September.

(S/B) Rubin. 6 Annalee Street.   C-132
d. 16 December.

Yudel Grimes (Gruns). 1 year.   C-306
95 Fortingale Street. *d*. 22 December.

1907   **Annie Lyszith (Lipsitz).** 28 years.   C-488
Belfast Asylum. *d*. 18 January.

Unknown child. 6 years. Mater Hospital.   C-487
d. 14 February.

(S/B) Blank. Child of George and Rachel,   C-486
Dundalk. *d*. 24 July.

Lleia Feldman. 15 years. Union Infirmary.   C-485
d. 1 August.

Fanny Grimes. 12 years. Children's Hospital C-484
Queen Street. *d.* 17 September.

Solomon Brown. 27 years. Lisburn. C-483
d. 2 October.

(S/B) Sireilmon. 31 Hanover Street. C-689
d. 20 November.

Abraham Freeman. Traveller. 62 years. C-119
d. 10 December.

Samuel Weiner. Traveller. 35 years. C-120
121 Cliftonpark Avenue. *d.* 13 December.

1908 **Polly Lauder.** 10 years. C-689
112 Fortingale Street. *d.* 12 January.

Ethyl Robinson. 9 years. C-688
14 Wellington Terrace, Lurgan. *d.* 2 February.

(S/B) Hodas. 33 Groomsport Street. C-688
d. 5 February.

Issac Levinson. 1 year. 26 Annalee Street. C-687
d. 17 May.

Israel Cohen. Tailor. 59 years. C-686
53 Fortingale Street. *d.* 30 May.

Robert Wilson. Traveller. 19 years. C-685
Union Infirmary. *d.* 6 June.

Gertrude Cohen and her (S/B) child. C-114
28 Jaffa Street. *d.* 24 June.

Elizabeth Landa. 1 year, 5 months. C-684
81 Crumlin Road *d.* 5 July.

Jacob Gross. Traveller. 73 Bristol Street. C-683
d. 9 August.

Myer Genns (Genn). Drapery traveller. C-116
58 years. 182 Old Lodge Road. *d.* 17 August.

Jesse Allen. 6 months. 24 Fortingale Street.   C-682
d. 21 August.

Louis Travers. Traveller. 18 years.   C-122
111 Bristol Street. *d*. 27 August.

Tomorrow Harris. 55 years.   C-121
180 Old Lodge Road. *d*. 4 October.

Celia Greenspohn. 47 years.   C-123
51 Fortingale Street. *d*. 11 October.

Nellie Millar (Miller). 5 years.   C-681
18 Hazelton Street. *d*. 18 December.

1909   **Rosina Stuart.** 9 years. 67 Hanover Street.   C-680
d. 21 January.

Wolff Cohen. 13 days. 2 Fairview Street.   C-679
d. 24 January.

Mairim Myers. Butcher. 70 years.   C-115
196 Old Lodge Road. *d*. 17 March.

Louis Bernstein. Traveller. 30 years.   C-117
Royal Victoria Hospital. *d*. 3 May.

Solomon Meneskorskey (Muneschevsky).   C-678
Traveller. 28 years. Union Hospital *d*. 17 May.

(S/B) Jacobs. 1 Cherryplace Terrace.   C-677
d. 25 May.

Leah Gorfunkle. 20 years. 96 Antrim Road.   C-124
d. 15 June.

Joseph Goldstein. Sailor. 23 years.   C-676
Abbey Sanatorium, Whiteabbey. *d*. 19 June.

Abraham Simon Blank. 6 months.   C-675
4 Fairview Street. *d*. 25 June.

Lena Cavalier. 52 years. 2 Alloa Street.   C-283
d. 29 June.

Aviea Kimineskey (Agnes Kimmesky).   C-674
23 years. Royal Victoria Hospital.
d. 4 September.

Albert Lewis. 13 years. 36 Dock Street.   C-284
d. 25 December.

Fanny Hyman. 1 week. 4 Vicinage Park.   C-673
d. 27 December.

1910   Freiederike Jaffé. *d*. 13 September 1909.   C-341
Cremated remains deposited 1910.

Meriam Halickman. 19 years.   C-672
53 Fortingale Street. *d*. 22 February.

John Myers. Tailor. Union Infirmary.   C-672a
d. 28 February.

Hilda Spain. 10 months. 85 Bishop Street,   C-285
Derry City. *d*. 5 March.

Abraham Purcell. 7 years. 37 Bristol Street.   C-486
d. 14 March.

Gertie Herbert. 94 years. *d*. 25 March.   C-286

(S/B) Frieze. 25 Hillman Street.   C-671
d. 19 April.

Mark Levi. Tailor 26 years.   C-287
37 Dargle Street. *d*. 19 April.

Mary Patchunski. 40 years. 10 Alloa Street.   C-288
d. 4 May.

Leah Fisher. 55 years. 24 Groomsport Street.   C-289
d. 12 May 1910.

Ida Sugarman. 30 years. 40 Perth Street.   C-290
d. 3 June.

(S/B) Hodes. 25 Dargle Street.   C-305
d. 28 November.

Lesbia Smith. 7 weeks. 2 Bedeque Street.   C-670
d. 16 December.

Bessie Jaffé. 24 years.   C-291
Royal Victoria Hospital. *d.* 26 December.

1911   **Mary Genn.** 59 years.   C-464
11 Twickenham Street. *d.* 18 February.
Burial order lists **C-460** *as grave number.*

Rebecca Ingleby. 28 years.   C-292
35 Eglinton Street. *d.* 31 March.

Henry Leuria. Tobacconist. 41 years.   C-293
8 Vicinage Park. *d.* 13 May.

Leah Zemmell (Zemmel). 4 years.   C-484
88 Hallidays Road. *d.* 3 September.

1912   **Deborah Sugarman.** 69 years.   C-465
114 Fortingale Street. *d.* 13 January.
Burial order lists **C-462** *as grave number.*

Leah Myers. 48 years. 18 Fleetwood Street.   C-466
d. 17 January.

Minnie Barnett. 9 months. 46 Carlisle Street.   C-467
d. 22 January.

Jessie Hodes. 21 days. 25 Dargle Street.   C-303
d. 9 February.

Lazarus Rubenberg. Draper. 45 years.   C-468
24 Vicinage Park. *d.* 22 March.

Ernest Myerowitz. 4 years. 1 Vicinage Park.   C-469
d. 8 April.

Rachel Lewis. 20 months.   C-294
70 Princes Street, Lurgan. *d.* 13 July.

Woolf Cohen. 78 years. 5 Kinnaird Street.   C-470
d. 24 August.

	Anne Summ. 65 years. Dundalk and 51 Avoca Street, Belfast. *d.* 12 October.	C-471
	Mary Ristorsky. 10 hours. 46 Groomsport Street. *d.* 6 December.	C-472
1913	**Isaac Travers.** 44 years. Mater Hospital. *d.* 23 May.	C-295
	Jennie Leuria. 15 years. 9 Vicinage Park. *d.* 31 July. Burial order lists **C-473** as grave number.	C-474
	Myer Friedlander. 73 years. 31 Foyle Street. *d.* 9 August.	C-296
1914	**Fanny Travers.** 45 years. 43 Bristol Street. *d.* 25 April.	C-297
	Lily Genn. 11 years. 31 Eglinton Street. *d.* 17 August.	C-475
1915	**(S/B) Brown.** 9 Lincoln Avenue. *d.* 23 January.	C-476
	Lea Solomon Ofstein. 24 years. 79a Divis Street. *d.* 20 March.	C-477
	Mary Rubins. 12 years. Church Street, Banbridge. *d.* 30 March.	C-478
	Mary Marda. 1 year, 6 months. 55 Fortingale Street. *d.* 8 April.	C-129
	Lena Pinker. 28 years. 16 Old Park Road. *d.* 18 April.	C-479
	Samuel Hyman. Tailor. 44 years. Belfast Municipal Sanatorium. *d.* 27 June.	C-298
1916	**Aaron Herbert.** Traveller. 63 years. 3 Wellington Street, Lurgan. *d.* 9 April.	C1-88

Israel Miller. Traveller. 68 years.   C1-87
3 Bandon Street. *d*. 26 April.

Fanny Watchman. 14 weeks.   C1-66
127 West Street, Portadown. *d*. 27 August.

Caroline Boas. 77 years. Broomfield,   C1-44
Windsor Park. *d*. 13 November.

1917   Herman Boas. 89 years. Broomfield,   C1-43
Windsor Park. *d*. 11 January.

Abraham Bernard Remz. 1 day.   C1-66
48 Fairview Street. *d*. 31 January.

Frances Remz. 4 days. 48 Fairview Street.   C1-65
d. 4: February.

Sydney Cohen. 11 months.   C1-65
25 Twickenham Street. *d*. 3 July.

Sarah Bernstein. 63 years. 3 Vicinage Park.   C1-86
d. 17 October.

Felix Harold Tibrach (Tlbrach). 4 months.   C1-64
56 Brookvale Street. *d*. 29 October.

(S/B) Myers. 42 Atlantic Avenue.   C1-63
d. 23 November.

1918   Milred Fineman. 45 years.   C1-85
175 Spamount Street. *d*. 18 March.

(S/B) Watchman. 47 Lower Bennett Street,   C1-63
Derry City. *d*. 13 April.

Tilly Livy (Levy). 51 years. 51 Dargle Street.   C1-84
d. 7 May.

(S/B) Herbert. 53 North Street, Lurgan.   C1-62
d. 11 May.

Rebecca Gordon. 65 years. 148 Peter's Hill.   C1-83
d. 31 July.

Joseph Hyman. Cabinet maker. 60 years.   C1-82
44 Fairview Street. *d*. 28 September.

Samuel Baker. Tailor. 27 years.   C1-81
4 Benwell Street. *d*. 5 October.

Florence Green. 16 weeks.   C1-62
23 Lincoln Avenue. *d*. 24 October.

Annie Turdledorf (Turtledorf). 29 years.   C1-42
49 North Street, Lurgan. *d*. 21 November.

Henry Tarshish. 25 years.   C1-40
68 Cromwell Road. *d*. 21 November.

Sophia Genn. 28 years. 7 Allworthy Avenue.   C1-41
d. 24 November.

Dora Lebowitz. 26 years.   C1-39
10 Cranburn Street. *d*. 13 December.

1919   **Gerty Kesler.** 23 years. St John's Home,   C1-38
Crumlin Road. *d*. 12 February.

Hepworth. 10 days. 134 Ormeau Road.   C1-61
d. 29 April.

Matilda Brown. 22 years.   C1-37
9 Lincoln Avenue. *d*. 5 June.

Martha Friedland. 41 years. Regent Street.   C1-36
d. 19 June.

Israel Remz. 18 months.   C1-61
48 Fairview Street. *d*. 27 October.

Isaac Goldfoot. Marine store dealer.   C1-35
2 Bellview, Landscape Terrace. *d*. 4 December.

Annie Yosselson. 88 years.   C1-79
22 Lincoln Avenue. *d*. 16 December.

1920   **Joseph Ruttenberg.** Traveller. 50 years.   C1-80
47 Eglinton Street. *d*. 18 January.

Rebecca Minnie Ruben. 12 weeks.   C1-60
14 Hawkins Street, Derry City. *d*. 2 February.

Joseph Myers. Rag merchant. 32 years.   C1-22
62 Crumlin Road and 42 Atlantic Avenue.
d. 10 April.

Myer Lukowsky. Draper. 43 years.   C1-20
38 Old Lodge Road. *d*. 13 August.

Robert Hodes. Butcher. 42 years.   C1-19
182 Old Lodge Road. *d*. 24 November.

1921   **Leah Sima (Simon).** 36 years.   C1-18
13 Hanover Street. *d*. 15 February.

Abram Genn. Traveller. 45 years.   C1-21
44 University Street and 31 Eglinton Street.
d. 12 March.

Sara Ruttenberg. 21 years. 14 Perth Street.   C1-17
d. 12 October.

Myer David Levine. 58 years.   C1-34
29 Thorndale Avenue. *d*. 29 December.

1922   **Moses Jacob.** Traveller. 55 years.   C1-33
244 Bishop Street, Derry City. *d*. 6 February.

1923   **Louis Freeman.** Traveller. 32 years.   C1-16
57 Avoca Street. *d*. 8 January.

1924   **Getty (Gerty) Elliott.** 63 years.   C1-15
24 Vicinage Park. *d*. 9 July.

1925   **Joseph Herbert.** Draper. 60 years.   C1-14
18 North Street, Lurgan. *d*. 17 November.

1928   **Leo Ruttenberg.** Draper. 59 years.   C1-12
14 Perth Street. *d*. 17 January.

Minnie Friedlander. 73 years.   C1-11
57 Eglinton Street. *d*. 26 May.

1929   Jennie Rebecca Herbert. 71 years.   C1-10
        28 Cliftonpark Avenue. *d.* 13 May.

        Leabe Millar (Libu Miller). 70 years.   C1-9
        39 Willowbank Gardens. *d.* 14 July.

1930   Joseph Summ. Draper. 75 years.   C1-8
        6 Dublin Street, Dundalk. *d.* 8 February.

        Annie Friedland. 60 years. 60 Regent Street.   C1-7
        d. 25 August.

1932   Julia Phillips. 87 years. 46 Harcourt Drive.   C-346
        d. 26 June.

1933   Samuel Cohen. 76 years. 46 Harcourt Drive.   C1-6
        d. 22 June.

1934   Bella Myers. 85 years. 57 Eglinton Street.   C1-78
        d. 3 June.

        Bernard Myers. Traveller. 75 years.   C1-77
        49 Hartwood Road, Southport, England,
        and 75 Vicinage Park. *d.* 20 December.

1937   Mark Ruttenberg. 78 years. 60 Cliftonville   C1-32
        Road and 57 Ponsonby Avenue. *d.* 26 July.

        Edith Herbert. 49 years.   C1-76
        18 Cliftonpark Avenue. *d.* 26 September.

1938   Yeth (Yetta) Rhoda Freeman. 84 years.   C1-75
        30 Cliftonpark Avenue. *d.* 18 January.

        Cecilia Jaffé. 78 years. 44 Indiana Avenue.   C1-31
        d. 15 April.

1940   Tema Fanny Genn. 66 years.   C1-74
        92 Botanic Avenue and Tudor House,
        Ballysillan Road. *d.* 20 February.

        Annie Librach. 51 years.   C1-5
        9 Brookhill Drive. *d.* 15 July.

1942   **Anna Leah Hodes.** 65 years.   C1-73
        371 Albert Drive, Glasgow and
        44 Cliftonpark Avenue. *d*. 21 January.

1943   **Lena Bogen.** 47 years.   C1-27
        21 Cliftonpark Avenue. *d*. 30 November.

1944   **Gabriel Genn.** Draper. 64 years.   C1-72
        25 Cliftonpark Avenue. *d*. 29 March.

1947   **Sophia Cohen.** 92 years. 46 Harcourt Drive.   C1-28
        d. 3 February.

1948   **Albert Cohen.** 85 years. Independent means.   C1-29
        46 Harcourt Drive. *d*. 15 January.

1950   **Sarah Rose Bogen.** 89 years.   C1-26
        21 Cliftonpark Avenue. *d*. 10 May.

1951   **Joseph Myers.** Commercial traveller.   C1-71
        61 years. 21 Strangford Avenue.
        d. 11 October.

1952   **Maurice Librach.** Linen merchant.   C1-25
        67 years. 9 Brookvale Drive.
        d. 20 January.

1954   **Fanny Herbert.** 86 years.   C1-13
        17 Mount Eden Park. *d*. 11 April.

1956   **Jack Fisher.** General dealer. 70 years.   C1-59
        Southport, England and
        3 Glantrasna Drive. *d*. 1 July.

        Molly Bogen. 65 years.   C1-69
        21 Cliftonpark Avenue. *d*. 1 August.

1959   **Abraham Herbert.** Draper. 78 years.   C1-57
        18 Cliftonpark Avenue. *d*. 14 January.

        Edith Rachel Bogen. 72 years.   C1-70
        21 Cliftonpark Avenue. *d*. 7 September.

1961   **Rachel Fisher.** 75 years. 3 Glantrasna Drive.   **C1-58**
         d. 13 June.

1964   **Abraham Herbert.** Draper. 60 years.   **C1-56**
         10 Cambourne Park. *d*. 10 June.

The Jewish graveyard had its own entrance from the Whiterock
Road and a small Tahara, often referred to in council minutes
as a synagogue or chapel. On the lintel above the bricked-up
door on the Whiterock Road is a Hebrew inscription which is
pronounced 'bethayim', literally meaning 'the house of life'.
However, since the noun 'life' in the singular is the same as 'life'
in the plural masculine, it can also be translated as 'house of the
living'. On 15 June 1972 the Tahara was broken into and wrecked
by vandals. As a result of ongoing vandalism right through the
1970s a decision was taken on 17 June 1981 to remove the doors
and remainder of the roof. The rest of the building disappeared
in the 1980s.

On 23 January 1884 the Cemetery Committee of the Belfast
Corporation passed a resolution prohibiting the erection of
headstones or monuments on graves in the Jewish section for the
burial of the 'poorer class of Jews'. The first burial in the Jewish
Poor Ground was Israel Cohen who died on 12 February 1884
and was buried in **C-150**. The January 1884 decision was finally

The Hebrew inscription on the lintel above the blocked entrance

reversed by the Belfast Corporation at its meeting on 1 March 1929 after pressure from Rabbi J. Shacter. On 22 February 1931, the Belfast *chevra kadisha* (burial society) erected a memorial stone on the Jewish Poor Ground to 'mark the plot therein individually and when desired'.

The memorial in the Jewish burial ground, erected 22 February 1931, with its Hebrew inscription

Jewish Poor Ground, Section C –
Acquired 1871
Grave layout 1884–1915

All names are spelt as they appear in burial orders.
When only a grave reference is given, this indicates an unused grave.

C-128	C-302	C-483 Solomon Brown 02.10.1907	C-668
C-129 Mary Marda 08.04.1915 Last burial in Jewish Poor Ground	C 303 Jessid Hodes 09.02.1912	C-484 Fanny Grimes 17.09.1907 Leah Zemmell 03.09.1911	C-669
C-130	C-304	C-485 Lleia Feldman 04.08.1907	C-670 Lesbia Smith 16.12.1910
C-131	C305 (S/B) Hodes 28.11.1910	C-486 (S/B) Blank 24.07.1907 Abraham Purcell 14.03.1910	C-671 (S/B) Frieze 19.04.1910
C-132 (S/B) Rubin 16.12.1906	C-306 Yudel Grimes 22.12.1906	C-487 Unknown child 14.02.1907	C-672 Meriam Halickman 22.02.1910 John Myers 28.02.1910
C-133	C-307	C-488 Annie Lyszith 18.01.1907	C-673 Fanny Hyman 27.12.1909
C-134	C-308	C-489 Louis Goldberg 23.08.1906	C-674 Aruea Kimineskey 04.09.1909
C-135 Harris Levinthal 07.07.1901	C-309	C-490 (S/B) Gordon 20.08.1906	C-675 Abraham Simon 25.06.1909
C-136 (S/B) Godea 30.04.1901	C-310 Jacob Smith 03.02.1904	C-491 (S/B) Eban 02.07.1906	C-676 Joseph Goldstein 19.06.1909

C-137 (S/B) Philip Hodes 03.04.1901	**C-311** (S/B) Hyman 17.01.1904	**C-492** Lea Hynman 29.03.1906	**C-677** (S/B) Jacobs 25.05.1909
C-138	**C-312** (S/B) Rapaport 06.01.1904	**C-493** Jane Diamond 02.03.1906	**C-678** Solomon Meneshorskey
C-139	**C-313** Sophia Writson 18.05.1903	**C-494** Bessie Eitman 25.06.1905	**C-679** Wolff Cohen 24.01.1909
C-140 (S/B) Sheir 08.03.1901	**C-314** (S/B) Jacobs 02.05.1903	**C-495** Morris Hynman 25.06.1906	**C-680** Rosian Stuart 21.01.1909
C-141 Fanny Robinson 25.02.1901	**C-315** Joseph Leventon 14.01.1903	**C-496** Henry Lewis 15.06.1905	**C-681** Nelli Millar 18.12.1908
C-142 Dina Cohen 18.12.1900	**C-316** (S/B) Sherlock 30.08.1902	**C-497** Joseph Daitch 06.05.1905	**C-682** Jesse Allen 21.08.1908
C-143 (S/B) Elliott 30.03.1900 May Morris 27.11.1900	**C-317** (S/B) Jacobson 25.08.1902	**C-498** Harry Winegood 12.03.1902	**C-683** Jacob Gross 09.08.1908
C-144 Mark Rutenberg 27.03.1900 (S/B) Davis 05.11.1900	**C-318** (S/B) Gorfunkle 12.07.1901	**C-499** Jacob Solomon 19.12.1904	**C-684** Elizabeth Landa 05.07.1908
C-145 (S/B) Rostow 17.11.1899	**C-319** Louis Blank 20.05.1902	**C-500** Paulina Gordon 12.12.1904	**C-685** Robert Wilson 06.06.1908
C-146 Isaac Solomon 09.09.1899	**C-320** Joseh Glasser 05.02.1902	**C-501** Ellina Harris 04.10.1904	**C-686** Israel Cohen 30.05.1908
C-147 Dalby G. Blank 08.01.1899	**C-321** (S/B) Sherskie 21.01.1902	**C-502** Edie Ratthaws 04.10.1904	**C-687** Issac Levinson 17.15.1908

C-148 David Wulfson 29.11.1898	**C-322** Sarah Paradise 03.09.1901	**C-503** Morris Samuel 26.09.1904	**C-688** Ethyl Robinson 02.02.1908 S/B Hodas 05.02.1908
C-149 Aaron Chipkin 11.11.1898	**C-323** Barry Benjamin 19.07.1901	**C-504** (S/B) Blank 16.08.1904	**C-689** (S/B) Sireilmon 20.11.1907 Polly Lauder 12.01.1908
C-150 Israel Cohen 12.02.1884 First burial in Jewish Poor Ground	**C-324** Benneh Rabimoutteh 08.11.1888	**C-505** (S/B) Jaffé 14.08.1890	**C-690** Clara Leinkram 15.12.1895
C-151 Abraham Rutenberg 06.08.1887	**C-325** Simon Lewis 12.03.1889	**C-506** Louise Miller 01.01.1891	**C-691** Abraham Elliott 09.01.1896
C-152 (S/B) Friedman 10.08.1887	**C-326** Rachel Silver 02.10.1889	**C-507** Maria Robinson 30.03.1891	**C-692** Henry Ruttenberg 24.03.1896
C-153 Goldfus Soul 23.03.1888	**C-327** (S/B) Lewis 12.01.1890	**C-508** Annie Ruttenberg 07.12.1891	**C-693** Samuel Edstene 02.06.1896
C-154 Benneh Gleazer 11.04.1888	**C-328** Emma Clarke 30.01.1890	**C-509** Abraham Laine 09.12.1891	**C-694** Louis Leinkram 31.10.1896
C-155 Abraham Rubinstein 26.10.1888	**C-329** Israel Sloan 12.08.1890	**C-510** (S/B) Krayzman 03.02.1892	**C-695** Catherine Glick 01.12.1896
C-156 Isaac Purcell 09.09.1892	**C-330** (S/B) Earlstein 26.10.1892	**C-511** (S/B) Bermstaym 29.11.1892	**C-696** (S/B) Leventhall 11.12.1896
C-157 (S/B) Brock 09.02.1893	**C-331** Michael Elliott 24.03.1893	**C-512** Abraham Ruttenberg 10.07.1893	**C-697** Blenny Barron 27.06.1897

C-158 Daniel Davis 11.04.1893	C-332 Haris Jacobson 15.08.1893	C-513 Jacob Cohen 23.11.1893	C-698 Liny Wolff 28.07.1897
C-159 Edih Berman 28.12.1893	C-333 Gershon Seilin 24.07.1894	C-514 Eihel Parke 04.11.1894	C-699 Rebecca Leinkram 02.08.1897
C-160 Sarah Berwitz 16.11.1894	C-334 Judah Herson 21.12.1894	C-515 David Fastovsky 22.01.1892	C-700 Nathan Rosenfield 17.09.1897
C-161 Davis Brooke 07.04.1895	C-335 Lazerus Cohen 04.02.1895	C-516 Aaron Elliott 05.06.1895	C-701 Mendel Parks 20.04.1898
C-162 Rose Rutenberg 09.07.1895	C-336 Leah Purcell 19.09.1895	C-517 (S/B) Bass 11.11.1895	C-702 (S/B) Millar 11.05.1898
C-163* Edward Boas 06.06.1881	C-337* Shulla Levine 26.06.1903	C-518* Bernard Grosse 17.12.1903	C-703

In 1898, Mr Vital and Mr Cohen, members of Belfast's Jewish community, lobbied for an extension of the Jewish graveyard. On 30 November 1898, a letter from Mr Jaffé, president of the Jewish Congregation, conveys thanks to the Cemetery Committee for the increase in burial ground which had been set apart for the Jewish community. The first burial in this extension took place on 24 December 1904.

On 1 March 1916, agreement was reached between the Belfast Corporation and the Belfast *chevra kadisha* for a third extension of the Jewish graveyard – extension C1 provided 116 new graves.

A *chevra kadisha* is a society that prepares a body for burial according to traditional Jewish practice. The office of the Belfast *chevra kadisha* was in the synagogue chambers, Annesley Street, Belfast. Its president was David Levinson of 6 Brookvale Avenue, vice-president was Hugh Solomon from 3 Lonsdale Street, and Joseph Brown of 9 Lincoln Avenue was honorary secretary.

---

* C-163, C-337 and C-518 are classed as proprietary roadside graves

Jewish burial ground extension, Section C –
Acquired 1898
Proprietary graves layout 1904–1915

All names are spelt as they appear in burial orders.
When only a grave reference is given, this indicates an unused grave.

		C-458
		C-459
		C-460
		C-461
C-107	C-281	C-462
C-108	C-282	C-463
C-109 Mollie Cohen 24.12.1904 First burial in this section	C-283 Lena Cavalier 29.06.1909	C-464 Mary Genn 18.02.1911
C-110 Kate Baker and her (S/B) child 13.04.1905	C-284 Albert Lewis 25.12.1909	C-465 Deborah Sugerman 13.01.1912
C-111 Leah Clarke 06.03.1906	C-285 Hilda Spain 05.03.1910	C-466 Lea Myers 17.01.1912
C-112 Helena Karp 12.06.1906	C-286 Gertie Herbert 25.03.1910	C-467 Minnie Barnett 22.01.1912
C-113 Sarah Lukowstie 25.09.1906	C-287 Mark Levi 19.04.1910	C-468 Lazarus Rubenberg 22.03.1912
C-114 Gertrude Cohen and her (S/B) child 24.06.1908	C-288 Mary Patchunski 04.05.1910	C-469 Ernest Myerwitz 08.04.1912
C-115 Mairim Myers 17.03.1909	C-289 Leah Fisher 12.05.1910	C-470 Woolf Cohen 24.08.1912
C-116 Myer Genns 17.08.1908	C-290 Ida Sugarman 03.06.1910	C-471 Annie Summ 12.10.1912

C-117 Louis Bernstein 03.05.1909	**C-291** Bessie Jaffe 26.12.1910	**C-472** Mary Ristofski 06.12.1912
C-118 Joseph Freeman 03.08.1905	**C-292** Rebecca Ingleby 31.03.1911	**C-473**
C-119 Abraham Freeman 10.12.1907	**C-293** Henry Leuria 13.05.1911	**C-474** Jennie Leuria 31.07.1913
C-120 Samuel Wiener 13.12.1907	**C-294** Rachel Louis 13.07.1912	**C-475** Lily Genn 17.08.1914
C-121 Tomorrow Harris 04.10.1908	**C-295** Isaac Travers 23.05.1913	**C-476** (S/B) Brown 23.01.1915
C-122 Louis Travers 27.08.1908	**C-296** Myer Friedlander 09.08.1913	**C-477** Leah Ofstein 20.03.1915
C-123 Celia Greenspon 11.10.1908	**C-297** Fanny Travers 25.04.1914	**C-478** Mary Rubin 30.03.1915
C-124 Leah Gorfunkle 15.06.1909	**C-298** Samuel Hyman 27.06.1915 Last burial in this section	**C-479** Lena Pinker 18.04.1915

Other members included A. Genn of 31 Eglinton Street, who was honorary treasurer, and Harris Brown of 9 Lincoln Avenue, Joseph T. Cohen of 2 Fairview Street, and Robert Miller of 34 Regent Street, who were trustees. The management committee were Bernard Myers of 6 Vicinage Park, Myer Vigader of 3 Annesley Street, Joseph Hurvitz of 46 Crumlin Road, Israel Serskey (Sherskie) of 5 Twickenham Street, S. Sugerman of 114 Fortingale Street, Max Rutenberg of 14 Perth Street, J. Glover of 15 Carlisle Street, Israel Miller of 3 Bandon Street, Wolf Cates (Klotz) of 162 Old Lodge Road, Max E. Millar of 3 Bandon Street, and Robert Gordon of 46 Annalee Street.

Jewish burial ground extension, Section C1 – Acquired 1916

Proprietary graves layout 1916–1964

All names are spelt as they appear in burial orders.
When only a grave reference is given, this indicates an unused grave.

C1-22 Joseph Myers 10.04.1920 Abraham Remz 31.01.1917	**C1-44** Caroline Boas 13.11.1916	**C1-66** Fanny Watchman 27.08.1916	**C1-88** Aaron Herbert 09.04.1916 First burial in this Section
C1-21 Abram Genn 12.03.1921	**C1-43** Herman Boas 11.01.1917	**C1-65** Frances Remz 04.12.1917 Sydney Cohen 03.07.1917	**C1-87** Israel Millar 26.04.1916
C1-20 Myer Lukosky 12.08.1920	**C1-42** Annie Turdledorf 21.11.1918	**C1-64** Felix Tibrach 29.10.1917	**C1-86** Sarah Bernstein 17.10.1917
C1-19 Robert Hodes 24.11.1920	**C1-41** Sophia Genn 24.11.1918	**C1-63** (S/B) Myers 25.11.1917 (S/B) Watchman 13.04.1918	**C1-85** Mildred Fineman 18.03.1918
C1-18 Leah Sima 15.02.1921	**C1-40** Henry Tarshish 21.11.1918	**C1-62** (S/B) Herbert 11.05.1918 Florence Green 24.10.1918	**C1-84** Tilly Livy 07.05.1918
C1-17 Sara Ruttenberg 12.10.1921	**C1-39** Dora Lebowitz 13.11.1918	**C1-61** (S/B) Hepworth 29.04.1919	**C1-83** Rebecca Gordon 31.07.1918
C1-16 Louis Freeman 08.01.1923	**C1-38** Gerty Kesler 12.02.1919	**C1-60** Rebecca Ruben 02.02.1920 Last child buried in Jewish burial ground	**C1-82** Joseph Hyman 28.09.1918
C1-15 Getty Elliott 09.07.1924	**C1-37** Matilda Brown 05.06.1919	**C1-59** Jack Fisher 01.07.1956	**C1-81** Samuel Baker 05.10.1918
C1-14 Joseph Herbert 17.11.1925	**C1-36** Martha Friedland 19.06.1919	**C1-58** Rachel Fisher 13.06.1961	**C1-80** Joseph Ruttenberg 18.01.1920

C1-13 Fanny Herbert 11.04.1954	C1-35 Isaac Goldfoot 04.12.1919	C1-57 Abraham Herbert 14.01.1959	C1-79 Annie Yosselson 16.12.1919
C1-12 Leo Ruttenberg 17.01.1928	C1-34 Myer Levine 29.12.1921	C1-56 Abraham Herbert 10.06.1964	C1-78 Bella Myers 03.06.1934
C1-11 Minnie Friedlander 26.05.1928	C1-33 Moses Jacob 06.02.1922	C1-55	C1-77 Bernard Myers 20.12.1934
C1-10 Jennie Herbert 13.05.1929	C1-32 Mark Ruttenberg 26.07.1937	C1-54	C1-76 Edith Herbert 26.09.1937
C1-9 Leabe Miller 14.07.1929	C1-31 Cecilia Jaffé 15.04.1938	C1-53	C1-75 Yetta Freeman 18.01.1938
C1-8 Joseph Summ 08.02.1930	C1-30	C1-52	C1-74 Tema Genn 20.02.1940
C1-7 Annie Friedland 25.08.1930	C1-29 Albert Cohen 15.01.1948	C1-51	C1-73 Leah Hodes 21.01.1942
C1-6 Samuel Cohhen 22.06.1933	C1-28 Sophia Cohen 03.02.1947	C1-50	C1-72 Gabriel Genn 29.03.1944
C1-5 Annie Lierach 15.07.1942	C1-27 Lena Bogen 30.11.1943	C1-49	C1-71 Joseph Myers 11.10.1951
C1-4	C1-26 Sarah Bogen 10.05.1950	C1-48	C1-70 Edith Bogen 07.09.1959
C1-3	C1-25 Maurice Librach 20.01.1952	C1-47	C1-69 Molly Bogen 01.08.1956
C1-2	C1-24	C1-46	C1-68
C1-1	C1-23	C1-45	C1-67

From the first burial of the stillborn Herschman, on 29 January 1873, to the very last burial of Abraham Herbert on 10 June 1964, a total of 295 remains have been buried here – including the cremated remains of Frederica Jaffé. Burial records show that, initially, the majority of deaths in the Belfast Jewish community were children. Of the 295 remains, 152 are children under 13 years with 110 of these being less than a year old. The last child to be buried was 3-month-old Rebecca Ruben from 14 Hawkins Street, Derry City, who died on 2 February 1920. Burial records reveal that the district around the Old Lodge Road in north Belfast was the first settlement area for Russian and Polish Jews. We also see that other popular locations were Dundalk, Lurgan, Armagh and Derry City.

Jewish burial records were recorded in a very haphazard way. The first twenty burials were registered normally in the main registers in chronological order. This practice changed on 2 October 1889 with the introduction of separate burial orders for Jewish graves; thereafter they were registered on the back pages of the main burial registers along with those buried in the military ground. Burial order 1a was issued for Rachel Silver who lived at 135 New Lodge Road and died on 2 October 1889; she is buried in Jewish Poor Ground **C-326**. The last recorded burial order was 274a, issued 11 June 1964 for 60-year-old Abraham Herbert of 10 Cambourne Park, Belfast. Abraham died on 10 June 1964 and is buried in grave **C-156**.

Frequent discrepancies show up when comparing those listed in the back pages of burial registers against the burial orders. This situation is further exacerbated by vandalism and destruction

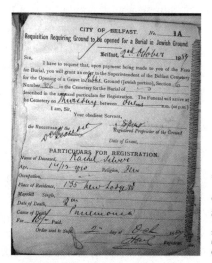

Rachel Silver, the first Jewish burial order

© Belfast City Council

of headstones which could have been used to corroborate the findings. There is no complete separate register for the Jewish burial ground.

The earliest Irish-Jewish connection dates back to 1079 when the Annals of Innisfallen record the arrival of five Jews from overseas. They were probably merchants from Rouen in France. In 1232 Henry III gave 'the custody of the Kings' Judaism in Ireland' to one Peter Rivall. Then, in 1496, a small

Abraham Herbert's burial order, the last burial in the Jewish section

number of Jews arrived following their expulsion from Portugal. In 1555 the Jewish William Annyas was elected mayor in Youghal, County Cork. Then there is David Sollom, a merchant in 1620, who owned property in County Meath. In 1718 members of the Portuguese Jewish community in Ireland founded a prayer room in Crane Lane, off Dame Street in Dublin. They also opened a cemetery near Ballybough Bridge, Clontarf, and a synagogue in 1746 for Dublin's 200 Jews. By 1778 there were a number of Jewish merchants in Cork City. The community was strengthened by the arrival of Jews from Germany and England in 1822, and by 1844 they obtained a provision in the Irish Marriage Act for the right to marry according to Jewish rites. The first Jews to settle in Belfast were German. About two thousand Russian and East European Jews arrived in Ireland from the 1880s onward.

In May 1882 repressive laws passed in Tsarist Russia contributed to the increase in Jewish migration, with a small number of Russian and Polish Jews finding their way to Belfast. In 1893 Max Veital founded the Belfast Hebrew Board of Guardians, and Mr Veital and Mr Cohen founded a Belfast

The last page of a burial register, showing details of Jewish burials

chevra kadisha, which is now the Belfast Holy Burial Society. In 1896 a Belfast Hebrew Ladies Foreign Benevolent Society was formed. During this period a number of houses were bought for families fleeing persecution and pogroms in Russia. North Belfast soon became the centre for the Jewish community in Belfast. A new prayer house was established in Jackson Street, between North Boundary and Hudson Streets, and a school was set up in Regent Street, which is in the Denmark Street–Carlisle Circus locality. By 1904 a new synagogue in

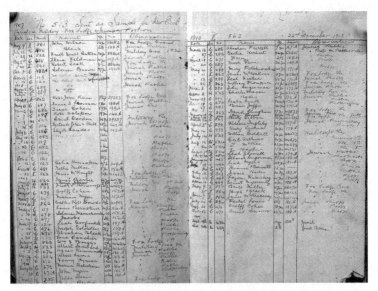

More entries from the back of a burial register

Annesley Street was opened by Otto Jaffé, son of Daniel (C-341). In 1907 a national school for Jewish children, the Jaffé Public Elementary School, was opened on the corner of Cliftonville and Antrim Roads. As a result of anti-German feeling, many Jews of German origin left Belfast during the First World War. During the Second World War a Jewish children's hostel was opened in Clifton Park Avenue.

In the 1950s there were about 6,000 Jews in Ireland, with 1,400 living in Belfast. Dublin had the largest Jewish community; Belfast had the second, with smaller communities in Cork, Derry, Limerick, and Waterford.

Well-known members of the Belfast Jewish community included Rabbi Herzog, who became the first chief rabbi of the Irish Free State. His son Chaim, born at 185 Cliftonville Road, was elected president of Israel in 1983. Jackie Morris from Cliftonville Drive became Israeli Ambassador to New Zealand and Harold Goldblatt was a founder member of the Ulster Group Theatre. The synagogue at 71 Great Victoria Street later became an Orange Hall and is now an Apostolic Church.

C-341; Daniel Jaffé; *d.* 21 January 1874

Daniel Joseph Jaffé died in Nice on 21 January 1874 in France. The burial register of 30 January 1874 records a Daniel Jaffé in section C, Jewish burial ground, but does not give a grave number. A study of the grave layout suggests his remains were placed in **C-341**.

A merchant from Hamburg in Germany, Daniel first visited Belfast to establish a business connection with the linen industry. Within ten years there were three Jewish linen houses operating in Belfast – Jaffé Bros., George Betzold & Co., and Moore & Weinberg. A Dublin Jewish minister, Julius Sandheim, administered to the Jewish community in Belfast and kept a register of births. In 1849 he registered Meir Levy, his first recorded entry. By 1869 there were twenty-one Jews living in Belfast. In 1864 a synagogue was built at 71 Great Victoria Street, funded by Daniel Jaffé. Its founder members were Mr Jaffé, Mr Weinberg, Mr Betzhold, Mr Boas, Mr Lippman and Mr Portheim. Joseph Chotzner conducted the opening service. Daniel lived in the synagogue which also

The Jewish burial ground today

contained a Jewish school where he taught religion. In 1874 a fountain was erected in the middle of Victoria Square, Belfast, in his memory. The fountain with its cast-iron octagonal canopy was moved in 1934 to the park at Botanic Gardens. In 2008 it was moved again to its current location, beside Victoria Square shopping centre.

In Hebrew the name Jaffé means 'beauty', and originates with an ancestor of Daniel, Rabbi Mordecai Jaffé, who was born in Prague in 1530. The Jaffé family comes from a long line of rabbinical scholars.

Otto Jaffé; *d*. 29 April 1929

Otto Jaffé, son of Daniel, was born in Hamburg on 13 August 1846. He became president of the Jewish community in Belfast and served as lord mayor of Belfast, 1899–1900 and 1904–5. He ran Jaffé Bros., linen manufactures, bleachers and merchants at Bedford Street and later at Donegall Square South.

He arrived in Belfast when he was 12 years old. His education, begun in Hamburg, continued at Mrs Tate's school, Holywood, and at the Royal University of Ireland. He became a member of the Belfast Corporation in 1892 and was elected mayor in 1899. In 1906 he became president of the Belfast Natural History and Philosophical Society. He was passionate about children's education and improving schools. He promoted the concept of technical education and raised funds for the acquisition of better equipment for Queen's College. He was buried at Golder's Green Crematorium in London.

C-120: Samuel Wiener; *d*. 13 December 1907

Samuel was a commercial traveller who lived at 121 Cliftonpark Avenue in north Belfast. The English inscription at the base of his headstone reads 'In loving memory of Samuel Wiener, Died 13th December 1907.' 'Tabeth 8th 5668' refers to the month, day and year of the Jewish calendar – December to January 1907–8.

There are twelve months in the Jewish calendar. These are:

Nisan	March–April	30 days
Iyar	April–May	29 days
Sivan	May–June	30 days
Tammuz	June–July	29 days
Av	July–August	30 days
Elul	August–September	29 days
Tishri	September–October	30 days
Cheshvan	October–November	29 or 30 days
Kislev	November–December	29 or 30 days
Tevet	December–January	29 days
Shevat	January–February	30 days
Adar	February–March	30 days

The Jewish year 5668 represents the number of years since creation, calculated by adding up the ages of people in the Bible back to the time of creation. Samuel died in the tenth month of the Jewish year.

CHAPTER 3

BELFAST – INDUSTRIAL POWER AND PRESBYTERIAN CITY

Beginning at the Cross of Sacrifice the third walk leads back to section C on the upper ring of the bell and for the most part contains itself within the bell's core. Symbolism is everywhere, of course, but do keep a special eye out for the huge variety of flowers that are etched into stone. The walk ends at the old drinking fountain at the intersection beside the Cunningham plot.

Here lie the rich and powerful – the movers and shakers of Victorian Belfast who pushed the city to the height of its industrial power, making it a prosperous corner of the empire. But the story contains more than unromantic nuts and bolts. We meet the first historians who recorded Belfast's past, as well as the initiators of Presbyterianism in Ireland. Belfast the Presbyterian city emerges through those former students of the Royal Belfast Academical Institution ('Inst'). This school, greatly influenced by the Enlightenment, produced a dynamic group of boys who went on to shape the intellectual and commercial life of Belfast – professors and industrialists, unionist ideologues and ministers of the Presbyterian Church, teachers and shipbuilders. There are also those connected to education whose contribution shaped the lives of millions of children throughout the world.

Unfortunate ocean liners are remembered, along with the sailors whose last port of call was Belfast, and those whose endeavours made the city a great sea port. The Irish language and Irish speakers are here, a reminder of the cultural complexity that existed in Victorian Belfast. You will also find a bit of Greek, Latin, German, Scots Gaelic and Welsh. Politics is everywhere – the story of James Craig, first prime minister of Northern

Ireland runs like a thread through the lives of many who lie here. Others mentioned include Garibaldi, the Italian patriot, Abraham Lincoln, the US President, John Mitchel, the Young Irelander, and Bulmer Hobson, the Irish Republican Brotherhood (IRB) devotee.

D3-57: John Kirk; *d.* 27 June 1930

John, who lived at 4 Mornington Crescent, Upper Newtownards Road, was 72 when he died. The son of a Presbyterian elder, he worked for a short time for the YMCA in Belfast. He then became a missionary in Etinan, Nigeria, where he served for twenty-five years. He arrived by canoe in November 1898 and left in May 1924. A man of many talents, he pioneered the mission work there, acting as preacher, schoolteacher and carpenter, as well as providing some medical help. The inscription on his headstone reads: 'One of the pioneers of the Qua Iboe mission. Opened work at Etinan 1899. His enduring monument is in the hearts and minds of African converts.'

Etinan is located in the Niger Delta near Calabar. In the late 1880s local people from the Ibeno region of the Delta contacted the Calabar Mission of the Free Church of Scotland, looking for a missionary. The Calabar Mission, unable to comply with their request, contacted Henry Grattan Guinness of the Harley Missionary Training College in London. One of the trainees at the college, Samuel Alexander Bill, immediately volunteered to travel to Nigeria. Samuel, a native of Belfast, was a member of the Ballymacarrett Presbyterian Church in east Belfast and was associated with the Island Street Mission Hall. On 14 September 1887, Samuel boarded a ship in Liverpool bound for Calabar, arriving there on 6 October. Soon after, he settled at the mouth of the Qua Iboe river where, along with local people, he built his own house and a church in the locality of Ubenekang. On 6 June 1890, Samuel left Nigeria and travelled to Liverpool, and then London, where he married Grace Kerr. The newly-wed couple soon afterwards returned to Nigeria where Grace gave birth to their first child. After two years and the birth of her second child, Grace returned home due to ill health. Once she regained her strength, she embarked on a speaking tour of churches throughout Ireland. It was at one of her meetings that she met John Kirk, who would later return with her to the Niger Delta. Today the Qua Iboe Church has grown to become one of the largest Christian churches in Nigeria, with a membership of over two million (see also **D2-194**: Reverend John Gillis Phillips, missionary for thirty years in Damascus, Syria).

In 1891 representatives of the Protestant churches in Belfast set up the Qua Iboe Mission Council to support Samuel Alexander Bill in his missionary work. The council helped to finance missionaries from the Belfast Presbyterian, Baptist and Quaker communities.

A-512: Robert John Welch; *d.* 28 September 1936

Robert was born on 22 July 1859 in Strabane, County Tyrone, the second son in a family of eight. His father, David, born August 1831, was a shirt manufacturer from Kincardineshire in Scotland. David settled in Strabane, attracted by the growth of shirt manufacturing in that part of north-west Ulster. In Strabane, he married Martha Graham, born in March 1840. Three years after Robert's birth his father became interested in scientific photography, first as a hobby, then, after moving in 1863 with his family to Enniskillen, County Fermanagh, as a profession. There, he commenced a long association with the landed gentry and the aristocracy and, in time, became the official photographer to the Marquis of Hamilton, later known as the first Duke of Abercorn. Eventually, David became the official landscape photographer to the Duke, who was also lord lieutenant of Ireland in 1866–8 and 1874–6.

Robert's early education occurred in private schools in Enniskillen and then in the model school, Newry, County Down. As a young boy, his father encouraged him to study geology and marine zoology through their many visits to the fossil shales and purple urchin rock pools at Bundoran. It was on these trips that he also began his lifelong interest in conchology, the science of molluscs. In Enniskillen, the young Robert first developed his interest in photography, which he combined with his deep interest in natural history. The first cameras Robert used were

most likely his father's; they required 10 x 12 inch glass plates.

In 1868 the Welch family moved to Newry where Robert attended the model school. Here he developed his love of science through the study of light, heat, magnetism and electricity. His headmaster Mr Watt gave him lessons in physiology, the science of functions and phenomena of living organisms. In Newry he also received special tuition in watercolour drawing. Between 1873 and 1879, Robert successfully completed examinations in drawing, geology and physiography awarded by the Science and Art department of the Council of Education.

In 1872 the family began a number of short-lived moves, first to Leamington Spa, then to Kingstown (now called Dún Laoghaire), Kilkenny, Kildare, Wicklow and Carlow, before settling in Bangor, County Down, in 1874, where his father added northern views to his series of Irish scenery and antiquities after completing an extensive series in southern Ireland. One of the oldest of Robert's photographs dates from this period – in September 1874 he photographed Donegall Square Methodist Church in the centre of Belfast. Following the death of his father in June 1875, the family moved from Bangor to 49 Lonsdale Street, situated between the Crumlin and Old Lodge Roads, in north Belfast; it was at this address that the family remained for the next sixty years.

In 1876 Robert was employed as a landscape operator and manager by the well-known Belfast photographer, artist, and naturalist, E.T. Church, of 53 Donegall Place. Prior to setting up his premises here in 1869, Church had worked for a Mr Henry Herring of Regent Street, London. Experiments in photography had begun in Belfast in the late 1830s, and by 1860 professional photography was firmly established in the city. In 1883, with his mother as his business manager, Robert left his employment with Church and set up on his own, using his home as his business address and photographic studio.

In this early period of his photographic career he specialised in geology, archaeology, topography and ethnography. One of his abiding interests was the city of Belfast. From the early 1880s he photographed the city streets at a time when the city was developing into one of the major industrial centres of the British Empire. By 1885 he was using 8½ x 6½ inch plates, as well as Ross's 7- and 10-inch portable symmetrical lenses combined with a 7-inch back lens. This was later replaced with a 6-inch Ross-Goerz lens. In developing his negatives he used pyro-ammonia, an old formula that gave clear detail to his photographs.

By the early 1890s he had become the official photographer for the Board of Public Works, for the Northern Railways of Ireland, and to the industrial giants of Belfast. These included the Belfast Rope Works and Harland and Wolff shipbuilders. From 1894 until the outbreak of the First World War, he was frequently used by Harland and Wolff to photograph their great ocean liners at every stage of the building process, and, in particular, during their sea trials. This included the sea trials of the *Titanic* in April 1912. His photographs of the launch of the *Olympic* on 20 October 1910 were reproduced worldwide. On 26 February 1914 he was appointed by Harland and Wolff to take the official photographs of the launch of HMHS *Britannic* at Queen's Island; this was followed two years later by an invitation from the Admiralty to be the official photographer for the launch of their light battle cruiser HMS *Glorious* at Queen's Island on 20 April 1916. Both these ships were to be lost at sea due to enemy action: on 21 November 1916 the *Britannic* hit a mine in the Aegean Sea and sank within one hour; HMS *Glorious*, by this stage a converted aircraft carrier, was sunk on 8 June 1940 returning from Norway when she and her escorts were intercepted by the German battle cruisers *Scharnhorst* and *Gneisenau*. At the launch of the monitor HMS *Sir Thomas Picton* on 30 September 1915, Robert lost his camera, and nearly his life, when he was caught up in the wash of the *Picton* as it came off the slipway.

From the 1890s onwards Robert's talent gained international recognition. At the Chicago World's Fair in 1892 he was awarded a diploma for the quality of his photographs. In that same year he was also awarded a special gold medal for scientific photographs at the Belfast Exhibition. At the Brussels Exhibition in 1898 he received a diploma for his views of the County Down railways, and, in 1900 he won a silver medal and diploma at the Paris Exhibition.

Alongside these awards came a growing number of prestigious appointments and membership of influential organisations. On 24 September 1895, he was elected a member of the Conchological Society of Great Britain and Ireland, on whose council he served from 1898–1900, 1907–8 and 1916–17, finally becoming the Society's President in 1922–3. On 1 June 1900 he was formally appointed Photographer for Natural History and Archaeology to Queen Victoria. In 1903 he was selected by HM Government Survey Department, London, to provide plates for the special memoirs on the Dublin, Belfast and Cork areas. The following year, he was elected as a Life Member of Royal Irish Academy for scientific photographic survey work in connection with fauna and flora, and archaeological survey work in connection with the Royal Society of Antiquaries (Ireland). Many years later he helped to organise the first ever meeting of the Academy held outside Dublin, when, in 1924, they met in Queen's University in Belfast. In 1922 he was elected president of the Conchological Society of Great Britain and Ireland. One of the last awards he received was an honorary degree of M.Sc. from Queen's University Belfast in 1925. Throughout his professional life Robert illustrated in whole or part over sixty scientific books, pamphlets and papers.

As joint editor of the journal, *The Irish Naturalist*, he frequently contributed to its pages.

Above all else, Robert Welch was a field naturalist. His deep love of the Irish landscape found its way on to his negatives, where the scenery, geology, botany, archaeology, and ethnography of Ireland remain caught in a moment of time as a monument to his deep curiosity and outstanding talent. He had joined the Belfast Naturalists' Field Club in 1880 and remained a member for the rest of his life. His activities with the club took him on numerous surveys where he conducted parties of naturalists from England and Scotland to the glens and bays of County Antrim and Rathlin Island. In 1908 he was elected as honorary secretary and, a year later, was made president. In 1911 he helped to establish the junior division of the club. He died at his home in 49 Lonsdale Street from the effects of an internal malignant tumour on 28 September 1936.

PHOTOGRAPHY IN BELFAST

In 1839 the Frenchman, Louis Daguerre, developed the chemical process of fixing images on metal plates. By 1841 Francis Beatty made a 'photogenic drawing' of the old Long Bridge that spanned the Lagan and the following year opened his first studio in Belfast. By the late 1850s Belfast had six professional photographers, a figure which doubled by 1864, and increased to fifteen by 1870. One of the first studios to be established was that of E.T. Church of 53 Donegall Place, which opened in 1869. Two years later James Magill, who owned a stationery shop at 2 Donegall Place, added a studio of his own to the premises. In 1880 Thomas Williams & Co from Plymouth set up a branch at 25 Castle Place, followed in the middle of that decade by the Glasgow firm of Turnbulls & Sons, who were to be found at 23 Garfield Street; furthermore, William Abernethy occupied several floors of 29 High Street in 1886 and employed up to twenty assistants. It was against this backdrop that Belfast's two outstanding photographers, Welch and Hogg, rose to prominence.

C-412: Griffith Lloyd; *d*. 14 August 1873

Griffith Lloyd was from Lasynys Fawr, near Harlech in Wales. The inscription on his Welsh slate headstone reads:

Yma y claddwyd	Buried here is
Griffith Lloyd	Griffith Lloyd
Lasynys Fawr Harlech	Lasynys Fawr Harlech
yr hwn a fu farw Awst 14, 1875	He died on 14 August 1875
trwy syrthio oddiwr hwylbren y	falling off the mast of the
Sydney & Jane, Porthmadog	*Sydney & Jane*, Porthmadog
yn 17 ml oed	at 17 years of age

B-49: Robert Arthur Wilson; *d*. 10 August 1875

A popular journalist, Robert Wilson wrote for the *Belfast Morning News* under the pseudonym Barney McGlone. Robert, the son of a coastguard, was born *c*. 1820 in Dunfanaghy, County Donegal, where he learnt Irish. In his youth he and his mother moved to Country Antrim. He taught for a short period in Kilmahamogue, five miles outside Ballycastle, and then went to the US where he worked as a journalist with the *Boston Republic*.

In 1847 he returned to Ireland and two years later was appointed sub-editor of *The Nation*. After leaving that newspaper in 1853, he was employed by the *Impartial Reporter* in Enniskillen. Shortly after he was appointed editor of the *Fermanagh Mail and Advertiser* which he wrote for under various names, such as Erin Oge, Young Ireland, Jonathan Oldmand and Barney McGlone. In 1865 he moved to *Belfast's Morning News*. He also wrote a regular column for the *Ulster Weekly News*, the weekly edition of the *Morning News*. In 1892 the *Belfast Morning News* became the *Irish News*. Robert was 55 when he died at 4 Wesley Place, Belfast; his burial record gives his age at 45.

B-22: Sarah Rachel Orr Hale; *d*. 7 May 1915

Sadie Hale was 29 when she lost her life while serving as a ship's typist on the SS *Lusitania*. She was buried in this grave on

12 May 1915 (see Frank Houston **A-15**).

The SS *Lusitania* was launched on the River Clyde on 16 June 1906, was 785 feet long and weighed 31,550 tons. Her maiden voyage took place 7 September 1907. She left New York on 1 May 1915, bound for Liverpool, carrying 1,257 passengers and 650 crew. That same morning, and alongside advertisements placed by the Cunard Line in the major New York newspapers giving details of the *Lusitania*'s departure, was an advertisement from the German Embassy in Washington. It stated:

> Travellers intending to embark on the Atlantic voyage are reminded that a state of war exists between Germany and her allies and Great Britain and her allies; that the zone of war includes the waters adjacent to the British Isles; that in accordance with formal notice given by the Imperial German Government, vessels flying the flag of Great Britain or the flag of her allies, are liable to destruction in those waters and that travellers sailing in the war zone on ships of Great Britain or her allies do so at their own risk.

The captain of the *Lusitania*, William Thomas Turner, was a veteran Cunard captain. Born on 23 October 1856 at Clarence Street, Everton, Liverpool, he had first gone to sea at the age of 13. He was initially appointed captain of the *Lusitania* in 1908, followed in 1910 by his appointment to the *Mauritania* and then in 1914 to the *Aquitania*. Shortly after the retirement of Daniel Dow, captain of the *Lusitania*, in April 1915, Turner was reappointed as captain of his old ship.

On 6 May 1915, as the *Lusitania* approached the southern tip of Ireland, Turner received a warning from the British Admiralty regarding German U-boat activity in Irish waters. Four further warnings were received that night. At 11.52 the next morning, he received another message regarding U-boat activity in the area he was sailing through. In such circumstances British Admiralty guidelines for captains instructed them to zigzag, operate at full speed, and stay away from headlands. Operating at a speed of only 18 knots, well below the *Lusitania*'s top speed of 25 plus, and moving in an undeviating course of 87 degrees or almost due east, the *Lusitania* presented textbook conditions for a submarine attack as she sailed within sight of the Irish coast.

Shortly before 1 p.m. on 7 May 1915, Karl Scherb, a young officer on *U-20*, was the first to sight the *Lusitania*. *U-20*, not yet a year old, was 650 tons with a crew of 4 officers and 35 men. The submarine had left Emden, its North Sea base, on 30 April 1915, with each of its torpedoes containing 290 lb of the high explosive trotyl. It could make a speed of 9 knots submerged and 15 on the surface. By 6 May *U-20* had already sunk two British merchant ships, the *Candidate* and the *Centurion*. At 2.10 p.m. on 7 May, 15 miles south of the Old Head, off Kinsale, West Cork, Kapitänleutnant Walther Schwieger, skipper of *U-20* and on his very first patrol, gave the order to fire a single torpedo at the *Lusitania* from a bow tube at a range of 700 metres. The torpedo hit the starboard side of the great liner just behind its bridge, sinking it in just eighteen minutes. Of the 1,907 passengers and crew on board, 1,198 were drowned, among them 128 Americans – 94 children died out of 140. It was estimated that over 1,000 passengers had survived the actual sinking but had then perished in the water. Rescue ships brought the dead and survivors to Queenstown, now Cobh, the first ships arriving soon after 8 p.m.

On 4 September 1915, almost four months later, *U-20* attacked and sunk the liner *Hesperian* – thirty-two passengers were drowned. Ironically, the *Hesperian* had earlier in its ill-fated voyage recovered the body of a *Lusitania* passenger from the sea. On 4 September 1917, two years to the day after he sank the *Hesperian*, Captain Schwieger died, while serving on *U-88* off the coast of Terschelling, one of the Dutch Friesian Islands. British mines sank his U-boat. In his role as U-boat captain he was responsible for the sinking of forty-nine ships, totalling 190,000 tons of allied shipping. Just six weeks before his death he had been awarded the highest German decoration, the Pour Le Mérite.

In early 1916, *U-20* was allocated the task of bringing Roger Casement to Ireland but it got as far as the North Sea, encountered engine trouble and was towed back to base, and so

U-19 brought him back instead. Raimund Weisbach, who had been torpedo officer on *U-20* when the *Lusitania* had been sunk, commanded *U-19*.

Captain Turner survived the sinking of the *Lusitania* and faced a board of inquiry which, given the enormous propaganda value of the sinking to the British, solely blamed the Germans. Turner was subsequently given command of a freighter, the *Ultonia*. In 1916 he again commanded a liner, the troopship *Ivernia*. However, when the *Ivernia* was torpedoed off Cape Manhattan on New Year's Day in 1917 by *UB-47*, under the command of Kapıtäinleutnant Steinbauer, Turner had to face another board of inquiry. He retired in November 1919 and died in Crosby, Liverpool, on Friday, 23 June 1933.

There are two more graves in Belfast City Cemetery which are connected to other ships lost at sea. These are **K-392**, Herbert Gifford, who went down on the *Titanic* on 14 April 1912, and **V1-5 Glen**, Robert Kelly, who went down on the *Princess Victoria* in the Irish Sea on 31 January 1953.

B-408, Robert Maxwell Macabe

B-408: Robert Maxwell Macabe; *d.* 23 April 1915

Robert was a soldier of the 8th City of London Battalion Post Office Rifles, and this family grave is designed as a war memorial – its plinth carries crossed swords and a regimental badge.

The grave is dominated by a broken column, which symbolises a young life cut short, an early grief, and usually represents the loss of the family head or the end of a family line. They often have a Masonic connection.

C-608: William Green; *d*. 3 August 1928

William Green was a linen merchant who lived at 'Orkla', Myrtlefield Park in south Belfast.

His headstone displays spiral symbols to the left and right of the inscription for his daughter-in-law Mary Johnston. The symbol on the right is a triskel, which consists of three interlocking legs with a threefold rotational clockwise symmetry. Its origins may be linked to the triple spiral ornamentation found on the rock face at the entrance to the prehistoric passage grave at Newgrange in County Meath. It is also found in early Christian books and in the fifth-century Lá Tene art, named after the Celtic site at Neuchatel in modern Switzerland. The four-armed symbol on the left may represent a version of the swastika combined with the spiral imagery of the triskel. The swastika is believed to derive from the wheel symbolising the sun; its four legs move in a clockwise direction, that is, sunwise. It may also represent the face of the cross that has four arms and could have originated as a sun symbol. The St Brigid cross is a good example of this.

F-230: Captain Norton Butler Alexander; *d.* 24 August 1873

Norton Butler Alexander lived at Vicinage Park, Lower Antrim Road, Belfast.

The old Irish inscription at the base of his headstone is a reference to one of the seven corporal works of mercy, '*Do bhí mé tinn agus thángabhar dom fhéachuin*' (When I was sick you came to visit me), taken from from the Bedell Bible, Matthew 25:36. The headstone inscription is in pre-standard print, pre-1950s.

F-230, Captain Norton Butler Alexander

—————— THE IRISH IN BELFAST ——————

In the 1790s, Irish was taught in the Belfast Royal Academy by Patrick Lynch from Loughlinisland, County Down. He was the last surviving member of his family, many of whom were teachers in Irish hedge schools, a form of education in rural Ireland in the eighteenth and nineteenth centuries whereby local educated men taught the community using mainly oral traditions. Lynch is said to have edited an Irish language magazine, *Bolg an tSolais*, first published in August 1795. More significantly, he is reputed to have taught Irish to the United Irishman Thomas Russell, who was subsequently immortalised in the popular poem 'The Man from God Knows Where'.

Thomas Russell was born on 21 November 1767 in Drumahane, in the parish of Kilshannig, County Cork. His father, John, was a lieutenant in the 83rd Infantry Regiment based in Mallow, County Cork. In the early 1770s, the family moved to Durrow, County Laois, and then in the early 1780s to Dublin. In early 1783, Thomas joined the 52nd Regiment of Foot, and in March that year embarked for India, where he remained until 1887. Between 1887 and 1890, he lived in Dublin. At the end of August 1790, he was posted to Belfast with the 64th Regiment of Foot. In Belfast, he befriended many radical republicans, having already met Theobald Wolfe Tone in Dublin on the 2 July 1790. He was a co-founder of the Society of the United Irishmen.

In January 1794, Russell became the first librarian of the Belfast Society for Promoting Knowledge (now the Linenhall Library). On 12 September 1798, he published a pamphlet entitled *A letter to the people of Ireland* on the present situation of the country. The pamphlet was viewed by the British authorities as highly seditious. Four days later, he was imprisoned in Newgate Prison in London. He remained there until March 1799, when he was removed with other leaders of the United Irish movement to Fort George, Scotland. He was released in June 1802. With Robert Emmett he planned a rising for 1803. He was arrested in Dublin and tried in Downpatrick, where he was hanged on 21 October 1803.

In the records of the Belfast Academical Institution, the Revd William Neilson is listed as a teacher of Irish from 1818 to 1821. The next teacher listed was Thomas Feenaghty, who taught in the school from 1833 to 1849.

In 1830, the Ulster Gaelic Society was founded with the objective of promoting Irish through classes, collecting manuscripts and organising the recording of the oral history of the Gaeltacht areas.

One of the key individuals in the Society was Robert Shipboy McAdam, a Presbyterian industrialist who was active in the promotion of Irish from the 1830s until his death in 1895. By the middle of the 1840s, Queen's College in Belfast (now Queen's University) had created a chair in Celtic studies. Many of those involved in the promotion of Irish were also members of the Belfast Natural History and Philosophical Society and the Belfast Naturalist Field Club. It was from the latter that the Belfast branch of the Gaelic League drew its membership after its formation on 19 August 1895 at the home of P.T. McGinley, 32 Upper Beersbridge Road, east Belfast.

The League was founded in 1893 with the objective of reestablishing Irish as a widely spoken language. In Belfast, the League laid the foundations for an Irish-language movement that survived the upheaval of the First World War, the partition of Ireland and repressive cultural policies by successive Stormont Governments during the twentieth century. By 1901, there were 2,500 citizens in Belfast who spoke Irish and English. From the 1895 formation of the Belfast branch of the Gaelic League through to the present, there has been a continuous and unbroken effort by Irish speakers and teachers to maintain the teaching of the Irish language in the city.

F-495: William McConnell Wilton; *d.* 29 March 1976

William McConnell Wilton was born at Glenbank, Derry, on 21 July 1900 and attended the model school there; he was commonly referred to as W.M. In 1914 the Wilton family moved to Belfast and, in the early 1920s, to Ligoniel village on the outskirts of north Belfast. In 1928 William purchased a carrier's business with an undertaking business attached. By the 1930s the undertaker's side of things had developed to such an extent that W.M. moved to new premises at Rosewood Buildings, Crumlin Road. The Wilton Funeral Company became the largest independent business of its type in Ireland and Britain. W.M. then lived at 658 Springfield Road. His interest in politics led to his election as a city councillor for the Court Ward on the Belfast Corporation on 15 May 1936; John William Nixon had previously held this seat. Wilton remained as councillor until 18 September 1946 when he lost to Clarke Scott by just two votes. On 9 February 1938 he stood as an independent unionist for the Stormont parliamentary

Thomas Henderson (**G2-71**) and William Wilton (**F-495**)

seat of Clifton in north Belfast, securing 5,600 votes, but lost
to the Ulster Unionist candidate, Major Hall-Thompson, who
polled 6,683 votes. On Friday, 24 August 1945, he was elected
to the Stormont Senate, a seat he held as an independent unionist
until 22 May 1953. Wilton was involved in a variety of social,
sporting and religious organisations. From 1934 he was a
member of the Belfast Board of Guardians representing the
Belfast district electoral division of Woodvale, a position he held
until 16 March 1939, when the board was dissolved by order of
the Stormont minister of home affairs, reducing the number of
guardians from 58 to 2. He was a director of Distillery Football
Club and a member of the Irish FA Council. In 1940 he was
installed as honorary president of Shankill Ambulance Division
of the St John's Ambulance Brigade. He was connected to the
Northern Ireland Show Jumping Association and possessed a
large collection of Scottish gigs, tub traps, jaunting cars, funeral
carriages and an original state coach. Fifty-six of his horses were
killed in the air raids on Belfast on the night of 15–16 April 1941,
when his stables and funeral parlour on the Crumlin Road were
almost completely destroyed. One of the most unusual sights of

that night was a stampede along the Crumlin Road of fourteen of his specially bred black draught funeral horses. A non-smoker, teetotaller and strict sabbatarian, he complained at a meeting of the Belfast Board of Guardians, on 24 September 1935, about the appearance of two advertisements from the board in a Sunday edition of the *Irish News*.

From an early age he was involved in the Presbyterian Church, initially with First Londonderry Presbyterian Church, and in Belfast with the Albert Street Presbyterian Church. Throughout his life William fused his Protestantism with his unionism; speaking at the unveiling of an Orange Arch at Wolff Street on the Newtownards Road on 10 July 1936, he declared that if the 'papishes in the north' did not like it here, they should go back home to the south. William McConnell Wilton died at his home, 227 Ballygomartin Road, Belfast, on Tuesday, 29 March 1976.

THE BOARD OF GUARDIANS

A bill of the British parliament, the Irish Poor Relief Acts 1838, provided for the building of workhouses in Ireland and the appointment of Boards of Guardians to oversee their administration. On 1 February 1839 the Belfast Board of Guardians held their first meeting in the Assembly Rooms, Commercial Buildings. On 26 March 1839 they secured a site of 12 acres on the Lisburn Road for the erection of a workhouse, purchased at a cost of £7,000 on 21 May 1839. Further land acquisitions increased the site to 30 acres. The workhouse opened on 11 May 1841. Today, the Belfast City Hospital occupies the site of the workhouse. (See I1-1/3 and 29/31 Glen, Abingdon Street Burial Ground.)

F-439: William Henry McLaughlin; *d.* 18 July 1920

William Henry was born in 1851, the son of Henry McLaughlin (born 1819), and educated at the old Belfast Seminary. While employed as a foreman carpenter by the contractor, James Carlisle (**J-465**), William's father had met William Harvey, also a foreman carpenter, while constructing the Crumlin Road courthouse. In 1853 Henry McLaughlin was offered a contract to build a new mill for the Rosebank Weaving Company. He immediately accepted the contract and approached Harvey with a proposition to form a new company. In 1853 the building firm of McLaughlin & Harvey was established with its new premises at 130 York Street. In 1889, following expansion of the business, it moved to Castleton, York Road. Castleton remained the company's headquarters until it relocated to Mallusk on the northern outskirts of Belfast in 1981.

After the death of his father, on 11 August 1871, William became the head of McLaughlin & Harvey. Under his leadership the business expanded, constructing many of the landmark buildings of Belfast. These included St Matthew's Church, the Royal Victoria Hospital, and the King Edward building. Outside of Belfast the company won the contracts to build Coleraine Town Hall and the railway stations at Portrush and Larne harbour. An important part of the company's business was the erection and improvement of local textile mills and other industrial buildings. This can be seen in the contracts from the industrial giants of the linen industry: W. Ewart & Sons, Ross Brothers, Edenderry Spinning Company, Broadway Damask, Northern Spinning, Ulster Spinning, J&S Johnston, W. Barbour & Sons, Falls Flex Spinning, and York Street Mills. McLaughlin & Harvey also built the College of Science in Dublin and constructed an extensive aluminium works on the Caledonian Canal in Scotland. They were specialists in the building of cinemas and had numerous contracts for this type of work in London and in many English towns.

Like most of his generation William was involved across a spectrum of religious and charitable organisations. He was a member of the Plymouth Brethren, the President of the Cripples Institute, and President of the Homes for the Blind on the Cliftonville Road. His interests included the Belfast YMCA and Shankill Road Mission. He was a life governor of the Royal Victoria Hospital and the Foster Green Hospital. His last public outing was his attendance at the unveiling of the *Titanic* Memorial in the grounds of Belfast City Hall on 26 June 1920.

F-439: George McLaughlin; *d*. 30 May 1900

George McLaughlin, aged just 22, died in the Boer War at Lindley, South Africa, on 30 May 1900. That day the 13th Battalion of the Imperial Yeomanry, the aristocracy-led unit, rode into Lindley, unaware that Boers led by Piet de Wet had taken the town. The 45th and 46th companies of the Imperial Yeomanry were raised in Ireland. The 45th, from the fox-hunting community, was known as the Irish Hunt Contingent; and the 46th was from Belfast. The 13th battalion retreated into a *kopje* (a small hill) outside Lindley and waited to be rescued. Lieutenant Hugh Montgomery was ordered to take sixteen men and occupy the west side of a kopje opposite the position held by the 46th. The Boers fatally wounded troopers Lackey, Martin, Walker and McLaughlin. Eventually the Battalion was forced to surrender – 80 soldiers were killed or wounded in this engagement and 530 captured. Among those captured were Lords Leitrim, Ennismore, Donaghmore and Longford, who had been shot in the neck. One of those killed was Sir John Power, whose family owned Powers Whiskey; he was shot while bringing three bandoleers containing 750 rounds of ammunition to the 46th company. Lieutenant James Craig (**J-18**), future Lord Craigavon and first prime minister of Northern Ireland, was also captured at Lindley.

De Wet's brother, Christiaan, was also responsible for the capture of another Irish unit. On 4 April 1900 he attacked the British garrison at Reddersburg, capturing 546 soldiers of the Royal Irish Rifles. During the Boer War 22,000 British and colonial soldiers lost their lives – of these 16,000 died from disease – while 7,000 Boer soldiers were killed and 28,000 Boer civilians, many of them children, perished in British concentration camps. The deaths of native Africans are unrecorded, but it is estimated that 20,000 Africans who worked for Boer families also perished in the concentration camps.

F-439: Arthur McLaughlin; *d*. 9 May 1915

There is a memorial inscription on the right stone surround of the grave for Arthur McLaughlin, the 20-year-old brother of George. He was a lieutenant in the 3rd Battalion Royal Irish Rifles, and died at Frommelles in northern France, when British and Indian units attacked German positions opposite Frommelles with the objective of capturing Aubers Ridge. Many British shells fired at the German lines proved defective; they were made in the USA and found to be filled with sawdust instead of high explosives. In the end 1,619 British army soldiers died at Aubers Ridge. At the same time the French army were attacking positions on Vimy Ridge, resulting in the death of 1,890 French Foreign Legion soldiers. Today at Vimy Ridge stands a memorial naming 11,500 Canadian soldiers killed on the battlefield in April 1917.

F-443: John Horner *d*. 25 October 1919

John McKelvey Horner was born in Belfast on 1 October 1858. He was educated at the Methodist College, then Sowerby Bridge, Yorkshire and finally in Germany. His father, who came to Belfast from Leeds, had been managing director of Brookfield Linen Company before beginning his own business at the Clonard Foundry on the Falls Road, which was eventually absorbed by James Mackie & Co. (**D-219**).

John was one of the main organisers of the Industrial Exhibition held in 1895 in the grounds of the White Linen Hall. A well-known botanist, he was appointed honorary treasurer to the Belfast Natural History and Philosophical Society in 1904–5 and in 1906–7. John was also a member of the Carlisle Memorial Methodist Church, a committee member of the Belfast Charitable Society, President of the Belfast Working Men's Club, and a senior member of the Masonic Order where he became a senior grand warden in the Provincial Lodge of Antrim, reaching the 28th degree.

He was 61 when he died at 'Drum Na Coll' on the Antrim Road. Drum Na Coll is most likely the anglicised form of *Droim na gColl* – 'the ridge/hill/top part of the hazel trees/grove'. John's burial order records his profession as machine hackle manufacturer. He bequeathed his collection of spinning wheels to the Belfast Museum, and is further remembered as the author of *The Linen Trade of Europe during the Spinning Wheel Period*, published by McCaw, Stevenson & Orr in 1920.

F-443: George Horner Gaffikin; *d.* 1 July 1916

On the right side face of the Horner obelisk is an inscription in remembrance of George Horner Gaffikin, major of the 9th Battalion Royal Irish Rifles, killed at the Battle of the Somme. The inscription ends 'Write me as one that loves his fellow men'. George, whose parents William and Georgina lived in King's Castle, Ardglass, County Down, is reputed to have led his men on to the battlefield waving an orange handkerchief.

As a captain, Horner Gaffikin sat on a court martial, which sentenced to death rifleman James Crozier from 80 Battenberg Street, on Belfast's Shankill Road. James, thought to be shell-shocked, went absent from his battalion for a week until he was arrested, court-martialed and executed by a firing squad. He was tied on hooks to a stake, blindfolded and shot at dawn on Sunday, 27 February 1916. Greater public awareness generated by the Shot At Dawn campaign – established in the early 1990s and which sought to secure a pardon from the British government for twenty-six Irish soldiers executed by firing squad – led to a statement from the British defence secretary, Des Browne, on 18 August 2006, that he would be seeking a 'statutory pardon' for British soldiers shot for military offences during the First World War – 6 of the 26 had a connection with Belfast.

──────── THE BATTLE OF THE SOMME ────────

Planning for the Somme offensive began in 1915. However, because of the intensity of the battle raging around the French fortress town of Verdun, which started on 21 February 1916, the date for the Somme offensive was brought forward by six weeks. One of its main objectives was to relieve the pressure on the French army which was being mauled at Verdun.

The Battle of the Somme began at 7.30 a.m. on 1 July 1916, when British and French armies attacked German positions along a 25-mile front. The battle began with the firing of a quarter of a million shells into the German trenches. On the first day the British army lost 1,000 officers, with 20,000 men killed and 25,000 seriously wounded. The scale of the offensive brought an immediate reaction from the German army which moved 60 heavy guns and 2 infantry divisions from the Verdun front to the Somme battlefield.

The first of July was a particularly gruesome day for the 36th Ulster Division (mostly recruited from the UVF) whose soldiers came from the Inniskilling Fusiliers, the Royal Irish Rifles and Royal Irish Fusiliers. Attacking along a 3,000 yard line, they suffered heavy casualties during their assault on the heavily fortified Schwaben Redoubt, the villages of Thiepval, Beaucourt and Beaumont Hamel. At the end of the first two days 5,553 were killed, wounded or missing, out of a total strength of 15,000. They had also managed to capture 600 German soldiers.

Dublin and Inniskilling Fusiliers, serving with the 29th Division on the left flank of the 36th, were also involved on the attack at Beaumont Hamel on 1 July. Another Irish division, the 16th, saw action on the Somme battlefield. Soldiers from the Leinster regiment, Munster Fusiliers, Connaught Rangers, Royal Irish Regiment, Royal Irish Rifles, Inniskilling Fusiliers and Royal Irish Fusiliers saw action at Ginchy and Guillemont. Between 3–9 September the 16th Division (many of whom were recruited from Redmond's Volunteers) lost 224 officers and 4,090 other ranks were killed, wounded or went missing. One of those killed was Tom Kettles, a lieutenant in the Dublin Fusiliers and a former Nationalist MP for East Tyrone. Many of the soldiers of the 6th Battalion of the Connaught Rangers came from the Falls Road in Belfast. Six days after the main assault on Ginchy and Guillemont, the 1st and 2nd Battalion of the Irish Guards suffered heavy casualties at Ginchy.

The Battle of the Somme raged for five months, ending on 18 November 1916, during which period the British, French and German armies fired 23 million shells. Just under a third of a million men lost their lives – 95,675 British, 50,729 French and 164,055 German soldiers. Add to this figure the 650,000 French and German soldiers killed at Verdun, between 21 February and 12 December 1916, and the death toll on these two battlefields amounts to just under a million.

F-527: Vere Foster; *d.* 21 December 1900

Vere Foster was the third son of Augustus John Foster, a senior diplomat in the British Foreign Office. Augustus John was appointed envoy-extraordinary and minister plenipotentiary to the United States in 1812. He subsequently served as British minister in Sweden, Denmark and Sardinia. The family home was at Glyde Court, Ardee, County Louth. Vere Foster was born in Copenhagen on 26 April 1819 when his father was British minister there. After his education at Eton and Oxford, he joined the British Foreign Office.

In 1842–3 he served with the British Diplomatic Mission in Rio de Janeiro, followed by service in Monte Video, Uruguay, from 1845–7. In Monte Video he got to know Garibaldi,

the Italian soldier and patriot, who in 1834 had been condemned to death for helping in a republican plot to seize Genoa but had escaped to South America; he was in command of a Genoese contingent under the protection of Britain. In 1848 Vere was appointed British attaché in Buenos Aires, but refused the post and subsequently severed his connection with the British Diplomatic Service.

He first visited Ireland

in 1847 at the height of the Famine and was so appalled by the poverty he witnessed that he spent the rest of his life working to alleviate the harsh conditions of the poor, concentrating particularly on the education of Irish children. During the mid-nineteenth century an Irish farm labourer was paid between £3 and £6 annually, and women were paid between 5 and 15 shillings every quarter. Poverty was so rampant that many thousands sought refuge in the workhouse system – the population of seven workhouses amounted to 110,000 paupers.

Vere was also deeply concerned about the conditions suffered by Irish emigrants on their journey to North America. Attempting to alleviate their hardship, he provided many of them with their passage money. He wrote, printed and widely distributed 100,000 copies of a small pamphlet *Work and Wages*, which outlined the benefit of seeking work in Canada and the United States, and advised emigrants on how to find employment, and where to get the financial assistance for their journey to North America.

Shrewdly perceiving the journey across the Atlantic Ocean to be only a first step, he gave support and material assistance to many, providing information on where to go on arrival, where to look for employment and the levels of wages that could be expected. To better gauge the terrible conditions faced on their journey, he actually travelled on the emigrant ships more than once. In Canada and the United States he visited many of the cities where Irish emigrants had settled, on one occasion meeting a young country lawyer, Abraham Lincoln. It is estimated that he spent approximately £25,000 of his own money in supporting emigrants.

He also maintained a deep interest in the education of children. In Ireland he provided financial support for the procurement of educational apparatus, which was then distributed among hundreds of schools. At the same time he sought to improve the condition of over 2,000 national schools. He campaigned for better standards of writing among school children, and in 1865 produced his own copybook, printed by the Belfast firm of Marcus Ward & Co. (**G-598**). Millions of these copybooks were produced. In 1868, he produced, with help from the Teachers' Associations, a pamphlet outlining teachers' views on the primary education of children – in effect a report on education in mid-nineteen-century Ireland. Vere was part of a small conference of teachers in August 1868, who met as a prelude to a larger meeting in December of that year, leading to the establishment of the Irish National Teachers' Organisation (INTO), the first all-Ireland trade union for teachers. Throughout his time in Belfast he was also a strong supporter of the Royal Hospital. He died at his residence, 75 Great Victoria Street.

I-104: James McKee; *d.* 5 May 1894

James McKee, who lived at 40 Castlereagh Street, Belfast, was born into a farming family in Kircubbin, County Down. When he first came to Belfast he taught at the Deaf and Dumb Institute on the Lisburn Road. A few years later he moved to the *Belfast News Letter* as a reporter, and shortly became chief reporter. His writing reflected the politics of the day, especially the issue of Home Rule and the rise of northern unionism. Among the public events he wrote about were the Great Unionist Convention and the Salisbury and Balfour demonstrations. Noted for his shorthand, he taught the Pitman system at the Belfast Shorthand Writers' Association. He died aged 40, from typhoid fever. At the graveside, Dr Richard Kane read a piece from the Scriptures. James was a member of Hills Gilhall Masonic Lodge Number 372.

At the very top of the monument there is an oil lamp symbolising knowledge and love of learning, and also representing life and time. A scroll with the ends rolled up symbolises a life that is unfolding like a scroll of uncertain length, with the past and future hidden. The lamp and scroll are sitting on two books.

—————— DRINKING FOUNTAIN ——————

George Smith and Co. of Sun Foundry, Glasgow, installed the drinking fountain in 1880. Even today, after so much vandalism and neglect, it remains a fine example of Victorian cast-iron workmanship.

Belfast City Cemetery drinking fountain

D-219: James Mackie; *d.* 12 April 1943

James Mackie came to Ireland from Scotland in 1843. He first worked in Drogheda, then in Bessbrook, eventually settling in Belfast. In 1846 he bought the Albert Street Foundry. His son James Mackie was born in 1864, when the family lived in College Gardens. When he turned 14, young James joined his father's company as an apprentice. In 1887, and following the death of his father that year, he became manager of the Albert Foundry. The main business of the company was the production of spinning and twisting machines for the linen industry. The company became known as James Mackie and Sons. In 1893 James and his brother Thomas bought 4 acres of land on the Springfield Road to build a factory for the production of textile machinery. Their new factory was called the Springfield Foundry. The company was highly successful, winning many contracts on the international market. During the First World War they produced thousands of shells which were used on the Western Front. Like many other factories the shortage of labour during the war forced it to employ women on its production lines. William Conor, a Belfast artist, painted Eillie Grey, a lathe operator in Mackies factory. By 1924, and with their new jute spinning machines, Mackies dominated the world market in the production of this type of textile machinery. With the outbreak of the Second World War, the factory very quickly became part of the armaments industry. The introduction of synthetic fibres in the 1960s triggered a steady decline in the fortunes of the company. In 1976 the Mackie family withdrew from the company and handed ownership of their factory over to a trust made up of their workforce.

E-41/2: Murphy Cross

This is another example of an Irish limestone cross. The figure on the shaft is St Andrew, and the inscription on the base of the cross tells us that Andrew Murphy, born on 23 January 1838, died on St Andrew's Day (30 November) in 1891.

The symbol on the face of the cross is the Christian lamb, representing Christ sacrificed for man. This is derived from John the Baptist, who, on seeing Christ, called out 'Behold the Lamb of God.' The lamb is carrying a cross with a pennant, a trophy of resurrection. The four symbols on the arms of the cross represent the four evangelists: St Marcus the winged lion, St Matheus the winged man, St Lucas the winged ox, and St Johanis the eagle. These symbols have two sources. In the Old Testament the prophet Ezekiel describes a chariot driven by cherubim. Each of the cherubim had four faces: the face of a cherub, the face of a man, the face of a lion and the face of an eagle. In the last book of the New Testament – the Book of Revelation or the Apocalypse – by John the Apostle, there is a reference to the throne of God surrounded by four living creatures, the lion, the ox, the man and the eagle. The Greek inscription at the base translates as 'That the just will shine like the sun in the kingdom of their father' (Matthew 13:43).

D-237/8: Robert Davison; *d.* 15 May 1897

Robert Davison lived on the Ormeau Road at its junction with Delhi Street. He came from Jaroslau in Russia, which is now in southeast Poland. He named his Belfast house Romanov, which was the family name of the Czar of Russia. There is an inscription on the left grave surround, at the base of the stone, in remembrance of his grandson Alexander Schneider, a captain in the Indian army, who was killed in action near Jandola, North Western Frontier, on 29 June 1921.

D-435/6: Alexander Corry; *d.* 12 October 1917

Alexander Corry who lived at Victoria Villas, Malahide Road, Dublin, was first engineer on the SS *WM Barkley*, which was sunk by a U-boat at 7 p.m. on 12 October 1917. The ship was a former collier belonging to John Kelly & Sons, Belfast, and was the first ship bought by the Guinness Brewery Group to transport their porter to Britain. They purchased three more, the *Carrowdore*, the *Clareisland* and the *Clarecastle*. She was torpedoed just off the Kish Lightship in Dublin Bay, losing 5 of her 13 crew and a full cargo of Guinness.

D-384: Fanny E.C. Ogilvie; *d.* 2 July 1894

On the headstone, Fanny Ogilvie is referred to as the daughter of 'Lieut Col Ogilvie 4th Royal Irish Dragoon Guards'. She died

D-384, Fanny E.C. Ogilvie

at the age of 86 at 31 Fitzwilliam Street, Belfast. On the face of the cross above the inscription can be seen in relief a ring. Inside the ring are the letters alpha and omega, the first and last letters of the Greek alphabet, which are the Christian symbol of god infinite and eternal. Taken from the first chapter of Revelations, sometimes called the Apocalypse, 'I am Alpha and Omega, the first and the last, the beginning and the end' (Revelations 22:13) or '"I am Alpha and Omega," says the Lord God, "who is, and was, and who is to come, the Almighty"' (Revelations 1:8).

On the back face of the cross in relief is 'He hath put a new song in my heart', taken from Psalm 40, 'Song of praise and prayer for help'.

D-245: Samuel Cleland Davidson; *d.* 18 August 1921

Samuel Cleland Davidson was born on 19 November 1846 in Ballymachan Farm, County Down, later the site of Glenmachan House, Belmont, Belfast. He was educated at the Royal Belfast Academical Institution. Leaving school at 15, he became an apprentice in the office of William Hastings, a civil engineer and a former town surveyor of Belfast. In 1864 he left Ireland and sailed for Calcutta to be an assistant manager on a large tea estate. It took him three weeks on a river boat to reach the estate which lay in the Cachar district of Assam, about 300 miles north east of Calcutta. Two years after arriving in India he became manager of the Burkhola estate of which his father was a co-owner. Following his father's death in 1869, Samuel inherited his share of the estate and bought out the other co-owners of the business. His experience on the tea plantations led him to invent cylindrical tea drying machinery; Richie Hart & Company in Belfast produced his early machines. Samuel was also a keen horseman and a member of one of the first European teams to introduce polo into Bengal from its indigenous home in the hill county of Manipur on the Indian-Burmese border.

A few years later he sold his estate and returned to Belfast, where in 1881 he founded the Sirocco Engineering Works. Beginning with one small workshop and seven workmen, the Sirocco Works was to become one of the key industrial sites in east Belfast. The company was a major producer of machinery used in India's tea plantations; it also produced centrifugal and propeller fans. An original fan with its accompanying machinery can still be found in the Royal Victoria Hospital, Belfast. During the First World War, Davidson developed a hand-held mortar. The company continued to produce fans and tea drying machinery into the 1970s, but by the 1980s decline in business led to the sale of the company to their main competitor.

Samuel Cleland Davidson was a staunch unionist and a supporter of the UVF. There is an inscription on the left hand stone surround to his son James, who was killed at the Battle of the Somme. James was general manager of the Sirocco Works until he enlisted in the 13th Battalion Royal Irish Rifles (1st County Down Volunteers) in September 1914.

A–38: Frederick Arthur Hurley; *d.* 30 November 1914

Frederick Arthur Hurley was the assistant director of irrigation, Main Road, Potchefstroom, Johannesburg in the Union of South

Africa. He lived at 152 Pine Street, Pretoria. He died as a result of a motorcar accident on 30 November 1914. His remains were returned to the family plot in Belfast, where they were interred on 22 January 1915. There is a considerable amount of documentation associated with the return of the remains: first, G.S. Whitelan, a resident magistrate, had to sign the order for burial; next, a South African death certificate was attached; then a letter from the undertaker, J. Swift, 165 Bree Street, Johannesburg, was issued; and, finally, a letter from the district surgeon of Johannesburg was drawn up, certifying that the body had been successfully embalmed.

A-15: Frank Houston; *d.* 7 May 1915

Lost on *Lusitania*, Frank was travelling steerage – the cheapest accommodation on a passenger ship, traditionally near the ship's rudder. (See **B-22** Sarah Hale.)

D-637: Florence Lewis; *d.* 23 August 1908
D-636: Albert James Lewis; *d.* 25 September 1929

Florence Hamilton was born in 1872. Her father was a Church of Ireland clergyman and Rector of St Mark's, 219 Holywood Road, east Belfast. Florence was educated at Queen's College, part of the Royal University of Ireland, getting an honours degree in Mathematics. She married Albert Lewis on 29 August 1894. They had two children, Warren Hamilton Lewis, born on 16 June 1895, and Clive Staples Lewis, born on 29 November 1898. The young family lived in Dundela Villas, off the Holywood Road – now the site of Dundela Flats. On 21 April 1905 they moved to Little Lea at 76 Circular Road. Her second son, Clive Staples, was to become known to millions as C.S. Lewis.

In 1908, just two weeks after his mother's death, C.S. Lewis was sent to school in England. For the next nine years, apart from a term in Campbell College, Belfast, in the autumn of 1910, he continued his education for the most part in Malvern College, Oxford. In November 1917 he was posted to the Western Front with the Somerset Light Infantry and was wounded at the Battle of Arras, 15 April 1918. He was hospitalised for a short period in the Liverpool Merchants' Mobile Hospital, Etaples, and then in Endsleigh Hospital, London. After the war he returned to Oxford, where he graduated with a first class degree. At Oxford he lectured on Medieval and Renaissance literature, and in 1954 became professor of these subjects at Cambridge. He was a theologian, religious broadcaster and writer, but is best remembered as the author of the Narnia stories. The first book, *The Lion, the Witch and the Wardrobe*, was begun in 1939 and only finished in 1949.

Albert James Lewis was born in Cork in August 1863. He was educated at Lurgan College and studied law with a firm of solicitors in Dublin. He qualified as a solicitor in 1885 and immediately set up his own law firm with offices at 83 Royal Avenue, Belfast. While much of his practice was as a prosecuting solicitor in the police courts, he also acted as sessional solicitor to the Belfast City Council and for the National Society for the Prevention of Cruelty to Children.

D-46: Mary Inglis; d. 22 September 1914

Mary was the wife of George Inglis, one of the founding members, and managing director of the Inglis Bakery Company. She lived at 'Kilmona', Adelaide Park, Belfast. The Inglis family stone in section C2-248 is listed and very well known but there is little to no public awareness regarding the Inglis connection to the stone of Mary Inglis.

Fl-379/380: Ulster Female Penitentiary

This plot contains the remains of the following seven women:

Sarah Gillespie	*d.* 30 September 1889, aged 76 years
Jane Johnston	*d.* 1 February 1890, aged 38 years
Ellen Haslett	*d.* 22 June 1891, aged 61 years
Rosena Hawthorn	*d.* 2 July 1892, aged 65 years

Louisa Johnston	d. 11 February 1902, aged 30 years
Jane McDowell	d. 14 May 1904, aged 50 years
Agnes Shannon	d. 18 October 1946, aged 75 years

In the early nineteenth century there were approximately 59 brothels and 236 prostitutes operating in the town of Belfast. The Ulster Female Penitentiary and the Ulster Magdalene Asylum were set up with the objective of rehabilitating them.

The Ulster Female Penitentiary opened in 1819 in York Lane in the vicinity of Donegall Street. A Presbyterian connection was made when Reverend John Edgar, minister of Alfred Street Seceding Church, raised funds for a new building. He soon collected £1,800 and was able to double that amount to build a new brick building at 14 Brunswick Street, which opened in 1839 and contained a laundry and accommodation for fifty-four women. The women had to work in the laundry and earned approximately £10 per year.

Dr Edgar died in 1866 and the name of the penitentiary was changed in 1892 to the 'Edgar Home'. By the end of the century the Brunswick site had become unsuitable. A new 'Edgar Home' was opened in 1902 in Whitehall Parade, off Sunnyside Street, on the Ormeau Road. This operated as a

A cast-iron shield for the Ulster Female Penitentiary

laundry until 1924 and eventually closed in 1932. Over the years a small number of inmates were given assisted passage to Canada.

The Ulster Magdalene Asylum, in Donegall Pass, founded by the Church of Ireland, opened in 1849. It had accommodation for fifty women and, like the Female Penitentiary, had a laundry. One of its early fundraisers was the Reverend Thomas Drew from Christ Church in College Square North. Drew Memorial Church on the Grosvenor Road, opposite the entrance to the Royal Victoria Hospital, was named after him. The Magdalene Asylum closed in 1916, by which time over three thousand women had passed through its doors. Today such institutions are referred to as 'Magdalene Laundries'.

While the lives of men are inscribed in detail on headstones and monuments, the lives of women are usually referred to only in the context of marriage or family – the minor or major achievements of women are rarely reflected in the inscriptions. In reality, the total anonymity of the women in the plot of the Ulster Female Penitentiary is not so far removed from the anonymity of the daughters and wives of the rich and powerful men who are buried in this cemetery.

B2-7: Wilhelmina Tredennick; *d.* 3 March 1891

Wilhelmina Tredennick was born at her family home, Fortwilliam, County Donegal, on 25 November 1837. Her interest in deaf people resulted from a story she was told about the Derry & Raphoe Institution for Deaf and Dumb, Strabane, which had been established in 1845 and subsequently destroyed by fire in 1856, resulting in the deaths of six deaf children. These children had not heard the shouting of others to evacuate the building. Shocked by the story, Wilhelmina accepted an offer from the Bishop of Derry in 1861 to act as secretary for the Strabane School for the Deaf in the Ballyshannon district. She was supported there by Mrs Cecil Frances Alexander, who composed poems and verses, which, with the help of the Reverend Samuel Smith, chaplain of the Royal London Association in Aid of the Deaf, eventually led to their publication in the periodicals *The Deaf and Dumb Magazine* and *Our Little Messenger*. Mrs Alexander used money from her early publications to support the building of the Derry & Raphoe Institution for Deaf and Dumb in Strabane. She is best remembered for her hymns 'All Things Bright and Beautiful', 'There is a Green Hill Far Away' and the great Christmas carol, 'Once in Royal David's City'.

In 1873, Wilhelmina established the Christian Deaf and Dumb Association of Ireland, renamed the Missions to the Adult Deaf and Dumb of Ireland in 1884. During a visit to Belfast in 1886, she was deeply troubled by the plight of unsupported deaf girls in the city. When she moved to the city in 1887 she opened the Central (Northern) Mission Hall for the Deaf at 7 Fisherwick Place on 9 November 1888, providing £121.3s.10d. of her own money for its furnishings. The new Mission Hall offered accommodation for approximately thirty deaf people, had a reading room, a coffee room, a room for Sunday services, and two classrooms, one for men and one for women. Wilhelmina became the Mission Hall's superintendent. She was 53 when she died of jaundice at the home of Mr Lavens M. Ewart of Glenbank House, Ballysillan in Belfast.

On 11 November 1906, the last religious service took place at 7 Fisherwick Place before the mission moved to its new premises at the former Hicks Metropole Hotel, at 5–6 College Square North. The new mission cost £4,000 and was aided by a bequest of £2,000 from Miss Elizabeth Agnes Moore of Manhattan in Derryvolgie, Belfast.

The first school for deaf people in Belfast was opened in the Congregational Church, Donegall Street East in 1830; its teacher was 17-year-old George Gordon. In 1834 the school, now called the Institute for the Deaf, Dumb and Blind, moved to King Street before moving a second time, in 1836, to new premises in College Street. In 1845 the institute was closed and its pupils moved to a new school on the Lisburn Road designed by the architect Charles Lanyon, now the site of the City Hospital. Thomas Colliers opened a small school in 1835, catering for seven boys and six girls. The first school for the blind in Belfast was the Asylum for the Blind in Biggar's Entry, opened in 1801 with thirteen pupils. (See **C-48 Glen**, Francis Maginn and **C2-37**, Reverend John Kinghan.)

A2-14: Hugh Robinson; *d.* 11 April 1890

Hugh Robinson, the eldest son of Samuel Robinson, a brush manufacturer, was born at 26 North Street, Belfast, in 1845. He was educated at the Royal Belfast Academical Institution and became an apprentice with Young & Anderson, wholesale drapers in Donegall Street. From an early age he nurtured a strong interest in natural history and in 1863 he enrolled in a series of natural history classes given by Professor Ralph Tate, a geology lecturer, and helped set up the Belfast Naturalist Field Club. From 1869–80 he acted as honorary secretary to the Field Club and for twelve years he was also secretary of the Belfast School of Art. From 1882–4 he was assistant secretary in the Royal Belfast Academical Institution, becoming its first registrar in 1884, a post he held until March 1890 when ill health forced him to resign. Hugh was also a member of the Royal Irish Academy, and an elder in Duncairn Presbyterian Church. He lived at 'Helen's View', Antrim Road, Belfast.

G1-547: William Osborne; *d.* 18 July 1923

William Osborne, an engineer from 55 Ashbourne Road, Liverpool, died aged 60 on 18 July from acute inflammation of the kidneys. William's headstone reminds us that inscriptions run across a broad spectrum. It carries the motto '*Pax in Bello*' (Peace in War), inscripted on to a circular buckled belt

G1-547, William Osborne

with a lion in its centre. The lion is taken from an early coat of arms of the Osborne family. A later version of the coat of arms carries the motto written on William's headstone. There are no other inscriptions on his grave.

I1–17–23 and 62–68: Catholic Poor Ground

A small piece of ground in section I1 is maintained as Catholic Poor Ground. Section I1 was opened for burials in the 1890s and may have been part of the land allocated for the burial of Catholics prior to the opening of the cemetery in 1869. It was possibly retained for that purpose in the aftermath of the dispute between the local Catholic bishop and the Belfast Corporation that led to Catholics being buried in Milltown Cemetery.

Hl-423: Private Charles Frederick Hughes; *d*. 14 July 1886

Charles Hughes, a private in the West Surrey Regiment, was only 20 when he was shot dead during the anti-Home Rule riots of 1886. He was first buried in **H1-80**, and then re-interred on 31 October 1886 in **H1-423**. Private Hughes was shot in the chest, at point blank range, in the early hours of 14 July, after a prolonged period of rioting in the brickfields between Divis Street and Shankill Road. His body was brought to Divis Street RIC barracks, which later became the Morning Star Hostel. Prior to this, two members of the RIC, Head Constable Gardiner and Sergeant Brady, had also been shot. Gardiner was rushed to the Royal Hospital but died at noon the following day; Brady was shot in the hip, the bullet passing straight through muscle.

Two men from the Shankill Road, Joseph Walker, an engineering worker, and his son, John, were arrested and accused of shooting Hughes, Gardiner and Brady. When arrested, the Walkers were very drunk – John was carrying 2lb of looted tobacco and his father was found in possession of twenty-nine live cartridges. At the Antrim Assizes, 29 March 1887, in front of an all-Protestant jury, Joseph Walker was found not guilty of murder but guilty of manslaughter. He was sentenced to twenty years of penal servitude. John was found not guilty and immediately left the court.

Beginning 3 June 1886, the riots lasted for over four months and left 32 dead and 371 injured. The first fatality was James Curran, a 17-year-old Catholic from the Short Strand, who drowned after being thrown off the dockside near the Alexander Graving dockyard in the shipyard.

Hl-151: Ernest Victor Todd; *d.* 4 October 1917

Ernest Todd was a soldier serving with the New Zealand Expeditionary Force. He was killed in action at Passchendaele in Belgium, 4 October 1917, after the German army launched a counter attack on British lines. The battle began on 31 July 1917 when nine British and six French army divisions attacked German lines along a 15 mile front. Their main objective was the capture of Passchendaele. This battle is remembered for the mud into which thousands of soldiers disappeared.

Passchendaele is a village that sits midway between the Belgian towns of Ypres and Roulers where, in late October 1914, the British and German armies began to dig lines of trenches. Extending in a semicircle around the historic town of Ypres, these trench lines became known as the Ypres Salient and saw some of the bloodiest battles of the First World War. The battles are known as the first, second, third and fourth battles of Ypres. First Ypres began on 19 October 1914 and lasted through to 22 November 1914. Second Ypres began 22 April 1915 and lasted to 25 May 1915. Third Ypres began on 31 July 1917 and lasted to 10 November 1917. The last battle, fourth Ypres, began on 28 September 1918 and finished on 2 October 1918. By this time this military vortex had sucked in hundreds of thousands of soldiers.

On 14 May 1915 Private J. Condon, aged 14, of the Royal Irish Regiment, was killed in the Ypres Salient. He is thought to be the youngest member of the British army to have died there. It was on the Salient that the Germans first used gas, discharging 168 tons of chlorine along a four-mile front at Langemark on 22 April 1915. A previous attempt by the German army in October

1914 to use the tear gas dianisidine chlorosulfonate at Neuve Chapelle had failed.

Among the British soldiers killed on the first day of Third Ypres was the Irish poet Francis Ledwidge, who had served with the Royal Inniskilling Fusiliers in Gallipoli and Salonika and had then been posted to the Western Front. Ledwidge was a friend of Thomas MacDonagh, who was executed by a British army firing squad for his part in the 1916 Easter Rebellion.

On 16 August 1917, the 16th Irish and 36th Ulster divisions, deployed alongside each other, suffered heavy casualties at Langemark, another battleground on the Ypres Salient; 7,816 soldiers from the two divisions were lost and wounded. Third Ypres finished 10 November 1917, by which time the British and French suffered 244,897 dead and wounded, while German dead and wounded amounted to over 400,000. Third Ypres is often remembered by its common name Passchendaele, its most bloody battleground.

B2-308: Dr John St Clair Boyd; *d.* 10 July 1918

John St Clair (pronounced Sinclair) Boyd, whose father part-owned Blackstaff Mill, was born on 9 December 1858. He was educated at Queen's College, Belfast, and then in Edinburgh and Paris. In 1886 he graduated from the Royal University with a masters degree and an MCh (Master of Surgery) and became a surgical assistant in the Birmingham and Midland Hospital for Women. On his return to Belfast he was appointed senior surgeon to the Samaritan Hospital, Lisburn Road, a position he held until 1907. A gynaecologist by profession, he was appointed in 1888 to the Hospital for Sick Children, Queen Street. In 1889 he obtained the post of gynaecologist at the Ulster Hospital for Women and Children in Fisherwick Place.

He was a liberal unionist and active in Irish language circles until his death, becoming the first president of the Belfast Gaelic League at its inaugural meeting on 19 August 1895, at the home of P.T. McGinley, 32 Upper Beersbridge Road. The League met at the Belfast Art Society at 49 Queen Street where classes were held on Wednesday nights. He also served as President of the Dublin Pipers Club. He lived at 'Chatsworth', 74 University Road, Belfast, and was 59 when he died.

B2-328: Major General A. H. M. Dickey; *d*. 11 May 1891

Adam Hugh Dickey was born on 8 October 1830. He lived at 'Laurine', Antrim Road, Belfast and was 69 when he died. His headstone refers to the Madras Staff Corp. In India, prior to the transfer of the Indian army from the East India Company to the British Crown, there were two types of officer – those who officered British line regiments and those who belonged to the Indian Service, in charge of regiments of the East India Company. In the latter, promotion was very slow. In 1861, to remedy this, immediately following the Indian Mutiny, officers of the Indian army were reorganised into three central staff corps – the Bengal, the Bombay and the Madras – filling a range of military and civilian posts.

D-9: Thomas Sinclair; *d*. 14 February 1914

Thomas Sinclair was born in Belfast on 23 September 1838, and educated at Royal Belfast Academical Institution and at Queen's College. In his early years he supported the Ulster Liberal Party, which founded the Ulster Reform Club. This club opened on 1 January 1885 in Royal Avenue, Thomas being one of its founding members. Following Gladstone's support for Home Rule in 1885, Sinclair moved towards unionism, becoming the first president of the Ulster Liberal Unionist Association, which was founded on 4 June 1886. On Friday, 30 April 1886, Thomas was the chairman of a meeting held by Liberals in the Ulster Hall in opposition to the Home Rule Bill. Gladstone's Home Rule Bill of 1886 was defeated on its second reading in the British House of Commons in the very early hours of 8 June by 343 votes to 313. In 1892 Sinclair promoted the concept of a Unionist Convention and duly became the driving force and one of the main organisers of the Ulster Unionist Convention held on 17 June 1892. The convention was organised to demonstrate Unionist loyalty to the

D-9, Thomas Sinclair

Crown and to protest against the imposition of Home Rule. Following the convention Thomas became chairman of The Watch Committee of the Ulster Convention League. On 13 February 1893, Gladstone introduced a second Home Rule Bill, which was passed by Westminster on Friday, 21 April 1893, but was defeated in the House of Lords on 9 September by 419 votes to 41. In the same year Sinclair became vice-president of the Ulster Defence Union and chairman of its Council. After the formation of the Ulster Unionist Council on 3 March 1905 he served as a member of its standing committee. He was also active in the West Belfast Anti-Home Rule Association.

He was involved in the third Home Rule crisis and was in attendance at the mass unionist demonstration held at James Craig's home on Saturday, 23 September 1911, when fifty thousand Orangemen and members of the Unionist Clubs were joined by thousands of spectators in a massive show of strength. It was at this meeting that the idea of creating a unionist army was suggested. Two days later, following a meeting of delegates from unionist associations and the Orange institutions, Sinclair was appointed to a 'Commission of Five' – its purpose was to frame a constitution for a Provisional Government of Ulster in the event of the Home Rule Bill being passed by the Westminster parliament.

By 1912 Edward Carson, the leader of Irish Unionism, and James Craig, the future prime minister of Northern Ireland, were discussing ways for unionists to enter into a solemn and binding oath to resist Home Rule. B.D.W. Montgomery, secretary of the Ulster Club in Belfast, suggested the Scottish

Covenant of 1643 as a model.

Thomas Sinclair wrote the first draft of the covenant. On 19 September 1912 Carson, standing on a stone outside the home of James Craig, read the new covenant to the standing committee of the Ulster Unionist Council.

Thomas Sinclair was central to the formation of Ulster unionism. He was also an active member of the Presbyterian church and was connected to Duncairn Church, which today is the home of an Irish language school. His family had a strong connection with Sinclair Seamens' Church, where Thomas was honorary treasurer. He was chairman of the Presbyterian Anti-Home Rule Committee. He lived at 'Hopefield', Antrim Road, Belfast. On the day of his funeral, 1,000 men representing the twenty battalions of the Belfast Division of the UVF led his funeral cortège from the Antrim Road to the City Cemetery. The formation led by the South Belfast Regiment was followed by the East and West Belfast Regiments, with the North Belfast Regiment alongside the hearse.

SCOTTISH COVENANTERS

Scottish Covenanters were seventeenth-century Presbyterians who, through a series of covenants, bound themselves to uphold the Presbyterian form of worship as the sole religion of Scotland. In their efforts to block the imposition of Anglican Church structures a large gathering of Presbyterians signed and adopted 'The National Covenant' in Greyfriars churchyard, Edinburgh, on 28 February 1638. There followed a period of political upheaval as the politics of the Reformation led to a civil war in Ireland, the emergence of Oliver Cromwell as a power in the English parliament, and the execution of Charles I in 1649. Two years after the restoration of Charles II in 1660 the English king declared the Covenants to be unlawful oaths. The Anglican Church was restored and Presbyterian ministers who refused to acknowledge the authority of the bishops were expelled from their ministries. A course of intense repression followed, and thousands of Presbyterians were killed during what is often referred to as 'the killing time'.

Significant unionist dates associated with Home Rule include:

May 1885	Southern Unionists form Irish Loyal and Patriotic Union
8 August 1885	Formation of Loyal Irish Union at the home of Sir Thomas Bateson
22 December 1885	Grand Lodge of Ireland instructs its secretary, Ellison Macartney, to convene a meeting of Ulster Conservative MPs on mobilising broad unionist support against nationalist movement
8 January 1886	Meeting in Constitutional Club, Belfast, sets up a committee to organise a public demonstration against Home Rule, to be held on 18 January 1886
9 January 1886	At a meeting in Omagh, the Northwest Loyal Registration and Electoral Association is formed
14 January 1886	Irish Conservatives MPs meet in St Stephen's Green Club, Dublin, to organise against Home Rule
25 January 1886	Irish Conservative MPs, along with fourteen British Conservative MPs, form a group active inside the British Conservative Party and pledge to resist Home Rule
22 February 1886	Lord Randolph Churchill is the main speaker at a public meeting of Conservatives and unionists in the Ulster Hall, Belfast. Earlier that day, in Larne, he had proclaimed that 'Ulster will fight, and Ulster will be right.'
8 April 1886	Gladstone introduces Home Rule Bill
9 May 1886	Lord Randolph Churchill repeats in a letter to a Glasgow Liberal Unionist his assertion that 'Ulster will fight, and Ulster will be right'

4 June 1886	Formation of the Ulster Liberal Unionist Committee in Belfast
8 June 1886	Home Rule Bill is defeated in the Westminster parliament by 30 votes
17 June 1892	Unionist Convention held in Belfast; 11,879 delegates attend
1 January 1893	First Unionist Club is formed in Templepatrick by Lord Templeton
13 February 1893	Gladstone introduces Second Home Rule Bill
13 March 1893	At a meeting in Lombard Street, Belfast, an Executive Committee of Unionist Clubs is set up
21 April 1893	The second reading of Second Home Rule Bill passed by Westminster parliament
2 May 1893	Unionist Clubs adopt their laws and Constitution
3 September 1893	Second Home Rule Bill is passed in the Westminster parliament by 301 votes for and 267 against
8 September 1893	Second Home Rule Bill defeated in the British House of Lords by 419 against and 41 for
22 October 1904	A conference of unionists in Belfast directs the secretary of the Irish Unionist Party to summon a meeting of Ulster unionists with the purpose of creating an Ulster Unionist Association
2 December 1904	A meeting of Ulster unionists decide to form an Ulster Unionist Council (UUC)
3 March 1905	At a meeting of Ulster unionists in the Ulster Hall, Belfast, the Ulster Unionist Council is formally constituted
21 February 1910	Edward Carson becomes leader of UUC

11 January 1911	Unionist Clubs reactivated
26 January 1911	First Unionist Club reorganised in Holywood, County Down
23 September 1911	Carson addresses 100,000 unionists at Craigavon, the home of James Craig
25 September 1911	Resolution is passed at meeting of UUC in Rosemary Hall, Belfast, to frame a constitution for a Provisional Government of Ulster in the event of Home Rule being passed through the Westminster parliament. A 'Commission of Five' is appointed to carry out this task
5 January 1912	Colonel R.H. Wallace, secretary of the Grand Orange Lodge of Ulster, applies to two local magistrates in Belfast for permission to drill and engage in basic military training. Orange lodges and Unionist Clubs begin to drill and train their membership in the use of arms. This represents the very early development stages of the UVF
9 April 1912	Edward Carson and Bonar Law, leader of the Conservative Party, review unionist and Orange Volunteers at the Balmoral Showgrounds, Belfast
11 April 1912	Asquith, the British prime minister, introduces the Third Home Rule Bill to Westminster parliament
19 September 1912	Standing Committee of the UUC adopts wording of the Ulster Solemn League and Covenant
23 September 1912	UUC adopts the wording of the Solemn League and Covenant
28 September 1912	Ulster Day, mass signing of the Ulster Covenant

January 1913	UUC decides to formally amalgamate all Unionist and Orange Volunteers into a single organisation known as the UVF
16 January 1913	Third Home Rule Bill passes third reading in Westminster parliament
31 January 1913	Third Home Rule Bill defeated in the British House of Lords; Special Commission of UUC present a draft report to Council for the setting up of a Provisional Government
24 September 1913	UUC, at its meeting in the Ulster Hall, Belfast, approves the establishment of a Provisional Government for Ulster
24 April 1914	25,000 rifles and 2,500,000 rounds of ammunition for the UVF smuggled through Larne
25 May 1914	Home Rule Bill passes its third reading in Westminster
18 September 1914	Third Home Rule Bill becomes law

D-203: William Henry Lynn; *d.* 12 September 1915

William Henry Lynn, who lived at 250 Antrim Road, was an outstanding architect. He was born on 27 December 1829 at St John's Point, County Down, where his father was a coastguard lieutenant. His youth was spent in Bannow, County Wexford, where he developed his talent as a painter of watercolours. In 1846 he was apprenticed to the famous Belfast architect, Charles Lanyon. In 1854, when he was only 24, he became a junior partner in Lanyon, Lynn and Lanyon, where he stayed until 1872. Lynn worked on many of Belfast's public buildings, the most notable being the Customs House. Other buildings designed by Lynn include Belfast Castle, the library of Queen's College (later Queen's University), Belfast Central Library, the Bank Buildings, Carlisle Memorial Methodist Church and the Belfast Water Commissioner's Office (now the Donegall Square North entrance

D-203, William Henry Lynn

to Marks & Spencers). One of his less well-known projects was the design for a lodge, which sat in the corner of Dunville Park at the junction of the Falls and Grosvenor Roads. His plans for this building were approved on 16 March 1892.

D-203: Samuel Terres Lynn; *d.* 5 April 1876

The younger brother of William Henry Lynn and a renowned sculptor, Samuel Terres Lynn lived at Crumlin Terrace, Belfast. He studied at the Belfast School of Art and then at the Royal Academy, London. He worked on the Prince Albert Memorial in Hyde Park. In Belfast he sculpted the statue of Prince Albert in Portland stone on the Albert Clock in the city centre, and the statue of Reverend Henry Cooke, which sits opposite the entrance to the Royal Belfast Academical Institution at College Square. His work also includes a white marble statuette of Master McGrath, the famous greyhound owned by Lord Lurgan, and the pediment above the Provincial Bank, College Street, Dublin. He died aged 41. This grave is listed as having special architectural and historic interest.

G-600: Robert Thompson; *d.* 3 August 1918

Robert Thompson was born on 1 February 1839 at Trouthbeck House, Ballylesson, County Down. A private education was followed by attendance at Purdysburn School and then with a Mr Charles Rennie at the Wellington Academy, Belfast. After leaving school he entered the linen business as an apprentice with Mr Edward Thomas; it was Edward Thomas who, in conjunction with James Kennedy, invented the first power loom for the manufacture of cambric and muslin goods. The first such loom was installed in their premises in Bedford Street. Robert Thompson eventually became the sole owner of Lindsay, Thompson & Co. of the Prospect Mills on the Crumlin Road, and the Mulhouse works on the Grosvenor Road. At the Prospect Mills the main business was flax spinning and linen thread manufacturing; while the main operations at the Mulhouse works were power loom weaving, bleaching and dyeing.

Like many other leading industrialists, Robert Thompson held a variety of positions in the commercial and civic infrastructure of Victorian Belfast. He was a member of the Harbour Board from 1893 and became its chairman in 1907, a position he held until his death in 1918. The naming of the Thompson dry dock was in recognition of his services to the Harbour Board. On 17 April 1907 he was appointed director of the Belfast and County Down Railway Company. For many years, he was president of the Ulster Flax Spinners Association. He

was also president of the Chamber of Commerce and chairman of the Board of Governors of Campbell College. A devoted Presbyterian, he regularly spoke on the platform in the Assembly buildings, Fisherwick Place, in the centre of Belfast. Throughout his life Robert Thompson remained an active unionist. Since the creation in 1885 of the Belfast North Westminster seat he had taken a keen interest in the affairs of that constituency. On 19 October 1909 the committee of the Divisional Unionist Association unanimously decided to recommend the adoption of Robert Thompson as their candidate to contest the North Belfast seat. In the general election on 20 January 1910 he polled 6,275 votes, against 3,951 votes for the Labour candidate, Robert Gageby. He was returned unopposed at the general election in December 1912.

Robert Thompson died at his home, Bertha House, on the Malone Road on Saturday morning, 3 August 1918.

THOMPSON DRY DOCK

The dominant industry of 1890s Belfast was the shipyards, where the largest ships in the world were built. Belfast was the birthplace of the great ocean liners of the Victorian era. By the 1890s it had become clear to the shipbuilders and the Harbour Board that a new dry dock was required for the fitting-out of these great ocean liners. Preparations began under the management of Thomas Ross Salmond, the resident engineer for Belfast Harbour between 1871 and 1892. On 25 July 1898 a Parliamentary Act was passed that allowed for major channel improvements and a new graving dock on the County Down side of Belfast Harbour. In 1900 a number of harbour commissioners visited Liverpool, Glasgow, Newcastle-upon-Tyne, Portsmouth, and Southampton to inspect the graving docks in those locations. The project was delayed for a short period before commissioners decided that the requirements of the port rendered the plans of 1898 redundant. On 26 July 1901 a new act, amending the 1898 Act, was passed, which allowed for the site and dimensions of a graving dock to be different from those originally proposed.

In 1903 the contract for the new graving dock was awarded to Walter Scott & Middleton of London. W. Redfern Kelly, resident engineer for Belfast Harbour, was in charge of its construction. However, due to the poor condition of the ground, excavation work was slow and dangerous. In the summer of 1905 the west wall of Alexander graving dock collapsed as a result of these excavations. Completed in 1911 at a cost of £300,000, the Thompson dock was the largest dry dock in the world. It was almost always left dry and would only be flooded in readiness for its next ship. When a ship was hauled into the flooded dock, the gate would be 'stabled' and the process of pumping out 26 million gallons of seawater would begin. This took two hours, by which time the ship would be resting on the keel blocks which ran along the middle of the dock floor. On 1 April 1911, the 45,000-ton *Olympic* was the first ship to be hauled into the new dock; on 3 February 1912, its sister ship, the *Titanic*, was brought into the dock. It was named the 'Thompson graving dock' by the lord lieutenant of Ireland, Lord Wimborne, on 20 May 1915, after Robert Thompson, who was chairman of the harbour commissioners at that time.

G-600: Samuel Herbert Hall-Thompson; *d*. 26 October 1954

Samuel Hall-Thompson, born in 1885 in Crawfordsburn, County Down, was the son of Robert Thompson, MP for North Belfast. He was educated at Methodist College, Belfast and Dulwich College, before joining his father's linen business, Lindsey Thompson & Co. At the outbreak of the First World War he enlisted with the Royal Engineers and then with the Royal North Downs (4th Battalion Royal Irish Rifles). He saw active service with the Mediterranean and Egyptian expeditionary forces. Soon after his demobilisation in 1919 he became an Area Commandant of the Ulster Special Constabulary, a position he held until 1922. In 1923 he was elected as a unionist councillor for the Clifton Ward of the Belfast Corporation. He was a founding member of the Belfast branch of the Junior Imperial League. By 1929 he was an MP in the Stormont parliament, representing the Clifton Division, north Belfast. With the outbreak of the Second World War he returned to the British army where he rose to the rank of lieutenant colonel in the Royal Ordinance Corps. Between 1939 and 1942 he was chief ordinance officer of Northern Ireland. In 1944 he was appointed minister of education in the Stormont parliament.

He is mostly remembered for the passing of the Education Act (1947), following the passing of the Butler Act in the Westminster parliament in 1944. The 1947 Act proposed to take away the power of the Protestant churches to recommend the appointment of Protestant teachers to state schools. Hall-Thompson's proposals, first published in December 1944, brought a storm of protest in their wake. The Catholic bishops accused him of favouring the state school system, while the Protestant churches accused him of making concessions to the Catholic Church and undermining the Protestant ethos of state schools. At a meeting of the Ulster Women's Unionist Council on 9 December 1946 he was shouted down and the crowd sang 'Derry's Walls'.

In 1949 he proposed to pay the national insurance and superannuation of Catholic schoolteachers. Basil Brooke, the prime minister of Northern Ireland, undermined this proposal, and told a protest meeting of the Grand Orange Lodge that he was going to amend it. Hall-Thompson resigned as minister of education soon after. In 1954 he lost his Stormont seat to an independent unionist, Norman Porter, secretary of the Evangelical National Union of Protestants. Ironically, Norman Porter's son, also Norman, wrote *Rethinking Unionism* (1996), which challenged unionists to 'move beyond their horizons by appropriating an inclusive vision of Northern Ireland and a broader notion of politics'. Hall-Thompson lived at 34 Cairnburn Road, Belmont, Belfast.

G-598: Francis Davis Ward; *d.* 5 March 1905

Francis Davis Ward was born on 8 August 1828, and lived at 39 Botanic Avenue, Belfast. He was the eldest son of Marcus Ward and headed the printing company, Marcus Ward & Co., set up by his father. The family had been involved with the manufacture of paper since 1802 when his grandfather, John Ward, in partnership with James Blow and Robert Greenfield, set up their new business at 97 Ann Street. By 1824, John Ward had founded his own company, John Ward & Co., in Ann Street, Belfast. He then expanded by acquiring paper mills in Comber, County Down, and Coleraine, County Derry. Following John's death in 1836, his son Marcus set up his own company, Marcus Ward & Co. By 1840 the new company had moved away from the manufacture of paper and began to develop a stationery and printing business. This successful change in direction necessitated a move in 1841 to new premises at 6 Cornmarket. From this point on the company developed a worldwide reputation for the quality of its work, especially in the field of colour lithography. Its capacity to remain at the cutting edge of printing technology while maintaining the highest artistic standards ensured its dominant position in the world market.

In 1847 Marcus Ward died, aged 41, leaving his business to his widow and sons Francis, John and William. By 1855 the company was once again on the move, this time to new premises in Donegall Place. Ten years later it established an office in Dublin where in 1865 they were introduced to Vere Foster (**F-527**). This was the beginning of a relationship that would dominate the company's business, and accelerate the rapid expansion of its printing capacity. Millions of Vere Foster copybooks were produced in the company's Belfast factory, where one of their steam-driven printing machines was capable of producing 16,000 copybooks daily. In 1874 a new factory was built on a 4-acre site on the Dublin Road, Belfast, but by then a serious dispute had broken out among the company directors, leading to John Ward retiring in 1876. Two years later, in August 1878, Vere Foster informed the company that he was withdrawing his contract. The company was dissolved in 1899 with a loss of over 1,400 jobs. In its heyday, Marcus Ward & Co. were world leaders in the production of illuminated books, calendars, greeting cards, illuminated stationery and children's books, many of which are now held in the Belfast Central Library.

C2-512: James Haslett; *d.* 18 August 1905

James Haslett, who lived at Princess Gardens near Queen's University, Belfast, was born in 1832. A son of Presbyterian minister, the Reverend Henry Haslett, pastor of Castlereagh Presbyterian Church, he was educated at Royal Belfast Academical Institution, and then served his time as a grocer and druggist with Mr William Dobbin, North Street, Belfast. He began the family chemist business with his brother John. A committed unionist, he was first elected to the Belfast Corporation in 1867 as a representative for the Smithfield Ward. In 1878 he became an alderman, succeeding Barney Hughes. A member of the Orange Order, he had joined Derby True Blues LOL 1959 in 1884. This lodge met in the old Derby Hall in Agnes Street, off the Shankill Road. He was also associated with St Matthew's Church Total Abstinence LOL 880, was a member of the Royal Black Preceptory (Mount Zion number 75) and was a trustee of Ballynafeigh Orange Hall. He was elected mayor in 1887 and again in 1888. In 1885 he was elected for the Westminster seat of West Belfast. In the general election of 1886 he lost his seat by 103 votes to Thomas Sexton. In 1896, following the death of Edward Harland MP, he stood for and won North Belfast. An active Presbyterian, he was an elder in May Street Presbyterian Church. Also an astute businessman, he held directorships in the Lagan Canal Company and the Whitehouse Spinning & Weaving Company.

G-20: Walter Tyrrell; *d.* 9 June 1918
John Tyrrell; *d.* 20 June 1918

There are two inscriptions on the surround to the right of the main stone. Remembered are Walter and John Tyrrell from Ballyholme, Bangor. Walter, who was only 19, was a wing commander in the RAF and a holder of the Military Cross; he was killed in France on 9 June 1918. John, also in the RAF, had a connection to the Royal Irish Fusiliers and was killed in France eleven days later, aged 23.

G-184/5: Richard Dawson Bates; *d*. 3 March 1881

Richard Dawson Bates, a solicitor and a councillor on the Belfast Corporation, was born on 14 November 1844. He died suddenly in the Westminster Palace Hotel, London, at the age of 36, leaving behind a wife and a young family. One of his children, Richard Dawson Bates (1876–1949) was secretary of the Ulster Unionist Council from 1906 to 1921, MP for East Belfast and Victoria Division 1921 to 1929, and the first minister of home affairs in the Northern Ireland parliament from 1921 until 1943.

G-182: Thomas Andrews; *d*. 26 November 1885

Thomas Andrews was born on 19 December 1813 at 3 Donegall Square South, Belfast. He came from a family of linen weavers and flour millers; his father was Thomas John Andrews, a linen merchant of Belfast. Educated at Belfast Academy, Donegall Street, and then at the Belfast Academical Institution, he left school before he was 15 to work in his father's linen business. However, a little while later he left Belfast and enrolled as a chemistry student at Glasgow University. In 1830 he travelled to Paris to work in the laboratory of M. Dumas, Professor of Chemistry in the Royal College. Returning to Ireland, he enrolled as a medical student in Trinity College Dublin, eventually finishing his education at Edinburgh with a diploma from the Royal College of Surgeons in April 1835, and graduating as a doctor of medicine (MD) in August of the same year. He was still only 22.

In 1832, as a result of his research during the cholera epidemic that ravaged Belfast, he published an important paper on the blood of cholera victims. His formal education completed, he returned to Belfast in 1835 to join the staff at the Belfast Academical Institution as Professor of Chemistry. In this period he was also a physician in the Belfast General Hospital. He was a member of the Royal Irish Academy and the Belfast Natural History and Philosophical Society. In 1846 he became vice-president of Queen's College, Belfast, where in 1849 he was also Professor of Chemistry, a position he held until 1879. The modern refrigerator was born out of his research on the liquefaction of gases. He was the first to understand that ozone was a form of oxygen. In 1869 he published 'The Church in Ireland', a paper advocating the disestablishment of the Church of Ireland. In 1880 he refused a knighthood.

Queen's College Belfast was designed by Charles Lanyon and opened its doors to students on 7 November 1849, with its formal inauguration taking place on 20 December. The college along with colleges in Cork and Galway constituted the Queen's University of Ireland. After the passing of an act in 1879, the Queen's University in Ireland was dissolved and replaced by the Royal University of Ireland.

G-197: Gustavus Heyn; *d.* 3 December 1875

Gustavus Heyn was born on 27 April 1803 in the Baltic seaport, Danzig, Germany. Situated in what was then the western Prussian region of Pomerania, its name was changed in the aftermath of the Second World War to Gdansk. As a young man Gustavus served as an officer in the Prussian army. He came to Belfast in 1825 where he founded a shipping company. He was a member of the Belfast Corporation, the Harbour Board, a treasurer and trustee of the General Hospital, later to become the Royal Hospital. His company held consular appointments for Russia, Prussia, Belgium, Spain and the Netherlands. The King of Prussia and the King of Belgium decorated him for his services to their countries. The inscription on his headstone refers to him as 'Chevalier De l'ordre De Leopold', a Belgian award; his Prussian decoration was the 'Knight of the Order of the Crown'. A prominent member of the Masonic Order, he was also involved in benevolent societies such as the Shipwrecked Fishermen and Mariners' Society. During his fifty years as a prominent citizen of Belfast, he became a naturalised British subject by a special Act of Westminster parliament. The Reverend Hamilton, best remembered as the grandfather of C.S. Lewis, officiated at his funeral service, which took place at St Mark's, Dundela.

G-420: Capt. H. C. F. Witt; *d.* 6 September 1874

Captain Witt, who died from consumption, was a sea captain, living at 15 Dock Street, Belfast. Gustavus Heyn is listed in the burial records as the owner of the grave. The German inscription on his grave reads:

Hier ruhet	Here rests
in	in
Gott der shiffs	God of the ship
Capt. H.C.F. Witt	Capt. H.C.F. Witt
Aus Rostock	of Rostock
Geb. den 9 ten Sept 1833	Born 9 September 1833
Ges. den 6 ten Sept 1874	Died 6 September 1874

There is a possibility that someone who spoke inadequate German dictated this inscription to the stonemason: '*Gott der shiffs*' does not make sense; '*Gott des schiffs*' (God of the Ship) or '*Gott dem schiff*' (God the Ship) may have been the intended meaning. In the word '*schiff*' the 'c' is silent; '*Geb.*' is an abbreviated form of '*Geboren*' (born); similarly, '*Ges.*' means '*Gestorben*' (died). There is another possible explanation if the inscription is read as:

Hier ruhet in Gott   Here rests in God
Der shiffs capt. H.C.F. Witt   The Ship's Captain H.C.F. Witt

In the Christian tradition the ship was often used as a symbol of the church, the mast of a ship being compared to a cross. For example, in the third century AD, St Hippolytus wrote, 'The world is a sea, in which the church, like a ship, is beaten by the waves, but not submerged.'

Rostock, situated in the Mecklenburg-West Pomerania area of north-eastern Germany (today Mecklenburg-Vorpommern), is a twelfth-century Baltic port with a long history of shipbuilding, the first German steam ship was built there. In the aftermath of the Second World War it became the main port of the East German state.

G-35: Henry Riddle; *d.* 30 January 1923

Henry Riddle was born on 4 December 1851. He received his early education at the Belfast Model School and the Belfast Academy. He was briefly an apprentice at the Milford Mill. In 1876 he entered Queen's College, Belfast, where he graduated with both a first-class honours and a Master of Engineering degree.

He worked for a time with Thomas Andrews (**G-182**). He began his career as an engineer in Riddle, Malcolm & Co., Hastings Street, Belfast, which later became known as Henry Riddle & Co. After the death of his brother James he became managing director of Alexander Riddle & Sons.

From 1911 to 1921 he was the honary treasurer of the Belfast Natural History and Philosophical Society, becoming its president in 1921 until his death in 1923. He represented St George's Ward on the Belfast Corporation from 1908 to 1920 and was a member of the Queen's University Senate from 1914 to 1923.

G-48: Walter Edwin Carson McCammond;
d. 30 August 1923

Walter McCammond was born on 31 July 1874. His father, William, had been the second lord mayor of Belfast in the years 1894–5. After a private education, he studied at the Belfast Royal Academy. On 7 March 1892 he was commissioned as a second lieutenant in the 4th Royal Irish Rifles, and was promoted to captain five years later on 13 August. He was promoted to major on 2 August 1902, and then to the honorary rank of lieutenant colonel on 1 March 1909. On 27 June 1908 the 4th Royal Irish Rifles transferred to the 3rd (Special Reserve) Battalion of the Royal Irish Rifles, formerly known as the Queen's Royal Antrim Rifles. In the aftermath of the 1916 Easter Rebellion the 3rd were ordered to Dublin to help suppress the rebellion. The regiment was subsequently quartered in the Victoria barracks, North Queen Street, Belfast. Between the beginning and the end of the First World War, 11,000 recruits were trained by the 3rd Battalion and then posted to the regular battalions of the Royal Irish Rifles serving in the 10th, 16th and 36th Divisions.

Walter McCammond represented Duncairn Ward on the Belfast Corporation from 1901 to 1903. He was vice-president of the Belfast Conservative Association, 1900 to 1906, and Worshipful Master Eldon Number 7 LOL. He joined the UVF at its inception and commanded its 5th North Belfast Battalion. He was also vice-president of the Belfast Rifle Club and president of the CPA Miniature Rifle Club. In the burial records his address is given as 60 Botanic Avenue and at 'Inisfale', Donegall Park, Belfast.

C2-250: James Kingsberry; *d*. 11 December 1891

James Kingsberry, born on 11 December 1844, was a coal merchant who lived at 278 Shankill Road, Belfast. He was active in the Masonic Order and was a member of the Thomas Valentine Masonic Lodge Number 21. He was also a member of the Orange Order LOL 1959. The shaft of the cross has very fine etching of flowers, with shamrock across its face.

C2-248: James Inglis; d. 28 August 1925

C2-248, James Inglis

James Inglis, whose family owned Inglis Bakery, was born in Scotland but came to Belfast where he and his brother George opened their bakery in Eliza Street in 1882. For the last thirty years of his life he lived at 64 Upper Leeson Street, Dublin. The family inscriptions are on the back of the stone. This monument with its panels in relief, and thought to be the work of Rosamond Praeger, is listed as having special architectural and historic interest.

C2, J1, K1 and D2: Grass roundabout on corners

In the original layout of the Belfast Cemetery, this site was earmarked as the location for a Catholic mortuary chapel.

C2-24/25: Rose Elizabeth Cameron; *d.* 27 February 1887

Rose Elizabeth Cameron, who lived at 74 Avoca Terrace, Springfield Road, died at the age of 34. She was the second wife of Allan Ewan Cameron, Town Inspector, Royal Irish Constabulary, whom she married on 16 November 1882. The couple had two children, Donald and Evan.

Allan Cameron was married four times: first to Greta Gumley; then to Rose Elizabeth (née Fitzgerald); after her death in February 1887, he married Zina Prosser; and his last wife was Alice Evans. The inscription on her stone reads 'Cameron of Lundavra'. At the base of the stone is Scots Gaelic, '*Sliochd Ian'ic Ailein*' (the descendants or the people of Ian McAllan). This may refer to Allan, the son of the clan chieftain, Donald Dubh of Lochiel, who lived in the early part of the fifteenth century.

C2-24/25, Rose Elizabeth Cameron

Cameron is one of the most famous of highland names thought to be derived from the Gaelic word *Cam-brun*, meaning crooked hill. It might also originate from *Cam-shron*, meaning a hooknose. Lundavra, from the Gaelic *lunn da bhraighe*, refers to a small mountain lake situated in the Mamore Hills, which rise above Fort William. *Lunn da bhraighe* could have one of two meanings – either the billow or wave between two uplands or a straight shaft between two uplands.

The history of Scotland is intertwined with the Cameron story. Ewen Cameron was the last highland chief to hold out against Oliver Cromwell. Donal Cameron, 'The Gentle Lochiel', was one of the first highland chiefs to declare for Bonnie Prince Charlie. He brought seven hundred of his clansmen to Glennfinnan where the prince raised his standard on 19 August 1745. The great-great grandfather of Allan Cameron was killed on 21 September 1745 at the Battle of Prestonpans, southeast of Edinburgh in Scotland. In 1793 it was an Allen Cameron who raised the 79th Regiment, which later become known as the Queen's Own Cameron Highlanders. It was Allan's grandfather who came to Ireland after a military career in India.

C2-29½
Frances Elizabeth Moffett;
d. 18 February 1958

Frances, who lived at 370 Ormeau Road, has the distinction of having a so-called half grave, which is very rare in the cemetery. These are small portions of spare ground located in sections where the numerical sequence of graves

C2-29½, Frances Elizabeth Moffett

has already been set. As these portions can be used as burial space they have to be placed in numerical sequence; taking an existing number and creating a new grave reference by adding a ½ achieves this. The use of the term 'half-grave' is for administrative purpose. The number 29½ is visible on the front right pillar of the surround.

C2-37: Reverend John Kinghan; *d.* 31 August 1895

John Kinghan was born on 4 February 1823 at Ballymacarn, near Ballynahinch in County Down. He completed his early education at Dr Blain's Academy in Arthur Street, Belfast, before moving to the Royal Belfast Academical Institution to study for the ministry of the Presbyterian Church. From 1845 he was engaged as a teacher by the Ulster Institution for the Deaf and Dumb on the Lisburn Road after its opening that year on 24 September. In 1852 he was licensed to preach by the Presbytery of Belfast. A year later he was appointed principal of the Ulster Institution. Reverend Kinghan was a strong supporter of the Belfast Workshops for the Blind and a councillor of the society for promoting home mission work among Belfast's blind. In 1857 he secured a schoolroom in King Street where, for the first time in Ireland, blind and deaf people could worship. The service was later moved to Great Victoria Street schoolhouse and then in 1858 to the Sandy Row area of Belfast. Reverend Kinghan continued as principal of the Ulster Institution until his death from cardiac failure in August 1895.

Jl-352: Walter Dorling Smiles; *d.* 31 January 1953

On the right panel of the stone is a memorial inscription to Walter Dorling Smiles who was lost on the MV *Princess Victoria* when she sank of the coast of Ireland on 31 January 1953.

Walter, the seventh of eleven children, was born in Strandtown, east Belfast, on 8 November 1883. His father, William Holmes Smiles, was the first managing director of the Belfast Rope Works. Dorling was his mother's family name; she was the sister of Mrs Beeton, famous for her cookery book. William was educated in Rossall School, Lancashire, and then served an apprenticeship in the engineering shop and offices of the Rope Works. This was followed by a job as assistant engineer in the Assam Tea Company, India, and then as divisional manager of the Moran Tea Company. When the First World War broke out in 1914 he qualified as a pilot and went to France as a sub-lieutenant in the Royal Naval Volunteer Reserve, attached to a naval armoured car division. He saw active service in France, Belgium, Austria, Russia, Romania, Persia and Mesopotamia. On 9 July 1916 his older brother William was killed in action on the Somme, and the following year his eldest brother Samuel was killed in action in Flanders on 16 August. That same year he married Margaret Highway of Didsbury, Manchester. In 1918 Walter was transferred to the machine gun corps with the rank of lieutenant-colonel. His experience in the armoured car division led him to write a book, *Armoured Cars and Modern Warfare*.

After the end of the war he returned to India in 1919 to become general manager in the Moran Tea Company. He came back to Ireland in April 1930 to live at Portavoe Point, Donaghadee. Here he became a member of Eldon Number 7 Orange Lodge. In November 1931 he was elected as a Conservative member for Blackburn, holding the seat until 1945, when he became the unionist member in the double-membered seat of Down. When double-membered seats were abolished in 1950 he stood for, and was elected as, the Unionist member for North Down, a seat he held until his death. In 1952 he was elected as chairman of the Ulster Unionist Parliamentary Party at Westminster.

J1-334: Thomas McKnight; *d.* 19 November 1899

Thomas, who lived at 28 Wellington Park, Belfast, was born on 15 February 1829 in Gainsborough, County Durham. After his early education at Dr Bowman's school in Gainsborough he entered the medical faculty at King's College, London, on 28 September 1849, leaving that institution in 1851. It was at King's College that he met and was heavily influenced by the Christian socialist, F.D. Maurice. Between 1851 and 1866 he wrote a number of books, including *History of the Life and Times of Edmund Burke, The Life of Henry St John, Viscount Bolingbroke*, a critical but anonymous biography of Disraeli, and *Thirty Years of Foreign Policy*, a defence of British Prime Ministers Aberdeen and Palmerston's foreign policies that culminated in the Crimean War. During this period he was a reader in a London publishing house and a leader writer for a London daily newspaper.

On 31 January 1866 he arrived in Belfast to take up the editorship of the *Northern Whig*, a daily newspaper established in 1824. The previous editor, Frank Harrison Hall, joined the staff of the *Daily News* as a leader writer and subsequently became its editor, a position he held until his resignation over the Home Rule policy of Gladstone. Just eighteen months into his role as editor of the *Northern Whig*, McKnight was confronted with the first political crisis of his career when, on 12 July 1867, a large number of Orangemen, led by William Johnston of Ballykilbeg, marched from Newtownards to Bangor in protest against the enforcement of the 1850 Party Processions Act. The act, which effectively banned all Orange marches, was introduced in response to a clash between Orangemen and agrarian Catholic 'Ribbonmen' on 12 July 1849 at Dolly's Brae, close to Castlewellan, County Down. As a consequence of a speech he made at the Twelfth meeting in Bangor, where he addressed many thousands of Orangemen, Johnston was charged at the Bangor Petty Sessions, on 4 September 1867, with infringements against the act. On 28 February 1868 he was sentenced at the Down Assizes in Downpatrick to a month's imprisonment, and to enter into a bail of £500, with two sureties of £500 each to be of good behaviour for two years. After sentencing, Johnston was immediately brought to Downpatrick jail. Released on Wednesday, 22 April 1868, Johnston became a hero of the Orange Order, and was nominated by the Belfast Working Men's Protestant Association as a candidate to contest the Belfast constituency in the parliamentary elections of 20 November 1868. Belfast was then an undivided constituency represented by two members. Johnston resigned his Belfast seat in 1878 but would win the Belfast South seat in 1885.

In the 1868 election McKnight gave the support of the Northern Whig to the Liberal candidate, Thomas McClure, and to William Johnston, both of whom were elected. In the years that followed, McKnight dealt with many of the political issues that dominated the latter end of the nineteenth century such as the disestablishment of the Church of Ireland, opposition to government plans for university education, the Irish land question and the rights of tenant farmers, and Gladstone's Home Rule policy. In 1896 he published his last book, *Ulster As It Is, or, Twenty-eight Years' Experience as an Irish Editor.* An early member of the Liberal Ulster Reform Club and the Ulster Liberal Unionist Association, Thomas McKnight moved away from support for the Liberal Party to supporting the cause of unionism. He died at his residence at 11 a.m. on Sunday, 19 November 1899. There is no headstone for his grave.

Belfast newspapers of the eighteenth and nineteenth centuries

- *Belfast News Letter* established 1737; daily (conservative)
- *The Belfast Courant* established 1745
- *Belfast Mercury* established 1783
- *Northern Star* established 1792
- *The Commercial Chronicle* established 1805
- *Belfast Mercantile Journal* established 1807 (neutral politics)
- *The Irishman* established 1818
- *Belfast Northern Whig* established 1824; daily (liberal)
- *The Vindicator* established 1839
- *Banner of Ulster* established 1842

- *Ulster General Advertiser* established 1842; issued free on a Saturday (neutral)
- *The Mercury* established 1851
- *Belfast Morning News* established 1855; daily (nationalist)
- *Belfast Weekly News* established 1855; issued on a Saturday (newspaper of the Orange Order)
- *Weekly Examiner* established 1855 (nationalist)
- *Weekly Northern Wig* established in 1858 (liberal)
- *Belfast Evening Telegraph* established 1870; daily (conservative)
- *Christian Advocate* established 1872 (evangelical journal)
- *Irish Educational Journal* established 1872
- *Belfast Weekly Telegraph* established 1873; issued on a Saturday (conservative)
- *Ulster Echo* established 1874; a half-penny evening paper (liberal)
- *The Witness* established 1874; Presbyterian weekly
- *Belfast Advertiser* established 1880; issued on a Wednesday (neutral politics)
- *The Irish News* established 1891
- *Blarney* comic journal; issued on a Saturday

The *Irish Baptist* magazine, the *Irish Church Directory and Year Book*, the *Irish Congregational Magazine*, and the *Irish Congregational Year Book* were also published in the city.

Kl-458: Reverend David Mitchel; *d.* 14 March 1914

Reverend David Mitchel, born in 1824, was an orthodox Presbyterian minister. He served in Warrenpoint Presbyterian Church and retired to his home at Hamilton Road, Bangor, County Down. His father Samuel was the brother of Reverend John Mitchel, a non-subscribing Presbyterian minister. David's first cousin was John Mitchel, a Young Irelander and author of the famous Republican publication, *The Jail Journal*.

The Mitchel family came from non-subsribing Presbyterians who

left Scotland and settled in Tory Island off the coast of Donegal. The
Reverend John Mitchel, who died in 1840, was a Unitarian and had
been a United Irishman. John Mitchel was born in Dungiven in 1815.
He received his early education in Derry and then in Newry when
his family moved there in 1822. In 1834 he successfully completed
a degree in law at Trinity College Dublin, and in 1836 he entered
the law practice of Mr Quinn in Newry. Here he met his future wife,
Jane Verner, whom he married in Drumcree Presbyterian Church
in February 1837. From 1840 to 1845 he lived in Banbridge and
worked for Mr Fraser, a Newry solicitor.

On 15 October 1842 *The Nation* newspaper of the Young
Ireland Movement was launched. Soon after, John Mitchel
became one of its contributors and by 1845 had become its editor.
In February 1848 he launched his own newspaper, *The United
Irishman*. On 21 March 1848 he was arrested and charged with
seditious libel. On 26 May 1848 he was tried in Dublin's Green
Street Courthouse under the Treason-Felony Act, convicted by a
packed jury and sentenced to fourteen years' penal servitude and
transportation the following day.

On 1 June he was brought to Spike Island, County Cork, and
boarded on a Man of War, HMS *Scourge*, bound for Bermuda,
where he arrived on 20 June. By April 1849 he was transported
on HMS *Neptune* to the Cape of Good Hope in South Africa,
arriving there in September the same year. Leaving Cape Town
on 19 February 1850, he was now bound for Van Diemen's Land,
arriving there on 6 April 1850.

Three years later, on 18 July 1853, he escaped from Van
Diemen's Land after being smuggled aboard the sailing brig, the
Emma, which immediately set sail for Sydney Harbour, Australia.
On 2 August he left Sydney aboard the *Orkney Lass* bound for
Hawaii, where he joined an American ship, the *Julia Ann*, which
brought him into San Francisco Harbour on 3 October 1853.

By 7 January 1854, while living in Brooklyn, New York,
he was once again publishing a newspaper, *The Irish Citizen*.
One week later, on 14 January, he began to write a column, 'Jail
Journal', for *The Irish Citizen*. In the American Civil War he
sided with the Confederates. His son Willy was killed at the battle

of Gettysburg, fighting with General Pickett's 1st Virginians. Another son, Major John Mitchel, commanding officer of Fort Sumter, died from shrapnel wounds.

John Mitchel remained in America until 1874, when he returned to Ireland. On 16 February 1875 he was elected MP for North Tipperary. Unseated by petition he stood again in the by-election held on 11 March 1875 and was re-elected. He died on 20 March 1875 and is buried in the Unitarian Cemetery in Newry, County Down.

K1 300/1: Berkeley Deane Wise; *d.* 5 May 1909

Berkeley Deane Wise, the son of James Lawrence Wise and Elizabeth Deane, was born on 2 October 1853 in New Ross, County Wexford. After his early education in England, he returned to Ireland and entered Trinity College Dublin in October 1871. Leaving Trinity prior to the completion of his degree, he became an apprentice in the engineers' office of the Dublin Wicklow and Wexford Railway; this was followed by his appointment to the position of assistant engineer in October 1875. During his time with the Dublin Wicklow and Wexford he worked on the development of the lines at Bray Head and the doubling of the line between Kingstown (now called Dún Laoghaire), Dalkey and the Westland Row station, Dublin.

After his appointment as chief engineer for the Belfast and County Down Railway in December 1877, Berkeley moved from his home at 26 Waterloo Road in Dublin to live at Salem Cottage, Knock Road in Belfast. From 1877, until he left the Belfast and County Down Railway in 1888, he modernised the infrastructure of the line, including the rebuilding of bridges, adding a signal cabin at Holywood station, and modernising the Queen's Quay Terminus in east Belfast. Conscious of the need for safety measures, he was responsible for the introduction of interlocking signals throughout the railway system under his care.

In April 1888, he obtained the post of chief engineer for the Northern Counties Railway following the death of Robert Collins, who had held the post. From his appointment to his retirement due to ill health in 1906, Berkeley once again modernised the infrastructure in his care. He rebuilt stations at Antrim, Belfast's York Road, Ballymena, Ballymoney, Carrickfergus, Glynn, Larne Harbour, Larne Town, Portrush, Troopers Lane, Whiteabbey and Whitehead. He continued the policy of a previous manager of the line, Edward John Cotton (L-426), by developing the tourism infrastructure, which was aimed at popularising the use of railways for recreation and leisure. Tea-rooms, promenades, bandstands, footbridges and new hotels were added to the growing development of the Northern Counties line. In May 1901 he launched the most remarkable of his tourism projects: the construction of a two-mile cliff path about 30 feet above the high-tide mark along the Gobbins cliffs on Islandmagee, County Antrim. The use of tubular suspension bridges to link various sections of the path helped create one of the most spectacular scenic walks on the island of Ireland. After his retirement in 1906 he lived with his sister at 18 Salisbury Terrace, Eglinton Street, Portrush, County Antrim, where he died on 5 May 1909.

His nephew, Freeman Wills Crofts, was one of the great fiction writers of the early twentieth century. He was born in Dublin on 1 June 1879, the son of a surgeon-lieutenant in the British Army Medical Service who had died abroad before Freeman's birth. His mother, Celia Frances (née Wise), later married Archdeacon Jonathan Hardy of the Church of Ireland, the vicar of Gilford, County Down. The family moved to Gilford, where Freeman lived in the vicarage. He was educated at Methodist and Campbell Colleges in Belfast. When he was 17 he became a civil engineering pupil of his uncle, Berkeley Deane Wise. Freeman remained a railway engineer until his retirement from the Belfast and Northern Counties Railway in 1929.

While recovering from a long illness in 1919, he began to write his first book, *The Cask*. Published in 1920, it sold over 100,000 copies. He wrote another 33 novels, 70 short stories and 27 plays. He will always be remembered for the character of Inspector Joseph French, introduced in his fifth novel, *Inspector French's Greatest Case*. His last book, *Anything to Declare*, was published in 1957. He died on 11 April of that year.

TRANSPORT IN BELFAST

The first railway line operated by the Belfast Railway Company opened in Belfast on 12 August 1839, nine years after the very first railway line between Liverpool and Manchester was launched. Journey times between Belfast and Lisburn took 18 to 20 minutes.

During the life of Berkeley Deane Wise a transformation of public transport in the city of Belfast was under way. On 28 August 1872 the first horse-drawn trams operated by the Belfast Street Tramways Company began to run from Castle Place to Botanic Gardens. On 28 September 1905 electric trams were used on the Falls Road to teach drivers; while, on 5 December of that year, the first operational electric tram service was formally launched in Belfast. The last operational horse tram had its last journey that very same day.

These improvements in the infrastructure of public transport continued right through to the late 1960s. On 4 October 1926 the first omnibus service ran from Castle Place to Cavehill Road. Twelve years later, on 28 March 1938, the very first trolley bus began its journey along the Falls Road. Ninety-six years after it first appeared on the roads of Belfast the last operational tramcar completed its final journey on 27 February 1954. The same fate befell the trolleybus on 12 May 1968.

The modernisation of Belfast's transport system kept pace across the spectrum of twentieth-century technological advances. As a result of aircraft development during the First World War, new Air Navigation Regulations came into force in 1919, which immediately led to the emergence of the civil aviation industry. On 22 February 1924 the Belfast Corporation commenced its negotiations to buy just under 50 acres of land at Taughmonagh from a Mr Archibald Willis and a Mr John Thompson for the price of £10,500. These 50 acres were situated between the Malone and Lisburn Roads in south Belfast. The first commercial flight from the Belfast Aerodrome at Malone was made on 30 April 1924, when a single engine DH-50 Aircraft G-EBFP left at 12.17 p.m. for Liverpool, landing there at 2.45 p.m. The last commercial flight from the Malone site took place on 8 June 1925. While the use of Malone airfield for commercial flights was short-lived, it was a very early indication of the impact that air travel would have in the decades following that first flight from Belfast in 1924.

Belfast City was to wait another thirteen years for its own airport when, on 16 March 1938, Belfast Harbour Airport was officially opened by the wife of the British prime minister, Neville Chamberlain. Infill used in the reclamation of the foreshore included the remains of the American cargo vessel, SS *Argenta*, which had been launched on 10 May 1919, and then bought by the Stormont government for £3,000 on 17 May 1922. It was used as a prison ship from 20 June of that year until 30 January 1924.

F2-616: Samuel Lawther; *d.* 9 June 1913

Samuel Lawther was born *c.* 1834 in Islandreagh in the neighbourhood of Antrim town. As a young man he came to Belfast and entered the service of a local shipping agent. In 1857 he established the firm of Samuel Lawther & Co., ship and insurance brokers, with offices at 2 Corporation Square. From this position he rose to become the owner of a small number of iron hull sailing ships, all built by Harland and Wolff. His first ship, built in partnership with Thomas Dixon, was the *E.J. Harland*, which weighed 1,333 tons, was launched on 20 April 1876, and was delivered on 1 June that year. It was followed by the *G.W. Wolff*, at 1,663 tons, which was launched on 28 September 1878; the *Walter H. Wilson*, which weighed 2,518 tons and was launched on 6 July 1882; the *W.J. Pirrie*, a 2,576-tonner, launched on 26 May 1883; and, finally, the *Queen's Island*, at 2,093 tons, which was launched on 22 September 1885. His involvement in the shipping trade continued to grow with a directorship in the Belfast Steamship Co., and the management by Samuel Lawther & Co. of the Belfast and Mersey Steamship Company, 21 Corporation Square in Belfast. He was one of the original shareholders of the White Star Line, investing in the new company by purchasing a number of shares, each costing one thousand pounds.

In addition to his business ventures, Samuel took an active interest in the local politics of Belfast. On 25 November 1872 he was first elected on a Conservative-Unionist ticket to represent Dock Ward on the Belfast Corporation. Ten years later he was returned as an alderman for that ward. He was a determined opponent of Home Rule and was involved in the unionist opposition to Gladstone's two Home Rule bills. With the extension of the municipal boundaries in 1897, when the number of wards increased from 12 to 15, he was able to win a seat in the Duncairn Ward as an alderman. In 1900 he stood as an Independent Conservative for the Westminster seat of South Antrim, where he was narrowly defeated by 588 votes. In 1902 he was elected as High Sheriff for the City of Belfast. As the chairman of the Corporation's asylum committee he played a major role in the acquisition of 88 acres of land lying between Purdysburn and Saintfield Road. He was also a member of the Harbour Board, from 1882 until 1909, and an advocate for better lighting of the Irish coast. In 1901 a new lighthouse was erected on Black Head, on the north coast at the entrance of Belfast Lough; and by 1903, as a result of his efforts, improved lights and fog signals were placed on the 'maidens', a group of nine rocks some six miles north of Larne. In his evidence in March 1907 to the Commission on Lighthouse Administration, he advocated the establishment of a central body under government control. In January 1910 he retired from business and public life, having been a member of the Belfast Corporation for thirty-eight years. He died from heart failure at his residence, Rath House, in Tullow, County Carlow.

In 1908 the Belfast Corporation authorised the establishment of a new Belfast asylum on the land at Purdysburn. In August 1913 patients were transferred from the old asylum on the Grosvenor Road to new accommodation in four new buildings referred to as 'villas' at Purdysburn. The site was described in Corporation publications as a Villa Colony. By the 1930s there were a total of seventeen villas with a hospital and sanatorium accommodating 1,320 patients.

D2-263: Francis Joseph Flynn; *d*. 31 October 1869

While it is generally correct to assume that, from its opening in 1869 the cemetery was only used by Belfast's Protestants, there are some Catholics to be found. Francis Joseph Flynn, a Catholic hotel manager of 67 Joy Street, Belfast, is the first Catholic mentioned in the burial records. On his burial order 'In Protestant Proprietary Grave' has been changed to 'In Roman Catholic Proprietary Grave'. Also in the burial records from 25 November 1869, reference is made to Mary Frazer in I–339, the first burial in Catholic Public Ground. Furthermore, there is a small plot of fourteen graves in section I1, referred to as Catholic Public Ground.

D2-194: Reverend John Gillis Phillips; *d*. 8 January 1909

John Phillips came from Clough, a small village in north Antrim. He was first employed in a solicitor's office in Ballymena, County Antrim, afterwards coming to Belfast to study for the Presbyterian ministry. He then moved to Jervis Street Mission in Dublin, staying there for three years. In 1877 he went as a missionary to Damascus in Syria, where he lived for thirty years. He died at his home, 'Hermon', in Osborne Park, Belfast. His eldest son followed in his father's footsteps by becoming a medical missionary for the Presbyterian Church in China. John's headstone is in the style of a rough-cut stone. Its inscription reads 'For thirty years, missionary of the Irish Presbyterian Church at Damascus, Syria.' At the bottom of the stone is an Arabic inscription with its English translation – 'God is love'.

D2-174: Lizzie Clarke; *d*. 1 April 1903
Henry Cooke Morrow; *d*. 11 January 1938

Lizzie Clarke from 104 Duncairn Street, Belfast, was buried at 2 p.m. on Saturday, 4 April 1903. The Morrow stone designed in the Art Nouveau style originally carried a bronze medallion, which has unfortunately been stolen.

D2-174, Lizzie Clarke

Henry Cooke Morrow, Lizzie's husband, was born on 27 August 1865. His father from Comber, County Down, started a family business in Clifton Street, Belfast, George Morrow & Sons, house painters, decorators and renovators. Henry's maternal grandfather, a MacNamara from Galway, had settled in County Down and was most likely Catholic and an Irish speaker.

In 1902 Henry was one of the founders of the Ulster Literary Theatre, whose origin can be found in the Protestant National Association. Bulmer Hobson, another founding member, had decided to use drama as a way of propagating his nationalist and republican views. Henry was both an actor and a playwright and is credited with writing eleven plays under the pseudonym Harry MacNamara. One of his earlier works, *The Mist That Does Be on the Bog* is a one-act play satirising the output of J.M. Synge, and was first performed in the Abbey Theatre, Dublin, on 26 November 1909. One of his best-known plays was *Thompson in Tír na nÓg*, the story of an Orangeman who is accidentally killed at the Battle of Scarva and then reawakens to find himself in the Celtic Valhalla, surrounded by a host of Irish heroes. The play was first produced in the Opera House, Belfast, on 9 December 1912.

Henry, who lived at 32 Victoria Road, Sydenham, in Belfast, was not the only talented member of his family; six of his seven brothers were known for their creative skills and their connection to the arts.

Albert Morrow, born on 26 April 1863, was an illustrator, designer and poster artist. He attended the Government School of Art in Belfast before moving to London as a result of winning a two-year scholarship to the South Kensington Art School. One of his best-known posters was of the actress Sarah Bernhardt. He died on 26 October 1927 in his home at West Heathly, Sussex, England.

George Morrow, born on 5 September 1869 in Belfast, was well known for his cartoons in the satirical magazine *Punch*, where they first appeared in 1906. He was eventually made a member of its staff and, for just under fifty years, contributed to its pages. He also contributed to the republican newspaper *Republic*, founded in Belfast in 1906 by Bulmer Hobson. One of his cartoons was later used as a postcard by the republican political and literary organisation, the Dungannon Clubs. George died at his home in Essex, England on 18 January 1955.

Jack Morrow, born on 26 February 1872 in Belfast, was a cartoonist who contributed to the *Republic* and the *Irish Review*, and worked alongside Bulmer Hobson in the Ulster Literary Theatre, designing costumes and sets; he was also a member of the Irish Republican Brotherhood. As with George, Jack's cartoons were also reproduced as postcards by the Dungannon Clubs. In the aftermath of the Easter Rebellion he was active as a republican cartoonist. In January 1919 he was jailed in Mountjoy jail for possession of government documents. He died in Dublin on 11 January 1926.

Fred Morrow staged, produced and acted in plays for the Ulster Literary Theatre. He was the sole producer of their plays until they merged in 1940 with the Jewish Institute Dramatic Society and the Northern Irish Players to form the Group Theatre. Fred, who lived at 59 Eglantine Avenue, died on 22 March 1949, aged 74. He is described in the burial records as a master painter, and is buried in **C2-480**.

Edwin Morrow, born on 7 February 1877 in Belfast, was a commercial, landscape and portrait artist. After attending the Government School of Art in Belfast he moved to the South Kensington Art School. A member of Dungannon Club number 4 in London, he also illustrated a postcard that was used by the club.* In 1906 his illustrations were used in a pamphlet on the United Irishman, William Orr; this was the first in a series of pamphlets by Francis Joseph Bigger entitled 'The Northern Leaders of '98'. Edwin died on 9 December 1952 at 23 Clapham Common, Clapham, Sussex.

Norman Morrow, born on 21 August 1879 in Belfast, was a cartoonist and illustrator. He also attended the Government School of Art. Later he was involved with the Ulster Literary Theatre as both an actor and a designer of their sets. He moved to London where he was involved with the Dungannon Club, which held its meetings in his Chelsea studio. The club later reproduced a cartoon by Norman in the *Republic* as a postcard. He died on 8 September 1917 at his home in Chelsea.

The Ulster Literary Theatre changed its name to the Ulster Theatre in 1915. By 1934 it had dissolved because of its inability to secure its own premises. In 1940 the Jewish Institute Dramatic Society along with the Northern Irish Players merged with ex-members of the Ulster Literary Theatre to form the Ulster Group Theatre.

The Government School of Design opened in Belfast on Thursday, 6 December 1849, occupying the northern wing of the Royal Belfast Academical Institution; the formal opening took place in April 1850. The school remained opened until December 1854 when it was forced to close due to lack of funding. In the first week of February 1856, under the new mantle, the Belfast School of Art, the establishment opened its doors once more, only to fall victim to funding issues again on 15 July 1858. On 17 October 1870 the Government School of Art was launched in the

---

* The Dungannon Clubs, federated societies for promoting non-sectarian republicanism, were formed in March 1905 by Bulmer Hobson and Denis McCullough of the IRB.

north wing of the Academical Institution, remaining there until Wednesday, 26 September 1901 when it moved to new premises at 170 North Street. Meanwhile, on 1 January 1901, a new act of the British parliament, the Agriculture and Technical Instruction Act, allowed for the setting up of colleges for the development of technical education. On 26 May 1902, work began on a new building on the corner of College Square East and College Square North to house the Belfast Municipal Technical Institute; work was completed in 1906. In September of that year, the School of Art left 170 North Street for the new Municipal Technical Institute, where it became known as the College of Art.

D2-164: William Charles Mitchell; *d.* 22 July 1894

William Charles Mitchell was born in Glasgow. At 30 he worked for Dunville & Co. Distillers; at 40 he set up his own distilling business, Mitchell & Co., at 84–6 Tomb Street, Belfast. His company had extensive business contacts throughout the British Empire. In 1891 he was elected president of the Belfast Chamber of Commerce. He was also a member of the Harbour Board and Chairman of the Irish Steam Navigation Company. He never forgot his roots and was president of the Belfast Scottish Association and a supporter of the Belfast Burns Club. He helped found the Belfast Benevolent Society of St Andrew. As a liberal unionist, he also belonged to the Ulster Reform Club.

J-18: James Craig; *d.* 20 April 1900

James Craig was born at Ballyvester, near Donaghadee, in County Down, on 7 May 1828. He was educated first by a tutor and then at Donaghadee School, before joining the Civil Service. At 19 he left the service to become a clerk with David Carmichael, a flour miller from Millisle in County Down. In November 1849 he obtained the post of book-keeper in the Comber linen mill of James Andrews & Sons. This was followed in 1856 by a move to Dunville's Distillery in Belfast. On 10 August 1858 he married Eleanor Gilmore Browne at the meeting house of the

Second Presbyterian Congregation in Rosemary Street. Around 1860 James became director and a partner in the Dunville's Distillery, making him a very rich man. The couple had eight sons and one daughter: Henry Cooke, William Dunville, Clarence, Vincent, Alice Eleanor, Charles Curtis, James, Edwin Ernest and Granville. The family lived at 'The Hill', Lower Sydenham, on the outskirts of Belfast. Shortly after 1871 they moved to a larger house, 'Craigavon', at Strandtown, now in east Belfast. Later they moved near Tyrella beach on Dundrum bay, County Down.

James, the seventh child of James and Eleanor, became a central figure in the development of Northern Irish unionism. He was born on 8 January 1871. His early education was at a preparatory school run by Reverend Charles McAlester in a room below the First Presbyterian (Non-Subscribing) Church in High Street, Holywood, County Down. From 1882 to 1887 he was educated at Merchiston Castle, Edinburgh. On his return to Ireland he entered the firm of Alfred M. Munster, General Brokers at 1 Victoria Street, Belfast. This was followed by a move to Foster & Braithwaite, a firm of stockbrokers in London, and finally back to Belfast, where in April 1892 he founded the family stock-broking business, Craigs & Co., on 36 Rosemary Street. He also helped set up the Belfast Stock Exchange. On 17 January 1900, he was commissioned into the 3rd (Militia) Battalion of the Royal Irish Rifles. Seven weeks later, on 6 March, he withdrew from the Belfast Stock Exchange. That same year he was posted with the British army to South Africa. James, now a lieutenant in the 46th Company 13th Battalion Imperial Yeomanry, was captured along with 530 soldiers of his battalion by Boers at Lindley on 30 May 1900. He spent three months in Nooightgedacht and was then released, after which he served as deputy assistant director of the Imperial Military Railways. In late 1901 he took command of D Squadron, 29th Battalion of the Imperial Yeomanry, commonly known as the Irish Horse. He returned to Ireland in 1902. He contested and was defeated by 152 votes in a parliamentary by-election for North Fermanagh on 20 March 1903. A member of the Ulster Unionist Council, he was also a District Master of Lacale, a Deputy Grand Master of Ireland and a member of the Apprentice Boys of Derry. In the 1906 British General Election he was elected as a member for East Down, holding his seat until 1918, when he was elected for Mid Down. He resigned this seat on his election to the Stormont parliament.

In the period of the Third Home Rule Bill, introduced to the British House of Commons on 11 April 1912, Craig became the second most important political figure in northern unionism and the driving force behind unionist opposition to Home Rule. On Saturday, 23 September 1911, unionists heard Edward Carson, on his doorstep, accept leadership of the Ulster Unionists. On Monday, 25 September Craig was appointed to a 'Commission of Five' whose purpose was to draw up a constitution in the event of Home Rule being passed by Westminster parliament. A year later Craig organised the political campaign centred on the Solemn League and Covenant which was made public at 'Craigavon' on 19 September 1912, culminating in its mass signing on 28 September (see **D-9**, Thomas Sinclair).

James Craig remained a central figure in the unfolding political crisis in Ireland. In the aftermath of the First World War he was instrumental in convincing the British government to set up the A-, B- and C-Specials and then ensured that the reorganised UVF would be absorbed into this new part-time police force. In March 1921 he became the leader of Ulster Unionism and went on to become the first unionist prime minister in the Stormont parliament, a position he held from 7 June 1921 until his death on 21 November 1941. One of the pallbearers at his funeral was Fred Crawford (**K-73/4**).

J-18: Eleanor Gilmore Craig; *d*. 6 May 1912

Eleanor was born on 12 September 1835. Her family was from Campsie in Stirlingshire, Scotland, and came to Ireland in the early part of the eighteenth century. Her grandfather William, born in 1767, owned the Clady Calico print works in Ballymather, County Antrim. He died on 24 July 1845. William had two sons Daniel and Robert (Eleanor's father). In the burial records her address at the time of her death is given as Craigalea, Studland Road, Bournemouth. Her eldest son, Henry Cooke Craig, died on 3 September 1930 and is buried in this plot in grave **J-19**.

J-454: Irene Winifred McKibbin; *d.* 5 January 1953

Irene Winifred McKibbin, of 'Lincluden', Finaghy, on the Lisburn Road in Belfast, was born on 3 June 1904. Irene's family owned H & J McKibbin, Builders, 375 Springfield Road. She was a teacher, and, for a number of years, taught in Malone Primary School. In 1924 she became a cadet of the 23rd Belfast Company of the Girl Guides. This was the beginning of her life-long association with the Guides. She later became captain of the 85th Belfast Company, followed by her appointment, in 1928, as commissioner for Woodvale. She continued to occupy a variety of senior positions, including commissioner for Malone, and Belfast County Secretary; for four years she served as Ulster commissioner for Rangers; and, by 1938, she had become skipper of the Sea Ranger ship, the *Whirlwind*. In 1947 she was awarded the Guides' Medal for Merit and became Belfast county commissioner.

She was 48 years old when she was killed in an air disaster at Nutts Corner Aerodrome on the night of 5 January 1953 while returning from a conference in London. Irene was one of 24 passengers and 3 crewmembers who lost their lives at Nutts Corner that night.

British European Airways Viking Aircraft, *The Lord St Vincent*, flight G-AJDL took off at 7.29 p.m. from Northolt, near London, on a scheduled flight to Belfast on 5 January 1953. Carrying 31 passengers, 420 kilos of baggage and cargo, it had a crew of four. At 8.53 p.m., just after crossing the Irish coast and flying at a height of 5,500 feet, it came under the control of Nutts Corner Aerodrome air traffic control. At 9.26 p.m. the captain was told to land on runway 28. The plane was approximately 3 miles from the runway, and at an altitude 90 feet above the flight's glide path, when rain clutter on the radar display screens at Nutts Corner obscured the radar image of the incoming aircraft. As the plane broke through the clouds, somewhere between 1,000 and 1,500 feet, the pilot told ground control he could see the runway's lights. Thirty seconds later they told him that he could take the option to overshoot. Visibility was around 4,400 yards but the aircraft's descent approach appeared slightly steeper than normal. It was 9.38 p.m. Just 1,790 feet short of the runway but 113 feet under its designated flight path, the plane struck five approach light poles taking the tops from the final three. It crashed into a field 250 feet beyond the poles, slewed across the ground for 82 feet, rising again before striking a stationary van containing radio beam equipment more than a 1,000 feet short of the runway. Out of control, it skidded on before demolishing a brick and concrete building housing instrument landing technology. The plane burst into flames. The trail of wreckage was strewn over a 150-yard area. One engine was flung 40 yards from the crash site and a propeller was found in a neighbouring field. The plane, with the exception of the tail, was destroyed by fire and 3 crewman and 24 passengers were killed.

Those killed in the tragedy were:

Mrs Patricia Auld, Westland Bungalows, Cavehill Road, Belfast.

Mr A.C. Barnes, The Glen, Pinner, Middlesex.

Miss Naomi Rose Brudno, 287 Lewisham Way, London, and 112 Fitzroy Avenue, Belfast.

Miss G. Clutsom, King's Road, Knock, Belfast.

Miss Eida Duarkan, Kansas, U.S.A.

Mr R.C. Easterbrook, Eastleigh Drive, Belfast.

Miss Dolores Griffen, Kansas, U.S.A.

Father Patrick Joseph Hackett, C.C., from Aughnacloy in County Tyrone, but based in Sidmouth, Devon.

Captain G.H. Hartley (pilot), North View, Eastcote, Middlesex, England.

Captain T.G.W. Haughton, Green Cottage, Cullybackey, County Antrim.

Mr R.D. Hayes (first officer), Malthouse Cottage, Sherlock Row, Twyford, Berkshire.

Mrs Jane Hill, Mount Daniel, Glen Road, Belfast.

Francis Kavanagh (sixteen month old baby), Fingle Glen, Luton.

Mrs Patricia Kavanagh, from Lagan Street in Belfast, but resident at Fingle Glen, Luton.

Mr J. Lawrence, Crescent Drive, Petts Wood, Kent.

Mr Douglas J. Maw, Wadham Road, Walthamstow, London.

Mr T.R.A. Merry (radio officer), Salling Lane, Yiewsley, Middlesex.

Mr C.H. Mishon, Wembley Park, London, and 105 Malone Road, Belfast.

Miss Agnes McConville, Rosemount, Drumlough, Rathfriland, County Down.

Mrs P.J. McGarvey, Tintagel, Balmoral, Belfast.

Miss Irene McKibbin, 'Lincluden', Lisburn Road, Finaghy, Belfast.

Mrs Elizabeth Pawlicz, Saltram Avenue, Maida Hill, Notting Hill Gate, London.

Mr L.A. Rees, Windsor Road, London and Eglantine Avenue, Belfast.

Master Brian Tweed (ten years old), Bangor, County Down.

Mrs Greta Tweed, Greyhound Hotel, Croydon, Bangor, County Down.

Mr E. Wiggins, Whiteley Avenue, Upper Norwood, London.

Mr Jeffrey Wilks, Wanstead, London and 29 Fitzwilliam Street, London.

Those injured in the tragedy were:

Mr Jack Brower, 146 Castallion Mansions, Maida Vale, London.

Miss Kathleen Browne, Suffolk, Belfast.

Mr Roy Fairclough, 3 Hill View Road, Cheltenham.

Mrs T.G.W. Haughton, Green Cottage, Cullybackey, County Antrim. (Her husband was killed in crash.)

Daniel Hill, 82 Glen Road, Belfast. (Daniel was ten years old and lost his mother in the crash.)

Mrs Prescott, Cleaver Avenue, Malone Road, Belfast.

Mr P. Scarlett, Dalmore Road, Dulwich, London and Finaghy Road South, Belfast.

Mr James Young (aircraft steward), 117 Joy Street, Belfast.

———— NUTTS CORNER AERODROME ————

Ten months after the beginning of the Second World War, the Airfields Board, founded by the British Air Ministry in 1923, explored a number of sites for new airfields throughout the North of Ireland. Between June and November 1940 they selected seven sites, among them Nutts Corner, 9 miles northwest of Belfast, in County Antrim. The new airfield was scheduled to be operational by April 1942, but, given the pressures of war, it was operational by July 1941. It was allocated to two squadrons of Coastal Command: the 120 Squadron flying Liberators, and the 143 Squadron flying Beaufighters. Nutts Corner remained under the control of the Air Force until Monday 16 December 1946, when it became a civil aerodrome; its first scheduled flight departed at 9 a.m. for Liverpool and London. Over the sixteen years of its commercial flight operations, there were a number of aircraft accidents. On 27 March 1951, a Douglas Dakota cargo aircraft crashed on takeoff with four fatalities. On 23 October 1957, a British European Airways Vickers Viscount, on an unscheduled flight from London, crashed on landing with a loss of seven lives. On 25 July 1959, an announcement was made at Westminster that Nutts Corner would close, and Aldergrove, located three miles from Nutts Corner, would become the new civil airport. The last flight from Nutts Corner left at 10.45 p.m. on 25 September 1963; the first flight into Aldergrove was a mail flight from Manchester, landing at 12.03 a.m. on 26 September 1963.

NJ-204: John Martin; *d*. 22 January 1912

John, born on 22 August 1846, was the son of Henry Martin who set up a building company in the late 1830s. Father and son became partners and founded H. & J. Martin & Co.

In 1879 the company moved to 163 Ormeau Road. Among the many buildings constructed by the Martins were the Opera House, the Ulster Museum building on Stranmillis Road and Belfast City Hall. The panels on the shaft and face of the Martin cross are covered in Celtic interlacing and Irish script is used for the inscriptions on the base of the cross.

J-204, John Martin

G-211/2: Sir Samuel Black; *d*. 18 April 1910

Samuel Black was born in Ballycastle on 26 June 1830. He was educated privately and then at Foyle College, Derry. In 1848 he joined the office of John Bates, solicitor and town clerk of Belfast (1842–55), as an apprentice, and in January 1853 he became a solicitor.

In 1859 he was elected for the St George's Ward on the Belfast Corporation, holding his seat until 1871. In the same year following the death of Mr Samuel Bruce, town solicitor, he was appointed to succeed him. By 1879 he was appointed town clerk after the death of Mr James Guthrie, who had held that position since 1856. Samuel remained town clerk for Belfast until his retirement in 1908. During his tenure of office, as town solicitor and town clerk, Belfast saw many changes and improvements – including the opening of public parks, the Free Library in 1888, the public baths, the introduction of horse-drawn trams in 1872 and electric trams in November 1905, the acquisition of the gas works in 1874, the purchase of the old White Linen Hall as a site for the new City Hall, the purchase of the old Albert Bridge that collapsed in 1886 and was replaced by a new bridge, the building of a new fish market and St George's Market, the building of the central fire station and the Albert Clock in 1867, the widening of the city's main roads, the River Blackstaff diverted and culverted, the 1888 Charter making Belfast a city, and the extension of the city boundaries in 1896. On his retirement Samuel Black received an annual pension of £2,000.

G-227: Henry Whitaker; *d.* 2 June 1912

Henry Whitaker was born in High Street, Belfast, on 22 May 1833. His father Joseph was a merchant in the city in the early part of the nineteenth century. Both his parents came from King's County, now County Offaly. Henry received his early education at Bullicks Academy in High Street, before moving to study pharmacy at Grattan & Co., Apothecaries, Chemist, and Aerated Water Manufactures, Medical Hall, Plough Buildings, in Belfast's Corn Market. This company, founded in 1825, was at the time the oldest apothecary in Belfast.

In 1854 Henry moved to Queen's College, and, in 1855, to the Apothecaries Hall, Dublin, where he became a licentiate in 1856. He continued his studies with the Royal College of Surgeons in England, obtaining the degree of MRSc in 1857. He subsequently took his MD degree with the Queen's University of Ireland and then moved back to Belfast as a partner in Wheeler & Whitaker, Apothecaries, High Street. In November 1869 he was elected to the Belfast Corporation, representing St George's Ward and holding the seat until 1890. In the early 1880s he became a lecturer in Sanitary Science at Queen's College, a position he held until 1890.

For most of his adult life Henry Whitaker was a staunch

Conservative and unionist, eventually becoming a member of Cliftonville Unionist Club. As an active supporter of the Conservative Association, he served as its treasurer for a short time. Henry also played an active part in many election campaigns: during the passage of the first Home Rule Bill in 1886, he travelled to the south of England to address numerous meetings arguing the case against the Bill. He was also a member of Eldon Number 7 Orange Lodge.

In 1890, following the death of Dr Samuel Brown, Henry was appointed medical superintendent officer of health for the Belfast Corporation, a post he held until 1906. During his sixteen years as medical superintendent, Belfast had the highest death rate in the industrial cities of Britain. Chickenpox, cholera, diarrhoea, diphtheria, German measles, influenza, measles, mumps, puerperal fever, scarlet fever, smallpox, tuberculosis, typhoid, typhus, and whooping-cough came with punishing regularity, killing thousands of Belfast's citizens. Henry's detailed and regular reports to the Corporation on the health of the city's populace are a stark reminder that, at the pinnacle of its industrial output, Belfast was rife with widespread poverty and misery. These horrendous social conditions continued right into the 1950s, long after Henry Whitaker had died as a result of an enlarged prostate and uraemia on the morning of Sunday, 2 June 1912, at his home on the Cliftonville Road.

G-631: Sir Daniel Dixon MP; *d*. 10 March 1907

Daniel Dixon, born in 1844, was the son of Thomas Dixon, a Larne merchant and ship-owner. He was educated in the Royal Academical Institution Belfast and then apprenticed to the firm of James Agnew, timber merchants, Chichester Street, Belfast. After serving his apprenticeship, he joined his father in the family business, Thomas Dixon & Sons, in Corporation Street. In 1867 his brother Thomas joined the company and the two brothers founded a shipping fleet, the Lord Line, and diversified into land development. Daniel lived at Ballymenoch, Holywood, County Down, but also had extensive land holdings at Glenville, County Antrim and at Ravensdale, County Louth. He held widespread business positions including managing director of the Irish Shipowner Company, chairman of Ulster Marine Insurance Company, chairman of the Harbour Board from 1904–7, director of the Ulster Steamship Company, and director of the County Down Railway Company.

Dixon first entered politics in 1871, being elected as councillor for the Dock Ward on the Belfast Corporation. In 1892 he became mayor, during which time Queen Victoria conferred on the city the title of lord mayor; he was the first councillor to obtain this new civic title. As a senior Belfast unionist he chaired a meeting on 8 April 1892 in the Central Hall, Rosemary Street, in order to organise the Great Unionist Convention of 17 June. He was knighted in 1892, resigned from the Corporation in 1894, and was High Sheriff for County Down in 1896. In 1901 he returned to the Corporation, representing Dock Ward and was again made lord mayor, a post he held in 1902, 1903, 1905 and 1906. In 1905 he was elected Unionist MP for North Belfast.

In 1729 the Irish parliament passed an act allowing for the establishment of a Ballast Office in Cork, Galway, Sligo, Drogheda and Belfast, instructing the Corporations in these towns to erect their Ballast Office after 25 April 1730. Again in 1785, an act of the Irish parliament established 'The corporation for preserving and improving the Port and Harbour of Belfast', otherwise known as the Ballast Board. On 21 June 1847 a new act of the Westminster parliament established the 'Belfast Harbour Commissioners', commonly called the Belfast Harbour Board.

H-112: Robert Wilson MacDermott; *d.* 8 January 1916

Lieutenant Robert Wilson MacDermott, the son of Reverend John MacDermott of Belmont Presbyterian Church, enlisted in the 8th Battalion Royal Irish Rifles. The 8th (Service) Battalion of the Royal Irish Rifles was raised in east Belfast in September 1914. It moved to Ballykinlar, in County Down, and again in July 1915 to Seaford on the Sussex coast. After training in the Aldershot Command, England, the battalion left Bramshott, 3 October 1915 and landed the following day at Boulogne in France. From 5 November 1915 to 3 February 1916 it was deployed with the 107th Brigade of the 4th Division. In February 1916 it rejoined the 36th Ulster Division.

MacDermott is believed to be the first officer of the 36th Ulster Division to be killed in action at the Western Front. However, Lieutenant Leigh Maxwell Anderson of the 9th Royal Irish Fusiliers, who died on 1 September 1915, may precede him, as may Lieutenant Francis Nicholas Andrews of the 15th Battalion (North Belfast) Royal Irish Rifles, who was killed on 11 October 1915. The first soldier of the 36th to be killed in action was Rifleman Samuel Hill (19557) of the 12th Royal Irish Rifles from Monkstown, Whiteabbey, County Antrim, and a member of the Central Antrim UVF, who died on 22 November 1915.

Robert McDermott's brother, William, a captain in the Royal Army Medical Corps during the First World War, died in the Royal Victoria Hospital, Belfast from typhoid fever. Another brother, John Clarke, was Lord Chief Justice of Northern Ireland from 1951 until 1971.

H-21: George Smith Clark; *d*. 23 March 1935

George Clark was born in Paisley, Scotland, on 8 November 1860 and was educated at Merchiston Castle School in Edinburgh. He served as a premium apprentice with Harland and Wolff and later joined Frank Workman in 1880 to form Workman Clark Shipbuilders. In 1907 he stood as a Unionist candidate in a Westminster by-election for North Belfast. He defeated the Labour candidate by a majority of 1,827 votes and went on to hold the seat until 1910. George was chairman of the Arms Committee, a secret part of the Ulster Unionist Council. After September 1913 this committee operated as a department of the Ulster Provisional Government.

Francis Elizabeth Clark, George's wife, who is also buried in this grave, was the daughter of Henry Matier, a linen merchant, in whose company, Matier & Co., George was also a director. The Matier family plot is in **H-23–5**, one grave removed from the Clark plot.

H-29: James P. Corry MP; *d.* 28 November 1891

Robert Corry, James's father, was born in 1800. By 1826 he established his own business importing timber from Canada, and had acquired his first ship, the 325-ton *Chieftain*. James was born on 8 September 1826, the year his father began his business. In 1840 Robert Corry bought his second ship, the *Summerhill*, and in 1843 he bought his third, the *Queen of the West*.

Robert had diverse business interests; apart from being a timber merchant and ship owner he was also involved in the building industry and owned a quarry. Many of his wooden-hull ships were built in Canada where wood was plentiful, keeping down the building costs. In 1859 the Corry business extended its shipping operation to Calcutta, in India, resulting in the transfer of the shipping activities to London. By the late 1850s the Corrys initiated a fleet replacement programme, aiming to substitute all their wooden-hull ships with the more modern iron-hulled vessels. The *Jane Porter* was the first iron-hulled ship built for the Corry's by Harland and Wolff. This ship was the first of twelve identical ships built by Harland, eleven of which were given a name prefixed by The Star of ...

H-31/2: Robert William Corry; *d.* 3 January 1919
Thomas Hughes Corry; *d.* 9 August 1883

Robert William Corry was the chairman of J.P. Corry & Co. He represented the Dock Ward on Belfast City Council. A dedicated Presbyterian, he was connected to Elmwood Church – now commonly known as Elmwood Hall and owned by Queen's University. The church was built in 1862 by Henry Martin (**J-204**) and designed by John Corry, a family member and London director in the firm of J.P. Corry.

H 31/2, Robert William and Thomas Hughes Corry

Thomas Hughes Corry, J.P.'s nephew, was born on 19 December 1859. He studied at Cambridge University and had a deep interest in botanical studies. He lived at 38 Warkworth Road, Cambridge. On the completion of his degree he lectured on botany at King's College, Cambridge and was appointed assistant curator at the University herbarium. In 1882 he was asked by the Royal Irish Academy to research the district around the Ben Bulben Mountain in County Sligo. On 9 August 1883, Thomas and a friend, Charles Dickson, a solicitor from Belfast, set out sometime between 10 a.m. and 11 a.m. in a light skiff to explore the flora, ferns and mosses of Lough Gill, which is located above the town of Sligo. The weather was dreadful. When they failed to return that evening Mrs O'Donnell of the Imperial Hotel, where the two men were staying, organised local people to search the lake. During the night an empty boat, keel up and containing nothing more than a few plants and associated notes was found. The following day, Sub-Inspector Lawless of the RIC organised a party to drag the lake. Search efforts were in vain. It was a local boatman from Hazelwood who, on Saturday, 11 August, recovered the bodies near Goat Island, the property of a Captain Owen Wynne. It would seem that tragedy struck at around 12.20 p.m., on 9 August, the time Thomas's watch stopped; Charles Dickson's watch had stopped at 1.13 p.m. On the return of Thomas Corry's remains to Belfast, a service was held in Elmwood Presbyterian Church and he was buried on 14 August 1883.

Samuel Alexander Stewart (**M-933**), an associate of Thomas Corry, published his *Flora of the North East of Ireland* in 1888. It bore the names of Stewart and Corry, despite Corry's death five years earlier.

The monument, which depicts a variety of plants and flowers, was designed in memory of Thomas. Beginning with the lower panel on the left hand side and travelling clockwise around the stone we find ivy and ivy seed, heart tongue, fern and blechnum fern, roses, rose buds and rose hips, acanthus leaf, ladder fern and lily of the valley, fox gloves, morning glory and passion flowers, laurel leaf, mistletoe and ivy, oak leaves and acorns, daffodils, white hawthorn, wheat and grapevine, primrose, bluebells, fern and primrose, acanthus, ladder fern, primroses, polyantha roses, blackberries or maybe raspberry, and finally passion flowers and leaf (see the Nicholl Monument **L-641–3**).

K-468/9: William James Pirrie; *d.* 7 June 1924

William James was born in Quebec on 31 May 1847. His father James, a Belfast man born on 27 November 1821, was sent to

K-468, William James Pirrie's original bust and plinth

Canada by his father, William, to develop a timber business. He married Eliza Swann Montgomery in Quebec on 28 June 1844.

Following his father's death in 1848, William James returned to Ireland with his mother and was raised in the village of Conlig, County Down. On 1 May 1858 he entered the Royal Belfast Academical Institution where he remained until June 1862. At the age of 15, he joined Harland and Wolff as a gentleman apprentice on 23 June 1862. Having worked his way up to the position of head draughtsman, he became a partner of Edward Harland and George Wolff in 1874. On 17 April 1879 he married his first cousin, Margaret Montgomery Carlisle. In 1893 he became a member of the Harbour Board and a councillor on the Belfast Corporation. By 1896 he was lord mayor of Belfast – the same year he and his wife inaugurated the Royal Victoria Hospital (RVH) Scheme to help raise funds to build a hospital. When the king and queen of England opened the RVH in 1903, Pirrie donated £11,000 to allow the hospital to open debt-free. Pirrie's connection with the RVH was recognised by naming ward 12 the 'Pirrie Ward', which has since closed.

By 1904 Pirrie had assumed total control of Harland and

Wolff. From his earliest days in shipbuilding he had foreseen the era of the great ocean-going liner. This vision was reflected in the partnership he created with the White Star Line and in the ships he built for that company. Starting with the launch of the *Oceanic* in 1899, the era of big transatlantic liner had begun. *Oceanic* at 17,293 tons and 705 feet long was followed by ships like *Celtic* at 20,904 tons and 700 feet long, *Cedric* at 21,035 tons and 702 feet long, *Baltic* at 23,876 tons and 725 feet long, *Adriatic* at 24,540 tons and 725 feet long, *Olympic* at 45,342 tons and 882 feet long, *Titanic* at 46,328 tons and 882 feet long and *Britannic* at 50,000 tons and 900 feet long. While most of these great liners have been forgotten, *Titanic* is still remembered because of that tragic first voyage. Luckily, illness prevented Pirrie from sailing on *Titanic*'s maiden voyage; however, his nephew, Thomas Andrews, the ship's designer, perished in the disaster.

Pirrie began life as a unionist and in 1893 he opposed Home Rule, but by 1912 he had become a supporter. On 8 February the same year, he chaired a public meeting of the Ulster Liberal Association at which Winston Churchill spoke. The meeting had been organised for the Ulster Hall but was moved to Celtic Park on the Donegall Road after the Ulster Unionist Council and the Orange Order threatened to prevent it taking place. In the same year, during the Kiel Regatta, he hosted a reception on his yacht for the German Kaiser.

On Saturday, 22 March 1924, he left with his wife Margaret for a cruise of South American ports, visiting Brazil, Argentina and Chile. His last port of call was the Chilean port of Valparaiso. He died at sea on the SS *Ebro*, off the coast of Havana, Cuba, on Saturday, 7 June 1924, on a return voyage to New York. His remains were brought from New York to Southampton on the White Star Liner *Olympic* and then from Liverpool to Belfast on the SS *Patriotic*. He was buried on Monday, 23 June 1924. He had residences at 'Ormiston', Belfast and at 24 Belgravia Square, London.

Pirrie was the pre-imminent Irish industrialist of his day. Through his efforts Belfast became a world leader in the technologies of the late Victorian period. He foresaw the emergence of the great ocean liners, and the replacement of coal-fired steam engines with oil-fired diesel engines; but his real genius was to turn a city and region lacking in raw materials into the 'silicone valley' of its day.

Pirrie's grave is of considerable historical interest to the citizens of Belfast. Originally the grave had a plinth with a bronze bust and four bronze plaques. Two of the plaques, reflecting the shipbuilding tradition of Harland and Wolff, referred to the SS *Venetian* and the RMS *Olympic*. As a result of vandalism the plinth and bronze were removed from the grave on 22 December 1992 and relocated in Queen's Island by Clarke Engineering & Co., acting on behalf of Harland and Wolff. Sadly, two of the plaques were stolen from Queen's Island during late September or early October 2003. A Castlewellan granite headstone replaced the original stone.

In late May 2006 the bust and plinth of William James Pirrie was brought from the yard at Harland and Wolff and erected on the lawn of the east wing of the Belfast City Hall, where it was unveiled by a member of the Pirrie family on 31 May.

The Pirrie-Carlisle plot contains ten graves. In **K-463–6** lie the remains of four members of the Carlisle family, **K-467–70** are Pirrie graves and **K-471–2** contain the remains of two members of the Neill family.

K-468/9: Margaret M. Pirrie; *d.* 19 June 1935

Margaret Montgomery Pirrie died aged 78 at her residence at 1 Carlos Place, London. She was born on 31 May 1857, the daughter of John Carlisle, head of the English department of the Royal Belfast Academical Institution and later headmaster of that school. Margaret received her early education from her father. In 1879 she married her cousin William James Pirrie.

A lifelong supporter of the Royal Victoria Hospital, she personally raised £100,000 pounds for the new building, which opened on 28 July 1903. She raised a further £100,000 to provide the hospital with an endowment fund. A bust of Margaret Pirrie donated to the RVH in 1934 was displayed in the main corridor.

Margaret was a Life Governor of the RVH and president of the hospital from 1915 until her death in 1935. She was on the Senate of Queen's University, and also served on the Board of Governors of the Royal Belfast Academical Institution, becoming its Lady President in 1931. She was a personal friend of the MP for West Belfast, Joe Devlin, and supported the liberal policy of Home Rule.

There were two wards in the RVH associated with the Pirrie family – ward 5, named 'Lady Pirrie', and ward 12, the 'Pirrie Ward'. In each of these wards there were thirty-four beds, each bed the result of a gift of £500 raised among Margaret's friends. She also raised £10,000 to have ward 6 named after her friend and personal physician, Professor Cuming. However these, and all the wards running off the main corridor, were demolished in June 2003 to make way for the second part of a major development on the RVH site.

Margaret's grandfather, the Reverend Henry Montgomery, founded the Remonstrant Synod. This synod emerged as a result of a theological dispute inside Irish Presbyterianism centred on Arianism. In the fourth century Arius of Alexandria taught that the second person of the Trinity did not have the same divine nature as the Father; therefore Christ was not truly divine. Those who promoted this concept in the Irish Presbyterian Church were called Arians. Henry was born at Killead, County Antrim, on 16 January 1788. Ordained on 14 September 1809 he was appointed to minister the congregation of Dunmurry that same year. In 1817 he joined the staff of the Belfast Academical Institution as headmaster of the English Department, retiring from that post in 1839.

Reverend Montgomery was an Arian. Opposition to Arianism was led by the Reverend Henry Cooke who raised the issue at the Synod of Ulster in 1822. The dispute raged on until 16 October 1828, when, at a meeting of Arians in Belfast, it was decided to publish 'A remonstrance against the proceedings of the Synod', declaring the intention of the Arians to secede from the Synod of Ulster. Seventeen ministers along with their congregations left the Synod in 1830 and formed the Remonstrant Synod. A hidden thread in this dispute reflected the political tensions between liberals and conservatives in Ulster Presbyterianism. Reverend Montgomery had United Irish connections, while the Reverend Cooke was a Conservative. Reverend Montgomery died on 18 December 1865 and is buried in Dunmurry.

K-464: John Carlisle; *d*. 19 January 1884

John Carlisle, born in 1822 in Saintfield, County Down, completed his early education at the Royal Belfast Academical Institution. He then became an inspector of national schools in the Ballymena area, and in 1861 joined the staff of the Royal Belfast Academical Institution where he became headmaster of its English department. From 1870 until his death he acted as secretary to the Board of Masters. John Carlisle was the father of Margaret Montgomery Carlisle, the wife of William James Pirrie, and Alexander Carlisle, manager of the shipbuilding works in Harland and Wolff, and described by William James Pirrie as the greatest shipyard manager in Europe.

United Irishman and Presbyterian William Drennan, who reputedly coined the phase 'the Emerald Isle', founded the Belfast Academical Institution, sometimes referred to as the Old Belfast College. The foundation stone was laid on 3 July 1810. By the winter of 1811 the main building and roof had been completed. On 1 February 1814 William opened the new school. The collegiate department of the school was opened in November 1815 and closed in October 1849 when Queen's College, Belfast opened. In November 1831, at the request of the Earl of Belfast, King William IV, the original 'Silly Billy', changed the name of the school to the Royal Belfast Academical Institution. Today the school is commonly referred to as 'Inst'.

K-447: George Benn; *d*. 8 January 1882

George Benn, who lived in Fortwilliam Park, Belfast, was born in Tandragee on 1 January 1801. His family moved to Belfast when he was 8. Here he was educated at Belfast Academy in Donegall Street, which had opened in 1785 with ninety scholars. From

March 1814 he was a pupil at the Belfast Academical Institution. His early interest in history was reflected in his 1819 essay, 'A History of the Parish of Belfast', for which he received a faculty prize of a gold medal. Soon after, his essay was published in the *News Letter*. In 1823, at the age of 22, he published anonymously *The History of the Town of Belfast* which was illustrated by a J. Thompson. He became a distiller and a farmer. In 1835, with his brother Edward, he bought an estate in Glenravel, County Antrim.

George Benn is remembered for his 1877 publication, *A History of the Town of Belfast from the Earliest Times to the Close of the Eighteenth Century*, which ran to 770 pages with maps and illustrations. He later published a supplement. Edward left a large collection of Irish antiquities to the Belfast Museum, which was then situated in College Square North.

George and Edward also established three hospitals in Belfast, the Benn Eye, Ear and Throat Hospital, the Samaritan Hospital and the Hospital for the Diseases of the Skin. Edward also added a wing to the Belfast Charitable Society in Clifton Street.

K-392: Herbert Gifford Harvey; *d*. 14 April 1912

This is the grave of James Thompson Harvey, a shipowner from Strandtown in east Belfast. On his headstone there is an inscription remembering his son, Herbert Gifford Harvey, a junior assistant second engineer on the *Titanic*. Herbert was born in Belfast on 4 February 1878; he was educated at Belfast Royal Academy and at Portora Royal School, Enniskillen. Having served his apprenticeship with the Belfast and Northern Counties Railway, he then joined the 46th Company of the Imperial Yeomanry and saw service in the Boer War. When he returned from South Africa he joined the shore staff of Harland and Wolff. He first went to sea as an engineer with Lowther Latta & Co. and then with the White Star Line. He served on the liners *Teutonic* and *Olympic* as assistant third engineer, before joining *Titanic*. On the night she sank he was last seen trying to help fellow engineer, Jonathan Shepherd, in boiler room five, where both had been working on the pumps.

IN LOVING MEMORY
of
JAMES THOMPSON HARVEY
BORN 3RD FEBRUARY 1841 DIED 25TH MAY 1909.
HIS WIFE
ELIZABETH GARSTIN GIFFORD
BORN 9TH FEBRUARY 1846 DIED 23RD JANUARY 1915.
HIS MOTHER
ANN HARVEY
BORN NOVEMBER 1807 DIED 2ND APRIL 1884.
THEIR SON
HERBERT GIFFORD
BORN 4TH FEBRUARY 1878
ENGINEER ON R.M.S. TITANIC WHO WENT DOWN IN THAT STEAMER
IN MID OCEAN DOING HIS DUTY 14TH APRIL 1912.
THEIR CHILDREN
NORMAN GIFFORD, MARGARET AND MARY,
WHO DIED IN INFANCY.
THEIR DAUGHTER
ANABEL NETTERVILLE
BORN 6TH MAY 1873 DIED 25TH FEBRUARY 1916.
THEIR SON
STANLEY St. GEORGE HARVEY
BORN 4TH DECEMBER 1874 DIED 31ST JANUARY 1961.

HARVEY

RMS *TITANIC*

Built by Harland and Wolff, the *Titanic* was the biggest and most luxurious ship of her day. The keel of the 46,328-ton ship was laid on 31 March 1909. She was launched twenty-six months later, on 31 May 1911. She was 885 feet long and 92.5 feet wide. With twenty-nine massive boilers she was capable of generating 50,000 horsepower with a capacity for 55,000 HP. With her triple screws she could reach a speed of 21–22 knots. She had two sets of four-cylinder reciprocating engines – each driving a wing propeller, a turbine driving the centre propeller, eight decks and was 175 feet high from keel to the top of her four huge funnels. She had a double bottom and was divided into sixteen watertight compartments, which were formed by fifteen bulkheads running across the ship. She carried sixteen wooden lifeboats and four canvas collapsible lifeboats lettered A, B, C and D, known as Englehardts. There were 8 lifeboats, numbered sequentially, on each side of the ship, 4 each on the port and starboard towards the bow and 4 each on port and starboard towards the stern. All the lifeboats together could hold 1,178 passengers. It took ten months to fit her out. Her sea trials were completed by 1 April 1912 and she arrived in Southampton on 3 April of that year.

She began her maiden voyage at twelve noon, 10 April 1912. Leaving Southampton she headed for Cherbourg, France, to pick up passengers, arriving there at 7 p.m. that evening. Two hours later she left Cherbourg and sailed to Queenstown (now Cobh). Arriving there at 12.30 p.m. on 11 April, she picked up more passengers and mail and left at 2 p.m. with 1,316 passengers and 891 crew aboard.

At 11.40 p.m. on Sunday, 14 April, the *Titanic* hit an iceberg in the North Atlantic at latitude 42° 46 N, longitude 50° 14 W. The ice tore through a line of steel plate ripping open six of her sixteen forward watertight compartments. Ten minutes later escaping air, pushed up by seawater pouring into the ship, forced up the number one hatch cover in the bow. In the forepeak locker, the compartment closest to the bow where the anchor chains are stowed, air was also forced up due to the tremendous pressure of seawater coming into the ship. At the same time water began to swirl around the foot of the spiral stairs in a passageway connecting the firemen's quarters with the stokeholds. Within ten minutes of hitting the iceberg, seawater was 14 feet above the keel and five of her six forward watertight compartments were flooded. At 12.05 a.m., twenty-five minutes after the collision, the order was given to muster crew and passengers and uncover the lifeboats. At 12.15 a.m. the first wireless call for help was made. At 12.45 a.m. the first emergency rocket was fired and at the same time the first lifeboat, number 7, was lowered. At 1.40 a.m. the last rocket was fired. At 2.05 a.m. the last boat, collapsible D, was lowered, and five minutes later the last wireless message was sent. At 2.20 a.m. *Titanic* sank with a loss of 815 passengers and 688 crew. At 3.30 a.m. passengers in the lifeboats saw the rockets of the *Carpathia*. At 4.10 a.m. the first lifeboat, number 2, was picked up. At 8.30 a.m. the last lifeboat, number 12, was picked up. The *Carpathia* rescued 705 passengers and crew.

The *Carpathia* was a Cunard liner bound from New York to Gibraltar, Genoa, Naples, Trieste and Fiume. She was carrying 150 first class and 575 steerage passengers. When her captain, Arthur Rostron, received a message for help from *Titanic* the *Carpathia* was 58 miles away. Normally capable of 14 knots Captain Rostron increased the speed of his ship to 17 knots. She arrived at *Titanic*'s last known position at 4 a.m. and immediately spotted a lifeboat. At 4.10 a.m. the first *Titanic* passenger, Miss Elizabeth Allen, came aboard Carpathia and by 8.30 a.m. the last lifeboat had been rescued. With 705 *Titanic* survivors on board, *Carpathia* set her course back to New York. At 8.37 p.m. on Thursday, 18 April, she docked at pier 54. Ten thousand New Yorkers watched her from the Battery in Lower Manhattan as she passed the Statue of Liberty. Another 30,000 waited for her as she slowly made her way to dock. At 9.37 p.m. *Carpathia* was moored and the gangplank lowered.

Captain Rostron was eventually awarded the Congressional Gold Medal by the President of the United States. A U-boat sank the *Carpathia* 120 miles of the Fastnet Rock on the Irish coast on 17 July 1918. After being hit by three torpedoes she sank at 12.40 p.m. with the loss of five of her crew.

K-289: Henry Arthur Newell; *d.* 10 October 1922

Henry Arthur Newell lived at 362 Antrim Road, Belfast. His early life was spent in Newtownmountkennedy, County Wicklow. He arrived in Belfast at 21 as a buyer for Lindsey Bros., manufactures and wholesale warehousemen, 8–14 Callender Street. In 1886 he started his own business, H. A. Newell & Co., clothiers and merchant tailors, which eventually moved to Royal Avenue. The monument at the Newell plot is a classic example of a family resting place designed as a war grave. The top of the stone with its inscription 'The Glorious Dead' is reflective of the Cenotaph in London. The inscription on the top panel of the stone remembers three soldier sons – Walter, David and George – who died during the First World War. On each side of the main stone are stone shells. The stone carried three regimental badges on its east face, which have since been stolen.

J-32/33: Elizabeth Reid; *d.* 17 August 1870

Elizabeth Reid of 28 Wellington Park, Belfast, was 30 years old when she died. Burial records refer to her as the daughter of the late Reverend James Seaton Reid, author of *History of the Presbyterian Church in Ireland.*

Reverend James Seaton Reid was born on 19 December 1798 in Lurgan, County Armagh. The Reid family were direct descendants of John Reid, a Presbyterian minister banished by Charles II to Bass Rock, 1.5 miles off the East Lothian coast of Scotland. The rock, a massive crag rising 350 feet out of the sea, contains an old fortress that was used as a prison between 1672 and 1688, first to confine the early Covenanters and then to hold Jacobites. During this period over forty religious/political prisoners died on the island. John Reid was eventually banished to Jamaica, later returning to Ireland to settle in Lurgan.

James was the twenty-first child of Forrest and Mary Reid. His father taught in the local grammar school. After his father's death and still only a young boy, he moved to Ramelton in County Donegal to live with his brother Edward, a Presbyterian minister. In 1813, at the age of 15, he entered Glasgow University where he graduated with a Master's degree in April 1816. By 1818 he was licensed to preach by the Presbytery of Letterkenny, County Donegal. On 20 July 1819 he was ordained in Donegore

Presbyterian Church, County Antrim. It was here that he decided to write a history of the Irish Presbyterian Church, but it was not until he was moved to Carrickfergus, where he was installed on 19 August 1823, that he began his research. In February 1826 he married Elizabeth Arrott, the daughter of the Belfast surgeon Samuel Arrott. Elected as moderator of the General Synod of Ulster in 1827, his term coincided with the climax of a bitter controversy raging inside the Irish Presbyterian Church over Arianism (see **K-468/9**). In January 1833 he was appointed Clerk of the Synod

It was not until 1834 that the first volume of his *History of the Presbyterian Church in Ireland* was published. Recognised immediately as an important piece of historical research, James was unanimously elected to membership of the Royal Irish Academy. His second volume, published three years later in June 1837, contained a number of rare documents relating to the Cromwellian period in Ireland. That July, the Synod of Ulster appointed him Professor of Ecclesiastical History, Church Government and Pastoral History in the Royal College, Belfast. Subsequently, he resigned as minister of Carrickfergus on 6 November 1838 and moved to Belfast. At the union of the Synod of Ulster and the Secession Synod held in the Third Presbyterian Church, Rosemary Street, on 10 July 1840 – which became the First General Assembly of the Presbyterian Church in Ireland – James was one of the clerks to the new Assembly. Another move followed when, on 2 April 1841, he became Professor of Church History at the University of Glasgow. Following extensive travel in Germany, France and Italy during 1845–6 he edited Murdock's translation of *Mosheim's Church History* in 1848.

James died in Edinburgh on Wednesday 26 March 1851 and was buried in Sighthill Cemetery, Glasgow. Only five of his eleven children survived him. His third volume, *History of Congregations of the Presbyterian Church in Ireland*, which at the time of his death was almost ready for publication, was completed by Professor the Reverend W.D. Killen, his successor to the Chair of Ecclesiastical History in the Belfast College.

J-24: James Seaton Reid; *d*. 3 May 1896

James Seaton Reid, the nephew of the Reverend James Seaton Reid, was born in Ramelton, County Donegal, on 7 July 1811, where his father, the Reverend Edward Seaton, was a Presbyterian minister. In 1823 he enrolled in the Belfast Academical Institution, afterwards moving to Edinburgh University where he graduated with a M.D. (Doctor of Medicine) in 1833. He moved to Derry City in November that year to set up his own practice, and was also employed as the House Surgeon in the City and County Derry Infirmary. In December 1836 he joined the staff of the General Penitentiary in Millbank. In 1840 he became attending physician to the General Hospital in Belfast and then, in 1846, was physician to the Belfast Union Hospital. He married Elizabeth Montgomery in 1850. Elizabeth's grandfather, James Montgomery, owned the apothecary at 28 High Street, Belfast. In 1857 James was appointed to the Chair of Materia Medica at Queen's College, Belfast, a post he held until 1890 when he was succeeded by William Whitla.

J-387: William Darragh; *d*. 20 December 1892

William Darragh, from 22 Queen's Street, Belfast, was born in the County Down town of Hillsborough, in 1813. The burial order records his age at his death as 89. William came to Belfast as a young boy. In 1844, at 31, he secured the job as curator of the Belfast Museum in College Square North through his association with renowned Belfast botanist William Thompson. He held this position until 20 June 1891 when he retired on a pension of £45 per annum. Samuel Alexander Stewart (**M-933**) succeeded William as Curator. William's grave is marked by a simple cast-iron shield set on a wrought iron surround.

–––––––– CENTRAL STEPS AND VAULTS ––––––––

These steps, completed by February 1867, were created as a central piece in the original design and layout of the cemetery. They link

The central steps, or 'Gallaher steps', as they are more commonly known

sections L and M with sections J and K. The steps were designed to emphasise the steep hill in this section of the cemetery. Initially called the Central Steps they are now commonly referred to as the Gallaher Steps, after Thomas Gallaher, the tobacco manufacturer who is buried in the vaults at the base of the steps. These vaults contain the remains of those families who dominated the industrial and financial life of Belfast at the end of the nineteenth century. The vaults, designed in high Victorian Gothic style, are listed as having special architectural and historic interest.

M-987: Edward James Harland; *d.* 23 December 1895

Edward Harland, founder of Harland and Wolff, and MP for North Belfast, lived at Glenfarna Hall, Enniskillen, County Fermanagh, where he died at the age of 64. Edward was born in Scarborough in May 1831, the sixth of eight children. His father, William, was a medical doctor with a keen interest in engineering, and was a pioneer in the development of the steam engine, having attempted to build a steam-powered road carriage in 1827. This interest brought him into contact with George Stephenson, the inventor of the steam railway engine, and resulted in 15-year-old Edward becoming an apprentice at the Robert Stephenson Company in Newcastle-on-Tyne, England. He worked a six-day week – 6 a.m. to 8.15 p.m. Monday to Friday; on Saturday he finished at 4 p.m. In his five-year apprenticeship he spent four years in the workshop and one in the drawing office. In 1850 he entered a competition organised by the Duke of Northumberland, offering a prize for the best design of a lifeboat. His design took the form of a small submarine powered by a hand-driven screw propeller at each end. In 1851 he moved to J. & G. Thompson, marine engine builders, Glasgow, where he rose to the position of chief draughtsman. In the autumn of 1853, still only 22 years old, he moved again, this time to work as manager for Thomas Toward, a shipbuilder on the Tyne in the North of England. In Christmas 1854 Edward arrived in Belfast where he became a manager in the shipyard owned by Robert Hickson on Queen's Island. Hickson also owned the Eliza Street ironworks. One of Edward's first actions as manager was to reduce the wages of the shipyard workers while demanding a higher quality of work – an action that very quickly led to a strike. Within four years Edward bought out Robert Hickson, helped by his friend, Mr G.C. Schwabe of Liverpool, whose nephew Gustav Wolff was Edward's private assistant.

Another friend, J. Bibby, gave him his first order for three steamers, the *Venetian*, the *Sicilian* and the *Syrian*. These three vessels, 270 feet long and 34 feet wide, were the forerunner of the long, narrow and flat-bottomed modern steamer. On 26 January 1860 Edward married Rosa Wann. Two years later, on 1 January, Gustav Wolff became a partner to Edward Harland; and on 11 April the company became Harland and Wolff. In its time the largest shipyard in the world, it introduced revolutionary change into the shipbuilding industry, and Edward Harland amassed a fortune.

Edward was a member of the Harbour Board from 1872 until 1887. In 1884 he became an alderman of the St Anne's Ward on the Belfast Corporation, a post he held until 1887. In 1885 and 1886 he was lord mayor of Belfast, and in 1889 he became MP for North Belfast, holding the seat until his death in 1895.

In its lifetime Harland and Wolff received 1,742 orders for new ships; only 93 of these orders were cancelled. The smallest boat, built in 1872, was a 9-ton river ferry for the Belfast Harbour Board. The largest ships were oil tankers with a gross tonnage of 172,000. The largest passenger liner was the *Britannic*, launched in 1914, with a gross tonnage of 48,158 tons. HMS *Eagle*, the largest aircraft carrier in the Royal Navy, was built there in 1951.

Gustav Wolff was born in Hamburg, Germany, in November 1834, to Moritz Wolff and his wife, Fanny Schwabe. When he was 14, Gustav moved to England and in 1850 he became an apprentice in the firm of Joseph Whitworth in Manchester. He moved to Belfast to work as a draughtsman for Robert Hickson. He joined the shipbuilding yard of James Harland as a manager of the drawing office, and was later made partner. He became a Member of Parliament and sat unopposed through five general elections. He died in London on 17 April 1913.

The earliest recorded ship built in the Belfast area was the 150-ton *Eagle Wing*. Built by Presbyterians fleeing from persecution, this ship was launched from the beach at Groomsport on the shore of Belfast Lough. She set sail for the Americas on 9 September 1636, but 1,000 miles across the Atlantic Ocean she was mauled by a ferocious storm. With her rudder broken, her sails torn, heavy seas sweeping over her round house and into her cabin, and severe leaking, she headed back to Ireland where she berthed at Carrickfergus on 3 November 1636.

In July 1791 William Ritchie, a shipyard owner from Ayrshire in Scotland, opened a yard in Belfast and employed 10 men. His first ship was the 300-ton *Hibernia*, launched on 7 July 1792. A decade later the yard employed 44 journeymen carpenters, 55 apprentices, 7 pairs of sawers, 12 blacksmiths and several joiners. In 1820, Hugh Ritchie and an Alexander McLaine opened another yard, and launched their first ship, the 200-ton *Belfast*, in the same year – the first steamboat built in Ireland. On 11 December 1838, another Belfast shipbuilding yard, Coates & Young, opened; they built the very first ironclad steamship, the *Countess of Caledon*.

J-462: Thomas Gallaher; *d*. 3 May 1927

Thomas Gallaher was born on 27 April 1840 on his father's farm at Templemoyle, County Derry. After a private education, he moved to Derry City as an apprentice with Osborne & Allen, general merchants of Waterloo Place. Here he quickly acquired the ability to make twist, pigtail, plug and other popular forms of tobaccos.

At the age of 17 he began his own business in Sackville Street, Derry City, by producing his own brand of roll pipe tobacco. By the age of 23, and as a result of his success he moved his business to Belfast. His first premises in Belfast were at the junction of Old Hercules Street and John Street. He then moved to Queen's Square and subsequently to a site in York Street, which later became the site of the Belfast Co-operative store. In 1896 he moved to a new site at 138 York Street, which sits between York Street, Meadow Street, North Queen Street and Earl Street. Thomas Gallaher, known worldwide as the 'Tobacco King', dominated the industry. His company acquired plantations and factories in Henderson, Kentucky and in Richmond, Virginia. In 1888 a new factory was purchased at 60 Holborn Viaduct, London, and a year later Thomas acquired a second factory in Clerkenwell Road. In 1902 the Gallaher Tobacco Company began its production of cigarettes. It also produced Mellow Virginia, Condor and Clan pipe tobaccos, Old Holborn 'roll-your-own tobacco', and Silk Cut cigarettes.

While he was the first in his business to reduce the hours of his workers from 54 to 47, and first to introduce annual paid holidays, Thomas will also be remembered for his role in the 1907 Belfast Dockers' Strike. As head of Gallaher Tobacco Co. and chairman of the Belfast Steamship Company, he played a leading role for the employers in the strike led by James Larkin, who had come from Liverpool in January 1907 to organise the National Union of Dockworkers. The strike began on Monday, 6 May 1907 when union members refused to work with non-union workers. Instructed to return to work by the union, the workers found their jobs taken by 'scab' labour brought in by the employers. Meanwhile the Royal Irish Constabulary in Belfast mutinied over pay and conditions – they were also unhappy over their role in the strike, which ended in July–August 1907.

Cigarettes had been produced in France since 1843, and ten years later by Susini's of Havana, Cuba. The London firm, Gloag's, of Depford Lane, introduced their hand-rolled cigarette in 1859. In 1881 a James Bonsack designed a cigarette rolling machine: the era of mass production had begun. In 1896, the Duchess of Clermont-Tonnerre was the first high society woman to smoke a cigarette in public at the Savoy Hotel in London, signalling the acceptability of smoking as a social habit and leading to the development of the women's market. Edward Bernays, the nephew of Sigmund Freud's wife Martha, used his knowledge of psychoanalytic concepts to market cigarettes to women as a symbol of female emancipation and independence. Bernays, regarded as the father of public relations, was hired in 1928 by the American Tobacco Company to promote its Lucky Strike cigarettes. Using the sympathy generated by the women's suffrage movement he promoted cigarettes as the new 'Torches of Freedom'.

The years 1906 and 1907 were a period of industrial upheaval in Belfast. On 10 May 1906 female spinners in the York Street mill demanded a 10 per cent increase in their wages. Four days later a large group of spinners refused to go back to work after their breakfast break. The strike spread to mills in Lisburn, Bessbrook, Newry, Ballymoney and Ballymena, and escalated further until 24,000 flax spinners and weavers were affected. This labour unrest, which ended in July 1906, was a precursor to the Belfast Dock Strike of 1907. On 26 April of that year, unskilled workers in the Sirocco Engineering Works went on strike. On the same day, Samuel Kelly, the owner of Kelly's Coal Boats, attempted to dismiss union workers employed at his coal quay, prompting a walkout by the majority of his workforce. On 6 May a small number of dockers went on strike, but over the following days the situation escalated when the employer began using blackleg labour from the port of Liverpool. The scene was now set for one of the most prolonged industrial actions in the history of Belfast. During the course of the strike elements of the Royal Irish Constabulary in Belfast mutinied in support of the workers. Negotiations to end the strike began on Wednesday, 14 August 1907, and ended at 6 p.m. the following day. By early September most, but not all, of the dockers had returned to work. Many of those who had walked off the quays in April of 1907 were victimised by the employers who refused to re-employ them when the dispute ended. Led by Jim Larkin, the strike was a defining period in the history of trade unionism in Ireland, and its experience influenced Larkin and James Connolly in their efforts to build an independent Irish trade union, registered on 4 January 1909, as the Irish Transport & General Workers Union (ITGWU).

J-465: James Henry Carlisle; *d.* 24 November 1882

James Carlisle was born on 22 September 1810 in Castledawson, County Derry. He began his working life as a journeyman carpenter. In or around 1832 he came to Belfast and began his business as a building contractor. In 1839 he married Anne Hall, the daughter of a wealthy cotton merchant. In a directory from 1843, a James Carlisle, builder, of 85 Donegall Street is mentioned. He lived in 'Enfield House', located in the triangle of land that sits at the junction of Crumlin and Oldpark Roads.

One of his major building contracts was for the courthouse on the Crumlin Road. Contracts for the building of spinning mills led him to form a partnership with a Phillip Johnston. The company Johnston & Carlisle owned the Brookfield Linen Mills on the Crumlin Road, where James was managing director. Following the resignation of a Councillor Lyons from the Belfast Corporation on 23 July 1859, James was elected unopposed as a City Councillor to represent Dock Ward. In the annual Corporation Elections held on 25 November that same year, he was re-elected, holding his seat until his death in 1882. He was a member of the Harbour Board from 1857 to 1875.

Throughout his life James maintained a strong relationship with the Methodist Church and was a member of the Primitive Methodist Society. Primitive Methodists were opposed to the administration of the Sacrament by Methodist ministers and consequently seceded from the main body of Methodists in 1818. This division lasted until 1878. James was responsible for supplying pews to a Primitive Methodist church in Academy Street and for the building of two Belfast city centre Methodist churches, in Donegall Square and Donegall Place. He secured fourteen acres of land at Vermont in the vicinity of Queen's College, for the building of the Methodist College which opened in 1868. Following the death of his son James, on 21 December 1870, he gave £25,000 pounds towards the building of the Carlisle Memorial Church, Carlisle Circus, in his memory. The church, designed by W.H. Lynn (D-203), opened on 12 May 1876. A school and hall were added to the church and opened on 23 November 1889. Carlisle Circus was named in the mid-nineteenth century after the Earl of Carlisle, who was Viceroy of Ireland.

The inscription on the Carlisle headstone is taken from the Bible, Hosea 13:14, 'I will ransom them from the power of the grave; I will redeem them from death.'

——— METHODIST COLLEGE, BELFAST ———

The idea of a Wesleyan grammar school in Belfast was first suggested in 1843 at a breakfast meeting in the city, then circulated to leading Methodists as a way of building support for the concept. When the idea was raised at the Methodist Conference in Belfast in 1844 the need for a new school was adopted in principle but alternative locations to Belfast were also suggested. Dublin, with a Methodist population twice that of Belfast, was finally chosen as the location for Wesley College, which opened in 1845. In 1863 the Methodist Conference offered Belfast Methodists a sum of £2,000 for their own school, provided they were able to raise a further £8,000 and that no building would begin until £10,000 had been subscribed. In that same year James Carlisle had secured and offered the city's Methodists 15 acres of land at Vermont on the Malone Road from a Miss Harrison for £21 per acre and a rental of £311.10s. per annum. Carlisle also donated £3,550 to the building fund for the new Wesleyan college.

In 1864 a report informed the Methodist Conference that a site had been secured in Belfast and that £9,564 had been subscribed. The architects, Fogerty of Dublin, won the contract to design the new school, and the foundation stone was laid on 24 August 1865. The ceremonial opening took place on 18 August 1868. On the following day, the first pupils arrived to begin their secondary education under the supervision of the establishment's first headmaster, the Reverend Robert Crook, LLD, who had previously been headmaster of the Dublin Wesleyan College in 1856. By 1869 there were 49 primary schools with a total of 2,647 pupils connected to the Methodist Church in Ireland. There was also another 61 Methodist children being educated in model schools.

M-495: Robert Lynd; *d.* 6 October 1949

Robert was born in Brookhill Avenue, off Cliftonville Avenue, Belfast, on 20 April 1879. His father, the Reverend R.J. Lynd, minister of May Street Presbyterian Church, was a moderator of the Presbyterian Church in 1888 and a leading unionist cleric. Robert was educated at Royal Belfast Academical Institution and Queen's College, later to become Queen's University, where he graduated in 1899. For a short time he was a reporter for the Belfast paper, the Northern Whig. At 21 he left Belfast for Manchester, where he began his career as a journalist with the *Manchester Daily Dispatch*. Three months later he moved to London, where he worked as a freelance journalist. By 1901 he was sharing a studio in west London with his friend, the Belfast painter Paul Henry. The son of a Presbyterian minister, Paul, born at 61 University Road, is remembered for his landscapes of the west of Ireland, in particular Achill Island, off the coast of County Mayo. It was Robert Lynd who first suggested to Paul that he visit Achill.

In London Robert joined the Gaelic League classes held in St Andrew's Hall, Oxford Street, where he learned and then taught others to speak Irish. Here he met and eventually married Sylvia Dryhurst, a novelist, critic and poet. They had two daughters, Sigle and Máire, whose first language was Irish. Through his Irish classes he met leading figures of the Irish nationalist community in London, among them Michael Collins and Roger Casement. In 1906 he wrote an article for the *Republic*, a weekly newspaper founded by his friend Bulmer Hobson. In 1908 he joined the staff of the *Daily News*, later the *News Chronicle*. His house in Hampstead became a meeting place for Irish writers and artists. He was a friend of James Connolly and wrote the introduction to Connolly's *Labour in Irish History*, and to *Islanders* by socialist republican Peadar O' Donnell. When James Joyce married Nora Barnacle on 4 July 1931, the wedding lunch was held in Lynd's London home. In 1946 Queen's University purchased a bronze bust of Robert Lynd for their library from Lady Kennet, widow of Scott of Antarctica. Robert was 70 years old when he died. He lived at 5 Keats Grove, Hampstead, London. Sylvia Lynd died on 21 February 1952. She was cremated, five days later, at Golder's Green Cemetery and her ashes were placed in her husband's grave on 3 March 1952.

Lord Lowry, former Lord Chief Justice of Northern Ireland from 1971 to 1988, is a nephew of Robert Lynd.

BULMER HOBSON

Bulmer Hobson, founder of the *Republic*, and a Quaker, was born in 1883 of Cromwellian planter stock who had settled in Holywood, County Down. He was educated at the Friends' School, Lisburn. In 1900 he founded the Ulster Debating Society for Boys which evolved into the Protestant National Association whose aim was to recruit Protestant youth into the national movement. In 1901 he joined the Gaelic League and soon after became secretary of the first County Antrim board of the GAA. As a way of popularising his political views he helped found the Ulster Literary Theatre in 1902. In the same year he established the scouting organisation Na Fianna Éireann. The following year he met republican Denis McCullough, Belfast organiser of the IRB, who recruited Bulmer into the organisation. That same year, Hobson, with other Ulster Literary Theatre members, launched a literary review *Uladh*. From November 1904 to September 1905 the magazine was published quarterly. In 1905 Hobson and McCullough founded a republican society, the Dungannon Clubs. Hobson, who became a member of the Supreme Council of the IRB, was also a founder member of the Irish Volunteers. He was opposed to the Easter Rebellion in 1916 and soon after left the IRB.

M-454: James Stelfox; *d.* 11 September 1910

James Stelfox, born on 23 June 1842, lived at 'Delamere', Chlorine Gardens, Belfast. He was manager of Belfast Gas Works from 1875 until 1907, succeeding his father, James, who had held this position since 1852.

The very first gaslights were turned on in Belfast on Saturday evening, 30 August 1823. From 1823 to 1874 gas production and distribution was the responsibility of the Belfast Light Company, after which it became the responsibility of the Belfast Corporation. The profits of the gas department were used to finance the building of the City Hall.

James combined his knowledge of technology with his understanding of classical architecture to produce the Gas Works office block, which still fronts the Ormeau Road; he is also responsible for the building of the middle section meter house lost during the Blitz of 1941. The monument of James Stelfox is a very good example of a Gothic window and Gothic architecture. This grave is listed as a having special architectural and historic interest.

L-156: Robert Boagh; *d.* 7 November 1877

Robert Boagh, who lived at Upper Crescent in Belfast, was born in Edinburgh in 1810. He was the son of a Church of Scotland clergyman, the Reverend John Boagh of Blackburn. In his mid-thirties Robert arrived in Belfast and was initially involved in the woollen trade, then the clothing business as a merchant tailor. He was the head of the Albion Clothing Company of High Street. In 1855 he was elected as city councillor for the St George's Ward to the Belfast Corporation, and became mayor in 1876. The life of Robert Boagh reflects the Victorian attitude towards public service: he was an active participant in the civic life of Belfast, involving himself in the many charitable associations that existed. From 1856 until his death, along with his friend W. H. Patterson (**L-136**), he was joint secretary of the Belfast Society for the Prevention of Cruelty to Animals. He was also a founder member of the Free Drinking Fountains Association, a committee member of the Belfast Royal Hospital, and treasurer of the Belfast Ophthalmic Hospital. Furthermore, he was connected to the Samaritan Hospital, the Ulster Hospital for Sick Children, the Sailors Home, the Midnight Mission, and Brown Street School. Robert died at the home of his son-in-law, a Mr Fleming, in Newington near Edinburgh. His remains were brought to Greenock via the Caledonian railway and then to Belfast on the Glasgow steamer, from where they were taken to the vestry of Elmwood Presbyterian Church.

L-153: Alexander Finley Herdman; *d.* 13 March 1875

Alexander, of 6 College Square North, died at the age of 34. The Herdman family owned flax spinning mills in Sion Mills and Belfast and had a strong connection with the Harbour Board – a Herdman Channel can be found at the end of Corporation Street. They were one of the first linen companies to introduce the spinning of flax by machinery. A member of this family, E.T. Herdman, spoke in support of resolution number 2 at the Unionist Convention of 1892. All the children were educated in Germany.

The architecture of the Herdman monument is Egyptian Revivalist, designed in the fashion of a lower framed gateway of an Egyptian Pylon (a monumental gate or door built in front of an Egyptian temple). Crowning the monument is a gorge or cavetto cornice decorated with symbolic bird wings. At the centre of the symbol is a disc with a Templar Cross in relief. Two falcon heads flank the disc, possibly the winged sun disk symbolising the Egyptian god Ra, carried on the wings of the god Horus, which originated with the Hittite people from Asia Minor and Syria. On each side of the monument are inverted torches representing death. In the Christian tradition the inverted torch symbolises the flame of eternal life and the resurrection. A single Corinthian column stands beneath the Herdman name. The column carries five sets of rings, each set containing four rings. An incised convex moulding, called a torus, runs along each side of the monument, continuing horizontally above the family name. It is designed to look like a series of linked bars with three incisions in each bar. An eight-petal flower, perhaps the cosmos flower, set in a ring fronts the small pillars that make up the surround.

The Templar Cross suggests that this is a grave of a senior Mason. The Knights Templar is an order of the Freemasons, which has its origins in a Masonic rite practised in Germany in the eighteen and nineteenth centuries. This Masonic link is reinforced by the use of the winged sun disk and the falcon heads which may also represent the two-headed eagle reputed to symbolise the '33 degree' – the highest order of the Ancient and Accepted Scottish Rite of Masonry. The Corinthian column, one of the Masonic 'Five orders of architecture' represents beauty. The importance of the number five is reflected in the five sets of rings. Five is a mystical number for the Masonic order and has various meanings: geometry is called the fifth science, in the old system of craft Masonry five brethren were required to constitute a Fellow Craft lodge, and there are five points of fellowship; to serve, pray for, keep the secrets of, defend and protect, and council and advise. The four rings may represent the four cardinal virtues: prudence, fortitude, temperance and justice. Thirty-four

L-153, Alexander Finley Herdman

incised bars make up the torus. Then again, the two central bars below the cornice appear to be joined as one, which brings the number down to thirty-three bars, linking it to the 33 degree.

The cosmos flower in the ring may represent law, order, harmony and truth in balance with the universe. The flower might also represent an eight-pointed star – the octagram – which is referred to as the Cross of St John. Its origins are found in the Maltese Cross, the symbol used by the Knights of Malta and by the Knights of St John of Jerusalem. Used during the crusades, it may have a Knights Templar connection. The eight points of the star are thought to represent the knightly virtues of tact, perseverance, gallantry, loyalty, dexterity, explicitness, observation and sympathy. They may also represent the eight beatitudes, from St Matthew's Gospel.

> How happy are the poor in spirit: theirs is the kingdom of Heaven.
>
> Happy the gentle: they shall have the earth for their heritage.
>
> Happy those who mourn: they shall be comforted.
>
> Happy for those who hunger and thirst for what is right: they shall be satisfied.
>
> Happy the merciful: they shall have mercy shown them.
>
> Happy the pure in heart: they shall see God.
>
> Happy the peacemakers: they shall be called the sons of God.
>
> Happy those who are persecuted in the cause of right: theirs is the Kingdom of Heaven.

The Herdman stone has still to reveal the full extent of its Masonic symbolism. The inverted torches and the three incisions on the bars of the torus require further research and explanation. It is listed as having special architectural and historic interest.

Plans for this monument were submitted to the Corporation on 25 July 1870. In the minutes of the Cemetery Committee, 17 April 1871, there is a reference to a Mr Lanyon, which may be Charles Lanyon, the architect. The name Gemmell on the right-hand base of the stone most likely refers to D.&J. Gemmell, Monumental Sculptors, from 10 Wellington Place, Belfast.

L-146/7: Thomas Gaffikin; *d.* 26 March 1893

Thomas, born on 3 July 1810, was a linen merchant with wide interests in the civic institutions of Belfast. He was a councillor on the Belfast Corporation, a member of the Harbour Board and Poor Law Board, and a founder member of the Working Men's Institute, Belfast. He was elected councillor for Cromac Ward on 25 November 1862, holding the seat until his retirement from the Corporation in 1874. In November 1875 he stood and was elected councillor for St George's Ward, a seat he held until his death. Thomas will always be remembered for his lecture, 'Belfast Fifty Years Ago', given in the Working Men's Institute on Thursday evening, 8 April 1875. In 1876 this lecture was printed by the *Belfast News Letter* as a pamphlet.

L-641–3: W. J. Nicholl; *d.* 29 July 1887

William John Nicholl lived at Rathmore, Greenisland, County Antrim. He was first connected to the firm of Foster Green & Co., before setting up his own company, Nicholls & Company. He was also director of the Sullatober Printing Company.

The Nicholl monument shows a variety of flowers and plants, all of which are highly symbolic, particularly in a religious sense. Below is a list of the symbolic meanings of some flowers and plants:

Acacia: immortality of soul
Acanthus: one of the oldest and most common cemetery motifs, acanthus is associated with the rocky ground where ancient Greek cemeteries were established
Daffodil: the flower of Easter
Dahlia: treachery and instability
Dead leaves: sadness, melancholy
Evergreens: everlasting life
Foxglove: insincerity
Geranium: steadfast piety
Hibiscus: delicate beauty
Holly: foresight
Ivy: attachment, eternal friendship
Ladder fern: sincerity and sorrow
Laurel leaf: glory and victory

Lily: innocence, purity, Resurrection and Easter

Lily of the valley: purity and humility

Mistletoe: affection, love

Morning glory: farewell, departure and mourning

Orchid: flower of magnificence

Passionflower: the Passion of Christ, faith and piety.
This is the most common flower found cut into the
headstones of Belfast City Cemetery. It originates
in South America and the Jesuits named it *Flos
Passionis* (passionflower), or *Flor de las cinco
llagas* (flower of the five wounds). Its floral
organs were thought to represent the symbols
and instruments of the Passion: ten petals for
ten faithful apostles; five stamens for the five
wounds of Christ on the cross; the corona is the
crown of thorns; the ovary is the hammer; and
the three styles are the three nails.

Passion fruit: hunger or feasting

Periwinkle: sweet memories and unerring devotion

Primrose: early youth and sadness

Rose: a single rose represents simplicity; a rosebud
represents beauty; climbing roses represent beauty,
hope and unfailing love.

Sheaves: the Divine Harvest, often represents the aged

Stephanotis: marital bliss, luck

Strawberry blossoms: foresight

Tree: the Tree of Life

Vine leaf and grapes: the blood of Christ, faith and piety

Wheat: the Resurrection of Christ

Wreath: with no beginning or end they represent eternal
life. They date back to the ancient Greeks who
crowned victors in the Pythian Games, held every
four years, with a laurel or bay crown. The wreath
was adopted by Christianity to signify victory of the
redemption.

Yew tree: sadness, eternal life

Not all of the flowers and plants on the Nicholl monument are easily identified but the central theme of the design seems to be the Passion, Death and Resurrection of Christ. Starting with the lower panel on the left hand side, and travelling clockwise around the stone we find the following:

Lower left panel: acanthus, single rose, rosebud or hip with leaf, passionflower, passionflower leaf, wheat, wallflower and leaf, rosebuds and leaf, daffodil, lily of the valley or

Solomon Seal, Passion Fruit, passionflower leaf, tubers of dahlia, orchid.

Left capitol: daffodil.

Upper left panel above capitol: single dahlia, daffodil or hibiscus, ladder fern, passionflower leaf, primrose, passionflower, passion fruit, lily of the valley, morning glory.

Panel immediately below pointed cornice: passionflower, passionflower leaf, morning glory.

Middle panel with roundel: The plants are all evergreens – mistletoe, holly, ivy, laurel leaf (set as a wreath in which the roundel is set). The roundel would have carried a dove, symbol of the Holy Spirit. The white dove is referred to in the story of the baptism of Christ, 'And John bore record, saying, I saw the Spirit descending from heaven like a dove, and it abode upon him' (John 1:32). When shown with an olive sprig, it means hope or promise.

Semicircular arched panel: morning glory, climbing roses.

Left cusp: Strawberry blossoms.

Right cusp: Ivy leaf with a cluster of berries.
Upper right panel above capitol: passionflower leaf, passionflower, rose, lily leaf and bud, wild geranium and geranium leaf.

Right capitol: rose.
Lower right panel: acanthus, wild rose or Rosa Hibernica, vine leaf and grapes, periwinkle, arum lily, foxglove, stephanotis, lily buds.

Base of monument: a bay wreath in relief.

Many questions arise when seeking to interpret this monument. While each flower has its own symbolic meaning, do plants and flowers grouped in panels have only one meaning? Can interpretation and meaning be found in the setting of one flower or plant beside another? Should the panels to the left and right of the columns be combined to have one meaning? Can the symbolism of the two capitols be combined in a similar way? Can the top panels be grouped together, and what is their relationship to the roundel that once carried a dove? It is a tribute to the ornate complexity of its stone carvings that, even now, it continues to elude full explanation. (See Corry Stone, H-31/2 for a similar design.)

L-709: Jane Skene Henderson; *d.* 7 December 1891

Jane Skene Henderson lived at Clanrye, Windsor Park, Belfast. She died of pneumonia when she was 48. There is a reference on the base of the headstone to 18-year-old Robert Henderson who was buried at sea. The inscription states that Robert, born on 16 October 1865, was drowned at sea, 15 May 1884, and his burial took place at latitude 17° 30, S, longitude 32° 21 W. This location is approximately 600 miles to the east of Brazil and 1,000 miles north of Rio de Janeiro.

L-705: Travers Robert Blackley; *d.* 28 September 1889

Travers Blackley, born on 20 March 1833, was a merchant who lived at Laurine, Antrim Road, Belfast. Robert came from a long-established County Roscommon family. The inscription on the plinth at the base of the cross refers to Travers as 'Late Major Royal Longford Rifles'. This was a militia regiment first raised in 1793 under the name of 'The Prince of Wales' Royal Longford Militia'. Stood down in the aftermath of the United Irish rebellion, the regiment was reformed in 1855 and in 1881 was absorbed into the 6th Battalion the Rifle Brigade.

L-704: Francis Lovell Speid; *d.* 6 December 1888

Francis Lovell Speid, born on 12 September 1856, was a captain in the Black Watch Regiment stationed in Willowbank Barracks, Belfast. In the 1887 Belfast street directory, this barracks, located less than half a mile from the cemetery on the Falls Road, near the site of the Willowbank Park, is referred to as 'New Military Camp'. In the 1901 directory the site is referred to as 'Willowbank huts'.

Lovell Speid died from typhoid fever caught while serving in the Royal Barracks, Dublin. He was commissioned into the Black Watch in 1876 and saw active service in Egypt in 1882 and in the Sudan in 1884. His headstone is a broken column resting on two slabs, which sit on a base. Cut into the front of the lower slab is a fine example of a sword and its belting. Cut into the upper slab are two campaign medals flanked by thistle, the national symbol of Scotland. The thistle dates back to Scottish King Alexander III and events connected to the Battle of Largs in 1263. According to legend, Viking raiders landed at Largs on the coast of Ayrshire to launch a surprise attack on the clansmen of the king. In darkness they removed their footwear in order to be as quiet as possible, not realising the ground was covered with thistle. Forced to keep walking, their cries of pain alerted the clansmen and the Norsemen were repulsed and defeated.

The medals are the 'Egyptian medal and three clasps' and the 'Khedive's Star'. Francis was awarded the Egyptian medal and the Tel-el-Kebir clasp for his part in the battle of Tel-el-Kebir in 1882, and the two remaining clasps for his service in

L-704, Francis Lovell Speid

the actions at El-Teb and Tamaii when his regiment took part in the Sudan Expedition of 1884. The Khedive's Star was awarded to him in 1882.

THE BLACK WATCH

General George Wade, an Irishman, was appointed commander in chief in Scotland in the aftermath of the 1715 Jacobite uprising. He raised six independent companies of Highlanders whose new recruits came from the Campbell, Grant, Frazer and Munro clans. These companies were loyal to the English government and were stationed across the highlands to pacify the rebellious highland clans. In 1739 the six companies plus four new companies became the Highland Regiment of Foot – the first British army regiment to use bagpipes and wear the kilt. The name 'Black Watch' is thought to originate in the regiments' role to 'watch' the highlands and in the dark colour of its tartan plaid.

L-668: William Marsh Burke; *d*. 20 April 1894

William Marsh Burke, born on 9 April 1859, was captain in the 1st Battalion, 51st Regiment King's Own Yorkshire Light Infantry stationed in Victoria Barracks. Through the cluster of military graves in this section emerges the story of Belfast as a garrison town. Many of these soldiers were based at Victoria Barracks, situated between the Antrim Road, Clifton Street and North Queen Street. The first military barracks built in Belfast in 1737 were located in the area we now call Barrack Street. Construction of the new infantry barracks in Carrickfergus Street, now North Queen Street, was begun in 1790 and they opened in 1796.

William Marsh was killed after being thrown from his horse under Holywood Arches in east Belfast. Captain Burke had first joined the Roscommon Militia and then in 1881 became a second lieutenant in the Yorkshire Light Infantry. He served in the Burmese expedition of 1886–7, and in the Zhob Field Force and Kiderzai expedition in 1890 under the command of

Sir George White. This was a small British expeditionary force sent to suppress the Pathan tribesmen in the Zhob Valley which sits in the north-eastern corner of Baluchistan, on the border between Pakistan and Afghanistan. The British built a fort there called Fort Sandeman.

Sir George White was born in Ballymena in 1835. In 1850, at the age of 15, he joined the British army at the Royal Military College, Sandhurst. In 1853 he left Sandhurst to join the 27th Inniskilling Regiment. In 1863 he was transferred to the Gordon Highlanders. On 6 October 1879 he won a Victoria Cross at Charasiah, about 12 miles from Kabul. He is best remembered as the officer who led the defence of Ladysmith, South Africa, which was under siege by a Boer army from 2 November 1899 to 1 March 1900.

Thomas Henry Burke, a relative of William Marsh Burke, was assassinated by 'the Invincibles', a group whose roots are to be found in the IRB. Thomas Henry, under-secretary for Ireland, was killed along with Chief Secretary Lord Cavendish in Dublin's Phoenix Park on 6 May 1882. William Marsh Burke was also related through his sister to Mr Jamieson, the explorer who lost his life on the Stanley expedition.

L-540: John Agnew; *d.* 27 September 1918

The inscription at the centre of the headstone is to the memory of 'Sgt John Agnew, Killed in action in Russia 27 September 1918'. John joined the American army in Michigan and served with the 339th Infantry Regiment. This regiment, along with the 1st Battalion of the 310th Engineers, the 337th Field Hospital and the 337th Ambulance Company (in total 4,500 men) were all part of the 85th Division of the American Expeditionary Force (AEF) which landed at Archangel in Northern Russia in early September 1918. The purpose of the landings was to secure the vast amounts of ordnance held by the Imperial Russian army in the region around the Russian ports of Archangel and Murmansk. Operating under British Command the AEF saw action against the newly-formed Red Army and remained in

Russia until August 1919. John was one of 174 AEF soldiers killed. He is buried in the Meuse-Argonne American Cemetery, Romagne, France.

He is also mentioned on another headstone. The family headstone of Agnew in O-675 carries an inscription to their son John, 'Serg. AEF Killed in action 27 September 1918. Buried in France.'

L-426: Edward John Cotton; *d.* 14 June 1899

Edward Cotton was born on 6 January 1829 in Rochester, Kent. His life's work was in railways. At 24 he moved from the Great Western and the Railway Clearing House in England to become the accountant for the Waterford and Kilkenny Railway. Thus began a long association with Irish railways. In 1857 he again moved to become traffic manager of the Belfast and Ballymena Railways and then general manager of the Belfast and Northern Counties Railway. From 1875 until 1884 he was manager of the Ballymena, Cushendall and Red Bay Railway. By 1886 he was also managing the narrow gauge Ballycastle Railway.

L-391: Gertrude Annie Taylor; *d.* 12 December 1916

Gertrude was a Voluntary Aid Detachment (VAD). Her stone reads 'On active service at First London Central Hospital, Camberwell'. Her service began in the UVF Hospital, Belfast, from February to May 1915. The UVF Hospital was opened in 1915 by Lord Carson in the Exhibition Hall near Queen's University. The Hall was given free of

L-391, Gertrude Annie Taylor

charge by the Belfast Corporation. From June 1915 to January 1916 Gertrude was at the General Hospital and from July to December 1916 she was at the London Central. She died, aged 37, from pneumonia contacted while serving in the London Central Hospital. (See Elizabeth du Mesney I-178.)

L-136: Robert Patterson; *d.* 14 February 1872

Robert Patterson, born on Easter Sunday, 18 April 1802, commenced his education at the Belfast Academy and then moved to the Belfast Academical Institution. On leaving the Academical Institution, he became an apprentice in his father's mill furnishing business (established in 1786), Robert Patterson & Co., High Street. A strong interest in natural history led him at 19 to help set up the Belfast Natural History Society.

On 4 June 1833 he married Mary Ferrar, whose father William Hugh Ferrar had been appointed in 1816 as the first stipendiary magistrate in Belfast. Mary traced her ancestry back to a Ferrar of Huntingdonshire, a captain in Schomberg's cavalry who fought with King William at the Battle of the Boyne, at Aughrim and at the Siege of Limerick.

On Tuesday, 27 January 1835, Robert was in attendance in the upper room of the museum of the Belfast Natural History Society in College Square North when Takabuti, the first mummy to arrive in Belfast, was unrolled. Thomas Greg of Ballymenoch donated this mummy. Reverend Edward Hincks, who deciphered the hieroglyphics, concluded that the name of the mummy was 'Kabooti', a daughter of a priest of Amun.

On 4 March of the same year, Robert gave a paper to the society on the insects discovered in the unrolling of the mummy. His first book, *The Insects Mentioned in Shakespeare's Plays*, was published in 1838. In 1846 he published the first volume of his popular textbook *Zoology for Schools*; the second volume followed in 1848. The Irish Commissioners of Education and the Council of Education in England adopted the two volumes as set books. In 1853, and in association with a number of eminent artists, he produced a set of coloured zoological diagrams, which were published by Day & Co., London. Robert lived at 6 College Square North, Belfast.

Marie Patterson, Robert's daughter, married a Dutch linen merchant, Willem Emilus Praeger. They had six children. On 25 August 1865 Marie give birth to her second child, Robert Lloyd Praeger. Robert Lloyd was educated at the Royal Belfast Academical Institution and then at Queen's College, where, in 1885, he attained a BA degree, and in 1886, a BEng (engineering degree). From 1886 to 1893 he was a civil engineer with the Belfast City and District Water Commissioners. A self-taught botanist from an early age, he became a member of the Belfast Naturalists' Field Club at the age of 11. A prolific writer and contributor to a range of journals he co-founded and edited the Irish Naturalist in 1892. In 1893 he joined the staff of the National Library of Ireland, Dublin, as an assistant librarian. Active as a field botanist until his death at 88, on 5 May 1953, he published a number of books but will always be remembered for the most popular, *The Way I Went*, which appeared in 1937.

On 15 April 1867 Marie Patterson give birth to her third child, Sophia Rosamond Praeger. Sophia Rosamond began her education at Sullivan School in Holywood, County Down. In 1886 she enrolled at the School of Art in Belfast, and then in October 1888 she enrolled for the Slade School of Fine Art in London. On her return to Belfast in 1894 she opened a studio at 1 Donegall Square West, moving the following year to Waring Street. This was followed by a move to Ballinderry and eventually, in 1914, she settled in Holywood. Throughout her career Rosamond wrote and illustrated twenty-five children's books – two of these were for the Belfast firm of Marcus Ward & Co. She also collaborated with her brother Robert Lloyd, providing sketches for two of his books. As a member of the Belfast Arts Society, she, along with other members, organised tableaux for a Gaelic League festival. A lot of her work depicts children. While she is best remembered for her sculpture, her work included figures, designs for the Irish Women's Suffrage Federation, First World War memorial plaques, portrait busts in bronze, and figurines, medals and garden sculpture. One of her best-known works is the panels on the front doors of the Carnegie Library on the Falls Road. Rosamond died on 17 April 1954.

L-136: William Patterson; *d*. 5 February 1918

William Patterson, born in College Square North on 1 August 1835, was the eldest son of Robert Patterson and the brother of Robert Lloyd Patterson (**I-319**). His early education began with a Reverend John Scott Porter in College Square East, followed by a move to the Royal Belfast Academical Institution in 1847, and then to Queen's College. He joined his father's mill furnishing business at 16. On 4 June 1858, at the age of 22, he married Helen Crossley Anderson, the daughter of John Crossley Anderson, owner of the Belfast Commercial Chronicle. A love of natural history inherited from his father led him to co-found the Belfast Naturalists' Field Club and become a member of the Belfast Natural History and Philosophical Society. Also a member of the English Dialect Society, he published, in 1877, under the auspices of that society, a bibliography of Anglo-Irish dialects. This was followed in 1880 by the publication, again under the auspices of the English Dialect Society, *A Glossary of Words and Phrases Used in Antrim and Down*. A keen painter and a member of the Belfast Art Society, he was competent enough to exhibit at that society's annual exhibition. He served on the board of the School of Art.

CHAPTER 4

THE BELFAST BLITZ, BOXERS, PLAYWRIGHTS AND H-BLOCK MEN

The fourth walk begins at the Cross of Sacrifice, its first stop being the war graves in section D Glenalina. Then it heads towards the Ballymurphy River that runs through Glenalina and makes its way up the slopes in the direction of Black Mountain. On reaching the perimeter wall of the Whiterock Leisure Centre, it heads back down the hill, once again crossing the Ballymurphy River, and retraces its steps on the city-side slopes of Glenalina to end at the Bell Yard, a few yards from Cross of Sacrifice.

The Glenalina meadows, at the base of Black Mountain, had been used for the bleaching of linen since the early decades of the nineteenth century. Its slopes, fed by a constant source of fresh mountain water, were an ideal location for a linen beetling and bleach mill. By the 1860s the site contained two large and four small mill dams, two beetling engines, a wading house, yarn lofts, a carpenter's house, an office and lapping rooms, a bleach mill with steam engines and boilers, a cottage, a gate lodge, a worker's house, a dwelling house and orchard. The two large dams were situated in what is now the location of the Whiterock Leisure Centre and Bleach Green Court. The first beetling engine was positioned below the two main dams, now the site of the leisure centre swimming pool. Two small dams existed in what are now sections P1 Glen, X1 Glen and Y1 Glen. The yarn loft and wading house were situated below the small dams, where the upper corners of sections O1 Glen and P1 Glen now meet. The main buildings of the bleach mill located below the yarn loft and

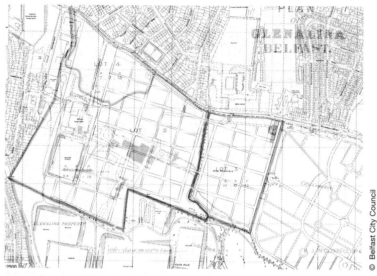

© Belfast City Council

An overlay map of the Glenalina section indicating the site of the Bleach Works

wading house occupied a site which is now sections H1 Glen, I1 Glen, O1 Glen and P1 Glen. The dwelling house, office and lapping room were sited to the south of the bleach mill, which is now the top of section J1 Glen and the bottom of sections R1 Glen and Q1 Glen. The orchard above the house, in what are now sections Q1 Glen and R1 Glen, was later developed as a bleaching green with its own small dam. Two small dams below the bleach mill fed the second beetling engine, in what is now the top end of Section V Glen.

In his report to the Parks' Committee on 15 July 1919, Daniel McCann, cemetery superintendent, writes 'I have been informed that the surveyors orders from you is to take down all the houses and erections on Glenalina. I would respectfully suggest that the office be allowed to remain as it would be useful when the upper portion is being worked.' The linen beetling and bleach mill and its out-buildings were eventually demolished in November 1919 and their stones used in the construction of the pathways in the new section. All the dams were filled in with clay and laid out as sections.

The war graves section in Glenalina

War Graves D-1/30 and D-102/128 Glen

This section has fifty-one new headstones remembering fifty-nine naval personnel who died during the Second World War. These graves were purchased on 26 March 1920 by commissioners acting on behalf of the Lord High Admiral.

In October 1979, 173 CWGC headstones in the City Cemetery were vandalised. The city council, in the week beginning 12 November 1979, removed to a store in Lady Dixon Park the vandalised stones along with the remaining stones in sections D, As, Bs, Cs and Ds, Glenalina and all the individual stones scattered throughout the cemetery – in total, 366 stones. A marker bearing a grave number was sunk into the ground behind each grave so that graves could be easily identified. It was thirteen years before the stones were put back on the war graves. The first was erected on 14 August 2002. On 10 October 2002, 6 headstones were erected in the first phase of a reinstatement programme. This was followed by the erection of a further 26 in the spring of 2003. In 2004 a further 254 headstones were erected, 61 were erected in May 2005 and 18 more were erected by 2006.

D-58/75, D-371/375, D-382 Glen

Plot used for the burial of the soldiers from the auxiliary cruiser *Otranto*.

At 11 a.m. on Sunday, 6 October 1918, HM auxiliary cruiser *Otranto*, in convoy from the USA, was seriously damaged after a collision with the 8,890-ton freighter *Kashmir*. During a severe gale that Sunday morning, the steering gear on the *Kashmir* had failed. The *Otranto*, at 12,124 tons and 554 feet long was the flagship of the convoy and was carrying over a thousand American soldiers. The destroyer *Mounsey*, also part of the convoy, was able to go alongside the crippled ship and take on board hundreds of soldiers. Of these, 27 officers, 239 sailors and 300 soldiers were landed safely in the North of Ireland. Among those were 30 French sailors from the three-masted French brigantine *La Croisine*, with which the *Otranto* had collided. The *Otranto* eventually sank twelve hours later, off the coast of the Scottish island Islay, with a loss of 335 soldiers, 11 officers and 85 crew. The remains of some of those lost were brought to Belfast and buried in the City Cemetery. The funeral cortège of 11 October 1918 set out from the Victoria Military Barracks in north Belfast and wound its way on to the Falls Road where it continued on to the cemetery. Forty-eight soldiers of the Northumberland Fusiliers flanked a gun carriage carrying the remains of Acting Sergeant Keller. All other remains were carried in a lorry, which followed the gun carriage. Two of those buried that day were brothers, Privates Floyd and James Evans. The firing party was made up of fifty soldiers from the Hampshire Regiment.

The *Otranto*, a passenger liner owned by the Orient Steam Navigation Company, was built in Belfast by the Workman Clark shipbuilding yard and launched in 1909. The boatswain mate on the *Otranto* was Peter Morgan of Belfast. Peter had served on the White Star liner RMS *Celtic*, which was built in 1901 by Harland and Wolff, and was torpedoed by a German U-boat on 31 March 1918 and then taken to Belfast for repairs.

What follows are the names of American soldiers of the 127th Field Artillery who were buried in City Cemetery. While most of the remains were eventually exhumed and returned for burial in the USA, a small number were returned to Brookwood Cemetery in Surrey, England. Brookwood was dedicated as an American War Cemetery in August 1937 and has 468 American servicemen buried there.

D-58   **Private Thomas McMahon.** Buried 14 October 1918. Exhumed and removed to Brookwood Cemetery, Surrey, 7 May 1929.

D-59   **Private S. Canevascini.** Buried 14 October 1918. Exhumed and removed to USA, 23 September 1920.

D-60   **Private Edward Keller.** Buried 11 October 1918. Exhumed and removed to USA, 23 September 1920.

D-61   **Private Floyd Evans.** Buried 11 October 1918. Exhumed and removed to USA, 27 April 1922.

D-62   **Private James Evans.** Buried 11 October 1918. Exhumed and removed to USA, 27 April 1922.

D-63   **Private Henry Kochler.** Buried 11 October 1918. Exhumed and removed to USA, 23 September 1920.

D-64   **Private Edward Kuchel.** Buried 11 October 1918. Exhumed and removed to USA, 23 September 1920.

D-65   **Private Oscar McDonald.** Buried 11 October 1918. Exhumed and removed to USA, 23 September 1920.

D-68   **Private James Corney.** Buried 11 October 1918. Exhumed and removed to USA, 23 September 1920.

D-69   **Private Charles Kaysner.** Buried 11 October 1918. Exhumed and removed to USA, 23 September 1920.

D-70   **Private Raymond Simpson.** Buried 11 October 1918 and removed to **D-59**, 23 September 1920. Exhumed and removed to Brookwood Cemetery, Surrey, 27 April 1924.

D-71   **Private Theodore Garner.** Buried 11 October 1918 and removed to **D-60**, 23 September 1920. Exhumed and removed to Brookwood Cemetery, Surrey, 27 April 1922.

D-72   **Private Alois Groska.** Buried 11 October 1918. Exhumed and removed to USA, 23 September 1920.

D-73   **Private Phillip Simon.** Buried 11 October 1918. Exhumed and removed to USA, 23 September 1920.

D-74   **Corporal Edward Knowlton.** Buried 14 October 1918 and removed to **D-63**, 23 September 1920. Exhumed and removed to Brookwood Cemetery, Surrey, 27 April 1922.

D-75   **Private Jessie Clifton.** Buried 14 October 1918 and removed to **D-64**, 23 September 1920. Exhumed and removed to Brookwood Cemetery, Surrey, 27 April 1922.

D-371   **Captain Fred Sturdevant.** Buried 17 October 1918. Exhumed and removed to USA, 23 September 1920.

D-372   **Private James M. Marshall.** Buried 14 October 1918. Exhumed and removed to USA, 23 September 1920.

D-373   **Private Ralph Davies.** Buried 19 October 1918. Exhumed and removed to USA, 23 September 1920.

D-374   **Private Aura Belk.** Buried 21 October 1918. Exhumed and removed to USA, 23 September 1920.

D-382   Private Joseph McCarthy. Buried 16 October
1918 and removed to **D-65**, 23 September 1920.
Remains removed to Brookwood Cemetery,
Surrey, 7 May 1929.

There are no headstones to mark these graves.

The following are three Catholic French sailors who also lost
their lives in the *Otranto* tragedy but who are buried in Milltown
Cemetery, grave **WE-9.B**. Their remains were brought from the
Union Hospital, now the City Hospital. A memorial cross was
raised in their memory but has since been badly damaged.*

Jean Marie Bougear, *d*. 13 October 1918, aged 16
Guillaume Denier, *d*. 14 October 1918, aged 32
Louis Cholou, *d*. 22 October 1918, aged 16

American Ernest P. George, a ship's carpenter on SS *Castle*,
was buried in **D-375.Glen**, on 19 April 1920. His remains were
exhumed and returned to America on 15 October 1920.

A-49 Glen: James Cooke-Collis; *d*. 13 April 1941

James Cooke-Collis lived at the Lodge, Dunmurry. He was born
in Castle Cooke, County Cork, on 7 May 1876. He was educated
at Cheltenham and joined the 5th Militia Battalion of the Royal
Irish Rifles in 1900. He saw active service with the British army
in South Africa where he was transferred to the 2nd Battalion of
the Royal Irish Rifles. He was seriously wounded at Dewetsdorp
(a small town named after Jacobus de Wet, father of the Boer
commander Christiaan de Wet). In 1908 he received a regular
commission, reaching the rank of captain. During the First World
War he saw action as a Brigade Major with the Mediterranean
Expeditionary Force and commanded the 80th Infantry Brigade
in Salonika and the Black Sea area. In this period he commanded

---

* The spellings of Bougear and Cholou are given here as they appear on their headstone.
However in *The War Dead of the Commonwealth, 1914–1918 & 1939–1945*
(CWGC, 2002), these are given as Bougeard and Cholon.

the 6th Battalion Royal Inniskilling Fusiliers (10th Irish Division) in France, Gallipoli and Palestine. He was Military Governor in Cairo.

By 1925 he was a colonel, in 1932, a major-general and then in 1935, general officer, commanding the Northern Ireland district, a post he held until his retirement from the army in 1938. In July 1938 he was appointed Agent for the Northern Ireland government in London. At his funeral, detachments of the Royal Ulster Rifles were drawn up at the cemetery gates. The cortège moved to the Mortuary Chapel for the burial service and then to the graveside where a volley was fired.

C-130 Glen: Joseph Richard Hall; *d*. 9 March 1927

Joseph Richard Hall was 84 when he died at his residence at 52 Cromwell Road in south Belfast. In the burial records Joseph is listed as an artist. Buried in the same grave is his son, Joseph Norman, an architect who lived at 16 Farnham Park in Bangor, County Down, and died on 8 April 1956.

The headstone, plinth and surround of the Hall grave are of particular interest, as they are all made from the red brick that is associated with the red clay used by McGladery of Belfast, whose brickworks were at Beechmount Street, off the Falls Road, and at 109 Limestone Road in north Belfast.

C-130 Glen, Joseph Richard Hall

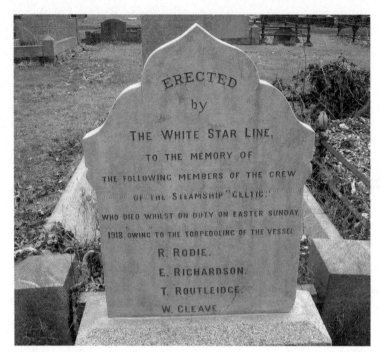

P-191 Glen, RMS *Celtic*

P-167/190/191 Glen: RMS *Celtic*

In **P-191 Glen** are the remains of the 'unknown man'. He was buried two months after he lost his life on the RMS *Celtic*, which was torpedoed by a German U-boat on 31 March 1918. Buried in **P-190 Glen** is 'Chief Boots' Charles Jeffers and in **P-167 Glen** is Stanley McDonald, an engineer on the ship.

The *Celtic*, built by Harland and Wolff, was launched on 4 April 1901 and delivered to the White Star Line on 11 July that same year. She was the 335th ship built by the yard and was the first of her class known as the 'Big Four'; the others were the *Cedric*, launched in 1902, the *Baltic* in 1904, and the *Adriatic* in 1907. On 26 July 1901, the *Celtic* left Liverpool on her maiden voyage to New York, arriving there on 4 August. Thirteen years to the day after her first arrival in the 'Big Apple', she was requisitioned for war service by the British Admiralty and, on 20 October 1914, was commissioned as an armed merchant cruiser with eight six-inch guns. On 4 December she was assigned to the 10th Cruiser Squadron. By 1916 she was decommissioned as an armed merchant cruiser and converted into a troop carrier. On 15 February 1917 she was badly damaged, and 17 people were killed, when she struck a mine laid by the German submarine *U-88*, off the coast of the Isle of Man. The *Celtic* was taken to Peel Bay, and then on for repairs to the shipyard in Belfast. Three months later, on 19 May, an attack on her by *U-57* failed; but she was again badly damaged in the Irish Sea on Easter Sunday, 31 March 1918, when *UB-77* scored a direct hit with a torpedo, killing 7 of her crew, all of whom are buried in the City Cemetery. The *Celtic* was then towed to Liverpool on 2 April and repaired there by Harland and Wolff employees. With the end of the First World War she returned to her role as a transatlantic passenger liner. She ran aground at Roche's Point when attempting to enter Cobh harbour, County Cork, on 10 December 1928. After unsuccessful efforts to re-float her, her owners sold the *Celtic* as salvage to Petersen and Albreck of Copenhagen.

UB-77 had been launched at the shipyard of Blohm & Voss in Hamburg on 5 May 1917 and commissioned on 2 October of that year. With a gross weight of between 500 and 600 tons, this class of U-boat was employed in the waters around Britain, Ireland and the Mediterranean. Between 2 October 1917 and 14 June 1918, *UB-77* was under the command of Kapitän Leutnant Wilhelm Meyer, who sank the very first troop ship transporting American army units to fight on the Western Front. The liner *Tuscania* had left Hoboken, New Jersey, on 24 January 1918 carrying 2,013 soldiers and a crew of 384. At Halifax, Nova Scotia she joined Convoy HX-20 bound for Le Havre on the northwestern coast of France. On 5 February she was seven miles north of Rathlin Island, when she was spotted by *UB-77*. At 5.40 p.m. two torpedoes were fired at the *Tuscania*; one missed, but one scored a direct hit. The *Tuscania* sank at 10 p.m. with a loss of over 200 soldiers and 30 members of her crew. *UB-77* later surrendered on 16 January 1919, and was broken up at Swansea.

P-292 Glen: A. Byford; *d.* 2 December 1918

Byford served with the 3rd Battalion Royal Inniskilling Fusiliers. One wonders at the story behind the inscription, which reads 'served as A.M. Bates'.

P-419 Glen: William Henry Dunning; *d.* 22 July 1920

William Henry Dunning was a 23-year-old labourer from 76 Bellevue Street, Shankill Road, Belfast. In the early part of the First World War, William had been a soldier of the 9th Battalion Royal Irish Rifles but was discharged in 1916. He was shot dead at 6.50 p.m. on 22 July 1920 in the vicinity of Cupar Street and Kashmir Road.

Between Thursday, 22 July and the early morning of Saturday, 24 July 1920, 18 people (3 women and 15 men) were shot dead in Belfast as a result of widespread political and communal conflict surrounding the partition of Ireland. On Wednesday, 21 July 1920, in the immediate aftermath of the 'Twelfth' holiday period, a mass meeting of Protestant shipyard workers took place at lunchtime outside the south yard of Workman Clark at Queen's Island. Following this meeting the workers began attacking Catholics employed there. Many of these Catholics were driven from their employment, some of them thrown into the Musgrave Dock. This expulsion of Catholic workers in the shipyard triggered similar expulsions across various factory sites in Belfast. Beginning in the Short Strand area, Catholics were driven from the Sirocco Works, and a number of Catholic-owned spirit grocers in the Lower Newtownards Road were looted and burned. In the west of the city, Catholics were attacked in the engineering firm of Combe, Barbour. Trouble also flared in the Clonard area of west Belfast when workers from Mackie's factory clashed with local Catholic residents. Over the following two days and nights, political strife, house-burnings and shootings raged across the streets of Belfast and beyond, including Lisburn, Banbridge, Dromore, Bangor and Newtownards. In just over a few days, thousands of Catholics were forced from their homes.

The names of those killed in Belfast from 22–24 July 1920 were:

Francis Finnegan, Lower Clonard Street

Bernard Devlin, Alexander Street West

Mrs Maggie Noade, Anderson Street

Reverend Brother Michael Morgan, Clonard Monastery

William John Downey, Roden Street

Joseph Giles, Kashmir Road

Alexander McGoran, Tralee Street

Thomas Robinson, Lucknow Street

Albert McAuley, Stanfield Street

William Godfrey, Argyle Street

William Dunning, Bellevue Street

James Stewart, Frome Street

William McKeown, Clonallen Street

James A. Conn, James Street

Mary Ann Weston, Welland Street

John McCartney, Lucknow Street

Nellie McGregor, Frome Street

Davis Dunbar, Silvo Street

The conflict ignited by the meeting on 21 July lasted for more than two years. Over 518 people died between 21 July 1920 and December 1922.

Hence the fatal shooting of William Dunning must be seen in the context of an Ireland in deep political turmoil generated by northern unionist attempts to consolidate their political dominance prior to the partition of Ireland, the armed struggle waged by the IRA, and the passage of a Westminster Parliamentary Bill known as the 'Better Government of Ireland Bill', commonly referred to as the Partition Bill. This bill, first announced in Westminster by David Lloyd George on 22 December 1919, entered its first reading in the House of Commons in February 1920. It was the fourth attempt by the British government to set up Home Rule in Ireland, and differed from the three previous Home Rule Bills in that it proposed the setting up of two parliaments in Ireland, one for the twenty-six counties and the other for the six north-eastern counties. The Bill became law on 23 December 1920 and took effect from 3 May 1921. On 19 May 1921 elections for a southern parliament of 128 members were held in the twenty-six counties, while on 24 May 1921, elections for a northern parliament of fifty-two members were held in the six counties. As a result of a boycott by republicans, the southern parliament failed to meet, while the northern parliament met for the first time on 7 June 1921. The partition of Ireland envisaged in the 'Better Government of Ireland Act' was further strengthened by a Treaty signed by British and Irish delegations on 6 December 1921.

Section As, Bs, Cs, Ds and Es and D Glenalina: Second World War

Two hundred and seventy-four military graves are located on the eastern bank of the Ballymurphy River, and are under the care of the CWGC. There are three women buried in these sections: one of them, Mary Rose Cuthbertson, was buried on 1 October 1943 and re-interred on 24 February 1948. There are also five unidentified service personnel buried here.

In the course of its history there have been many soldiers and airmen of different nationalities buried for a short period in the cemetery, including German, Free French, Belgian, American, Canadian, New Zealand soldiers and a member of the Dutch Merchant Marine. Three members of the Norwegian merchant navy are buried in Sections T1 and V1 Glen.

On 20 June 1940, the IWGC reserved graves in section **Es-42/74 Glen**. On 12 February 1942 they were reallocated to the American forces. They contained the remains of forty-two American service personnel who were exhumed and re-interred to Lisnabreeney, Castlereagh, on 24 May 1944.

During the war the cemetery contained soldiers, sailors and

airmen of the German armed forces. In the Belfast area there was a POW military hospital in Campbell College, Orangefield – referred to in burial documents as Orangefield POW Hospital – and a POW camp in Holywood, County Down.

Section As Glen

This section contained four German soldiers. It also contains airmen from New Zealand and Australia.

As-157 Glen: Oberfeldwebel Alfred Rinn; *d*. 5 February 1945; German army

Alfred Rinn, POW number B 71040, aged 44 and from Giessen in Germany, died of pulmonary tuberculosis at the Military Hospital, Campbell College. He was interred on 8 February 1945, then re-interred to **Es-205 Glen** on 26 February 1948, and exhumed for reburial on 17 July 1962. His unit was Ld. Schützen Zug 23/1 (x1).

As-158 Glen: S/Gefreiter Wilhelm Thöne; *d*. 7 March 1945; German army

Wilhelm Thöne, POW number B 24399, aged 42, died at the Military Hospital, Campbell College. He was interred on 10 March 1945, then re-interred to **Es-206 Glen** on 26 February 1948 and exhumed for reburial on 17 July 1962.

As-159 Glen: Obergefreiter Herbert Lisser; *d*. 22 March 1945; German Air Force

Herbert Lisser, POW number A 58170, aged 21, died at the Military Hospital from cardiac failure as a result of his war wounds. He came from Richthofenstrasse 51, Bremen. He was interred on 24 March 1945, then re-interred to **Es-207 Glen** on 26 February 1948 and exhumed for reburial on 18 July 1962.

As-160: Unteroffizier Gerhard Geier;
d. 25 March 1945; German Air Force

Gerhard Geier, POW number B 19042, aged 27, died of a fractured skull at the Military Hospital, Campbell College. He was interred on 27 March 1945, then re-interred to **Es-207 Glen** on 26 February 1948 and exhumed for reburial on 18 July 1962.

Section Cs
This section contained a German soldier, a soldier of the Free French and two soldiers of the 2nd Belgium Brigade.

Cs-26 Glen: Obergefreiter Friedrich Selbach;
d. 26 July 1945; German army

Friedrich Selbach, aged 38, from Anna Graben 33 in Bonn, died at Orangefield Military Hospital. He was interred on 28 July 1945, then exhumed on 18 July 1962 and re-interred at Cannock Chase, Staffordshire, England.

Cs-86 Glen: Sgt. Ernest Almoyroc;
d. 25 September 1940; Free French Forces

Ernest Almoyroc, aged 23, an airman of Aviation Française attached to the British army in Gambia, died of cut eye and blackwater fever at the Military Hospital, Campbell College. He was interred on 28 September 1940, then exhumed on 15 November 1950 for reburial in France.

© Belfast City Council

Registration details of Second World War German servicemen

Cs-93 Glen: Pte. Leon Maton;
d. 9 March 1945; Belgian army

Leon Maton, aged 23, 1st Battalion, Second Brigade, Belgian army, from 43 Rue de la Croix de Pierre, St Gilles, Brussels, died of meningitis at the Military Hospital, Campbell College. He was interred on 13 March 1945 and then exhumed on 8 October 1949 for reburial in Belgium.

Cs-94 Glen: Sgt. Joseph Vandecraen;
d. 16 March 1945; Belgian army

Joseph Vandecraen, aged 24, number 2 Company, 3rd Belgian Infantry Battalion, 2nd Belgium Brigade, died at the Massereene Hospital in Antrim. He was interred on 20 March 1945 and then exhumed on 8 October 1949 for reburial in Belgium.

Section Es

This section contained three German soldiers and two German sailors.

Es-181 Glen: Obergefreiter August Kreinbring;
d. 25 May 1945; German army

August Kreinbring, POW number B 4246, aged 29, was held at Market Hill, County Armagh. He was interred on 29 May 1945 and then exhumed on 13 July 1962 and re-interred at Cannock Chase, Staffordshire, England.

Es-182 Glen: Gefreiter Rudolph Blume;
d. 25 May 1945; German army

Rudolph Blume, POW number B 4534, aged 34, was held at Market Hill, County Armagh. He was interred on 29 May 1945 and then exhumed on 13 July 1962 and re-interred at Cannock Chase, Staffordshire, England.

The common burial register for German and Allied military

Es-183 Glen: Obergefreiter Wilhelem Jungclaus; d. 27 May 1945; German Navy

Wilhelem Jungclaus, POW number A 811180, aged 42, was held at Elmfield Camp, Guilford, Portadown. He was interred on 30 May 1945, exhumed on 16 July 1962 and re-interred at Cannock Chase, Staffordshire, England.

Es-184 Glen: Obermaat Rudolf Schwarz; *d.* 29 May 1945; German Navy

Rudolf Schwarz, POW number A 939273, aged 53, died in Orangefield POW hospital. He was interred on 1 June 1945 and then exhumed on 16 July 1962 and re-interred at Cannock Chase, Staffordshire, England.

Es-185 Glen: Ober/Kan Wilhelm Dalbeck; *d.* 23 July 1945; German army

Wilhelm Dalbeck, POW number A 438606, aged 33, was a POW in Palace Barracks Holywood, County Down. He was interred on 25 July 1945 and then exhumed on 16 July 1962 and re-interred at Cannock Chase, Staffordshire, England.

2c WHITEROCK ROAD

The Corporation had built a small lodge in what is now Section M Glen. This was to become 2c Whiterock Road. It was demolished sometime during 1972.

T-233 Glen: Faiz Hamed Mohamed; *d.* 7 May 1929

Faiz Hamed Mohamed, a 24-year-old medical student from San Ferando, Trinidad, lived at 105 Portallo Street, off the Woodstock Road in east Belfast.

He studied at Napasina College, Trinidad, and then at Queen's University, Belfast. He entered the Faculty of Medicine at Queen's in 1926, having matriculated through the Scottish Universities Entry Board and is listed in the 1929–30 University Calendar. He died in his third year at Queen's, from pulmonary tuberculosis.

His grave marker, erected by the overseas students at Queen's, has an inscription and a crescent moon and star. It gives his date of death as 7 May 1924. In the burial records his religion is described as Mohammedan. There are two other Muslims, both sailors, buried in the cemetery: Coonjee Moideen, *d.* 5 September 1933 (**Z-217 Glen**) and Abdul Moghy, *d.* 24 June 1941 (**T1-145 Glen**).

AI-90 Glen: Matilda Gould; *d.* 27 June 1966

Just before 11 p.m. on the night of 10 May 1966 a petrol bomb was thrown through the window of 50 Upper Charleville Street in the Shankill Road area of Belfast. Matilda Gould, a 77-year-old who lived in the residence, was badly burned and immediately rushed to the Royal Victoria Hospital where she died as a result of her injuries on 27 June 1966. It later transpired that a loyalist group, known as Ulster Protestant Action (which later changed its name to the UVF), was actually attempting to petrol-bomb a Catholic-owned pub next door to Mrs Gould's house. On the same night a Catholic household in Northumberland Street and St Mary's Teacher Training College on the Falls Road were also petrol-bombed.

Matilda Gould was the first person injured, and the first woman to die, in this phase of the Irish conflict, which had begun with a UVF attack on the home of independent unionist Stormont MP John McQuaid on 16 April 1966. This attack was a bogus one, meant to give the impression of an active IRA. Moreover, it was intended to deepen the political crisis by retarding the reforming efforts of the Unionist prime minister, Terence O'Neill, which included the introduction of measures aimed at giving the Catholic population political rights.

One month after the petrol bombing of the home of Matilda Gould, Patrick Scullion, who lived at 2a Oranmore Street in the Clonard area of Belfast, became the first victim of the conflict to be murdered. He died on 11 June from a gunshot wound he had received on 27 May while on his way home from the Conway bar in Milford Street. Patrick is buried in Milltown Cemetery in grave **ZF-113.A.**

E1-470 Glen: Terry Enright; *d.* 11 January 1998

Terry Enright was shot dead by loyalists on the night of 11 January 1998. He was 28 years old and married with two children. Terry was a sportsman who played with, and coached, his local Gaelic football club. He worked in the community sector where he was a driving force in a programme that sought to develop the skills of young people through outdoor activity and environmental awareness. Following his death, a foundation was set up to 'follow his example in creating opportunities for young people to build their self esteem and confidence'.

Terry Enright, a victim of an assassination squad, is one of several Catholic assassination victims buried in the cemetery. Their deaths are reflected through the inscriptions and references found among the headstones in the upper slopes of Glenalina and in the reserve paths at the lower end of the cemetery. The majority of Belfast's Protestant victims of the Troubles were buried in Roselawn cemetery in east Belfast.

E1-589 Glen: Gerald Duffy; *d.* 30 November 1989

Gerald's inscription, 'I told you's I was sick', captures the black humour of the Belfast wit.

A similar epitaph was used by Spike Milligan, the legendary comedian, who died on 27 April 2002, and was buried at St Thomas's Church cemetery in Winchelsea, East Sussex. Before his death he told his family that the epitaph on his headstone should read 'I told you I was ill.' Whilst the Chichester diocese objected to the use of Milligan's epitaph, a compromise, in which the epitaph would be written in Irish, was reached. Milligan's headstone now reads: '*Duirt mé leat go raibh mé breoite.*'

L1-267 Glen: Wee Boon Ann; *d.* 11 January 1952

Described in burial records as 'Chinaman' Wee Boon Ann, his name has been phonetically recorded. He was the chief cook on board MV *Lingula*, which was berthed at the Alexander Jetty, Belfast docks. Wee Boon Ann hanged himself. There is no headstone on this grave.

K1-354 Glen: Liam Andrews; *d.* 6 February 1996

Liam Andrews was born on 14 September 1913 in Springfield Village in the locality of Woodvale, Belfast. Liam has the distinction of being baptised twice: once as a Catholic in St Paul's Cavendish Street and as a Protestant in Christ Church, College Square North. He attended Springfield Road Primary School and left there at 14 to work in Springfield Road laundry.

In his early twenties he began his lifelong affair with the Irish language and also began to study art at Belfast Art College. Over the years Liam painted landscapes of old Belfast, the Belfast

docks and travellers. On 4 February 1972, Liam, his wife Anna and their seven children were forced by loyalists to move from their home at 513 Springfield Road to 4 Ballymurphy Parade, where he involved himself in a range of community projects. The Irish inscription on his headstone reads:

Anseo	Here
faoi Shuaimhneas Dé	in the peace of God
atá	is
Liam, Céile ionúin Anna	Liam, dear husband of Anna
Ealaíontóir agus Gael	Artist and Gael
a d'éag 6 Feabhra 1996 aois 82	who died 6 February 1996 age 82

'*Ealaíontóir agus Gael*' (Artist and Gael) is a reminder of the two great passions in his life. The inscription on the base of the stone reads, '*Is Mise an tAiséirí agus an Bheatha. Eoin 11:25*' (I am the Resurrection and the Life. John 11:25).

M1-245 Glen: Lionel Strutt; *d*. 13 March 1938

Lionel was a First World War soldier of the Canadian Expeditionary Force. While the stone appears to be the standard CWGC headstone, 2ft 8in by 15ft, it is in fact a larger stone at 3ft 1in by 18in. This may be a family headstone modelled on the traditional CWGC stone.

A study of First World War headstone inscriptions in the cemetery reveals a number of references to Belfast men who fought in the Canadian army. Links between Ireland and Canada have historically been very strong, and were reflected in the large numbers of Irishmen who enlisted to fight with Canadian regiments in the First World War.

On 6 August 1914 the Canadian army began to assemble volunteers for a Canadian Expeditionary Force, with the first Canadians arriving for training in Britain in mid-October. By February 1915 the 1st Canadian Division was deployed on the Ypres Salient. In all, five Canadian divisions fought on the Western Front: 418,000 soldiers served with the Canadian Expeditionary Force; just over half were casualties (210,000), and of these 56,500 were killed while on active service.

T1-211 Glen: Emily, Sammy, Billie, Jim, Peggy and Sally Douglas; *d*. 16 April 1941

Emily, aged 29, William, aged 9, Margaret, aged 5 and Sarah, aged 1, died at 8 Ballynure Street, Belfast, on the night of the 15–16 April 1941 during an air raid by the Luftwaffe. While the headstone lists five children, the grave contains only three children and their mother. There is no reference to Sammy or Jim; it is probably safe to assume that the remains of these two children were never identified or found. (See **V-47/48 Glen**, Blitz Plot.)

T1-Glen

This section contains the graves of foreign sailors who died in Belfast during the Second World War. Edgar Kardo, an Estonian aged 27, was an Able Seaman on SS *Salena*, which was berthed in the Clarendon Dock. He died on 28 March 1942 and was buried in **T1-407 Glen**.

Karl Samuel Stranne, aged 34, and from Kabelgatan, 13c Gothenburg, Sweden, was a chief officer on SS *Solstadd* berthed at Queen's Quay. He drowned on 14 November 1941 and is buried in **T1-311 Glen**.

There are no headstones marking these graves.

T1 and V1 Glen

Three members of the Norwegian Merchant Marine are buried here.

V1-225 Glen: Halvard Halgjem *d*. 6 December 1942, aged 45.

T1-312 Glen: John Jansen *d*. 13 December 1941, aged 29.

T1-309 Glen: Karl Rygve Karlsen *d*. 20 December 1941, aged 52.

U1-414 Glen: Dirk Kranenburg; *d*. 10 July 1940

Dirk Kranenburg was a sailor in the Dutch Merchant Marine, and was 17 when he died on 10 July 1940. His remains were exhumed on Monday, 28 September 1964 and re-interred in the

Netherlands Field of Honour, Paddington (Mill Hill) Cemetery, London. There is no headstone on this grave.

V1-5 Glen: Robert Kelly; *d*. 31 January 1953

Robert Kelly, a ship's engineer from 47 Wallasey Park, off the Oldpark Road, perished on the MV *Princess Victoria*, which went down off the Copeland Islands during a storm on Saturday, 31 January 1953. The *Princess Victoria (IV)* – one of the first roll-on, roll-off ferries – left Stranraer at 7.45 a.m., 31 January 1953, carrying 128 passengers and fifty-one crew. She immediately encountered a rough sea and was badly battered by heavy waves. Shortly after 10 a.m., the sea forced the stern doors inward and the car deck was quickly flooded. For the next four hours the ship made slow progress across the North Channel to a point off the Copeland Islands at the mouth of Belfast Lough. Rescue services were hampered by the severe storm conditions and had difficulty locating the damaged ship. While the ferry floundered close to the mouth of Belfast Lough rescue services were concentrated in an area not far from the Scottish coast. Finally, at 2 p.m. the ship capsized. There were just 44 survivors – 10 crew and 34 passengers. All were male. Of the 135 lost, the bodies of 32 crew and 68 passengers were recovered.

Robert Kelly was buried on 4 February 1953. James Curry, Roden Street, Belfast, employed by Short Bros. & Harland at their Wig Bay Factory, who was travelling home on the *Princess Victoria*, was another victim. He is remembered on the headstone of the Curry family **E-167 Glen**.

The captain of the *Princess Victoria*, James Ferguson, received a posthumous George Medal. Radio operator David Broadfoot received a posthumous George Cross; he had sent out a total of sixty radio messages, the first at 9.46 a.m. and the last at 1.58 p.m.

Because the storm was so wild, it is now referred to as the 'Great Storm of '53'. A combination of winds of up to 119 miles per hour and a high tide made it one of the worse storms of the twentieth century which claimed the lives of fishermen off the Scottish coast, passengers on the *Princess Victoria (IV)*, and villagers living in the coastal communities along the east coast of England – all victims of the mountainous seas generated by the hurricane conditions on that night. Over 300 men, women and children lost their lives, 210,000 were made homeless, and 200,000 acres of farmland ended up under water. In Holland 1,800 people lost their lives.

X1-39 Glen: Chris (Fargo) Wilson; *d*. 6 January 1999

Another interesting inscription: 'God created the world but our dad carried the brick.'

X-227 Glen: Victor Beausart Mitchell; *d*. 31 January 1953

Victor Beausart Mitchell, from 1 Colchester Street off the Donegall Road, another passenger of the *Princess Victoria*, was buried on 5 February 1953 (See **V1-5 Glen**).

Z1 Glen: Baby Public

In May 1945 this section was allocated as Poor Ground and the first burial took place on 23 May 1945 in **Z-21**. Between 23 May and 23 June 1945, thirty-seven infants were buried in this grave. In 1954 the Belfast Corporation decided that from January 1955 the section would be used solely for the burial of infants.

There are a number of babies buried in this plot who died by drowning soon after their birth. Infanticide was a regular occurrence in Belfast up to the late 1950s. In the burial records of Section **Z1** a number of references are entered as 'unknown child found in …' The locations include Twin Basin, Belfast Harbour, Blackwater River, Stranmillis Locks, Albert Quay, Springfield Dam, Waterworks and Loop River. One of the last entries is for an infant found in the Blackwater River on 28 November 1957.

A2-404 Glen: Pat Finucane; *d.* 12 February 1994

Pat Finucane was born on 12 March 1949 at 27 Sevastopol Street, Belfast. He began his primary education at St Finian's, 61 Falls Road, moving to St Mary's Grammar School, Barrack Street, and finally to Trinity College, Dublin.

In 1968 the Finucane family moved from Sevastopol Street to Percy Street, which runs between Divis Street and Shankill Road. During the political upheaval in August 1969, the family were forced by loyalists to leave their home. Pat, who went on to become a prominent human rights solicitor, was shot dead by two members of the Ulster Defence Association (UDA) at his home on Sunday night, 12 February 1989. Since his death there have been consistent allegations of collusion between his murderers and British state forces. One of the guns used to kill him was stolen from British army barracks by a soldier of the Ulster Defence Regiment. A British agent, Brian Nelson, a member of the UDA, claimed he had targeted Pat but had informed military intelligence that he was doing so.

The Finucane family continue in their campaign to uncover the truth about the circumstances of Pat's murder.

L2-46 Glen: Julie Livingstone; *d.* 13 May 1981

Julie Livingstone, the youngest in a family of 13 children (she had 8 brothers and 4 sisters), lived at 118 Carrigart Avenue, Lenadoon in Belfast. She was born on 18 November 1966 and lived with her family in 124 Dover Street.

Late on the evening of 15 August 1969, the Livingstone family were forced by loyalists to flee from their home, and moved first to Carryduff, on the outskirts of Belfast, and then, after a few months, relocated to the Divis Flats, where they stayed for a year. It was then that the family home was set up at 118 Carrigart Avenue. Julie attended Oliver Plunkett Primary School in Lenadoon and Cross & Passion Secondary School on the Glen Road. She was just 14 when she was wounded by a plastic bullet at 7 p.m. on 12 May 1981.

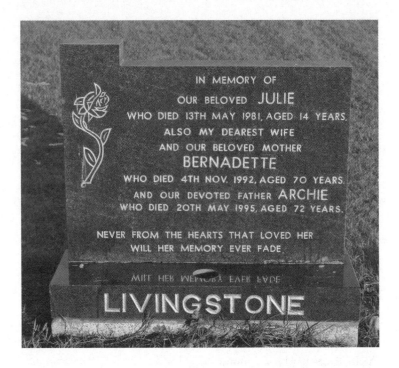

IN MEMORY OF
OUR BELOVED JULIE
WHO DIED 13TH MAY 1981, AGED 14 YEARS,
ALSO MY DEAREST WIFE
AND OUR BELOVED MOTHER
BERNADETTE
WHO DIED 4TH NOV. 1992, AGED 70 YEARS.
AND OUR DEVOTED FATHER ARCHIE
WHO DIED 20TH MAY 1995, AGED 72 YEARS.

NEVER FROM THE HEARTS THAT LOVED HER
WILL HER MEMORY EVER FADE.

LIVINGSTONE

Early on the evening of the fatal incident, Julie and her friend Nuala Lowry set out on an errand to a shop located near the junction of Lenadoon Avenue and Stewartstown Road. On returning to Lenadoon they passed a small protest, mainly of women and children blocking the Stewartstown Road. The protest was a local response to the news that republican hunger striker Francis Hughes had died. At around 7 p.m. Julie and Nuala passed on the inside of a hedge running parallel to the Stewartstown Road, which separated them from the protesting women and children. It was then that two British army Saracen armoured vehicles of the Prince of Wales Regiment, driven at speed, approached the protesters and scattered the women and children. As the armoured cars passed, two plastic bullets were fired by the army. Moments later Julie was found lying directly behind the hedge with a serious head injury caused by one of the bullets. She was immediately rushed to the Royal Victoria Hospital, where she died the following day.

─────── RUBBER AND PLASTIC BULLETS ───────

Often referred to as baton rounds, rubber and plastic bullets are a mixture of truncheon and bullet. The first baton rounds were made from teakwood and were an inch long. Later versions were 7½ inches long and 1½ inches in diameter. They were first used during the 1967 anti-colonial protests in Hong Kong, when the deaths of eighteen protesters were attributed to their use.

On 2 August 1970, the British army used a new version of the baton round against nationalist residents on the New Lodge Road, Belfast. This new bullet was made from hard rubber, measured 6 inches in length and was 1½ inches in diameter. Before their withdrawal in 1975, when they were replaced by a plastic (PVC) bullet, 55,834 of these baton rounds, commonly referred to as rubber bullets, were fired. The new plastic bullet, 3½ inches long and 1½ inches diameter, was introduced in August 1972, but not used until 7 February 1973. At first it was used sparingly. Between February 1973 and the end of 1974, 258 plastic bullets were fired. When, in 1975, it replaced the rubber bullet altogether, 3,500 were fired in that year. Between 1 January and 11 November 1981, the year of the hunger strikes, 29,665 plastic bullets were fired, the greatest number ever. Of these 16,656 were fired in May alone.

Since the introduction of baton rounds on 2 August 1970, 17 deaths have been attributed to their use. Of these, 11 have occurred in the Belfast area. Six of those killed are buried in Milltown. The first casualty was 11-year-old Frank Rowntree from Divis Flats, Belfast who was hit with a rubber bullet on 20 April 1972 and died several days later. The last was 15-year-old Seamus Duffy from the Short Strand, Belfast, who was hit with a plastic bullet on 9 August 1989.

KILLED BY RUBBER BULLETS

Francis Rowntree. 11 yrs, *d.* 23 April 1972, Belfast   PA -516.B[*]

Tobias Molloy. 18 yrs, *d.* 16 July 1972, Strabane

Thomas Friel. 21 yrs, *d.* 22 May 1973, Derry

[*] Buried in Milltown Cemetery

KILLED BY PLASTIC BULLETS

Stephen Geddis. 10 yrs, *d.* 30 August 1975, Belfast   BB-549.B[*]

Brian Stewart. 13 yrs, *d.* 10 October 1976, Belfast   X-419.B[*]

Michael Donnelly. 21 yrs, *d.* 10 August 1980, Belfast   O-530.B[*]

Paul Whitters. 15 yrs, *d.* 25 April 1981, Derry

Julie Livingstone. 14 yrs, *d.* 13 May 1981, Belfast   L2-46 Glen

Carol Ann Kelly. 12 yrs, *d.* 22 May 1981, Belfast   B1-417 Glen

Henry Duffy. 45 yrs, *d.* 22 May 1981, Derry

Nora McCabe. 33 yrs, *d.* 9 July 1981, Belfast   B1-403 Glen

Peter Doherty. 33 yrs, *d.* 31 July 1981, Belfast   UF-62.A[*]

Peter McGuinness. 41 yrs, *d.* 9 August 1981, Belfast[**]

Stephen McConomy. 11 yrs, *d.* 19 April 1982, Derry

John Downes. 23 yrs, *d.* 12 August 1984, Belfast   E-533.B[*]

Keith White. 20 yrs, *d.* 14 April 1986, Portadown

Seamus Duffy. 15 yrs, *d.* 9 August 1989, Belfast   P1-85 Glen

---

R1-125 Glen: John George Thomas; *d.* 5 December 1936

John was 76 when he died. He lived at 37 Leadbetter Street, Old Lodge Road, Belfast, and was a sailor and labourer. This grave was purchased by the British Legion Benevolent Society under a scheme for those who died 'in straitened circumstances'. This scheme was opened to families or institutions who applied to the corporation for a new grave at a reduced rate. The grave was first purchased and then an application would be made to the corporation for a reduction. Applicants had to answer twelve questions on the financial and family status of the deceased. Details on property, debts or liabilities, funeral expenses, family or dependants were required. If successful the applicant would receive a refund. The grave contains the remains of three other men all described as ex-service men. There is no headstone on this grave.

---

[*] Buried in Milltown Cemetery

[**] Buried in Carnmoney Cemetery

R1-128 Glen: Richard Mussen; *d.* 27 December 1936

Richard Mussen, who lived at 22 Dundee Street, on the Shankill Road, Belfast, was born in 1860. His father, also Richard, was a farmer from Hillhall, Lisburn in County Antrim. In 1875, at the age of 15, Richard enlisted with the 27th Regiment of Foot, later known as the Royal Inniskilling Fusiliers. Three years later, on the outbreak of the Anglo-Zulu War in Natal, South Africa, he was transferred to the Second Battalion 24th Regiment of Foot, Warwickshire Regiment, later known as the South Wales Borderers. Richard was one of sixty-five survivors of that regiment when it defended the mission station at Rorke's Drift against a force of between four and five thousand Zulu warriors. The Second Warwickshires were initially supported by a small detachment of the Natal Native Contingent who, minutes before the commencement of action, fled the mission station. This left a British force of just 139. Of these, 110 were soldiers of B Company, including 30 incapacitated soldiers, thus leaving the company with a cohesive fighting unit of just 80 soldiers. Action began at 4 p.m. on the afternoon of 22 January, when the first wave of six hundred Zulu warriors attacked the south wall that joined the mission hospital and storehouse. This was the first of a series of Zulu attacks, which lasted until 2 a.m. on 23 January. Sporadic musket fire from the Zulu snipers continued until 4 a.m. However, by this point the Zulus were exhausted – they had been on the move for the previous six days, and without food for the last two. Their capacity to fight had also been undermined by many casualties, including the loss of 370 of their warriors. At 8 a.m. on 23 January the small British force at Rorke's Drift were relieved by a large British force under the command of Lord Chelmsford.

In the aftermath of the action on 22 and 23 January 1879 eleven Victoria Crosses and five Distinguished Conduct Medals were awarded to the defenders of the mission station at Rorke's Drift. The soldiers still hold the record for the highest number of Victoria Crosses awarded to a regiment of the British army for a single action.

The year after Rorke's Drift, Richard was invalided home.

However, in 1914, at the age of 54, and along with his four sons and two sons-in-law, he enlisted with the 9th West Belfast Battalion of the Royal Irish Rifles. He was drafted for home service and was stationed in Ballykinlar and Clandeboye, both in County Down, where he worked on munitions. In the aftermath of the First World War, he became a 'riveter's holder up' in the Harland and Wolff shipyard, but was forced to retire due to bad health. Richard was a member of St Luke's Parish Church, Northumberland Street, and the Belfast Harbour LOL 1883 (Black Chapter). On his death, he was given a full military funeral, his remains being borne on a gun carriage along the Shankill Road.

THE ANGLO-ZULU WAR

In 1824 the British established a trading post at Port Natal, on the eastern seaboard of Southern Africa, now the city of Durban. By the 1840s, and with the extension of British economic and trading interests in the hinterland of the port, the British colony of Natal emerged along the southern borders of Zululand. The growth of the colony was accelerated with the discovery of diamonds in 1867, and of gold in 1871. This immediately led to tensions between the British and local Zulu tribes. Attempts at creating a confederation of joint control between the Zulu chiefs and the British failed, hampering the expansion of the economic interests of the Natal colony. Furthermore, the political tensions in Natal coincided with a British strategy for Southern Africa that sought to amalgamate two Boer Republics, independent African territories, and two British colonies into a more cohesive political and economic entity. Zulu opposition to British expansion into Zululand was therefore seen as a threat to this strategy. Minor incidents between the Zulu and Boer settlers along the Natal Zululand border gave the British the pretext to issue an ultimatum to the Zulu King Cetshwayo on 11 December 1878: he was to disband his army and Zululand was to lose its independence. As anticipated by the British, Cetshwayo rejected the ultimatum, and the invasion of Zululand by the British became inevitable.

The invasion was planned for January 1879. Three attacking columns were to invade Zululand from Transvaal and Natal with the objective of converging on Ulundi, the home of the Zulu king. On the 11 January, a column of 4,000 men, under the command of Lord Chelmsford, crossed into Zululand, but, on 22 January, the British suffered a humiliating defeat at their base camp at Isandlwana when it was attacked by 20,000 Zulu. Throughout the first six months of 1879, there were eleven major battles between British and Zulu forces. The war lasted until the final battle at Ulundi on 4 July 1879, when a British force of 5,000 troops defeated 20,000 Zulu warriors. By the end of the war the British had lost 1,700 soldiers while Zulu losses were in excess of 10,000. The defeat of the Zulu army at Ulundi broke the back of native resistance to British expansionism into their homeland and brought about the end of an independent Zulu nation. By September 1879, the British had successfully mopped up all pockets of Zulu resistance. The Connaught Rangers were the only Irish regiment on active service during the Anglo-Zulu war.

R1-141: Thomas Henry Sloan; *d.* 11 October 1941

According to many sources, Thomas Henry Sloan was born in Belfast in 1870; however, as his burial record cites his age as being 69 when he died in 1941, it is safer to surmise that the actual year of his birth was either 1871 or 1872. He was a semi-skilled worker in the platers' shed of Harland and Wolff shipyards, first as a red leader and then as a sub-contractor for the cementing of ship floors. Thomas was a member of the Amalgamated Union of Labour, the Worshipful Master of St Michael's Total Abstinence Orange Lodge 1890, and No. 7 Black Sir Knights Masonic Lodge. He was also one of the leading figures in the Belfast Protestant Association (BPA) and a Protestant evangelical lay-preacher who regularly held lunch-hour meetings for shipyard employees at his workplace.

At the Belfast County Orange demonstration in Castlereagh on 12 July 1902 there was sustained heckling from the assembled crowd during the speech of County Grand Master Colonel Saunderson MP, the leader of the Irish Unionists in Westminster. As the heckling increased, Thomas Sloan mounted the platform to ask Saunderson whether he voted against the inspection of convents. His query related to the passage of a Parliamentary Bill that provided for the inspection of convent laundries. Saunderson's reply of 'Certainly not' was refuted by Sloan who immediately replied, 'then the press of Belfast must be liars'.

Following the death on 17 July 1902 of William Johnston of Ballykilbeg, MP for Belfast South (see McKnight **J1-334**), and a legendary figure in the Orange Order, Sloan, with the encouragement of his co-workers, was immediately nominated by the BPA to contest the vacant seat as an independent unionist. He promptly received the support of a number of Orange lodges, including the Springfield Temperance LOL 948 and the Tyrone True Blue LOL 497. Among the temperance societies backing his campaign were the Independent Order of Good Templars, and the Rechabites. His supporters included some unexpected names: there are suggestions that William James Pirrie, chairman of the Board of Harland and Wolff, annoyed at his failure to secure the nomination of the Conservative and Liberal Unionists to contest Belfast South, may have provided funding for Sloan's election campaign. On election day, Pirrie's brother-in-law stated in a letter to the Northern Whig that he was supporting Sloan. Trade union support was provided in the persons of Belfast Trades Council members Alexander Boyd, Worshipful Master of Donegal Road Temperance LOL 731 and organiser of the Municipal Employees Association, and John Keown, Chairman of No. 1 branch of the BPA.

On 13 August, five days before the election, a meeting of the Grand Lodge of Belfast passed a resolution condemning the behaviour of Sloan at the 12 July Castlereagh demonstration; they also appealed to the Orangemen of south Belfast not to elect Sloan as representative for their constituency. During his campaign, Sloan accused the unionist leadership of being soft on the ritualists of the Church of Ireland and the menace of Rome, and of opposing temperance measures. Sloan won the election with a majority of 826 votes over his rival C.W. Dunbar Buller, the candidate of the Unionist Party.

The internal process initiated by the meeting on 13 August dragged on until 17 August when Sloan received a letter, asking him to appear before the Grand Lodge of Belfast to offer a written apology. His refusal to apologise led to his being suspended from the Orange Order for two years. At the same meeting, the warrants of three private lodges were withdrawn: Queen Victoria Memorial Temperance LOL 700, Donegall Road Temperance LOL 731, and Guiding Star of Sandy Row LOL 1026. Several Orangemen who supported Sloan were also suspended. Sloan's next move was to appeal to the Imperial Grand Lodge of Ireland, whose meeting was convened in Armagh city in early June 1903. The appeal was unsuccessful.

Resentment about the Order's treatment of Sloan surfaced at a meeting on 11 June 1903 on the 'plains' (now the Botanic Gardens in Belfast), which was attended by eight thousand Orangemen. Three resolutions were passed at the meeting: the first called for the creation of an Independent Orange Institution; the second instructed a committee to organise for 12 July demonstrations that year; and the third stated that no apology should be made by the expelled lodges to the Orange leadership. The first demonstration of the new Independent Orange Order (IOO) took place at Dundonald on 12 July that year. Resolutions proposed by Sloan called for the inspection of all convents, opposed the setting up of a sectarian – that is, Catholic – university, and resisted any modification of the declaration, made by the British monarchs at their accession, repudiating the doctrine of transubstantiation as superstitious and idolatrous.

By 1904 membership of the IOO had grown to 2,000 and comprised 55 lodges. Its Imperial Grand Lodge of Ireland was inaugurated on 20 February 1904. By 1905 the number of lodges increased to 71. At its Grand Lodge meeting on 3 June 1905, its principal officers were authorised to draft a manifesto for the IOO. Just over five weeks later, on 13 July 1905, Robert Lindsay Crawford, Grand Master of the IOO's Grand Lodge of Ireland, used a meeting at Magheramorne in County Antrim to issue a document of over 3,000 words, now referred to as the 'Magheramorne Manifesto', which called for an end to religious conflict and appealed to Catholics and Protestants to unite around a shared nationality. It attacked clericalism of all kinds in Irish politics, rejected 'clerical control of schools', called for compulsory land purchase, the transfer of such land to tenant farmers, and supported the claims of town tenants. It also attacked the UUC, describing unionism as a discredited force. The Manifesto was seen by many as a challenge to the dominant leadership of big house unionism and indicative of a radical trend within a section of the unionist working class. The unionist press very quickly denounced it, and its signatories Lindsey Crawford, the Reverend D.D. Boyle, James Mateer and Thomas Sloan, were condemned by the *Belfast News Letter*, the *Belfast Evening Telegraph*, and the *Northern Whig*. While the majority of the IOO membership endorsed the manifesto, a small number of members defected, including John Keown, Sloan's backer in the 1902 by-election and member of No Surrender Independent Orange Lodge ILOL 4. From the very beginning, Sloan appears to have had an ambivalent attitude towards the manifesto, and he eventually dissociated himself from its contents in a letter to the *Belfast News Letter* on 1 January 1906.

As the general election of 1906 approached, Sloan attempted to rebuild his relationship with the UUC, who, regardless, nominated Lord Arthur Hill to contest the Belfast South seat on their behalf. During the election campaign Sloan received the support of the Belfast Trades Council, which assisted him in winning the seat on Thursday, 8 February 1906 with a majority of 816 votes. He remained MP for South Belfast until the general election of January 1910 when he lost by 2,219 votes to the unionist candidate James Chambers. Eleven months later, Chambers again won the seat with an increased majority of 2,722. These losses signalled the end of Sloan's political career, the downward spiral of which ran parallel with the weakening of the IOO, whose decline in membership since 1908 had been accelerated by the emergence of a more cohesive UUC, preparing for its onslaught on the Third Home Rule Bill.

— THE BELFAST PROTESTANT ASSOCIATION —

The Belfast Protestant Association (BPA) was founded in 1894 by the fundamentalist lay preacher Arthur Trew to oppose 'Romanism' and the growth of 'Ritualism' in the Church of Ireland. The political mindset of the BPA was a combination of fundamentalist Protestant views and unionist ideology. Trew lived in Dublin but spoke every weekend on the Custom's House steps in Belfast, a city he eventually settled in. The nature of BPA public activity can be found in the official minutes of the Westminster parliament Hansard for 29 March 1900. In a question by Samuel Young, MP for Cavan East, the secretary of state for the Home Department was asked if he 'was he aware that a man calling himself "Ex-monk Widdows" had been preaching under the auspices of the BPA and that his real name was Nobbs, who had been sentenced in Toronto, Canada, to five months' imprisonment and then in 1888 to ten years' penal servitude and that Widdows, alias Nobbs, was never a monk'.

Trew was active in street agitation, opposing Wolfe Tone commemorations and Catholic public ceremonies in Belfast. Along with the secretary of the BPA, Richard Braithwaite, he was charged with disrupting a Corpus Christi procession from St Patrick's Church in Donegall Street to St Malachy's College on the Antrim Road on Sunday, 9 June 1901. On 25 July, Trew was sentenced to twelve months to be served in Crumlin Road jail, while Braithwaite was sentenced to six months. Trew was released on 18 July the following year. During his imprisonment, Thomas Sloan had taken over Trew's position as leader of the BPA. In 1905 the organisation fielded a number of candidates in the Belfast local elections. They remained active until 1920 and sometimes used the name 'Ulster Protestant Association'. In this very late period of their existence, they had evolved into a murder gang, and by 1922 were eventually broken up by the Stormont administration.

P1-356 Glen: Sisters of Adoration

The first burial in this plot took place on 3 February 1987. Theodelinde Dubouche, who was born in Montauban, France, on 2 May 1809, founded the order Sisters of Adoration. She was 16 when she discovered her talent for painting and began her studies in art. When she was 23 she moved with her parents to Paris and continued to develop as a painter. One of her paintings, *The Martyrdom of Saint Philomena*, was completed in 1838 for the Cathedral of Bayeux in Normandy. Ten years later she moved with her father to be near the Carmelite Convent in Rue d'Enfer, Paris. In June 1848 she made a proposal to the Mother Prioress to create a Third Order of Carmel. On 6 August 1848 the Order was formally established, and by July 1853 the Third Order of Carmel had evolved into the Sisters of the Adoration. This order came to Belfast in 1980 and occupied the Bon Secour Convent at 63 Falls Road, which had been a convent since 1879.

P1-292/6 and P1-319/26 Glen: Good Shepherd Convent

The first burial of an inmate of this convent took place here on Thursday, 27 August 1987. The first burial of a sister was on Tuesday, 26 July 1990.

In 1867 the Bishop of Down and Connor invited the Good Shepherd nuns to Belfast to open a refuge for young women. One year later they opened a house at Ballynafeigh at the top of the Ormeau Road. In 1869 they opened their convent on eight acres of land rented from Mr Carolan. New buildings were added in 1893 when the sisters opened the first steam laundry in Belfast and in 1906 when they built a new convent. They originally provided residential care for thirty teenage girls but eventually were able to accommodate 140 women and girls. One of its residents, who had entered when she was 14, was still there sixty years later. The laundry closed in 1977. This stone is unique in the sense that it is inscribed on both sides, carrying on its east face the inscription 'The Contemplative Sisters of the Good Shepherd' and on its west face the inscription 'In loving memory of all those who died at St Mary's Good Shepherd Convent Belfast.'

I1-1/3 and 29/31 Glen: Abingdon Street Burial Ground

In this plot lie eighteen unknown remains lifted in August 1986 from an old paupers' graveyard situated at Abingdon Street playground off the Donegall Road. The first burials in this plot took place at 9.30 a.m. on Wednesday, 13 August 1986, when eight remains were buried. The following day another eight remains were buried at 10 a.m. The last two burials took place at 10 a.m. on Friday, 15 August 1986.

The Abingdon Street burial site belonged to the workhouse on the Lisburn Road. This institution opened on 11 May 1841 at a cost of £7,000. It housed 1,000 inmates and was situated on the site now occupied by the City Hospital. Dr Thomas Andrews (**G-182**), its first doctor, was paid £60 per annum. Burials took place in this paupers' graveyard up to the 1920s. Burial records indicate that from May 1908 remains from the workhouse were sent to Dundonald Cemetery. In the burial records of the City Cemetery there is an entry for 31 July 1917, which reads 'ten from Union' – the Belfast Union Workhouse. On average ten remains per fortnight were thereafter sent for burial from the workhouse.

The Abingdon Street burial ground

I1-286 Glen: Johan Evald Isaksson; *d*. 8 April 1945

Johan Isaksson, from Rora in Sweden, was an engineer on board a steamer berthed at Belfast. There is no headstone on this grave

B1-372 Glen: Kieran Nugent; *d*. 3 May 2000

Kieran Nugent was born on 12 September 1957 in Merrion Street, in the Lower Falls area of Belfast. He was the eighth child in a family of six boys and five girls. His father, Michael John Nugent, from Crossmaglen, County Armagh, had joined the merchant navy in his early teens. He later joined the Royal Navy and was on active service during the Second World War. At the start of the war he came to Belfast where he met Mary O'Hara Davey, of 55 Merrion Street. The couple were married on 17 December 1945.

Kieran first attended St Paul's school, Getty Street, and then St Joseph's Primary, Slate Street, and finally St Peter's Intermediate School, Britton's Parade – all in the Falls area. In 1974 Kieran was interned without trial in Long Kesh prison camp, and released in 1975. He was arrested in May 1976 and held in Crumlin Road jail. On 14 September 1976 he was the first prisoner sentenced under new laws which treated republican prisoners as common criminals. On his arrival at the H-Blocks in Long Kesh, Kieran refused to wear the prison uniform. Thus began the blanket protest, which eventually led to the IRA hunger strikes of 1980 and 1981. Kieran, who lived in Rossnareen Avenue, Andersonstown, died at the age of 42 and is buried with his parents, Michael John and Mary.

In 1972 Special Category Status (Political Status) was granted by the British government to republican and loyalist prisoners in the North of Ireland. One of the conditions of Special Category Status was the right of a prisoner to wear their own clothes. In January 1975 Lord Gardner, in his report to the British government, recommended ending the Status. Consequently, from 1 May 1976, republican and loyalist prisoners were to be treated as common criminals and were now to wear prison uniform.

B1-203 Glen: Rinty Monaghan; *d*. 3 March 1984

Rinty was born on 21 August 1920 and lived for most of his life at 32 Little Corporation Street. He began his professional boxing career at 14 and by 1938 had fought and won twenty-one fights – he lost his twenty-second fight when pitted against Glasgow's Jackie Patterson. In 1945, he became the Irish Flyweight Champion when he knocked out Bunty Doran. In 1946, in a non-title fight with Jackie Patterson in the King's Hall, Belfast, he forced the Glaswegian to retire in the seventh round. In October 1947 he won the NBA (America) and IBBC version of the World Title when he beat Hawaiian Dado Marino at the Harringay Arena, London; three months earlier he had lost a fight with Marino on a technicality.

In March 1948, at the King's Hall, he became the undisputed World Flyweight Champion when he knocked out Jackie Patterson in the seventh round. Patterson held the World, British and British Empire titles and Rinty became Ireland's first World Champion since Jimmy McLarnin in 1934.

In April 1949 in the King's Hall he successfully defended his title, easily out-pointing the Frenchman Maurice Sandeyron, and adding the European title to his British, Empire and World titles. Soon after, in the Hippodrome, Great Victoria Street, he fought and won his fight with the Italian boxer Otello Belardinelli. In September 1949, in the King's Hall, he fought Terry Allen of Islington, London. The fight ended in a draw. Six months later he retired as undefeated World Champion at the age of 30 because of a lung complaint. In 1952, under the management of Frank McAloran, he attempted a comeback but the boxing authorities refused him his licence.

In his sixteen-year professional career Rinty Monaghan won 51 fights, drew 6 and lost 9. In 1969 he was the first Irish boxer to be honoured by the Boxing Hall of Fame. He will always be remembered for his rendition of 'When Irish Eyes are Smiling', sung at the end of his fights.

C1-31 Glen: Sam Thompson; *d*. 15 February 1965

Sam Thompson was born, the seventh of eight children, in east Belfast in 1916. He grew up in Montrose Street, which runs between the Albertbridge and Newtownards Roads. His father was a lamplighter. Leaving school at 14, he became an apprentice painter in the shipyard, and then for a short time was employed by the Belfast Corporation where his trade union activities led to his dismissal. He remained a trade unionist and joined the Northern Ireland Labour Party, standing as the Labour candidate for South Down in the 1964 elections. Sam Thompson had a heart attack and died, aged 48, while visiting the Labour Party Headquarters in Waring Street, Belfast. He lived at 55 Craigmore Street in the Donegall Pass area of Belfast.

He began to write in 1956 and was encouraged in his endeavours by Sam Hanna Bell, a BBC producer. He wrote a number of radio features for the BBC. On receiving his first cheque from the BBC he immediately bought himself a typewriter. By 1959 he was writing full-time. His interest in amateur dramatics  led him to act for stage and television and helped to develop his skills as a playwright. He wrote three full-length plays: *Over the Bridge* in 1958, *The Evangelist* in 1963, and *Cemented with Love* in 1965.

He is best remembered for *Over the Bridge*, which reflected the sectarian realities of the Belfast shipyard. It was given to the actor Jimmy Ellis, the artistic director of the Ulster Group Theatre. Ellis brought the play to the group's reading committee who, by a majority of votes, approved its production. Public controversy flared after Ritchie McKee, board chairman of the Group Theatre, intervened on behalf of the Board and withdrew the play two weeks before it was due to open. McKee was also chairman of the Belfast Arts Theatre and chairman of the grant-awarding agency, Council for the Encouragement of Music and Arts. His brother was a unionist lord mayor of Belfast. As a result of the controversy, Harold Goldblatt, a founder member of the Group, resigned in May 1959, along with two others, Jimmy Ellis and Maurice O'Callaghan. Thompson and Ellis then set up a new company and set about producing the play in another venue. It finally opened at Belfast Empire Theatre, running for six weeks and playing to a total audience of forty thousand. The life of Sam Thompson is captured in his inscription 'His was the voice of many men.'

D1-156 Glen: David Cowan Boyd; *d.* 24 October 1939

David, from 90 Urney Street, off the Shankill Road, was the first soldier to be buried in the cemetery, following the outbreak of war in September 1939. There is no headstone on this grave.

V-47/86 Glen: Blitz Plot Memorial Stone

This memorial stone was unveiled on Monday, 22 October 1951 by the lord mayor of Belfast, Councillor J.H. Norritt, to remember the 154 unidentified men, women and children killed in the air raids of April and May 1941. On the night of Easter Tuesday, 15 April 1941, 123 were killed; an additional 31 died on 4 May. The first burials in this plot took place on 21 April and the last on 29 May. There were three major air raids by the Luftwaffe on Belfast in 1941, on the nights of 7–8 April, 15–16 April and 4–5 May. The most devastating raid in terms of life lost was the second one, when it is estimated that up to 900 people died.

The remains in this plot came from Duncairn Gardens, Heather Street, Cambridge Street, Blythe Street, Thorndyke Street, Hogart Street, Mountcollier Road, Ballynure Street, Avoca Street, Walton Street, Disraeli Street, Ambrose Street, Manor Street, Whitewell Road, Urney Street, Argyle Street, Eastland Street, Vandyke

V-47/86 Glen, Blitz plot memorial stone

Gardens, Unity Street, Percy Street, Louisa Street, Annadale Street, Ballyclare Street, Westbourne Street, Avondale Street, Sydney Street West, Isoline Street, Westcotte Street, Ravenscroft Avenue, Cliftonville Road, Mossvale Street, Templemore Avenue, Tower Street, and Wilton Street.

W-382/6, 407/410 Glen: Identified and unclaimed victims of the Belfast Blitz

This section contains 34 remains of those killed in the air raid on 16 April 1941, who were identified but not claimed by their families. Many families may not have been able to cover the cost of having a relative re-interred in a family-owned grave. The remains here came from Ballynure Street, Percy Street, York Street, Estorial Park, Pernau Street, Sussese Street, Hogarth Street, Glencoe Park and Sheridan Street.

The cemetery also contains 104 remains of those who were killed in the Blitz and who were buried in family graves scattered throughout the Glenalina section. There is no headstone on this grave.

X-389/394, 413/418 Glen: Home for the Blind, Cliftonville

There are twelve graves in this plot. The first burial took place on 24 January 1930. The Home for the Blind moved in 1901 from Hope Street in the centre of Belfast to 26–30 Cliftonville Road, where it provided accommodation for thirty women and twenty men. In 1983 Hearth Housing Association, well known for its restoration of old buildings, bought the property.

The buildings were designed by a young architect called Thomas Jackson, who built a number of classical villas for the city merchants in the Clifton area of north Belfast. Thomas lived at 28 Cliftonville Road, which was burned down in 1982.

Section Ds and Cs Glenalina

Those parts of these sections on the western bank of the Ballymurphy River contained a bothy with its own yards and sheds, which were demolished by the Corporation in 1971.

L-363: Margretta Bowen; *d.* 8 April 1981

Margretta Bowen, born in Dublin on New Year's Day 1880, died, aged 101. She married Matthew Campbell and they moved north in 1921. She began painting, at 70, under her maiden name Gretta Bowen, to distinguish herself from the work of her artist son George Campbell. Her style of painting is described as

'primitive'. Another son, Arthur, who died on 20 March 1994, was also a well-known painter and photographer. Among his many works are two books of old photographs, *Return Journey* and *Looking Back*.

Section F: Poor Ground Glen

In January 1929, Section F Glen was allocated as Poor Ground. On 5 January 1929 the first burial to take place was a stillborn infant called Wylie, buried in F-695.

E-223 Glen: Constable Charles Anderson; *d.* 9 October 1933

Charles Sillery Anderson was a 33-year-old police constable based at Cullingtree Road RUC Barracks, in the Lower Falls Area of Belfast. He was shot while guarding a house at 18 Roumania Street in the area. He was from Westmeath and had fought in the First World War. He joined the RUC in 1926 and served for six years in Cullingtree Road Barracks. On the night he died, he came on duty at 10.45 p.m. along with Constable John Fahy. At 11.10 p.m., a group of men approached the two constables from the direction of Servia Street and called for the RUC men to 'put them up'. When Constable Anderson went for his revolver he was shot in the hand and abdomen. He was rushed to the Royal Victoria Hospital but died shortly after 2 a.m. At the inquest into his death a verdict 'that death was due to gunshot wounds wilfully inflicted by some person or persons unknown' was returned. This was the second member of the RUC from Cullingtree Road Barracks to be mortally wounded at this time. On 28 February 1933, Constable John Ryan was shot dead at the corner of Durham Street during the railway strike.

C-48 Glen: Francis Maginn; *d.* 16 December 1918

Born in Mallow, County Cork, on 21 April 1861, at the age of 5 Francis contracted scarlet fever and lost his hearing. As a young man he briefly taught at the Royal School for the Deaf in Margate. He subsequently went to the National Deaf Mute College in Washington, USA, later renamed Gallaudet College. It was there that he developed his ideas for a similar college for deaf people in Ireland and Britain. In 1888 Francis became the first superintendent of the Ulster Institute for the Deaf in Fisherwick

C-48 Glen, Finger-writing on Francis Maginn's gravestone

Place, Belfast. In 1890 he proposed that an association for the deaf and dumb be set up in Britain. In the early 1900s he published a pamphlet *Guide to the Silent Languages of the Deaf*, which contained 80 drawings, 2 alphabets and a poem about deafness. He lived at 24 Eglantine Avenue and was described in the 1917 Street Directory as 'Chaplain to the Deaf and Dumb'.

There are two forms of sign language in Ireland and Britain, Irish Sign Language (ISL) and British Sign Language (BSL).

The top of the stone depicts finger-writing. The two fingers of the right hand sit on two fingers of the left hand, representing the letter F. The three fingers of the right hand sit on the palm of the left hand, representing the letter M.

THE BELL YARD

This was the location of a bell which rang to inform the public that the cemetery was about to close. Generations of cemetery staff believed that the bell came from the old White Linen Hall, which occupied the site of the present Belfast City Hall. Photographs of the White

Linen Hall show a tower above the main entrance with a four-faced clock. The bell is thought to have belonged to this clock. In his 1896 report, the Town Surveyor of Belfast records that 'The new Fish Market has been completed and opened. The clock, removed from the Linen Hall, has been erected over the entrance opposite May Street.' An article in the *Belfast Telegraph*, dated 28 April 1922, reports that the clock of the White Linen Hall inscribed, 'Robert Neill, 1821, still ticks of the hours in its new position at the Fish Market, Oxford Street.' It is most likely that the bell, separated from the clock after the demolition of the White Linen Hall in 1895, was sent to the cemetery some time early in the twentieth century. However, it disappeared from the cemetery in the early 1970s.

It was not until May 2004 that a bell, thought to be the cemetery bell, was recovered in west Belfast. There are a number of clues linking the bell to the cemetery. First, two pillars in the bell yard supported the cemetery bell and the recovered bell is hung on a crossbar, which has two bearings at each end. Second, when the bell was dust blasted a layer of green (parks) paint was discovered. Third, there is an arm at an angle of the crossbar used to pull the bell. This is probably a part of the original clock mechanism, which allowed the bell to be rung independently of the striking lever. Fourth, a blacksmith made the fittings on the crossbar, which indicates that the bell is certainly old. Last but not least, there is Geordie, a foreman who worked in the cemetery long before the bell disappeared, and who identified the recovered bell as that which hung in the Bell Yard.

The foundation stone for the White Linen Hall was laid in 1783 and the building was opened in 1784. A cupola above the main entrance was added in 1815. On Wednesday, 18 January 1893, the Improvements Committee of the Belfast Corporation decided to give notice to the tenants of the White Linen Hall to quit their holdings by 1 November 1893; the site was to be the location of a new Belfast City Hall. It was last used to hold an industrial exhibition organised by the Working Men's Institute in January, February and March 1895, and was demolished when the exhibition ended. In his 1896 report, the Town Surveyor of Belfast states 'The Linen Hall site has been cleared of old buildings and the site sown in grass.'

In the history of Belfast there have been a number of Linen Halls. The first was opened in Cooney's Court in 1739. It was replaced in 1754 by the Brown Linen Hall, which existed on the site of St Ann's Church, Donegall Street, now occupied by St Ann's Cathedral. This building was closed and a new Brown Linen Hall was opened on the west side of Donegall Street in 1773. The terms Brown and White signified the colour of the linen sold in the Linen Halls.

© OSNI / LPS

An aerial photograph of Glenalina with the footprint of the Bleach Works clearly shown, 1967

CHAPTER 5

THE FIRST WORLD WAR

The First World War, more than any other historic event, dominates the family headstones in the City Cemetery. The fifth walk is therefore constructed to give a sample of the First World War memorial inscriptions found in the lower end of the cemetery. It begins in section O, just inside the main gate and finishes in section L1 along the perimeter wall of the Falls Park.

The First World War began on 4 August 1914 and formally ended on 11 November 1918. When the British Expeditionary Force went to France in 1914 it numbered 220,000; by the end of the war there were 1,999,000 British soldiers in Flanders and France. During the course of the war 380,000 British soldiers had been killed outright on the field of battle, 150,000 had died from wounds received on the battlefield, 145,000 had disappeared, presumably lost in battle, 175,000 had been taken as prisoners of war and 32,000 had died as a result of non-battle accidents.

Over 200,000 Irishmen served with the British army; many more served in the armies of Australia, Canada, India, New Zealand, South Africa and the United States. Corporal E. Thomas, of the 4th Royal Irish Dragoon Guards, is reputed to have fired the first shots at German soldiers on the morning of 22 August 1914 in the village of Casteau, 3 miles northeast of Mons. Lieutenant Maurice James Dease, from Gaultstown, County Westmeath, won the first Victoria Cross of the war, on 23 August 1914. It is also reputed that a soldier from the 5th Royal Irish Lancers was the last British soldier killed on the day the war ended, by which time over 35,000 Irishmen had lost their lives.

Irish units of the regular British army went to France with the British Expeditionary Force in August–September 1914. These included the North Irish Horse, Munster Fusiliers, Irish Guards, Irish Dragoon Guards, Royal Irish Rifles, Royal Irish Regiment, Royal Irish Lancers, Royal Irish Hussars, Royal Irish Fusiliers, Dublin Fusiliers, Inniskilling Fusiliers, the Leinster Regiment and the 2nd Battalion Connaught Rangers. On 13 August 1914, the war correspondent, George Curnock, was watching the soldiers of the British Expeditionary Force march through the French port of Boulogne when he heard the Connaught Rangers sing one of their marching songs 'It's a Long Way to Tipperary'. A report of this was carried in the *Daily Mail*, 18 August 1914, and

Cross of Sacrifice

the song became one of the most popular of the First World War.

Many regular Irish battalions were in India prior to the beginning of the war, but by December 1914 they had been posted to the Western Front; these included the Royal Irish Fusiliers, Munster Fusiliers, Dublin Fusiliers, Inniskilling Fusiliers, the Leinster Regiment and the Royal Irish Regiment. The 1st Battalion Connaught Rangers arrived in France in October 1914 with a corps of the Indian army and the 1st Battalion Royal Irish Rifles arrived from Aden.

On 7 August 1914 Lord Kitchener, Britain's secretary of war, using his famous slogan, 'Join your country's army', made a public request for 100,000 volunteers; by the middle of September 1914 almost 480,000 men had signed up. They represented the first great surge of recruitment for Kitchener's new army. By the end of 1914, 82 battalions had been raised in Ireland. On 9 May 1915, the 9th Scottish Division was the first division of Kitchener's first new army to embark for France. In the first two years of the war, over 3,000,000 men volunteered and 5 new armies were formed.

The first Irish division recruited from Kitchener's volunteers was the 10th and they landed at Suvla Bay in the Dardanelles, on 7 August 1915. Two other Irish divisions were formed in this period, the 16th, recruited from Redmond's National Volunteers, and the 36th Ulster, recruited from the UVF. These three divisions suffered heavy losses in Flanders, France, Mesopotamia and Turkey. Soldiers from Belfast served in all three of these divisions. They also fought with the kilted regiments of the Highland Division, with the London Irish and London Scottish in the Church Lad Battalion of the Kings Royal Rifles, with the Tyneside Irish in the Northumberland Fusiliers, in the Royal Scots, and in the Post Office Rifles.

Five battalions of the Royal Irish Rifles were raised in Belfast. These were the 8th (East Belfast Volunteers), 9th (West Belfast Volunteers), 10th (South Belfast Volunteers), 14th (Young Citizen Volunteers of Belfast), and the 15th (North Belfast Volunteers).

In a study of this period clear examples emerge of how politics seeped into and shaped the Irish divisions of Kitchener's new armies. Six hundred Catholic men from the Falls Road refused to join the 36th Ulster Division, as it was associated with the UVF; instead, they joined the 6th Battalion Connaught Rangers. Likewise, Catholics from the Glens of Antrim, rather than joining the 36th, crossed the sea to Scotland and enlisted with the Cameron Highlanders. Many UVF men, not wishing to wait for the formation of the 36th Ulster Division, joined the 10th Irish Division, which was formed in August 1914.

Soldiers from Belfast served on every major First World War battlefront and in the armies of the American Expeditionary Force, as well as in companies from Australia, Britain, Canada, India, New Zealand and South Africa. They died in Flanders, France, Gallipoli, Germany, Greece, Italy, Mesopotamia, Russia and Palestine, on land, in the air and in the sea. All these battlefields are mentioned in the inscriptions.

The oldest soldier remembered is 46-year-old Thomas Stephenson, who also fought in the Boer War; the youngest is James Robinson, who was 17 when he died on 10 August 1915.

Robert Stephenson, the father of Thomas Stephenson (O-513), served as a sergeant with the 44th (Essex) Regiment and fought in the Crimean War, while William John McNabney, a First World War soldier who died from his wounds on 6 January 1941, lost his son Thomas on 4 July 1940. Thomas had been serving with the Royal Navy on the HMS *Foylebank*.

N-750: Richard Jefferson, Canadian Infantry; *d.* 3 June 1916, Hooge, Flanders.

N-704: Arthur Bourke, Royal Irish Fusiliers; *d.* 9 May 1915, Aubers Ridge.

P2-873: William Lavery, Australian Infantry, Australian Imperial Force; *d.* 9 August 1915, Gallipoli.

This force was raised in August 1914 and by December the same year had been sent for training to Egypt. Here they were joined by the New Zealand Expeditionary Force. The two forces then became the Australian and New Zealand Army Corps but are known by their common name, ANZACs.

I-576: Thomas Telford, Machine Gun Corps; *d.* 12 March 1919, Grantham Military Hospital.

The Machine Gun Corps was formed in October 1915.

O2-327: John Warnock McLean, Royal Irish Rifles; *d.* 1 January 1915, Laventie, France.

Section H: Roll of Honour Ground

In 1914 a portion of ground, later described as 'the Roll of Honour' ground, was allocated for the burial of First World War soldiers. The first burial in this plot was Rifleman Sturgeon, of the Royal Irish Rifles, who died on 1 December 1914.

C3-799: W.J. Gillespie, Royal Navy; *d.* 15 October 1914, HMS *Hawke.*

C3-Island: Cross of Sacrifice.

Designed by Sir Reginald Bloomfield, it was erected to remember the soldier dead of First World War.

B-22: Sadie Hale, Merchant Marine; *d.* 7 May 1915, SS *Lusitania.*

B-408: Robert Maxwell Maccabe, Post Office Rifles; *d.* 23 April 1915, Givenchy.

F-439: Arthur McLaughlin, Royal Irish Rifles; *d.* 9 May 1915, Frommelles.

On the right surround there is an inscription for his brother George who died at Lindley, South Africa, on 30 May 1900.

F-443: George Horner Gaffikin, Royal Irish Rifles; *d.* 1 July 1916, Somme.

I-93/4: Donard Irvine, Royal Irish Rifles; *d*. 1 July 1916, Somme.

K-346: Edward Workman, Royal Irish Rifles; *d*. 26 January 1916, Le Touquet River Lys.

Edward was awarded the Military Cross (MC). This decoration was introduced on 28 December 1914 and was only given to junior officers at the rank of captain and below. During the First World War 37,081 MCs were awarded.

K-289: Walter Newell, Black Watch; *d*. 10 July 1915.

Headstone refers to Old Military Cemetery, Wangerie, Lavantie as burial site. CWGC lists Rue-David Military Cemetery, Fleurbaix, as gravesite. Headstone includes his brothers, David, who died on 13 March 1916, and George, who died on 7 August 1917.

H-439: Reverend John Davis, Royal Army Medical Corps; *d*. 22 July 1917, Amara, Mesopotamia.

H-45/46: Cecil Reginald Crymble, Royal Irish Fusiliers; *d*. 10 November 1914, Houplines, Flanders.

Crymble has the distinction of being the first member of Queen's University to be killed during the First World War.

H-112: Robert Wilson MacDermott, Royal Irish Rifles; *d*. 8 January 1916, Somme.

MacDermott is often referred to as the first officer of the 36th Ulster Division killed in action on the Western Front.

D-215: John Thompson Robinson, Royal Welsh Fusiliers; *d*. 8 September 1918, Ploegsteert, Flanders.

CWGC lists death as 8 September 1916.

D-237/8: Robert Davidson, Kings Liverpool Regiment; *d.* 8 October 1916, Somme.

A2-381: Henry Barton, Black Watch; *d.* 25 August 1917, Ypres, Flanders.

F1-54: Thomas Millar, Royal Navy; *d.* 27 May 1915, HMS *Majestic.*

The battleship *Majestic* was off West Beach, Gallipoli Penisula, when it was torpedoed by the German *U-23*. On 20 July 1915 *U-23* was torpedoed in the North Sea by the British submarine *C-27*. To avoid capture by the enemy *C-27* was blown up by her crew in Helsingfors (Helsinki) Bay on 5 April 1918.

G1-21: Harold Alexander McCrea; *d.* 25 August 1923.

Headstone reads 'As a result of service in Great War'.

G1-109: Richard Shaw Purdy, Royal Inniskilling Fusiliers; *d.* 11 September 1916, Ginchy.

G1-149: Ralph Ireland, Royal Navy; *d.* 19 January 1917, HMS *Southampton*, North Sea.

H1-151: Ernest Victor Todd, New Zealand Expeditionary Force; *d.* 4 October 1917, Ypres, Flanders.

G-17: Lawrence McKisack, Royal Flying Corps;
d. **13 November 1916.**

G-20: Walter Tyrrell, Royal Air Force; *d.* **9 June 1918, France.**

Headstone includes his brother John, who was killed on 20 June 1918.

G-34: David Moore Riddell, The King's Liverpool Regiment; *d.* **23 September 1917.**

Died in the Officers' Hospital, Dublin, from wounds received at Trones Wood, on 12 July 1916.

D2-410/11: Adam Primrose Jenkins, Royal Irish Rifles;
d. **28 August 1928.**

Headstone reads 'As a result of wounds.'

J1-352: William Alan Smiles, Royal Irish Rifles;
d. **9 July 1916, Somme.**

K1-443: Harold Hardy, Royal Irish Rifles;
d. **15 April 1918, Kemmel Hill, Flanders.**

L1-548: Fred Eakin, Royal Fusiliers; *d.* **18 August 1916, Edinburgh War Hospital.**

Fred died from wounds received on 20 July 1916.

M1-1024: Thomas Malcomson Greeves, Royal Naval Air Service; *d.* **23 December 1917, France.**

M1-855: Arthur Galway Morrow, Royal Irish Rifles (YCV); *d.* **1 July 1916, Somme.**

G2-180: William Edwin Davey, Royal Fusiliers;
d. 7 October 1916, Gueudecourt, France.

G2-474: John McIlroy, Royal Irish Rifles; *d.* 15 June
1915, Hooge.

Headstone has inscription for his brother Samuel who died on
1 July 1916.

G2-562: Arthur Mitchell; *d.* 13 February 1925, Military
Hospital, Belfast.

Arthur was a recipient of the DSO (Distinguished Service Order)
and Croix De Guerre.

F2-433: Alexander Kerr, Royal Navy; *d.* 12 March 1917,
HMS Submarine *E-49*, coast of Shetland Islands.

L-391: Gertrude Annie Taylor, VAD; *d.* 12 December
1916, First London Central Hospital, Camberwell.

P-160: William Bridgett, Royal Irish Rifles; *d.* 7 June
1917, Spanbroekmolen Messines, Flanders.

Q-646: John Heatherington Dickson, Royal Air Force;
d. 14 August 1918, France.

N-104: Robert Wallace McConnell, Royal Lancaster
Regiment; *d.* 9 April 1916, Sanna-L-Yat, Mesopotamia.

CONCLUSION

One of the graves on the third walk is the plot of the Ulster Female Penitentiary. Seven women are buried in this double grave which is marked with a small cast-iron shield bearing the name of the penitentiary. We know little of the lives, or the dreams of the women buried in the plot and can only guess at the circumstances which drove them into prostitution and thence into the penitentiary.

The owners of this plot intended that these women remain anonymous. However, later generations of Belfast citizens sought to identify the seven women, and in doing so pay homage to the women of Victorian Belfast. In the confrontation between our lack of knowledge and our need for knowledge about these women, we realise that there is little difference between the anonymity imposed in a grave inscription by an institution, and the anonymity imposed in an inscription by 'her loving husband'. How ironic that the nameless women of the female penitentiary symbolise the repression and neglect of the history of all women of Belfast. Such neglect needs to be confronted and replaced with interest and exposure. Prostitute and teacher, suffragette and heiress, mill worker and wife, daughter and artist, nun and nurse, all their histories are revealed in the exposure given to the seven women of the Ulster Female Penitentiary.

The Belfast City Cemetery is more than a burial site or a collection of headstones and monuments. On the inscriptions on headstones and in the varied symbolism, hidden among the pauper dead, buried with the rich and powerful, are countless historical treasures.

The cemetery tells us about education, or lack of it; about the mill workers and their struggles and the great gulf that separated them from the mill owners; about industrialist and their industries; about the poor, kept out of sight and out of mind; about separate gates and underground walls; about the Presbyterian mercantile elite. We encounter stories of world wars – the young soldier killed on a far away battlefield, men of the Luftwaffe and Wehrmacht, submariners and men with kilts and bagpipes, soldiers and administrators of empire, emigration from Russia and a new life for Jewish families in Belfast. We find lack of education for women; the wasted lives of children; the ravages of cyclical disease, doctors and their hospitals; solicitors and human rights lawyers. We meet Orangemen and Orange women; members of the Masonic order (their symbolism discreet but ever-present); see the rise of Ulster unionism, the role of UVF gunrunners and their political leaders; are shown the republican blanket man, the assassinated Catholic, artisans and craftsmen, historians and writers, clergymen and the lone parish priest, heretics and lunatics, stone crosses and monuments, flowers in all their beauty cut in stone, obelisks and urns, anchors and headstones, sandstone, limestone, granite and slate, the soil from which we came and to where we return.

In death every soul in the cemetery demands to be heard. They are the historical foundations on which we view our past and as such they enrich our present with the stories of their lives. So be curious about the dead in Belfast City Cemetery – they have much to offer us.

APPENDICES

APPENDIX 1

The Falls Park

Prior to the opening of the Belfast Cemetery in 1869 the Belfast Corporation decided that 57 acres of the new Falls Road site were surplus to the requirements of the new cemetery. They passed a resolution, 1 November 1869, to establish a public park using the surplus land. However, as the surplus land was outside the borough, this resolution was ultra vires. By 1872, a new Act of Parliament, the Public Parks (Ireland) Act (1869), Amendment Act (1872) gave the Corporation the legal right to establish, maintain and regulate parks. The Provisional Order Confirmation Act (1873) allowed the council to proceed in the planning of a new park. Soon after, 13 of the 57 acres were to be returned to the cemetery.

On 22 December 1875, the Cemetery Committee's report for the January 1876 council meeting states, 'The Parks Committee having lodged to the credit of the Burial Fund the sum of £5,000 in payment of the purchase money of the lands on which the Falls Park has been established. Your committee have signed cheques to pay off mortgages on the Burial Fund to that amount.' The new park, formally named the Falls Park, opened its gates to the public in January 1876. In 1877, Barney Hughes donated £50 for the erection of a drinking fountain. The Rangers lodge, costing £230, was erected in 1879 and by 1887 a new bridge was built over the river that ran through the centre of the park. Work began on the bandstand in August 1900 and on the bowling green in January 1901. During the First World War, and until 1921, 145 allotments were rented out to the Garden Plots' Association. By the 1920s, 5 football pitches, 2 tennis courts and 2 cricket creases had been added to the facilities in the park.

APPENDIX 2

Proprietary graves by section, Belfast Cemetery 1869

Proprietary graves were located in sections A to S in the inner core; sections A1 to M1 located along the proposed southern boundary, now the Falls Park; sections A2 to H2 located on the main avenue which runs along the westward rim of the bell. K2 to Q2 located along the Whiterock Road perimeter. (There is no section E2).

A study of these sections reveals the underlying class ethos found in the layout of the new cemetery. Sections D, E, G, H, K, L, M, I, are all located inside the bell. The inner core of the graveyard contains the majority of 'select' and 'class 1' graves. These were the graves sold to the elite of Victorian Belfast.

Those who could only afford to buy one of the cheaper graves were buried in the rear sections of the bell or outside the bell, but still within sight of the rich and powerful.

Paupers' graves were located at the very back of the new cemetery, outside the bell and out of sight, and alphabetically listed as Sections A, B, D, E, F, G, H, I, J.

APPENDIX 3

Memorial stones listed as having special architectural and historic interest

Q-660/1	Phillips cross
D-203	William Henry Lynn
C2-248	Inglis stone
Sections J and K	Gallaher vaults
L-153	Herdman monument
M-454	Stelfox monument
Q-723	Alan Campbell Carson

Originally, there were eight memorial stones listed, the eighth being the Pirrie stone, **K-468/9**. This stone was removed by Harland and Wolff as a result of vandalism.

APPENDIX 4

First World War memorial inscriptions on family headstones

In the Belfast City Cemetery I have found 253 family headstones which carry inscriptions in memory of 254 military personnel, 4 members of the merchant marine, 2 nurses and 2 civilians, who lost their lives during the First World War. Nine of these stones carry inscriptions for two brothers; the Newell stone (**K-289**), which appears to be a family grave designed as a war memorial, carries inscriptions for three brothers and the Corry/Osborne stone (**D-435/6**) carries inscriptions for an uncle and nephew. The Lees stone (**I-571**) carries inscriptions for two cousins. The McLaughlin stone (**F-439**) carries an inscription for a soldier of the Boer war and a First World War soldier. Two soldiers, Agnew and Holywood, are each remembered on two headstones.

Some stones carry the name of battlefield sites; others carry the location of military graveyards which were used to inter the remains of soldiers from neighbouring battlefields. These graveyards were often located in the vicinity of a field hospital. Inscriptions often relate 'killed in action' or 'died of wounds' and give no other details. Many soldiers were killed in the daily grind of trench warfare and are remembered on memorials scattered along the Western Front.

The confusion of battles where thousands of men lost their lives is, in a small number of cases, reflected on family headstones where dates of death differ from the dates held by the CWGC. In the cases of two soldiers there is no location of death. Many soldiers who received wounds on the Ypres Salient were removed to hospitals in northern France. The largest number of First World

War inscriptions refers to the Somme and the Ypres Salient.

Among the 254 military personnel remembered are 91 soldiers of the Royal Irish Rifles – 5 of these soldiers have YCV (Young Citizen Volunteers) inscripted on their headstones. There are 17 Royal Irish Fusiliers, 17 Inniskilling Fusiliers, a member of the Tank Corp, a driver in a Horse Transport Coy, 6 Royal Navy sailors (1 being a submariner), 4 sailors of the Merchant Marine, a soldier of the Royal Marine Light Infantry who died on HMS *Indefatigable*, 5 airmen of the Royal Flying Corps, 1 of the Royal Naval Air Service and 3 from the Royal Air Force. There are two women mentioned, both VADs involved in hospital work. There are 17 Canadian soldiers, 2 Australians, 3 New Zealanders, 1 Indian Army Reserve who served with a Gurkha Regiment, a soldier of the 2/21 Battalion Punjabis (Indian army), 1 South African soldier, 1 soldier of the American Expeditionary Force and 3 POWs who died in Germany. There are Dublin Fusiliers, a Connaught Ranger, a Munster Fusilier, a soldier of the London Irish Rifles, a Welsh Fusilier, a soldier of the Durham Light Infantry, a Northumberland Fusilier, and a soldier of the Post Office Rifles. There are the 'kilted regiments' – the Black Watch, Cameron and Seaforth Highlanders, along with the Royal Scots, the Border Regiment and the King's Own Scottish Borders.

There are a few inscriptions which refer to brothers whose dates of death are very close. The Malone brothers (**K-273**) died within three months of each other in 1917. The Tyrrell brothers (**G-20**) died within eleven days of each other in 1918.

There are 5 inscriptions for 1914. The number increases in 1915 to 31. The largest number of inscriptions for any one year is 1916, which has eighty-eight. The figure decreases in 1917 to sixty-six, with a further decrease in 1918 to fifty-two. There are six for 1919, three for 1920, two for 1921, two for 1923, one for 1924, two for 1925, one for 1927, one for 1928, one for 1929, one for 1938, and one for 1941. Long after the end of the First World War, soldiers continued to die from wounds received during that conflict. There are a small number of inscriptions, which reflect this.

Of the 79 inscriptions which remember the Royal Irish Rifles, there is one for 1914, six for 1915, forty-four for 1916 and seventeen for 1917, while 1918 has nineteen, 1919 has one, as does 1925. There are twenty-five for 1 July 1916, the first day of the Battle of the Somme.

Summary of names by year found on inscriptions on family headstones

CWGC refers to the Commonwealth War Graves Commission

1914	**H. Carlisle,** Irish Guards *d.* 14 September with British Expeditionary Force. Marne River	P2-581
	W. J. Gillespie, Royal Navy *d.* 15 October. HMS *Hawke*	C3-799
	Robert Macpherson Adair, Royal Irish Rifles *d*: 25 October. France	E-430
	James Green, civilian *d.* 1 November *Inscription reads 'Submarined 1914'*	Q-215
	Cecil Reginald Crymble, Royal Irish Fusiliers *d.* 10 November. Houplines, Flanders	H-45/46
1915	**John Warnock McLean,** Royal Irish Rifles *d.* 1 January. Laventie, France	O2-327
	George Morris, Gloucestershire Regiment *d.* 7 February. France *CWGC gives Ypres, Belgium as memorial site*	K-224
	Walter McCurry, Royal Army Medical Corps *d.* 14 March. Ypres, Flanders	D2-362
	Charles Bell, Royal Irish Fusiliers *d.* 23 April. France *CWGC gives Ypres, Belgium as memorial site*	D3-59
	Robert Maxwell Maccabe, Post Office Rifles *d.* 23 April. Givenchy, France	B-408
	John Crangle, Royal Irish Fusiliers *d.* 30 April. Ypres, Flanders	B-407

Sadie Hale, Merchant Marine *d.* 7 May.   B-22
SS *Lusitania*

Frank Houston, civilian *d.* 7 May.   A-15
SS *Lusitania*

Gordon William Lockhart,   L1-501
NZ Expeditionary Force *d.* 8 May.
Cape Helles, Dardanelles

Robert Magee, Princess Patricia's   H2-227
Canadian Light Infantry *d.* 8 May.
Ypres Flanders

Joseph Wilson, Kings Royal Rifle Corps   G-413
d. 8 May. Hooge, Flanders

Arthur Bourke, Royal Irish Fusiliers   N-704
d. 9 May. France

Arthur McLaughlin, Royal Irish Rifles   F-439
d. 9 May. Frommelles
The family headstone has an inscription for
his brother **George** *d. 30 May 1900*
 at Lindley, South Africa

William Leigh Maxwell, Balugh Light   J-213
Infantry *d.* 9 May. Gallipoli
CWGC shows Royal Marines

Victor Gadd, Royal Navy *d.* 15 May 1915.   M-317
HMS *Goliath*, Dardanelle Straits
Victor is described as Boy 1st Class. HMS Goliath
was torpedoed by the Turkish destroyer
Muavenet-I-Milet *off De Tott's battery, Dardanelles*

Charles Ernest Cooke, Royal Irish Fusiliers   J-245
d. 26 May. Ypres
CWGC lists date of death as 25 May 1915

Thomas Millar, Royal Navy *d.* 27 May   F1-54
HMS *Majestic* torpedoed, Gallipoli Peninsula

John McIlroy, Royal Irish Rifles   G2-474
d. 15 June Hooge, Flanders
Headstone has inscription for his brother
Samuel *d. 1 July 1916*

James Davison, Royal Engineers *d.* 16 June   M2-508

Edwin Blow Kertland, Royal Irish Fusiliers   E-123
d. 16 June. Hooge, Flanders

James Denning Willis, Black Watch   D-305
d. 10 July, France
CWGC gives Rue-David Military Cemetery,
Fleurbaix as gravesite

Walter Newell, Black Watch *d.* 10 July   K-289
Wangerie, Lavantie
CWGC lists Rue-David Military
Cemetery, Fleurbaix as gravesite. |
Headstone includes his brothers **David**
d. 13 March 1916, and **George,**
d. 7 August 1917.

Richard Reid, Royal Inniskilling   P-343 Glen
Fusiliers *d.* 6 August. Dardanelles

William Lavery, Australian Infantry   P2-873
Australian Imperial Force *d.* 9 August.
Gallipoli

John Gallagher, Royal Irish Rifles   L-223
d. 10 August. Gallipoli

James Henry Robinson, Royal Irish Rifles   L1-262
d. 10 August. Gallipoli

William Bloomer, Royal Inniskilling   H-166 Glen
Fusiliers *d.* 15 August. Dardanelles
See also his son, **W. Bloomer,**
Royal Inniskilling Fusiliers
d. 18 February, 1943 in Burma

Joseph Smyth, Black Watch   N-448
d. 25 September. Loos, France

Robert Hamilton, *d.* 13 October   G-335 Glen

Samuel McCracken, Canadian Infantry   M1-847
d. 20 October. Flanders

John Archibald McReynolds,   B-60 Glen
Royal Irish Rifles *d.* 22 December. France

1916 **Robert Wilson MacDermott,**   H-112
Royal Irish Rifles *d.* 8 January. France
MacDermott is often referred to as the first
officer of the 36th Ulster Division killed
in action on the Western Front

Edward Workman, Royal Irish Rifles   K-346
d. 26 January. le Touquet River Lys, France
Edward was awarded the Military Cross (MC)

James McBurney, *d.* 4 February France   A2-436

John Beck McDowell, Royal Fusiliers   H2-710
d. 13 March. Givenchy, France

David Newell, Royal Fusiliers, *d.* 13 March.   K-289
Buried, Cambrin Pas de Calais, France
Inscription includes his brothers **Walter**
d. 10 July 1915, and **George** *d. 17 August 1917*

John K. Bell, Royal Irish Rifles   P-353 Glen
d. 29 March. Miraumont, France

Robert Wallace McConnell, Royal   N-104
Lancaster Regt *d.* 9 April. Sanna-L-Yat
Mesopotamia

Neville Dutton Clarke, Royal Irish Rifles   I-23
d. 18 April, buried Belfast City Cemetery
CWGC lists date of death as 10 April 1916

Tom Martin, Royal Irish Rifles *d.* 6 May.   B2-340
France

Herbert Curran, Royal Fusiliers   P-313
d. 7 May. France

William James McCausland, Royal Marine   M1-18
Light Infantry *d.* 31 May. HMS *Indefatigable*,
Battle of Jutland

Richard Jefferson, Canadian Infantry   N-750
d. 3 June. Ypres, Flanders

Samuel Gorman, Royal Irish Rifles   C-16
d. 6 June. France

Robert McCalmont Pettigrew,   M-280
Royal Irish Rifles *d.* 10 June. France

Sidney Johnston, Canadian Infantry   **J1-31**
d. 13 June. Flanders
Sidney was the son of John A. Johnston,
Superintendent of the Harbour Police, Belfast,
a force first appointed in 1824.

John Henry Davis, Royal Army Medical   **H2-628**
Corps *d.* 21 June. Liverpool, England

Harry Whelan Holywood, Seaforth   **J1–66 Glen**
Highlander *d.* 29 June. St Eloi, France
Harry is remembered on a second
headstone, **L2-38**

Ernest George Boas, Royal Irish Rifles   **B-95 Glen**
d. 1 July. Somme, France

Samuel Bond, Royal Irish Rifles   **A2-219**
d. 1 July. Somme, France

George Burns, Royal Irish Rifles   **A-426**
d. 1 July. Beaumont Hamel, France

William Bustard, Royal Irish Rifles   **O-180 Glen**
d. 1 July. Thiepval, France

James Samuel Davidson, Royal Irish Rifles   **D-245**
d. 1 July. Thiepval, France

George Dunwoody, Royal Irish Rifles   **H1-439**
d. 1 July. Somme, France

George Horner Gaffikin, Royal Irish Rifles   **F-442**
d. 1 July. Somme, France

Albert Gibson, Royal Inniskilling Fusiliers   **A-502**
d. 1 July. Somme, France

William Henry Gregg, Royal Irish Rifles   **G-591**
d. 1 July. Somme, France

Robert Victor Hamilton, Royal Irish Rifles   **R-537**
d. 1 July. Somme, France

Robert John Johnston, Royal Irish Rifles   **O-557**
d. 1 July. Somme, France

James Johnston, Royal Irish Rifles   **C3-782**
d. 1 July. Thiepval, France

James Laughlin, Kings Liverpool Regiment   **B-17/18**
d. 1 July. Somme, France

Archie Lemon, Royal Irish Rifles   **O-13 Glen**
d. 1 July. Thiepval, France

Sidney Todd Martin, Royal Inniskilling   **B-9**
Fusiliers *d.* 1 July. Thiepval, France

Harry McCashin, Royal Irish Rifles (YCV)   **H-247**
d. 1 July Somme, France

Thomas McCurry, Royal Inniskilling   **M2-20**
Fusiliers *d.* 1 July. Somme, France

Samuel McIlroy, Royal Irish Rifles   **G2-474**
d. 1 July. Somme, France
Headstone includes his brother
John *d. 1 June 1915*

Thomas McIlvenny, Royal Irish Rifles   **I1-134**
d. 1 July. Thiepval, France

Richard McNamara, Royal Irish Rifles   **C3-783**
d. 1 July. Somme, France

George Molyneux, Royal Irish Rifles   **C2-59/60**
d. 1 July. Somme, France
The name on the headstone reads
Molyneaux

Arthur Galway Morrow, Royal Irish   **M1-855**
Rifles (YCV) *d.* 1 July. Somme, France

James Mullan, Royal Irish Rifles   **C-155 Glen**
d. 1 July Thiepval, France

James Murdoch, Royal Irish Rifles   **M-488**
(YCV) *d.* 1 July. Somme, France
CWGC lists a **James S. Murdock**
14th Royal Irish Rifles,
date of death 1 September 1916

Douglas Hill O'Flaherty, Royal Irish Rifles   **Q-670**
d. 1 July. Somme, France

Samuel Porter, Royal Irish Rifles   **I1-83**
d. 1 July. Somme, France

Robert Rodgers, Royal Irish Rifles   P2-472
(YCV) *d.* 1 July. Somme
Headstone has inscription for brother **James**
d. 30 April 1918

Charles Slacke, Royal Irish Rifles *d.* 1 July.   G-631/2
Thiepval, France

Donard Irvine, Royal Irish Rifles   I-93/4
d. 1 July. Somme, France

George C. Keenan, Royal Irish Rifles   H1-387
d. 2 July. Somme, France

John Kells, Royal Irish Rifles *d.* 2 July.   N2-337
Somme, France

William George McCaw, Royal Irish   N2-108
Rifles *d.* 2 July. Somme, France

T. Sillars, Royal Irish Rifles *d.* 2 July   N-134 Glen
Grandcourt. France

David Bertram Corbett, Royal Irish   B-100 Glen
Rifles *d.* 3 July. Martinsart, France

John Stewart McClinton, South Lancashire   B-386
Regiment *d.* 5 July. Thiepval, France

William Clarke McConnell, Royal Irish   K-378/9
Rifles *d.* 8 July. Somme, France
CWGC lists date death as 9 July 1916

Robert Kernaghan, Royal Irish Rifles   R-451
d. 9 July. Somme, France

William Alan Smiles, Royal Irish Rifles   J1-352
d. 9 July. Ovillers, France

Robert McMaster, Royal Inniskilling   N-242 Glen
Fusiliers *d.* 10 July. Somme, France

John Stanley Knox, Royal Inniskilling   C2-345
Fusiliers *d.* 11 July. France

James C. Campbell, Black Watch   B-13 Glen
d. 14 July. Longueval, France

William Thomas Lyons, Royal Lancaster   N-456
Regt *d.* 18 July. Somme, France

Headstone has inscription for his brother
Robert Victor *d. 24 March 1918*

Victor Harold Robb, Royal Irish Rifles   **I-39**
d. 22 July
CWGC lists date of death as 3 July 1916

Hugh Corry Osborne, West Yorkshire   **D-435/6**
Regiment *d.* 24 July. Somme, France
CWGC lists date of death as 23 July 1916.
Inscription refers to his uncle **Alexander Corry**
d. 12 October 1917 on SS WM Barkley

William Kinnear Dobbin, Royal Fusiliers   **C-10/11**
d. 27 July. Delville Wood, France

Frederick John Carton, Canadian Infantry   **G2-158**
d. 3 August. Ypres, Flanders

Oliver Bradshaw, Canadian Infantry   **B2-139**
d. 11 August. Flanders

Fred Graham, Cameron Highlander   **B1-245**
d. 16 August. Flanders
CWGC lists date of death as 17 August 1916

Fred Eakin, Royal Fusiliers   **L1-548**
d. 18 August. Edinburgh War Hospital
Died as a result of wounds received
20 July 1916

Adam Clarke Capper, Royal Irish Rifles   **C2-443**
d. 9 September. Somme, France

Joey Harper, Royal Inniskilling Fusiliers   **B2-241**
d. 9 September. Givenchy, France

William Morgan, Royal Inniskilling   **F2-116**
Fusiliers *d.* 9 September. Somme, France

Richard Shaw Purdy, Royal Inniskilling   **G1-109**
Fusiliers *d.* 11 September. Ginchy, France

Willie Haveron, Royal Scots   **M-676**
d. 15 September. Somme, France

John Clarke, Canadian Infantry   **O-39 Glen**
d. 26 September. Northern France

John Bradley Grierson, Canadian Infantry   Q-63
d. 27 September. France

William Edwin Davey, Royal Fusiliers   G2-180
d. 7 October. Gueudecourt, France

Robert Davison, Kings Liverpool Regt   D-237/8
d. 8 October. Somme, France

Harold Richards, Essex Fusiliers Canada   L1-515
d. 21 October

Trevor Moutray Bennet, Royal Flying Corps   J1-352
d. 10 November. France

Lawrence McKisack, Royal Flying Corps   G-17
d. 13 November. Buried in City Cemetery

William Lowson, Royal Scots   A2-23
d. 17 November. Beaumont-Hamel, France

Joseph Weir, Border Regiment   F2-472
d. 18 November. France

John Campbell, Canadian Infantry   G1-71
d. 25 November. France

J. H. Ghion, Royal Irish Rifles   C-119 Glen
d. 25 November. Buried in City Cemetery

Joseph Samuel Cully, Royal Engineers   C-131 Glen
d. 28 November. Belfast

Charles Ferris Beverland, Royal   H1-126
Inniskilling Fusiliers *d.* 4 December. France

Archie Maginnes, Royal Irish Rifles   H2-94
d. 7 December. Somme, France
CWGC lists death as 7 December 1915

Gertrude Annie Taylor, VAD   L-391
d. 12 December. London Central Hospital,
Camberwell

Richard Ernest Sweeney, Army Service   K1-428
Corps *d.* 21 December. Karasouli, Greece

John Gordon Crymble, Royal Irish Fusiliers   E-444
d. 28 December. Bailleul, France

1917 **Walter MacDonald,** *d.* 1917, France   **E-143 Glen**
   No other details known

   Ralph Ireland, Royal Navy *d.* 19 January.   **G1-149**
   HMS *Southampton*, North Sea

   Reginald McConnell, Kings Own Scottish   **G-192**
   Borderers *d.* 22 January. Arras, France

   Elizabeth du Mesney, VAD *d.* 14 February.   **I-178**
   Waverley Abbey Military Hospital
   Burial records give her name as
   Winifred Elizabeth Atkinson

   John Jack, Canadian Machine Gun Corps   **J1-267**
   d. 12 March. France

   Alexander Kerr, Royal Navy *d.* 12 March.   **F2-433**
   HMS *E-49*, coast of Shetland Islands

   James A.V. Currie, London Regiment   **J-41 Glen**
   d. 13 March. Arras, France

   Robert Alfred Brown, Seaforth Highlander   **N-368**
   d. 9 April. Arras, France

   Robert James Johnston, Black Watch   **M2-331**
   d. 9 April. France

   Hugh Charles Allen, Black Watch   **Q-632**
   d. 23 April. Fampoux, France

   Alexander Turnbull, Royal Flying Corps   **K1-388**
   d. 25 April. France

   Frederick Williamson, Gurkha Rifles,   **H-393/4/5**
   and Indian Army Reserve *d.* 10 May. India

   William Adolph Malone, Cheshire Regiment   **K-273**
   d. 16 May. Ploegsteert Wood, Flanders
   Headstone includes his brother
   Bristow Miniss *d. 16 August 1917*

   David Collins, Black Watch *d.* 17 May.   **G-447**
   Arras, France

   Jim Marshall, Royal Inniskilling Fusiliers   **E1-397**
   d. 19 May. Arras, France

Alfred Douglas Kennedy, 2nd Canadian   K1-10/11
Mounted Rifles *d*. 20 May. France

George Stanley Sinclair, Royal Irish Rifles   F-227/9
d. 28 May. Peronne, France

Robert Galway Hume, Merchant Marine   I-38 Glen
d. 6 June SS *St Paul*.

William Bridgett, Royal Irish Rifles *d*. 7 June.   P-160
Spanbroekmolen Messines, Flanders

Sydney Downey, Royal Irish Rifles *d*. 7 June,   G-12
Spanbroekmolen Messines, Flanders

Richard Dixon, Royal Irish Rifles *d*. 7 June.   P-227
Messines, Flanders

William Ferris, Royal Irish Rifles *d*. 7 June.   M-941/2
Messines, Flanders

Arthur McBride, Royal Irish Rifles *d*. 7 June.   K-408
Messines, Flanders

George Brankin, Royal Irish Rifles (YCV)   L-319
d. 8 June. France

William Charles Brown, Royal Army   G-84
Medical Corps *d*. 30 June. Buried in
City Cemetery

Jack Crichton, Canadian Infantry   B2-531/2
d. 5 July. France

Isaac McConnell, Royal Engineers   J-78
d. 9 July. Flanders

Rev John Davis, Royal Army Medical Corps   H-439
d. 22 July. Amara, Mesopotamia

William Doggart, Canadian Highland   P2-918
Infantry *d*. 26 July. France

Alfred Squire Taylor, Royal Army Medical   H-35
Corps *d*. 31 July. Flanders

Harold Edwin Todd, Yorkshire Regiment   I1-245
d. 1 August. Ypres, Flanders

Richard Ivan Robson, Royal Irish Rifles   K-572
d. 6 August. Ypres, Flanders

George Newell, Royal Irish Rifles   K-289
d. 7 August. Ypres

John Cowan Adams, Royal Field Artillery   G1-423
d. 11 August. Flanders

Cyril Cullen, Royal Irish Fusiliers   N-539
d. 16 August. Ypres, Flanders

Walter Stanley Gimson, Kings Own   P-288
Yorkshire Light Infantry *d.* 16 August.
Langemarck, Flanders

Adam Darley Hill, Royal Irish Rifles   M-278
d. 16 August. Frezenberg, Flanders

Hugh Kennedy, Royal Irish Rifles   K-178
d. 16 August. France
Inscription reads 'Killed in action in France';
CWGC lists Tyne Cot Memorial on Ypres Salient

Bristow Malone, Royal Irish Fusiliers   K-273
d. 16 August. Ypres, Flanders
Headstone includes his brother **William Adolph**
d. 16 May 1917

William Mathew Seymour, Royal Irish   C-224 Glen
Fusiliers *d.* 16 August. Ypres, Flanders

Samuel Smiles, Royal Irish Rifles   J1-352
d. 16 August. Flanders

Robert Alexander Scilley, Canadian Infantry   C2-124
d. 21 August. Lens, France
Inscription includes his brother **James Frederick,**
killed in action 22 January 1918

Henry Barton, Black Watch *d.* 25 August.   A2-381
France
Inscription reads 'Killed in action, France';
CWGC lists Tyne Cot Memorial on
Ypres Salient

David Stanley Wilkinson, Royal Flying Corps   E-450
d. 26 August. Flanders

Victor Harold Morgan, The King's Liverpool   F-356
Regiment *d.* 6 September. Ypres, Flanders

David Hall, Royal Field Artillery   B3-766
d. 20 September. Flanders

James Gray Ronaldson, The Queen's   G1-186
(Royal West Surrey Regiment)
d. 20 September. Menin Road, Flanders

David Moore Riddell, The King's Liverpool   G-34
Regiment *d.* 23 September

Herbert Nixon, Australian Imperial Force   K1-371
d. 1 October. Zonnebeke, Flanders

Ernest Victor Todd, New Zealand   H1-151
Expeditionary Force *d.* 4 October. France
Inscription reads 'Killed in action, France';
CWGC lists Tyne Cot Memorial on Ypres Salient

John Magee Freckelton, Royal Field   G1-565
Artillery *d.* 11 October. Flanders

Alexander Corry, Merchant Marine   D-435/6
d. 12 October. Dublin Bay
Inscription refers to his nephew **Hugh Corry**
Osborne, *killed in action 24 July 1916*

Robert James McCullough, Cheshire   K-345
Regiment *d.* 22 October. France

Johnston Tate, Royal Irish Fusiliers   C2-98
d. 7 November. Palestine

John Hamilton, Royal Irish Rifles   G2-533
d. 22 November. Cambria, France

George York Henderson, Royal Irish Rifles   M-947/9
d. 22 November. France

Thomas Simms, Royal Irish Rifles   O-463
d. 22 November Cambria, France
Inscription reads 'Killed in action
22 November in Cambria'; CWGC lists
Tyne Cot Memorial on Ypres Salient

Cecil Vincent Boyd, Royal Irish Rifles   M-960
d. 23 November. Cambria, France

Hugh Fisher, Royal Munster Fusiliers   P2-212
d. 23 November. Flanders

Robert Rankin, Royal Irish Rifles   H1-97
d. 23 November. Cambrai, France

Robert Loyd Thompson, Royal Field   H-474/5/6
Artillery *d.* 1 December. Cambrai, France

William Wilson McBride, Royal Garrison   C2-275
Artillery *d.* 5 December. Northern Italy

Bass Durant Capper, Royal Flying Corps   K-29
d. 6 December. Buried in City Cemetery

John Doonan, London Irish Rifles   O-415 Glen
d. 23 December Palestine
Headstone includes his brother Frederick J.
Doonan, *late 9th Battalion Royal Inniskilling
Fusiliers, d. 10 July 1923*

Thomas Malcomson Greeves, Royal   M1-1024
Naval Air Service *d.* 23 December. France

Thomas Taft, Durham Light Infantry   H-412
d. 23 December. France

1918 James Frederick Scilley, Royal Irish Rifles   C2-124
d. 22 January. St Quentin, France
Inscription includes his brother Robert
Alexander, *killed in action 21 August 1917*

John Brown, Royal Irish Rifles   H1-130
d. 21 March. St Quentin, France

Edward Burnside, Royal Irish Rifles   F2-518
d. 21 March. St Quentin, France

Robert Thompson Finnegan, Army Service   H2-714
Corp *d.* 21 March. St Quentin, France

Dalton Prentor, Royal Irish Fusiliers   F-47
d. 21 March. St Quentin, France

John Crawford Thompson, Royal Irish   D2-407
Rifles *d.* 21 March. France

Andrew Veighey, Royal Irish Rifles   N-266 Glen
d. 21 March. Pozieres, France

Norman Lowden, Royal Inniskilling Fusiliers   Q-28
d. 22 March. St Quentin, France

James G. Marks, Seaforth   C-37/38 Glen
Highlanders *d*. 23 March. Lebucquiere,
France

Robert Victor Lyons, Royal Irish Rifles   N-456
d. 24 March. Somme, France
Headstone includes his brother
William Thomas *d. 18 July 1916*

William Frederick MacHutchison, Royal   C2-76
Dublin Fusiliers *d*. 27 March. France

William Thompson, Royal Irish Rifles   R-498
d. 27 March. France

Unknown sailor, *d*. 31 March. SS *Celtic*   P-191

Robert Bodie, Merchant Marine   P-191 Glen*
d. 31 March. SS *Celtic*

William Gleave, Merchant Marine   P-191 Glen*
d. 31 March. SS *Celtic*

George Richardson, Merchant Marine   P-191 Glen
d. 31 March. SS *Celtic*

Samuel Routledge, Merchant Marine   P-191 Glen*
d. 31 March. SS *Celtic*

Stanley MacDonald, Merchant Marine   P-167 Glen
d. 31 March. SS *Celtic*

Jim Murray, Northumberland Fusiliers   A-33 Glen
d. 11 April. Flanders

Harold Hardy, Royal Irish Rifles,   K1-443
d. 15 April. Kemmel Hill, Flanders

Henry Murray, Royal Irish Rifles   L-710
d. 15 April. Messines, Flanders

James Stuart Steele, Royal Fusiliers   R-228
d. 24 April. Hangard Wood, France

Fred Lewis, Royal Irish Rifles *d*. 29 April.   L-653
Flanders

---

*On these headstones the names are incorrectly spelt: Bodie as Rodie, Gleave as Cleaave, and Routledge as Routleidge

James Rodgers, Royal Engineers   P2-472
d. 30 April Ypres, Flanders
Headstone includes his brother **Robert**
d. 1 July 1916

George Cecil Molyneaux, Royal Air Force   H-14 Glen
d. 11 May. Buried in City Cemetery
*Based at Ruislip in Middlesex (later London
Heathrow Airport). He was 21 when he died.
Belfast address was 10 Ulsterville Gardens.*

Samuel McAllister, Royal Army Medical   D-323 Glen*
Corps (POW) *d.* 15 May. Roye, France

Walter Tyrrell, Royal Air Force *d.* 9 June.   G-20
France
Headstone includes his brother
John *d. 20 June 1918*

James Leathem, Army Service Corp   M-317
d. 18 June. France

John Marcus Tyrrell, Royal Air Force   G-20
d. 20 June. France
Headstone includes his brother
Walter *d. 9 June 1918*

Kenneth Malcolm Agnew, Royal Irish   N-81
Rifles (POW) *d.* 25 June Hanover Germany

John Douglas Hazelton, Canadian Infantry   B-73/4
d. 25 June. France

Ashley Albert Miln, Royal Irish Rifles   K2-136
(POW) *d.* 19 July. Germany

James Ireland, Royal Field Artillery   H1-543
d. 24 July. Buried in City Cemetery

Robert McIntyre, East Yorkshire Regiment   K1-422
d. 25 July. France

William Percival Vint, Machine Gun Corps   I-11/12
d. 5 August. France

---

*Between August 1914 and November 1918, 175,000 soldiers of the British Expeditionary
Force were taken prisoner in France and Flanders. Approximately 14,000 of them died
while being held captive.

John Heatherington Dickson, Royal Air
Force, *d*. 14 August. France   Q-646

William Browne, Royal Irish Rifles
d. 18 August. France   N-34 Glen

James Lowry Lees, Tank Corps
d. 23 August. France
Headstone includes his cousin **Lowry Lees**
d. *16 October 1918*   I-571

Edward Leslie Marshall, Royal Inniskilling
Fusiliers *d*. 1 September. France   N-92

William Timbey, Royal Irish Fusiliers
d. 4 September. Flanders   B-352 Glen

William Frederick Vance, Royal Irish
Fusiliers *d*. 5 September. France   Q-49 Glen

Robert Shaw, Royal Irish Fusiliers
d. 6 September. Bailleul, France   M1-74

John Thompson Robinson, Royal Welsh
Fusiliers *d*. 8 September. Ploegsteert, Flanders
CWGC lists death as 8 September 1916   D-215

George Donnelly, Royal Irish Rifles
d. 9 September. France   H2-520

John Agnew, 339th Infantry Regiment
American Expeditionary Force
d. 27 Sept. Russia
*John is also remembered on the Agnew
family headstone* (**O-675**)   L-540

Francis Henry Hall, Royal Irish Fusiliers
d. 30 September. Ypres, Flanders   I-129

James B. Johnston, Royal Naval Volunteer
Reserve *d*. 8 October Cambrai, France   I1-9

Samuel Kerr, Royal Inniskilling Fusiliers
d. 8 October. Le Oatelet, France
Headstone includes his brother
James *d*. *28 October 1920*   N-486

Stanley Law, Connaught Ranger
d. 9 October. France   N2-405

Robert Spence, Royal Irish Rifles   **I-362**
d. 15 October. France

Lowry Lees, London Scottish Regiment,   **I-571**
d. 16 October. Ypres, Flanders
CWGC gives date of death as
14 October. Headstone refers to his
cousin James *d. 23 August 1918.*

Alexander Kerr, Royal Irish Rifles   **Q-85 Glen**
d. 25 October. Ypres, Flanders
See also Robert Kerr
d. 15 December 1940 ·

Harold Percival Nixon, Wiltshire Regiment   **H2-553**
d. 26 October. Flanders

Robert Mortimer, Royal Irish Rifles   **C-42 Glen**
d. 27 October. Fargo Military Hospital,
Salisbury Plain

Harry Leebody Weir, Royal Irish Rifles,   **O-540**
(POW) *d.* 28 October
Cologne Germany

William McCormick, Royal Irish Fusiliers   **L1-647**
d. 3 November. Flanders

Arthur McClelland, 4th Horse Transport   **G2-134**
Coy, Army Service Corps *d.* 10 November.
Cambrai, France

Samuel Gatensby, Royal Irish Rifles,   **H3-55**
d. 24 November. Buried in City Cemetery

1919 **Stanley Nixon,** Royal Air Force   **N-318**
d. 1 January. France
CWGC lists his regiment as 'Princess
Patricia's Canadian Light Infantry'

Herbert Barnes, 4th Hussars   **M1-1002**
d. 22 February.
Buried in the City Cemetery
Herbert's family is listed in the British
military records as serving continuously
with the 4th Hussars since 1715

Thomas Stephenson, Royal Irish Rifles   O-513
d. 2 March
Thomas was awarded the Distinguished
Conduct Medal (DCM). His headstone lists his
regiment as the 14th RIR. CWGC lists his
regiment as the Royal Irish Fusiliers.
He had been a soldier for 27 years and had
seen service in the Boer War.
His father is mentioned on the headstone as
serving at Alma, Inkermann and Sebastopol in
the Crimean War and at Pekin Taku Forts in 1860.
Thomas was born at Falls Park.

John Warnock Bingham, Royal Army   I-112
Medical Corps *d.* 10 March. France

Thomas Telford, Machine Gun Corps   I-576
d. 12 March. Grantham Military Hospital

Robert Bingham, Royal Irish Rifles   J1-6
d. 4 October
Robert served as batman to Tom Kettles, the
Nationalist MP for East Tyrone who was killed
in action at the Somme in September 1916

1920 **John Charles McKillop,** New Zealand   I1-29
Rifle Brigade *d.* 24 July. New Zealand

James Fielding Kerr, Royal Inniskilling   N-486
Fusiliers *d.* 28 October
Headstone includes his brother **Samuel**
d. 8 October 1918

Dickson Graham, Royal Garrison   P-21 Glen
Artillery *d.* 28 December. Buried in City Cemetery

1921 **Robert Polley,** Royal Irish Fusiliers   J-38 Glen
d. 17 February
Headstone has inscription for
Victor Polley, *killed on active service*
3 March 1945

Alexander Schneider, 2/21 Punjabis,   D-237/8
Indian army *d.* 29 June
Alexander is buried in Jandola in Pakistan

1923   **Frederick J Doonan,** Royal Inniskilling.   **0-415**
Fusiliers *d.* 10 July
Headstone includes **John Doonan,** *London*
Irish Rifles, d. 23 December 1917. Palestine

Harold Alexander McCrea, *d.* 25 August   **G1-21**
Headstone reads 'As a result of service
in Great War'

1924   **John James Wilson,** *d.* 31 March   **B-185 Glen**
Headstone inscription reads 'From illness
received in the Great War'

1925   **Arthur Mitchell,** *d.* 13 February.   **G2-562**
Military Hospital Belfast. Buried in
City Cemetery
Arthur was a recipient of the Distinguished
Service Order (DSO) and Croix De Guerre

Charles Henry Kinch, Royal Irish Rifles   **C-66 Glen**
d. 17 October

1927   **Hugh St Claire Roy,** Royal Inniskilling   **Q-233 Glen**
Fusiliers and Royal Air Force
d. 12 November

1928   **Adam Primrose Jenkins,** Royal Irish   **D2-410/11**
Rifles *d.* 28 August
Headstone reads 'As a result of wounds'

1929   **Hugh Ferris,** South African Heavy Artillery   **M-94**
d. 17 July Vence, France

1938   **Lionel Strutt,** Canadian Expeditionary **M1-245**
Force *d.* 13 March

1941   **William John McNabney,** *d.* 6 January   **A-750**
Headstone reads 'from war wounds';
it also carries an inscription to his son
Sub-Lieut Engr Thomas McNabney
d. 4th July 1940 on HMS Foylebank

APPENDIX 5

Second World War

The Second World War began with the invasion of Poland on 1 September 1939, and ended at midnight on 7 May 1945 in Europe, and on 14 August 1945 in Japan. It had enormous social, political and military consequences for the citizens of Belfast. In July 1940, there were plans to evacuate 17,000 Belfast children to the countryside, but these plans were never fully successful, with only half of the designated children being moved; of these, more than half returned to the city by early months of 1941.

An indication of how the war would hit the streets of Belfast came on the night of 30 November 1940, when a lone German aircraft, using high definition aerial photography, surveyed the city. On the night of the first Belfast Blitz, 7 April 1941, when a small force of German bombers targeted the Harland and Wolff shipyards and the docks area; there were thirteen fatalities. This first raid was followed by a more devastating raid on the night of 15 April, when 180 German bombers dropped 203 metric tons (1 metric ton equals 1,000 kilograms) of high explosive bombs and 800 firebomb canisters over north Belfast. It is estimated that as many as 1,000 people perished that night. This was followed by an even larger raid by 200 German bombers on the night of 4 May, when 207 metric tons of bombs were dropped on the city along with 95,992 incendiary bombs. This time, the German bombers targeted the city centre, the docks and the Harland and Wolff shipyards; 191 died that night. A small raid by three German bombers over east Belfast took place on the night of 5 May, with a loss of 14 people in Ravenscroft Avenue. The impact of the Blitz on the city was enormous; by the end of May, over

200,000 Belfast citizens had left for the country, 53 per cent of the housing stock was destroyed or damaged, and many thousands of residents slept out on the hills around Belfast.

Given the increasing demand for armaments, Belfast's factories were in full production. By January 1943 the rise in the number of women employed in engineering had reached a figure of over 12,000. War conditions and the pressures of long hours spent on the shop floor led to a strike in the shipyards and aircraft factories, beginning on 25 February 1944; the strike lasted until 8 April 1944. By December of that year the workforce at Harland and Wolff had reached its all-time high of 38,801.

Throughout the Second World War many Belfast men and women saw active service with the British army, navy and air force. The City Cemetery contains 274 Second World War burials under the care of the Commonwealth War Graves Commission. There are also forty-one family headstones which carry an inscription to British soldiers, sailors and airmen who died in the years between 1939 and 1945. As well as 19 inscriptions for the air force, 19 for the army, and 3 for the navy, there is 1 for a merchant marine, and another for a flying officer in the Royal Canadian Air Force. The very first soldier buried after the outbreak of the War was David Cowan Boyd (**D1-156**) from 90 Urney Street, Shankill Road. He died on 24 October 1939 at the Military Hospital in Holywood, County Down. Units connected with the north of Ireland fought in every theatre of the war; these included the North Irish Horse, the Royal Inniskilling Fusiliers, the Royal Ulster Rifles, the Royal Irish Fusiliers, and The Royal Inniskilling Dragoon Guards.

Second World War memorial inscriptions on family headstones

† *Indicates a reference on headstone to First World War casualty.*

1939 **Denis Dermott Kane,** Royal Air Force   M-945
      d. 3 November

1940 **Leonard Edgar,** Royal Artillery   L-242
      d. 23 May. France

Robin Scott, Royal Artillery   K-244
d. 27 May. Dunkirk, France

John Edward McCullough, Royal   W-36 Glen
Naval Volunteer Reserve *d.* 10 June.
HMS *Acasta*

John Boyle, Pioneer Corps *d.* 15 June.   Q-236 Glen
Dunkirk, France

Samuel Sanderson, Royal Air Force   H-89 Glen
Volunteer Reserve *d.* 9 August

John Calvert, Royal Engineers,   I-53
d. 10 October. Chatham, England

Frederick Mc Dowell, Home Guard   Q-494
d. 15 October. Fulham, London

John Haveron, Royal Naval Volunteer   E-219 Glen
Reserve *d.* 29 November. HMS *Javelin*

William Scott McCrum, Royal Artillery   N-305
d. 3 December

David Mills, Royal Air Force Volunteer   A2-484
Reserve *d.* 9 December

Robert Kerr, Royal Irish Rifles,   Q-85 Glen[†]
d. 15 December
see **Alexander Kerr,** *d. 25 October 1918*

1941 **William James Sheeran,** Merchant Navy   F1-292
d. 24 March. SS *Agnete*

John W Bradley, Royal Air Force.   P-91 Glen
d. 15 October

Alfred Mandale Fisher, Royal Air   F-430/1
Force Volunteer Reserve *d.* 6 December
Operations at Sea

1942 **John Hutchinson,** Royal Army Service   B-574
Corps *d.* 24 January. Benghazi, Libya

Bryan Desmond Kane, Royal Horse   M-945
Artillery *d.* 7 March. Heliopolis, Egypt

William Luney, Royal Air Force   L-347 Glen
Volunteer Reserve *d.* 1 April

Robert Reid, Royal Inniskilling Fusiliers   E1-25
d. 18 April. Rangoon, Burma

John Hagan Jeffrey, Royal Air Force   B1-813
Volunteer Reserve *d.* 11 August

George Rodway MacDonald,   I-15
Royal Air Force, *d.* 20 October

Charles Henry Barton, Royal Air   A2-381[†]
Force Volunteer Reserve *d.* 7 November.
India
CWGC list Singapore as place of death

James Cardwell, Seaforth Highlanders   O-203 Glen
d. 31 December. Alamein, Egypt

1943 **William Frederick Bloomer,** Royal   H-166 Glen
Inniskilling Fusiliers *d.* 18 February, Burma
See also his father **W. Bloomer,** *Royal Inniskilling
Fusiliers* d. *15 August, 1915   Dardanelles*

David J. Boyd, Royal Air Force   A-217 Glen
d. 15 August. Malta

William Moore, Royal Artillery   G1-537
d. 29 September

William Frederick Neill, Royal Air Force   J-455
d. 3 November. Düsseldorf, Germany

Ronald St Clair Douglas, Royal Corps   B-368 Glen
of Signals *d.* 26 December

1944 **John Frederick Nelson,** Royal Air   L1-304 Glen
Force Volunteer Reserve *d.* 7 February.
Cassino, Italy

Thomas Henry Boomer, Royal Ulster Rifles   H3-636
d. 8 February

Robert Irvine Johnston, Royal Air Force   J-224
Volunteer Reserve *d.* 25 April

William Gibson, Dorset Regiment   V-138 Glen
d. 1 July. Normandy, France

Edward Workman Lindsay, Royal Air   K-346
Force Volunteer Reserve *d.* 12 August.
Bay of Biscay

William Holt Conroy, Royal Navy   I-550
d. 21 August. HMS *Kite*

Joseph Millar Parkinson, Royal Canadian   G1-215
Air Force *d.* 12 September. Milan, Italy

William Cummings Taylor, Royal Air Force   K-64
Volunteer Reserve *d.* 29 September.
POW aboard a Japanese ship

1945   **George A. Martin**, Royal Air Force   B2-341[†]
Volunteer Reserve *d.* 28 April

Kenneth Thompson, Royal Ulster Rifles   N-159 Glen
d. 7 April. Oldenzaal, Holland

Robert William Stanley, Royal Air Force   B2-475
Volunteer Reserve *d.* 3 June. Burma

William John Bell, Royal Artillery   Q-71 Glen
d. 25 July

Alfred Ernest Lloyd-Dodd, Royal Irish   B-19
Rifles *d.* 30 July

William J Alexander, Royal Air Force   B-146 Glen
d. 13 September, Kirkee, India

George Wilkinson, Royal Air Force   L-185 Glen
Volunteer Reserve *d.* 16 October.
Naples, Italy

FURTHER READING

In researching the history of Belfast City Cemetery I have used a wide range of source material. The reading list below is a selection of that material, which I hope will be helpful to the reader who wishes to develop their interest in the fascinating history of the cemetery and, by extension, Belfast.

Anson, Peter F., 'The Building of Churches', *The New Library of Catholic Knowledge* vol. IV. (London/New York: The Caxton Publishing Company, 1965)

Bardon, Jonathan, *Belfast: An Illustrated History*. (Belfast: Blackstaff Press, 1995)

— *A History of Ulster*. (Belfast: Blackstaff Press, 2001)

Barton, Brian, *The Blitz: Belfast in the War Years*. (Belfast: Blackstaff Press, 1999)

Beckett, J. C. *Belfast: The Making of the City 1800–1914*. (Belfast: Appletree Press, 1983)

Blaney, Roger, 'Dr John St. Clair Boyd', *Journal of the Federation for Ulster Local Studies*, vol. 9, no.18 (1984)

Boyd, Andrew, *The Rise of the Irish Trade Unions, 1729–1970*. (Tralee: Anvil Books, 1972)

— *Holy War in Belfast*. (Belfast: Pretani Press, 1987)

Boyle, J.W., 'The Belfast Protestant Association and the Independent Orange Order 1901–10', *Irish Historical Studies*, vol. XIII, (1962–3)

Brett, C.E.B., *Buildings of Belfast, 1700-1914*. (Belfast: Friar's Bush Press, 1985)

Byrne, Ophelia, *The Stage in Ulster from the Eighteenth Century. (*Belfast: The Linenhall Library, 1997)

Cameron, Stephen, *Death in the North Channel. The Loss of the Princess Victoria, January 1953*. (Newtownards: Colourpoint Books, 2002)

Caul, Brian Francis, *Maginn: His Life and Times*. (Ulster Local History Trust, 2006)

Clarke, Richard, *The Royal Victoria Hospital Belfast. A History, 1797–1997*. (Belfast: Blackstaff Press, 1997)

Coate, Leslie, Y*pres 1914–18: A Study in History Around Us*. (Horsham: L.D.C. Publications, 1995)

— *The Somme 1914–18: A Study in History Around Us*. (Horsham: L.D.C. Publications, 1996)

Commonwealth War Graves Commission, *The War Dead of the Commonwealth (also Foreign National and Non World War Burials): Belfast (Balmoral) Cemetery, Belfast (Dundonald) Cemetery, Belfast (Milltown) Roman Catholic Cemetery, Belfast City Cemetery, Knock Old Cemetery, Shankill Cemetery*. (CWGC, 2002)

Conlay, Iris; Anson, Peter F., 'The Art of the Church', *The New Library of Catholic Knowledge Vol. IV*. (London/New York: The Caxton Publishing Company, 1965)

Crawford, Fred. H., *Guns for Ulster*. (Belfast: Graham & Heslip Ltd., 1947)

Crossland, Bernard; Moore, John S., *The Lives of Great Engineers of Ulster Vol. 1. (*Holywood: Priori Press, 2003)

Curl, James Stevens, *A Dictionary of Architecture*. (Oxford: Oxford University Press, 2000)

— *The Victorian Celebration of Death*. (Stroud: Sutton Publishing, 2001)

— *The Art & Architecture of Freemasonry. An Introductory Study*. (Woodstock & New York: The Overlook Press, 2002)

— *Classical Architecture. An Introduction to its Vocabulary and Essentials, with a Select Glossary of Terms.* New York/ (London: W. W. Norton & Co., 2003)

Daniels, Rod, *In Search of an Enigma: The 'Spanish Lady'.* (National Institute for Medical Research. www.nimr.ac.uk, 1998)

Deane, Arthur, (ed.), *The Belfast Natural History and Philosophical Society, Centenary Volume, 1821–1921. A Review of the Activities of the Society For 100 Years With Historical Notes, And Memoirs Of Many Distinguished Members.* (Belfast: Belfast Natural History and Philosophical Society, 1924)

Dixon, D. Roger, *Marcus Ward and Company of Belfast.* (Belfast: Belfast Education & Library Board, 2004)

Doherty, James and Tom Thompson, *Standing Room only. Memories of Belfast Cinemas.* (Belfast: Lagan Historical Society, 1997)

Evans, E. Estyn and Brian S. Turner, *Ireland's Eye: The Photographs of Robert John Welch.* (Belfast: Blackstaff Press, 1977)

Farrell, Michael, *Northern Ireland: The Orange State.* (London: Pluto, 1976)

Farseth Youth and Community Development Ltd., *Ireland's V.C's. A comprehensive list of Irishmen who were awarded The Victoria Cross.* (Cultural Traditions Group, 1995)

Gilbert, Martin, *First World War.* (London: Harper Collins, 1994)

Haggar, Reginald G., *A Dictionary of Art Terms. Architecture, Sculpture, Painting and the Graphic Arts.* (Dorset: New Orchard Editions, 1984)

Hamilton, Thomas, *History of Presbyterianism in Ulster.* (Kilkeel: Modern Missionary Trust, 1982)

Harbison, Peter, *Irish High Crosses.* (Drogheda: The Boyne Valley Honey Company, 1994)

Holmes, Finlay, *Our Irish Presbyterian Heritage*. (Publications Committee of the Presbyterian Church in Ireland, 1985)

Jackson, Tabitha, *The Boer War*. (London: Channel 4 Books, 2001)

Jeffery, Keith, *Ireland and the Great War*. (Cambridge: Cambridge University Press, 2000)

Johnstone, Tom, *Orange, Green and Khaki: The Story of the Irish Regiments in the Great War, 1914–18*. (Dublin: Gill & Macmillan, 1992)

Jordan, Alison, *Who Cares? A History of Charitable Associations in Victorian and Edwardian Belfast*. (Belfast, 1993)

Jordan, Alison, *Margaret Byers: Pioneer of Women's Education and Founder of Victoria College, Belfast*. (Belfast: The Institute of Irish Studies, 1990)

Keneally, Thomas, *The Great Shame: A Story of the Irish in the Old World and the New*. (London: Chatto & Windus, 1998)

Killen, William Dool, *History of Congregations of the Presbyterian Church in Ireland and Biographical Notices of Eminent Presbyterian Ministers and Laymen*. (Belfast and Edinburgh: Cleeland & Gemmell, 1886)

— *The Language and Poetry of Flowers*. (Belfast & New York: Marcus Ward & Co. Ltd, 1877)

Larmour, Paul, Belfast: *An Illustrated Architectural Guide*. (Belfast: Friar's Bush Press, 1987)

Leher Ernst and Johanna, *Folklore and Symbolism of Flowers, Plants and Trees*. (New York: Dover Publications, 2003)

Lucy, Gordon, *The Great Convention. The Ulster Unionist Convention of 1892*. (Lurgan: Ulster Society Publications, 1995.)

Lynch, John, *Forgotten Shipbuilders of Belfast*: *Workman Clark, 1880–1935*. (Belfast: Friar's Bush Press, 2004)

Lynd, Robert, *Galway of the Races: Selected Essays*.
(Dublin: Lilliput Press, 1990.)

MacCarron, Donal, *Landfall Ireland. The Story of Allied
and German Aircraft Which Came Down in Éire in
World War Two*. (Newtownards: Colourpoint Books, 2003)

Mackenzie, Kenneth R. H., *Royal Masonic Cyclopaedia, Parts I
and II, 1877 (facs)*

Magee, Jack, Barney. *Bernard Hughes of Belfast, 1808–1878.
Master Baker, Liberal and Reformer*. (Belfast: Ulster
Historical Foundation, 2001)

Maguire, W.A., *Caught in Time: The Photographs of Alex Hogg
of Belfast 1870–1939*. (Belfast: Friar's Bush Press, 1986)

McConnell, Charles, *The Ships of Harland and Wolff*.
(Carrickfergus: Carmac Books, 2004)

McNeill, Mary, *Vere Foster, 1819–1900. An Irish Benefactor*.
(Newton Abbot: David & Charles, 1971)

Moriarty, Theresa, *Doffers & Dockers: Women's Industrial
Struggles in Belfast 1906–1907*. (Northern Ireland:
Unison, 2007)

O'Hare, Fergus, *The Divine Gospel of Discontent: Story of the
Belfast Dockers and Carters Strike 1907*. (Dublin:
Connolly Bookshop, 1981)

Pakenham, Thomas, *The Boer War*. (London: Abacus, 2000)

Preston, Diana, *Wilful Murder. The Sinking of the* Lusitania.
(London/New York: Doubleday, 2002)

Richardson, Hilary and John Scarry, *An Introduction to Irish
High Crosses*. (Cork: Mercier, 1990)

Royal Belfast Academical Institution, *Centenary Volume
1810–1910*. (Belfast: McCaw, Stevenson & Orr Ltd., 1913)

Royle, Trevor, Crimea. *The Great Crimean War, 1854–1856*.
(London: Little, Brown & Company, 1999)

Scott, Robert, *A Breath of Fresh Air. The Story of Belfast's
Parks*. (Belfast: Blackstaff Press, 2000)

Snoddy, Theo, *Dictionary of Irish Artists of the Twentieth Century.* (Dublin: Merlin, 2002)

Stewart, A.T.Q., *The Ulster Crisis. Resistance to Home Rule, 1912–1914.* (Aldershot: Gregg Revivals, 1993)

Strawson, John, *Gentlemen in Khaki. The British Army 1890–1990.* (London: Secker & Warburg, 1989)

Symington, Brian and John Carberry, *British and Irish Sign Languages: The Long Road to Recognition.* (Belfast: The Linenhall Library: 2006)

Walker, Brian and Alf McCreary, *Degrees of Excellence: The Story of Queen's, Belfast, 1845–1995.* (Belfast: The Institute of Irish Studies, 1994)

Wilson, A. N., *C. S. Lewis. A Biography.* (London: Flamingo, 1991)

HOW TO GET THERE

Black taxis

Most of the black taxis travelling to west Belfast from the
Castle Junction depot pass the Falls Road gate at the front
of Belfast City Cemetery.
For timetable information call 028 9031 5777

Translink bus service

Translink timetable information is available online
www.translink.co.uk
Alternatively call 028 9066 6630

Opening times

For details on opening times please call the
Belfast City Cemetery office, 028 9032 3112

IMAGE ACKNOWLEDGEMENTS

Group shot of Belfast Cemetery employees, reproduced by kind permission of Belfast City Council.

Map of the Jewish burial ground, 1901, reproduced by kind permission of Belfast City Council.

Map of the RVH and the Belfast District Lunatic Asylum, reproduced from the *c*. 1900 Land & Property Services / Ordnance Survey of Northern Ireland® map.

Map of the townland of Ballymurphy, 1832–3, reproduced from the 1833 Land & Property Services/Ordnance Survey of Northern Ireland® map.

Map of the townland of Ballymurphy, 1857, reproduced from the 1857 Land & Property Services/Ordnance Survey of Northern Ireland® map.

Minutes of the Belfast Corporation's Cemetery Committee, 5 October 1869, PRONI LA/7, reproduced by kind permission of Belfast City Council and PRONI.

Queen's University section of the Poor Ground, reproduced by kind permission of Belfast City Council.

Registration details of Second World War German servicemen, reproduced by kind permission of Belfast City Council.

Thomas Henderson and William Wilton, PRONI LA/7/ 50E/1, reproduced by kind permission of Belfast City Council and PRONI.

INDEX

ALSO BY TOM HARTLEY

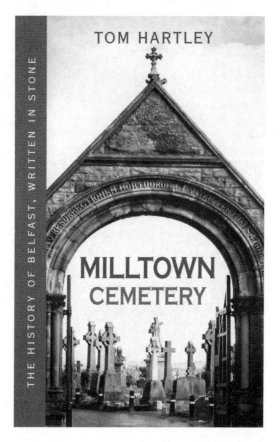

eBook
EPUB ISBN 978-0-85640-733-8
KINDLE ISBN 978-0-85640-750-5

Paperback
ISBN 978-0-85640-925-7

www.blackstaffpress.com